ALSO BY GLENN KENNY

Anatomy of an Actor: Robert De Niro

A Galaxy Not So Far Away:
Writers and Artists on Twenty-Five Years of Star Wars (editor)

Made Men

THE STORY OF *GOODFELLAS*

GLENN KENNY

HANOVER
SQUARE
PRESS

HANOVER
SQUARE
PRESS™

Recycling programs
for this product may
not exist in your area.

ISBN-13: 978-1-335-01650-8

Made Men

Library of Congress Cataloging-in-Publication Data has been applied for.

Hanover Square Press
22 Adelaide St. West, 40th Floor
Toronto, Ontario M5H 4E3, Canada
HanoverSqPress.com
BookClubbish.com

Printed in Italy by Grafica Veneta

To Claire, with all my love

Table of Contents

"Treachery is beautiful if it makes us sing."

—**Jean Genet,** *The Thief's Journal*

Prologue:
MARTIN SCORSESE, DECEMBER 1989

"I ran into Paul Schrader in the hall the other day, he's finishing his movie. I said to him, 'It figures I see you here, we're the only two guys who are gonna work through Christmas. Everyone else is clearing out.'"

Martin Scorsese was referring to the man who wrote the screenplay for his galvanizing 1976 movie *Taxi Driver*, with whom he'd subsequently worked on *Raging Bull* and *The Last Temptation of Christ*. Schrader himself started directing features in 1978, forging an idiosyncratic path with films that often mixed searching spirituality with sexuality and violence. But he never shook, or tried to shake, the association with Scorsese. The *Raging Bull* experience, which saw De Niro and Scorsese rewriting Schrader's script almost from scratch, had bruised Schrader's feelings somewhat, but the two men retained an affinity with, and an affection for, each other. More to the point, fifteen years after they first worked together, they were still as consumed by filmmaking as they had been then. Schrader was finishing his disturbing, Venice-set *The Comfort of Strangers*, written by Harold Pinter from a novel by Ian McEwan. Scorsese was caught up in assembling a picture called *Goodfellas*. (At this time, and for some time after its release, it was, as you'll see, rendered in print as *GoodFellas*. This changed over the years. No one to this day, to my knowledge, can pinpoint when it changed or why.) Both pictures would see release in the fall of 1990.

Scorsese mentioned this run-in to me before we ourselves got to work. He had set aside a couple of hours so we could start on an essay to which he would attach his byline. In 1989 I was working at a magazine called *Video Review*, which would be celebrating its tenth year of publication in 1990. That it had survived for ten years as a consumer magazine was a testimony to a lot of things, and mainly to the fact that home video and home theater in the late '80s was a sufficiently hot topic to sustain a regular readership of a few hundred thousand.

For the 10th Anniversary Issue, we were soliciting the opinions of various ostensible luminaries and visionaries on how home video had affected life and culture, and what effect it would have in the future. I should emphasize again that this was 1989. "Home video" meant VHS, and maybe a little bit of laser disc; the DVD, video streaming, oversize flat-screen TVs, critically acclaimed original programming on cable, the whole "is TV better than movies" debate: all of this was in the future. What seemed to me, and to everybody else, the distant future. Most of the predictions we would run were in the form of sound bites solicited in phone interviews (J. G. Ballard: "I look forward to the day when specialty video producers—the equivalent of Sun Records and the like in the music business twenty, thirty years ago, and the equivalent of small publishers in the book trade—really can begin to reach out to the public." Paula Abdul: "The big movie musical will return to prominence in this decade, as recording artists take the video music concept one step further."). But for the keynote address, so to speak, I thought Martin Scorsese would be ideal. The filmmaker was also a well-known film *lover*, passionately concerned with film preservation, and a great proponent of home video as a medium, however initially imperfect, for movie appreciation.

So I got the number for his office and called. I was greeted by Julia Judge, his assistant at the time. I laid out what we wanted to do, and I also stipulated that if Scorsese had neither the time nor inclination to sit down and write such a piece himself, I would be delighted to come up to the office, interview him, and construct an "as told to" piece. Either way, I said, we would pay Scorsese three thousand dollars, for a thousand-word article.

"Three thousand dollars?" Judge responded, sounding impressed. I wasn't aware of it at the time, but the director was still trying to bounce back from personal financial crises dating from earlier in the decade.

His cinematic output continued, but the fieriness that distinguished his prior pictures frequently took a different and sometimes less volatile form. His critical profile seemed to have diminished ever so slightly during this time, as well. In 1985's *After Hours* he experimented with a form of proto-indie, guerrilla filmmaking. In 1986 *The Color of Money* was a sequel to *The Hustler*, and starred Paul Newman and a very up-and-coming Tom Cruise—a solid film, with solid returns. He worked for his old friend Steven Spielberg directing an episode of the latter's attempt to revive the *Twilight Zone* television series; he was sought out by megastar and future King of Pop Michael Jackson to make a music video; he contributed to the anthology film *New York Stories* with fellow graying eminences Francis Coppola and Woody Allen. (Scorsese was the youngest of the three.)

And he was also able to achieve, finally, his passion project for many years, an adaptation of Nikos Kazantzakis' novel *The Last Temptation of Christ*, which attracted the wrong kind of controversy at the wrong time, controversy of the sort—one would think—to make Scorsese look like a troublemaker in the eyes of the studio heads. To make matters worse, the controversy did not translate into box-office success by any metric.

I can't say that Scorsese was feeling as if he was standing on shaky ground when I came along with the *Video Review* offer.

But I'll always remember being struck by the enthusiasm with which my offer was accepted. (Another well-known writer I was pursuing for the project was demanding five dollars a word and a free video camcorder, neither of which *Video Review* was willing, finally, to cough up for him.) Judge soon got back to me taking up the offer, and stipulating that Scorsese would indeed be too busy to sit down and write it himself. (Often when the director has a magazine article or op-ed piece with his by-line attached, he's done it with the assist of a writer; for many years the critic and director Kent Jones, who also worked for a period as Scorsese's video archivist, filled that role.) We set a date for the third week of December.

Scorsese's office at the time was in the Brill Building, the legendary then-entertainment-industry cynosure on the outer edge of Manhattan's Times Square. Its reputation was built around the fact that it once held the offices of song publishers, many of whose staff and freelance songwriters in the '50s and '60s would become superstars after doing time there (Carole King, Neil Diamond, etc.). The structure also housed offices for television and film producers, and various technical facilities, as well. Scorsese's editing suites for *Goodfellas* were in the same building, which made the place ultraconvenient for the filmmaker. His office was not much to look at: it was a big open space with linoleum floors and pale green walls and a couple of square pillars; Judge sat at a desk in more or less the middle of the room. Scorsese himself had a small office built into the corner of the room, and after I was introduced to him that's where we settled. I had a tape recorder and a legal pad. We didn't spend too much time on small talk, merely observing the coming of the holiday and the fact that we were all still working, before getting down to business.

The man immediately struck me as yes, intense, but also warm, friendly, considerate. I asked him a question: "When did you first hear about home video?" and off he went. He stood as he spoke, paced around a bit, and every now and then, after he had gone off on a long tangent, he would take a hit off an inhaler of asthma medication.

Eventually we talked about the work in progress. There was a sense, almost palpable, of his delight that he was trying something really new, and also a slight sense of trepidation, as in "What are they gonna make of this?" And of course the postproduction work on this new film was consuming.

Getting back to the subject of our essay, he revealed, not surprisingly, an enthusiasm for home video because of its ability to let the user create a library of films, and cross-reference it at his or her convenience. He told a charming story about watching the original Universal *The Mummy*, directed by Karl Freund, with one of his daughters, and then leapfrogging to James Whale's *The Bride of Frankenstein*. He discussed issues that would continue to be hot buttons even into the age of DVDs and Blu-rays, e.g., how ultrawidescreen movies should be presented on home screens. He also bemoaned, as filmmakers did and do, what he called "the shorter attention span encouraged by television and video." But he recognized that everything is, or can be, relative: "You realize sometimes as you're making a film that today's audience may not sit for a shot of a certain length. This may not change the way I'll make a picture. Whatever the pace, if it's right for the shot or scene, that's the way it's got to be—as in *The Last Temptation of Christ*, where a number of sequences take on the tone and mood of the desert. When I was in Morocco I got a real sense of timelessness, of everything moving at 120 frames per second—extreme slow motion, almost like a trance. That's part of the effect that I wanted from the movie, and it's part of the reason the movie is two hours and forty-six minutes long. I decided that certain elements of *Temptation* would be fast, fine. But in the desert, there's a sense of mysticism you experience that often comes in a trancelike manner." This led him, again, to the movie he was currently editing. "As for my new film, *Goodfellas*, even if it's two and a half hours long, I'm hopeful it will be one of the fastest-paced pictures ever made, because it tells a story in a style heavily influenced by documentary TV reporting and these new tabloid shows." After we were finished with the formal part of the interview, Scorsese continued to enthuse about the movie. "In a way, it's the most like television I've ever done," he said, sounding a little surprised with himself. "Not just *The Untouchables*—the late '50s–early '60s TV series, not Brian's film," he clarified, referring to the 1987 movie directed by his old friend Brian De Palma and featuring Robert De Niro in the role of Al Capone. "In terms of the narration, I love that staccato, rat-a-tat thing you get sometimes with Walter Winchell on the old series. And that continues, I think, into today's true-crime and exposé television shows, a kind of tabloid approach. That's definitely part of what's informing the style of this movie."

At the end of our session, I handed the director my then-new hardcover copy of the book *Scorsese on Scorsese*, which he signed: "To Glenn Kenny/Thanks & appreciation/Martin Scorsese/1989."

Despite his familiarity with the movie's milieu, the scenario of *Goodfellas* did not have entirely the same kind of personal pull that such stories as *Raging Bull, New York, New York*, and yes, even *Taxi Driver*, had at the time for the filmmaker. There's no real Scorsese surrogate in *Goodfellas*. But there's a near-anthropological interest in the manners and rituals of the modern gangster's world. Practically voyeuristic, you could say. And that perspective is shot through with a good deal of "memory-play" material, derived from Scorsese's childhood and teen years. Two movies subsequent to *Goodfellas*, 1995's *Casino* and 2013's *The Wolf of Wall Street*, cast a similar eye on the actual crimes that gangsters commit and how they commit them, to the extent that *Wolf*'s immersive depiction of the depraved Dionysian modes of its characters' existences proved off-putting to some critics. Despite the squalor and tension and ultimate betrayals depicted in *Goodfellas*, there were similar worries at the time of its release that Scorsese did not emphasize sufficiently just how thoroughly corrupt his protagonists were. One reason the movie took so long to edit was because of the nuances of perspective that Scorsese and his longtime editor, Thelma Schoonmaker, tucked into the film's overall structure.

For all the excitement that Scorsese expressed about what he was doing, he was a little uncertain, sheepish even. He again mentioned that he wasn't sure how the picture would be received. He certainly didn't give the impression of knowing that he was redefining the gangster movie.

Because that's what *Goodfellas* would end up doing, despite its not making a megafortune at the box office (its returns were such that Warner Brothers considered it a modest success). The movie took gangsters off the wobbly pedestal popular culture erected in honor of *The Godfather* movies and made them into something like "regular" guys. Henry Hill begat Tony Soprano; Tony's own creator pretty much admits as much. And the movie wound up, through exposure on cable and yes, home video, a cultural touchstone that's still quoted to funny and/or horrifying effect to this day.

And today, Scorsese's offices are only about a dozen or so city blocks from the Brill Building. But in a sense they're a world away, occupying a floor in a deluxe East Side building, complete with a temperature-controlled screening room and an extensive video library. It's arguable that it is the office that *Goodfellas* built.

One:

NICK, AND NORA, AND OTHERS

There's a way in which the entirety of *Goodfellas* is contained in its opening scene.

The movie begins with a 1969 Pontiac Grand Prix seen from behind, driving fast down an otherwise empty road. The camera veers to the left and pulls past the car, as if it's another vehicle trying to overtake this one. The next shot is a static title card: "New York, 1970." Then a shot of the Pontiac's inhabitants, seen in wide angle as if through the front windshield, over the steering wheel. Three actors play three tired characters. Ray Liotta drives; riding shotgun is Robert De Niro, who looks as if he's napping; in the back seat, very still, sits Joe Pesci. It's clear from their stances that these men are, if not brothers, "part of a crew" as it will be stated later. They're comfortable together.

A foreign sound hits our, and their, ears. An insistent, even desperate, banging. "What the fuck is that?" Liotta says. "Is it a flat?" asks Pesci, now somewhat animated. "Better pull over and see."

The car pulls over; we see its back end, sidelong, in a medium shot. The three men get out of the car and line up, looking at the trunk. The car's taillights suffuse them in red. They look like they're stepping out of, or into, a garish Italian horror movie.

There's a cut to a plain head-on shot of the car's closed trunk. A more ordinary director would just let that shot lie. Instead, the camera tracks in, slowly, from the right side; Scorsese and cinematographer Michael Ballhaus make its lens a curious consciousness in and of itself. Following is a reverse angle shot of the three men, De Niro, Pesci, and Liotta, lined up looking at the trunk. Pesci reaches into his sport jacket; we presume he's going to pull out a gun. Instead, he takes out a terrifyingly long and sharp butcher's knife. The camera pans right as Liotta approaches the rear of the car, warily, keys in hand. Inside, wrapped in a bloody sheet, is a man with blood all over his face, rasping, "No." Pesci approaches, knife ready to strike, furious: "He's still alive, the fucking piece of shit," as he stabs through the sheet several times.

De Niro, whose face has until now had an expression one could read as disapproving, steps up, revolver in hand, and fires four bullets into the body. The trunk is all white sheet drenched in blood; we can barely make out the now definitively dead man's head. The whole frame is turning red.

Liotta is then alone, still bathed in the red of the car's taillights; he looks off-frame at his companions and moves to close the trunk. In voice-over, he says, "As far back as I can remember I always wanted to be a gangster." As he closes the trunk the camera tracks in on him, resolving in a medium close-up; he's gazing into the distance with a "what the fuck just happened" look on his face (a look likely shared by anyone watching the movie for the first time) as the blaring, almost comical horns of the intro to the 1953 Tony Bennett song "Rags to Riches" come up. The shot freeze-frames Liotta in close-up. Only then does the movie's title appear; these letters are red on black.

In less than three minutes, the movie simultaneously establishes a realistic intimacy, putting you right in the car with those characters, and uses stylization as a distancing effect that's nevertheless anything but neutral in its temperature—the horror-movie lighting, and the mordant irony of "always wanted to be a gangster" as the punch line to this mystifying, squalid bloodbath.

Goodfellas is frequently cited as the most realistic American movie about organized crime ever made. In a sense, it is. But it is a great movie about organized crime because, among other things, it constantly pushes beyond ordinary realism.

In fact, the movie's director, Martin Scorsese, does not make movies that are by any yardstick objectively realistic. Rather, he makes movies that explicitly reflect his own perception. In the late '80s he recounted to an interviewer, "I read in the *Village Voice* that Jim Jarmusch, who made *Stranger Than Paradise* and *Down by Law*"—knowing, aesthetically offbeat, minimalist comedies with long, static shots of characters standing, or sitting, around talking—"said something like, 'I'm not interested in taking people by the hair and telling them where to look.' Well, I do want them to see the way I see. Walking down the street, looking quickly about, tracking, panning, zooming, cutting, and all that sort of thing. I like it when two images go together and they move."

His way of seeing is evident in the first three minutes of *Goodfellas*. After the Warner logo, the movie's titles begin; these were designed and executed by Saul Bass, in this case in collaboration with his wife, Elaine. The opening titles are somewhat reminiscent of those Bass designed for Hitchcock's 1960 *Psycho*: stark white typeface over black. Each title—"A Martin Scorsese Picture," the principal cast's names, etc.—zips at high speed from right to left, and is followed by a copy of that card, now static, for a few seconds, centered on the screen; on the soundtrack, the whirr of cars passing underscores the movement. The first set of opening credits ends with the text: "This film is based on a true story."

Goodfellas, indeed based on a true story, is a movie as much about Martin Scorsese's relationship to its subject as it is about its subject. While the director's movies, up until this point, had often featured crime and criminals in their worlds, *Goodfellas* was—arguably—his first gangster movie proper. (Because of the proximity of the characters in *Mean Streets* and *Raging Bull* to mob interests, some consider those gangster pictures, or closely akin to them.) But it made such an impression that in the world outside of informed cinephilia, Scorsese is often referred to *solely* as a maker "of gangster movies."

Once it backs away a little from the grotesqueries of its opening scene, the movie is acute in detailing the lure of the lifestyle. (The voice-over line immediately following the first is "To me, being a gangster was even better than being president of the United States," which is even funnier/sadder now than it was then.)

Scorsese has frequently recollected watching gangster movies with his friend, the screenwriter and critic Jay Cocks. He tells a story of the first time they looked at the Howard Hawks picture *Scarface*, made in 1932 and starring Paul Muni. All but forgotten today, the film became such a touchstone for both the *Cahiers du Cinéma*–influenced critics of the '50s and '60s and the so-called "movie brats" who transformed Hollywood in the 1970s that the 1983 remake directed by Brian De Palma (himself once one of those self-same movie brats) was considered authentically sacrilegious at the time it was announced.

"There's a wonderful scene where all these cars line up out-side a coffee shop, the guys get out, kneel down, and fire into the shop with machine guns, wrecking everything," recalled Scorsese. "This goes on for a long time. Then Paul Muni says to George Raft, 'What are they shooting with?' and he replies, 'Tommy guns.' Muni then says, 'Great, I'll go get one,' and he comes back with a gun and starts firing with it! Jay and I looked at each other and both said, 'We really love these guys.' It's strange that we don't normally like people who are killing other people, but the way they're presented in this film is ex-tremely glamorous."

Scorsese encountered Nicholas Pileggi's book *Wiseguy*, an inside-the-mob chronicle, in the winter of 1986. Here, for the first time, a mob soldier, Henry Hill, willingly and with no state or federal coercion, told all to Pileggi, an investigative reporter since the late 1950s. Scorsese had grown up in New York's Little Italy in the 1940s and '50s, when it was rife with Italian Ameri-can mobsters. The book, Scorsese recalled, depicted "something I knew from my own experience":

"I grew up on the East Side, which was a very closed commu-nity of Sicilians and Neapolitans, and it took me years to work out what was happening among the organized crime charac-ters. But I was aware of these older men and the power they had without lifting a finger. As you walked by, the body language would change, you could just feel the flow of power coming from these people, and as a child you looked up to this without understanding."

In *Mean Streets*, his critical breakthrough feature of 1973, Scorsese positioned this world of power on the periphery of the immediate world of its aimless young male characters. Char-lie, the central figure among them (played by Harvey Keitel), is halfheartedly running collections for his minor-mobster uncle while protecting his irresponsible hellion friend Johnny Boy

(De Niro) from an inept wannabe loan shark. In *Goodfellas*, too, the locus of power is at a remove. Its central figure, Henry Hill, is a mob "soldier" who, because he is only half-Sicilian, can never be a "made man" or a fully "protected" member of the mob. (Given that the guy in the trunk in the movie's opening scene, Billy Batts, was himself a made man, one thing the story ultimately reveals is that this whole concept was a critical fallacy in mob life.)

Scorsese's interest in the mob was a two-way street: Henry Hill frequently recounted how he "kidnapped" the reclusive mob underboss Paul "Paulie" Vario (Paul Cicero in *Goodfellas*) to show him *Mean Streets*, so impressed was Hill by the accuracy of its depiction of life among the Little Italy mooks. Vario was reportedly similarly impressed.

"The only reason I was able to write *Wiseguy*," Nicholas Pileggi tells me, "is because Henry Hill defied the FBI, and the marshal service, by giving me his telephone number, so I was able to reach him while he was in the witness protection program."

At the time of our meeting, Pileggi is eighty-five years old but has the bearing of a man at least twenty years younger. Trim, energetic, and voluble, the onetime journalist now makes his living writing and consulting on television series and movies, and divides his time between Los Angeles and Manhattan's Upper East Side.

He grew up in Brooklyn's Bensonhurst neighborhood, an area that, like Scorsese's East Side, was watched over if not entirely ruled by the Italian American mob. "I grew up in that world, in that environment. My father had come here, as a young man, from Calabria—we're Calabrese, my mother, too. He was a musician, played trombone in the movie theaters, in the days before sound film. There was a lot of work for guys like my father.

Being Calabrese, he came over with people who later emerged as major organized-crime figures, like Albert Anastasia, and Frank Costello, and Joe Adonis, and they were all Calabrese. This set them apart from the Sicilian Mafia, which was moving into New York around the same time. And later on, as the mob wars began, these were all people my father knew. And I knew of them; it was an environment that I felt comfortable with and I always had access to them."

But he wasn't tempted to enter their way of life. Instead, he was seduced by literature and writing. "I went to Long Island University, was the Class of '55, if you can believe it—so many years have passed! I was an English major, and I had great teachers who would take us through line-by-line analyses of *Ulysses*, of T. S. Eliot. I just loved it. I worked for the school newspaper. Soon I decided I want to live in the city, without really knowing what I wanted to do there."

Pileggi's cousin, the writer Gay Talese, had gotten a job as a copy boy at the *New York Times* before having to complete an ROTC commission. He gave Pileggi's father a tip, which he passed on to his son, which was that the AP was hiring.

"The address was 50 Rockefeller Plaza, I was so naive, coming from Brooklyn, and I thought I was looking for an A&P, as in the supermarket!" Soon Pileggi sussed out that he was being directed to the then-headquarters of the Associated Press, where Joe Kelleher hired him as a messenger/copy boy. "That's how easy it was!" Pileggi marvels today.

At the AP, the atmosphere was defined by shoe-leather reporters, with whom Pileggi eventually found himself working. "If you were a police reporter, you knew first-grade detectives, and your sister was married to a cop. It was very blue-collar, and very connected in that way. This was long before Woodward and Bernstein. The police reporters at the time all had that kind of street experience, most of them had never gone anywhere near a college campus. I was unique among the police reporters in that way. And I fell into covering this world that I grew up in, the world of crime.

"This is before Valachi," Pileggi says, referring to the mobster Joe Valachi, who testified before a Senate committee on organized crime in 1963, and whose story became the subject of a 1968 book by Peter Maas. "This is the middle '50s; the Kefauver Committee had come up but nobody really paid attention. And so I wound up covering these guys before they were being covered." And the mob guys would talk to him, because they knew him. They would use him as a sounding board for inter- and intramob dish, and because Pileggi knew everybody, he always had choice morsels to feed in order to get choice morsels back.

"These guys would gossip about the other family, they would tell you about theirs, then I'd go to the other guys they'd been talking about and ask them about that—and they liked talking to me. Remember, there are five 'families' in New York City and there's not much in the way of newspaper articles, there's no internet. They find things out only by meeting somebody at a social club, or going for a walk...now that I've put myself in the mix, they can ask me, 'What's going on with the Chin?' and so on. While reporting, I also became their communications facilitator, one they trusted." ("The Chin" was Vincent/ Vinnie "the Chin" Gigante, a mobster who in the late 1960s famously faked insanity to avoid arrest and prosecution, a tactic that worked out pretty well for him until the 1990s, when he was tried and convicted for murder; he subsequently died in prison in 2005.)

Pileggi cultivated that trust socially. One of the through lines in the movie *Goodfellas* is the importance of food in Italian American social life. Pileggi won the trust of mobsters not just through neighborhood and family connections—he made an impact via their appetites, too.

"Just as I began that job, my father took me to a restaurant in Little Italy called Paolucci's, on 149 Mulberry Street. And they were Calabrese. And my father asked Mr. Paolucci to make sure I ate properly. I had started out working the night shift, so I would get to the restaurant after work at about three in the afternoon, before they'd opened. So I had to knock at the door and they'd let me in. It wasn't a restaurant that had an off-the-street clientele. They didn't want strangers. Really, the only people who ate there were Mafia bosses and Mafia guys. And when they saw that I was there, they asked the owner, 'Who's that?' and they said, 'Oh, that's okay, that's Nicola's son.' I wound up having dinner in there, or lunch in there, or early dinner in there, with every mob boss on Mulberry Street. And they would recognize me. So if I was walking down the street and Aniello Dellacroce"—the Gambino crime family underboss nicknamed "the Tall Guy"—"was standing outside the Ravenite Social Club, I would nod, he would nod. And as life went on, I started asking the Pauluccis to make dishes that my grandmother made. There was one dish ended up on the menu called Pork Chops Pileggi. Which is sautéed pork chops, sliced potatoes, onions, and hot vinegar peppers. All sautéed together. And all these mob guys loved it and began ordering it. Which also furthered my cachet. And my access."

One would think both the cachet and the access would diminish once Pileggi's stories were published on a regular basis. He laughs wryly when I bring up the idea. "At the Associated Press all those years, I never got a byline. That was just the way it was done; it was a wire service and all stories were just credited to the Associated Press. And these guys didn't even have any idea of what the Associated Press, or the AP, was. They didn't know that the seven newspapers in New York at the time were using *my* stories, usually combining them with bits of their own staffers' reporting, and giving those reporters the byline—Eddie Kirkman at the *Daily News*, say—with an 'additional reporting' credit going to the Associated Press. So there was never any trouble."

If the mob guys had no idea what Pileggi was up to, newsroom insiders had taken notice. In 1968 Clay Felker founded *New York* magazine, and invited Pileggi on staff. As much as Pileggi loved his affiliation with the AP (he now refers to his stint there as among the happiest years of his career), Felker offered him more freedom, more scope, longer pieces (and a byline). It was the right move at the right time. "By then, 1968," Pileggi observes, "the mob is really a big story."

Public awareness of Italian mob activities had expanded in 1957. The so-called "Apalachin Meeting," a summit of mobsters convening in Upstate New York, was descended upon by law enforcement, resulting in the detainment and indictment of well over fifty mob bosses. In 1968 Peter Maas's book *The Valachi Papers*, spurred by the 1963 testimony of Joe Valachi, was published and became a bestseller. (The book was turned into a not-terribly-successful 1972 mob picture starring Charles Bronson, a credible movie tough guy but not a particularly credible movie Italian American.) Mario Puzo's novel *The Godfather*, fictionalizing a boatload of mob lore, would be published in 1969, and become a bestseller.

This public exposure was ostensibly tearing at the fabric of the mob code of ethics—a code that *Wiseguy* and subsequently *Goodfellas* would reveal had always been sheer bluster, anyway. *Omerta* and such notwithstanding, mobsters loved seeing approximations of themselves in bestselling books and on movie screens. So Pileggi no longer needed the anonymity that had shielded him so effectively.

"Instead of looking at *The Godfather* like this curse, they loved it," Pileggi says of the crew he wrote about in *Wiseguy*. "They were empowered by it. Henry Hill told me he and the guys all got in a car and drove from Long Island to Manhattan to the Paramount Theater to see the first screening of *The Godfather*. This is a car full of gangsters, guns under their car seats. Henry said, 'I came out of the theater, I was so happy to be a gangster. I never wanted to be anything else.' This was his validation."

"I think *Wiseguy* would have been a very different book had Henry Hill not been Henry Hill," Pileggi says. It wasn't just that Hill, who was hidden by the feds after assisting in cases against Paul "Paulie" Vario and Jimmy "the Gent" Burke among others, had approached Pileggi (initially through an attorney) not just ready but eager to talk. It was Hill's *ability* to talk, and to remember.

After the initial contact, which led to Hill's flouting of his protected-witness status, Pileggi learned that Hill had both the vocabulary and the memory of a born storyteller. "I had asked a hundred mobsters, 'What was your first big score on the numbers?' And they would say, 'I don't remember.' Didn't remember the score, didn't remember what they did with the money, shrugged, and said, 'What the hell, you're talking twenty years ago, I don't remember.' Henry Hill, I asked the same question, 'What was your first big score with the numbers?' He said, 'I got six hundred dollars.' I said, 'What'd you do with the money?' He said, 'I bought a yellow Bonneville convertible, it was the greatest day of my life. I've played the numbers ever since.' I mean, that's golden.

"These mob guys, most of them, had lived a life of not telling stories. They had dedicated their lives to being monosyllabic. Henry was the opposite. He was the Irishman.

"He was playing to the crowd. He would dance. And the

wiseguys liked him for that. The fully Italian guys didn't hold anything against him, because he was not one of them.

"He was like the court jester."

That vivid voice spoke to Pileggi, and so, too, to Scorsese. When Scorsese tried to contact Pileggi about getting the rights to the book and adapting it, Pileggi was skeptical. Not about *Wiseguy*'s potential as a movie, but as to whether the calls he was getting were actually from Scorsese.

"I had seen all of his movies, down to his great documentary about his parents, *Italianamerican*. So doing a movie with him was a kind of dream I didn't think could necessarily come true. He first called from Chicago, while he was in the middle of directing *The Color of Money*."

Pileggi wasn't at his *New York* magazine office when the first call came; the receptionist gave him a pink slip with the message when he came in. "I got this message to call Marty Scorsese." Pileggi laughs at the memory. "I *knew* that it was bullshit, I knew it was David Denby, my friend who at the time was the movie critic for the magazine. The son of a bitch. He knew how much I loved Marty's movies because we had seen a bunch of them together. So I figured if I called the number I'd just get Denby, and Denby was gonna bust my balls, so I didn't call.

"And then, next day, there was the same message, and again I didn't call."

Pileggi and the writer Nora Ephron had been romantically involved for some time by the mid-'80s, and Ephron's career in film as a screenwriter, and later director, was well on its way. They married in 1987. "I think the only reason she even talked to me and got married to me was that she was fascinated by this world of mobsters that I wrote about, because it was the opposite of hers," Pileggi says of Ephron, fondly and kiddingly.

"The day I didn't return the call for the second time, I got home that night, and Nora was home, and she says to me, 'Are you crazy?' And I said, 'What do you mean, am I crazy?' She said, 'Why won't you call Marty Scorsese?' And I said, 'That's not Marty, that's Denby busting my balls.'"

Ephron informed him no, it was Marty—a crew member on *Money* who had worked with Ephron had called her to ask what was up. Chastened, Pileggi called Scorsese immediately.

"I couldn't think of anybody I'd rather have make a movie out of this book. And once we spoke, that was it."

This despite the fact that at the time, Scorsese could offer Pileggi nothing beyond his desire to make the book into a movie. "He said, 'I can't do it right away,' because there was no deal, and he had to finish *Money*, and then he really needed to get *The Last Temptation of Christ* squared away. But I didn't care. We made a handshake deal over the telephone, so to speak."

Once the book was out of galleys and in bookstores in the early spring of 1986, offers intensified. "The book was huge, and a lot of people were coming at me. I threw them all out. I told my agent, we're not selling it. A whole slew of directors wanted to do it, and would have done it instantly. Including Brian De Palma, and I like Brian, and I like his movies. But I just knew this was Marty's material, that this was where he was *from*, in a way that Brian wasn't."

Pileggi held faith that Scorsese was the filmmaker to do justice to *Wiseguy*, and he was proven more than correct. But because Pileggi waited, a different movie about Henry Hill made it into theaters before *Goodfellas*.

My Blue Heaven, directed by Herbert Ross and produced and distributed by Warner Brothers, the same studio that put together *Goodfellas* (this despite Scorsese already having a production deal with Touchstone in place), opened in theaters on August 17, 1990, a full month before the Scorsese/Pileggi collaboration. It stars Steve Martin as Vincent "Vinnie" Antonelli, a New York mobster enrolled in the witness protection program; Rick Moranis plays Barney Coopersmith, his neat-as-a-pin, by-the-book, tenderhearted FBI keeper.

This broad comedy relocated its mobster to California rather than the Midwest. Made well before fusion cuisine and such hit the West Coast, it finds Vinnie perplexed on a visit to a supermarket where not only can he *not* find arugula, but where no one has heard of it. "Arugula! I haven't had arugula in SIX WEEKS," he cries. Shades of the lament of the exiled Hill at the end of *Goodfellas*: "Can't even get decent food. Right after I got here I ordered some spaghetti with marinara sauce and I got egg noodles with ketchup."

The screenwriter of *My Blue Heaven* is Nora Ephron.

"She was the daughter of playwrights, screenwriters," says Pileggi. "It was a very refined world. So I just brought her along. And everybody she met [from Pileggi's world], and I tell you, she met major people, they loved her. So she wound up being included in lots of—well, I wouldn't say mob meetings, but dinners. Like the ninetieth birthday of a mob boss from Las Vegas, in Staten Island, we'd get in the car. She loved meeting these people, and as they got to know her movies, the wives really connected to her." Prior to writing *Heaven*, Ephron based her screenplay for 1989's *Cookie*, a comedy about the feisty daughter of a mob boss, on Nina Galante. Nina was the daughter of mobster Carmine Galante, and in the 1970s she served as her dad's chauffeur. ("She was the best wheel man in the city," Pileggi insists.)

Pileggi stayed close to Henry Hill after the publication of *Wiseguy*, indeed, up to the end of Hill's life. Hill kept up with the showbiz trades and became very animated when word about a possible movie based on *Wiseguy* came up. "A lot of the conversations were 'how's the book doing, where's the movie now, when am I going to get a paycheck,' that sort of thing."

Sometimes in the early days of their association, when Hill called, one of Ephron's boys from her marriage to Carl Bernstein, then in their preteens, would answer the phone, and the caller would announce himself as Henry. That was the name by which they knew Ephron's father, Henry Ephron. So they'd say hello, and hand the phone to their mom.

"And they would spend a lot of time on the phone," Pileggi says. "She was fascinated, because, like anybody else, you want to know, how do you live in the witness protection program? He got a little more far-fetched with her than he did with me. I think because it was clear to him that she found it so entertaining, he made some things up."

Heaven is a broad, amiable farce, which ends with its mobster character turning local hero by dedicating the proceeds of a new criminal scam to a youth baseball construction project—an ending probably more inspired by the exigencies of Hollywood narrative than Hill's own yarn-spinning.

When it came down to writing a screenplay for the movie whose title Scorsese and Pileggi changed to *Goodfellas*, because a mob-themed television series called *Wiseguy* had started airing in 1987, the collaborators began by concentrating on what they could subtract from Henry Hill's story. "Marty said, 'You go with the book, and I'll go over the book again, and let's each pick out the movie from the book. Where is the movie in this book?' I said okay. So I went and I made up my breakdown of scenes. And he made his, and when we compared them, they were identical. We left out Henry's stint in the army for instance. For the writer and the director to come out with the identical same vision for what the movie is in the book, I don't know whether that happens every day."

Some portions of the process nevertheless mystified Pileggi, who manned the typewriter during the writing sessions. "You know, in the script somewhere, you're gonna see, typed on the side, the word *cream* in a parentheses. And the author had no idea what Marty was talking about, because he was not following rock music. I was too busy following Frank Sinatra stuff." It would be a few years before Pileggi would know what Scorsese meant.

Two:

PLAYERS

In his 1994 autobiography *The Kid Stays in the Picture*, the eccentric film producer and Hollywood executive Robert Evans coined, or probably revived, this adage: "There are three sides to every story: your side, my side, and the truth."

One component of this story is indisputable. That a lengthy excerpt from *Wiseguy* appeared, illustrated by vivid paintings by Larry Gerber (some seeming to anticipate specific shots in the movie version), in the January 26, 1986, edition of *New York* magazine.

At the time, Scorsese was in Chicago, shooting *The Color of Money*, as was the film's producer, Barbara De Fina, who was married to Scorsese. "I was getting my mail sent to me, and I subscribed to that magazine," De Fina says. "So I was going through my mail…and Marty didn't read *New York* magazine, he didn't like it. I found the *Wiseguy* article, and read it, and I put a little yellow Post-it on it. I said to him, 'This looks like fun, this looks interesting.' I didn't hear anything for a while, and only found out later that he and his assistant were frantically trying to reach Nick. He never told me what was going on. Because I would have just called the book publisher and said, 'So who's repping the book?'"

This dovetails with Pileggi's story of not answering phone calls reputed to be from Martin Scorsese and, it turns out, actually were from Martin Scorsese. In Pileggi's telling the next step was an agreement to collaborate on the screenplay and then defer the making of the film by a couple of years after Scorsese was given the opportunity to finally make *The Last Temptation of Christ*.

In January of 1986 the film producer Irwin Winkler, who'd worked with Scorsese on *New York, New York* and *Raging Bull*, was living in Paris. Winkler was producing Bertrand Tavernier's *Round Midnight*, in which Martin Scorsese had an acting role, playing an avid but ruthless jazz nightclub owner in the film's New York–set-and-shot sequences. Winkler writes, in his book *A Life in Movies*, "My ritual was to visit the English-language bookstore WH Smith on the rue de Rivoli every Monday afternoon. There I could get the Sunday *New York Times*, the *New Yorker*, and *New York* magazine. One week when I picked up *New York* magazine I devoured the excerpt from Nick Pileggi's book *Wiseguy* while standing in the aisle. I knew Nick from the 1960s, and when I called him in New York, he said his book hadn't been sold and that the agent handling the film rights was Bob Bookman at CAA in Los Angeles. When I reached Bookman, he said he had several interested buyers and was preparing to auction the book. I called Bookman's boss, Michael Ovitz, then the most powerful man in Hollywood (according to the cover story of *Time* magazine). Ovitz told Bookman to sell *Wiseguy* to me and then quietly asked me to help him sign Martin Scorsese as a client.

"When I had a celebratory call with Pileggi, he told me he'd heard that Marty Scorsese was interested in the book. I hadn't worked with Marty since *The Last Temptation of Christ*"—Winkler here refers to the abortive 1982 attempt to get the film made— "and when we connected, he told me that yes, he wanted not only to direct the film but also to write the script with Pileggi. Scorsese and Nick Pileggi started working up an outline for the film, and I gave them my notes as they moved toward a script. Marty, however, got the go-ahead on the long-delayed *Last Temptation*, so we put aside *Wiseguy* for a year and a half until he finished that film."

When I interviewed Irwin Winkler for the first time in 2019, he told more or less the same story with some additions.

"We'd get all the magazines and newspapers from New York, and…I picked up *New York* magazine, and I read the excerpt of Nick's book, and I thought, This is a movie. I called his agent, a guy named Sterling Lord, who I think is still around, he's like ninety-six years old or something." As of this writing, Sterling Lord is still around, and one hundred years old.

"I knew Sterling from my relationship with Jimmy Breslin, who was a client of his back in the day. And he told me that he was selling it in conjunction with CAA, but basically CAA was really handling it day to day. So I called Bob Bookman, who was a CAA literary agent. Bookman told me that they had a lot of offers and a lot of interest in Pileggi, and then I called Mike Ovitz, and Mike said, 'Okay, we'll sell it to you.' At the same time the chairman of Warner Brothers, Ted Ashley, had read the same excerpt and told [Warner executive] Terry Semel to go after it. After I bought the rights, Terry Semel, boy, he jumped right in, and wanted to develop it."

In a November 1990 *Rolling Stone* interview, which author Anthony DeCurtis notes took place in "the apartment [...] where [Scorsese] lives with Barbara De Fina, his fourth wife" (no mention that she is the credited executive producer of the film he and Scorsese will discuss), Scorsese said, "I read a review of *Wiseguy* when I was directing *The Color of Money*, and it said something about this character Henry Hill having access to many different levels of organized crime because he was somewhat of an outsider."

Scorsese told Richard Schickel in the book *Conversations with Scorsese*, "When I was doing *The Color of Money* in Chicago, I was reading the *New York Review of Books* and saw a review of a book by Nick Pileggi called *Wiseguy*." Murray Kempton's laudatory essay on *Wiseguy*, titled "Hood's Progress!" appeared in the May 8, 1986, edition of the *New York Review of Books*. "It seemed like Nick was taking us through the different levels of purgatory and hell in the underworld, like Virgil or like Dante. Irwin Winkler said, 'Are you interested in that?' I said yes and he bought it for me."

Less frequently quoted than the front end of Robert Evans' maxim is its continuation: "And no one is lying. Memories shared serve each differently."

Who found the material, who pursued the material and how, who bought the material, whose account is true or accurate: these might not seem consequential questions now. But they have definite implications on the other side of the film's making and marketing, and in the wake of relationships that sustained, and relationships that broke, in the years after.

Winkler's tidbit about Michael Ovitz's request to bring Scorsese to the talent agency CAA (Creative Artists Agency), which Ovitz headed at the time, ties in interestingly with Scorsese's own recollections of Ovitz. Speaking with Schickel about the 1986 *The Color of Money*, he said, "Michael Ovitz at that time was representing Cruise. He called me and said, 'Why don't you use Tom Cruise?' Cruise had been in Michael Chapman's film *All the Right Moves*"—Chapman was Scorsese's very inspired and trusted cinematographer on *Taxi Driver* and *Rag-*

ing Bull, and a friend; *Moves* was his directorial debut—"And I thought he was very good. I said, 'Sure, let's put him in as the young pool player.'"

Money had been developed by Scorsese's then-agent Harry Ufland, in conjunction with Ovitz. In conversation with Ovitz, he asked Scorsese, "What do you want done most?" The answer was *The Last Temptation of Christ*, which had been set up at Paramount in 1982 until Barry Diller pulled the plug on it in preproduction. Scorsese recounted the conversation with Ovitz to Schickel: "And he smiled. Mike was a genius at what he did, and a person who likes a challenge. He said, 'I'll get it made for you.' I didn't think he would. I didn't think he could."

But Ovitz could, and did. He set the film up at Universal as a one-off deal. (Albeit one that would require, at some point, Scorsese to make another picture with the studio in the future; that would become *Cape Fear*.) Tom Pollock, always an adventurous producer, then in a power position at that studio, took it on and it got made more or less as Scorsese had wished. It's one of the director's greatest pictures. It did poorly at the box office, and was met with vociferous, persistent, and largely ill-informed protests on release. It did not, however, result in another term in what industry wags call "movie jail" for Scorsese, as the troubled box-office failure, 1982's *The King of Comedy*, had. By bringing in *The Color of Money* on budget, and that film having been a minor hit, Scorsese had proved that he could function within the system. He was not a persistent Problem Filmmaker. In addition, his development deal with Touchstone could not be affected by *Last Temptation*. But, as the various players converged around Pileggi's book, the chips fell so that *Wiseguy* ended up with Warner Brothers rather than Touchstone. Not inapt, given Warner's gangster movie pedigree—they were the studio behind such classics as *Little Caesar*, *The Public Enemy*, and *White Heat*, to name but a few.

Speaking of players, and chips, Harry Ufland, the aforementioned Scorsese agent, who had been an executive producer on *Temptation*, called Winkler about *Goodfellas* at one point. "He said, 'You know, I gotta be a producer,' and I said, 'I don't want any partners,'" Winkler says. "And he backed off."

Joe Pesci was one of the first to be cast. He was reluctant when first approached. Scorsese visited Pesci at his home, and in conversation Pesci—who made a huge impression as Jake LaMotta's brother Joey in *Raging Bull* and was from a milieu not dissimilar to Scorsese's own—worked out ways to make the character of Tommy his own. An anecdote from his own life fueled what was to become one of the movie's most quoted scenes.

Looking at *Something Wild* you can understand why Ray Liotta wanted to play Henry Hill so bad. In that 1986 film directed by Jonathan Demme, Liotta played a character named Ray Sinclair. Sinclair is the ex-boyfriend of Melanie Griffith's Audrey, and he's got a wicked grin and a terrible temper that explodes in shocking violence at the movie's climax. The role garnered critical plaudits and a Golden Globe nomination for Liotta, then in his early thirties.

Looking at *Goodfellas* you cannot imagine anyone else playing Henry Hill. Scorsese wanted him. Winkler wasn't convinced. "I didn't think he had the charm to capture the audience after all the drugs, stealing, and womanizing that Henry practiced," Winkler writes, "but Marty kept insisting, and I kept putting it off, and one night Margo"—Margo Winkler, the producer's wife, herself an actor—"and I were having dinner at a restaurant in Santa Monica with my friend Dick Zanuck when Ray Liotta came over to our table and asked to speak to me. In a ten-minute conversation he (with charm and confidence) sold me on why he should play Henry Hill. Marty was right."

Lorraine Bracco had a connection to Scorsese by dint of her

marriage to Harvey Keitel, who'd acted in four prior Scorsese movies, all crucial ones: *Who's That Knocking at My Door, Mean Streets, Alice Doesn't Live Here Anymore,* and *Last Temptation.* She and Keitel lived at the time in the same Tribeca property as Robert De Niro and Scorsese's first assistant director Joseph Reidy; that property was owned by Chuck Low, who cameoed as a restaurant patron mocking Rupert Pupkin in *The King of Comedy* and would play Morrie in *Goodfellas.* Which is not to say that Bracco's part came about through coincidence, happenstance, or nepotism. She was an accomplished actor who was building a solid résumé, but she also had the freshness of a relative newcomer. As it happened, she had auditioned for a role in Scorsese's *After Hours* some years prior, and while she did not get it, Scorsese told her how much he'd liked what she did and that he would keep her in mind for future roles. In a 2017 interview with the *Guardian,* she recalls being dubious: "Like the date who says he'll call you, right?" But years later, Scorsese called, inviting her to his apartment, where he and Ray Liotta waited. "The three of us have a nice drink. That was my audition."

The Warner executive Terry Semel had floated Tom Cruise and Madonna for the parts of Henry and Karen, a suggestion that was privately ridiculed by the film's makers at the time and may now be ridiculed by many more. Winkler was careful, in recounting his own disdain for the idea, to not have it reflect on Cruise himself: "I asked [Mike Ovitz] if Cruise had even read the script, since he was so wrong for the part (and Cruise is an actor who has a very good sense about what roles he should play). Did Cruise want to be a cokehead?" As for Madonna? "And Madonna we wouldn't discuss."

Paul Sorvino had doubts about playing Paul Vario, the mob boss whose name would later be changed to Paul Cicero. The voluble character actor was curious about why he was approached to play someone so quiet. And while he'd portrayed criminals before, he had never played such a killer. At a Tribeca Film Festival Q&A commemorating the making of the movie, Sorvino said, "The real difficulty there was the inner life…that weird bifurcation of character. When they're home, they're family people. When they're out, they're shooting people." His doubts continued in the run-up to the shoot. "I was quitting after almost four weeks and we were supposed to start three days later and I called my manager and said, 'Get me out of this, I can't do it.'" One day, feeling some frustration at being unable to tie a tie properly, or feeling some spinach in his teeth (Sorvino's recollection is like anyone else's in its changeability), he caught an unguarded look at himself in the mirror, and the unpleasant look on his face gave him the key to playing Paulie.

In his book Winkler tells of a phone call in which Barbara De Fina complained that the studio was delaying a green light for the production, and that if one was not forthcoming, Scorsese would move to another picture. Winkler went to Terry Semel, who told him that "with our casting of Ray Liotta and Joe Pesci and our budget of $16 million he couldn't okay the film unless we had a major star for the other lead. After a lot of arguing, Semel said that if I gave him my word that we would get a major star for the third role, he would give *Goodfellas* the okay. I promised but really had no idea who would play Jimmy Conway. Marty had an idea. He called me the next day and had spoken to Bob De Niro, and we had our star."

The teaming of director Scorsese and actor De Niro is one of the most storied and lauded in American cinema, world cinema even. Anyone who's seen the pair together, as recently on panels to promote *The Irishman*, can detect the affinity and good humor that flows between them. Their films together, even one as mixed as *Cape Fear*, bristle with energy and virtuosity.

The two men cannot help but be personally close, but they are not as close personally as pop-culture conventional wisdom implicitly maintains. ("People who think that Bob and Marty hang out…" Barbara De Fina said to me, with an eye roll, during one of our talks.) They have close friends in common, including the screenwriter and critic Jay Cocks, who helped introduce the two in 1971; it was at a Christmas party hosted by Jay and his wife, the actress Verna Bloom, at which Scorsese and De Niro formally met. (Both men recollect running into each other in the neighborhood when they were growing up.) Brian De Palma, who could count De Niro as his discovery (he cast the very young actor in the 1963-shot comedy *The Wedding Party*, a college film De Palma codirected with Wilford Leach and Cynthia Munroe; the movie did not see any kind of release until 1969), was also in attendance at the event.

Looking at the films Scorsese and De Niro made together with a consideration of how they ended up being made, the story that emerges is one of some affinities, but also a large percentage of shared self-interest. They first collaborated on *Mean Streets*, for which Harvey Keitel, having played another Scorsese surrogate in the 1967 *Who's That Knocking at My Door*, had been chosen for the lead. De Niro has recalled in interviews bring miffed that he had not been considered for that role until he saw what he could do with the irrepressible Johnny Boy. De Niro says that at the time he was "competitive," and the way he almost steals the movie from each of the main male actors (the others are David Proval and Richard Romanus, both superb) shows just how competitive.

Paul Schrader's script for *Taxi Driver* had kicked around a bit before Scorsese became the director; there had once been a possibility that Jeff Bridges would play the title role. Once Scorsese signed on as director, De Niro had two big things going for him: his work in *Mean Streets* and his Oscar-winning role as young

Vito Corleone in *The Godfather Part II*. The casting had a logic beyond the pair's personal desire to work together again. With *New York, New York*, the *Taxi Driver* momentum yielded a project that was probably the most personal iteration of the relationship between the director and the actor, both of them pouring a lot into the conception of Jimmy Doyle, the sax player who's an inspired creator and a near-impossible person. And that film precipitated a crash-and-burn for Scorsese.

It was at the director's hospital bed, after a drug-related collapse, that De Niro brought the *Raging Bull* project up to Scorsese. Scorsese has spoken in interviews of his difficulty in finding his way into the material. Once Scorsese had regained some of his health and he and De Niro retreated to the Caribbean to rework the script, he was able to give it a full commitment. But shooting the film wound up beating up Scorsese's health again.

And it was De Niro who brought *The King of Comedy* to Scorsese. In a note on the front page of one of the scripts of *The King of Comedy* (which De Niro had bought while it was still a novel by the film critic Paul D. Zimmerman, who subsequently transformed it into a treatment, then a screenplay), De Niro wrote, "Marty: Don't always want to be weird or crazy."

The subsequent film was, for Scorsese, whose asthma was acting up, hard to shoot: "I was coughing on the floor and sounding like a character from *The Magic Mountain*," Scorsese told Ian Christie and David Thompson. "It got so bad that some days I wouldn't get there until 2:30 in the afternoon [...] We were shooting in New York and there were maybe five trailers, which you had to park in a certain way because the teamsters wanted this and the police wanted that. Finally, if you wanted to move, the entire company had to go along like a caravan through the city streets in the daytime. We didn't get one break from anybody there, or at least that's how it felt. If we wanted something, we had to pay for it and pay a lot. It was like making a film with a dinosaur: the tail was so big it was wagging and slamming into everything, perhaps not intentionally, but destroying things as in a Godzilla movie."

De Niro doesn't think that it was the difficulty of making *The King of Comedy* that broke up the collaboration for several years. "I had a good time making it," he said with a wry shrug. In fact, he does not read much of anything into the hiatus (he reads only slightly more into the twenty-year pause between *Casino* and *The Irishman*). The actor does not process his career in terms of things like landmark roles. He's a working actor who goes where the work is. The pronounced box-office failure of *The King of Comedy* raised more crucial questions for Scorsese than whether he'd be able to work with De Niro again. It raised questions as to whether he'd be able to work at all. Retrenching took the form of the black comedy *After Hours*, a project brought to him by actors-turned-producers Griffin Dunne and Amy Robinson, who'd had some indie success in backing the John Sayles film *Baby It's You* in 1983. Robinson had played Theresa in *Mean Streets*. Shot in a semiguerrilla style not entirely dissimilar to the mode of *Mean Streets*, *After Hours* testified to Scorsese's continued vitality. ("On the first day of shooting I realized happily that I had no time to sit down or wait in my trailer," he told Christie and Thompson. "If I was sitting down there was something wrong!")

But it was Paul Newman's approach to the director that ended up becoming *The Color of Money*, a sequel to Newman's 1961 classic *The Hustler* and the project that helped deliver Scorsese from "movie jail."

And during this period, with films such as *Midnight Run*, De Niro became what his one-time agent Harry Ufland had predicted he would never become: a mainstream movie star.

In my interview with him for this book, the only time that De Niro got defensive was when I observed that when Scorsese came to him about doing *Goodfellas*, De Niro was in a different position in Hollywood than he had been when *The King of Comedy* wrapped. "How so?" he asked. "Well," I sputtered, citing *Midnight Run*, "there's more money, more leverage." "There's more attention, that's for sure," he responded. He shrugged as if to allow the point, but it was clear that discussing the business as such was not something he was interested in. But when *Goodfellas* was coming together, De Niro was a player, regardless if he was outsourcing the ins and outs of his deals.

And when Scorsese spoke to Amy Taubin in one of the first interviews to promote *Goodfellas*, he frankly told her, "I want to be a player." ("To be a player in Hollywood, you have to take a lot of bruising," he added.) Immediately after *The Color of Money*, Scorsese made *Life Lessons*, one-third of *New York Stories*, an anthology movie with other minimovies by Francis Ford Coppola and Woody Allen. Starring Nick Nolte and Rosanna Arquette (who had worked with Scorsese on *After Hours*), the knotty tale of an old painter and his young assistant/love interest/erotic obsession, inspired in part by episodes from the life of Dostoevsky, is a New York story without physical violence or crime, something Scorsese has rarely done since. (*The Age of Innocence*, set in old Manhattan, is a notable exception. And both *Life Lessons* and *The Age of Innocence* bristle with emotional violence.) The extent to which Scorsese made *Goodfellas* with the aim of realizing the ambition he revealed to Taubin is unclear. But the fact is that when Scorsese approached De Niro to play Jimmy Burke, as the character was still called, for that was the criminal's real name, their professional dynamic was substantively different than it had been at the wrap of *The King of Comedy*. It was he who had to ask De Niro this time.

De Niro recalls reading *Wiseguy* while on the set of *We're No Angels*, the 1989 release directed by Neil Jordan from a script by David Mamet. A remake of a minor 1955 crime comedy directed by Michael Curtiz in which Humphrey Bogart and Aldo Ray are escaped convicts masquerading as priests, the movie

mainly consists of De Niro and Sean Penn doing imperson-
ations of Bowery Boys Huntz Hall and Leo Gorcey. (During
my interview with De Niro I neglected to inquire whether this
was intentional.)

"I was in Canada, and I read the book on a weekend. I knew
I couldn't play Henry, I was too old to play. I remember it was
on a weekend and I went out to one of the islands near Van-
couver, and I called Marty, I remember, and said, 'You know,
what about the part of Jimmy?' And he said, 'Yeah, yeah.' And
that's how it started. And then I started working on it right after
I wrapped *Angels*. I flew to New York, I had to get ready right
away, because they had already started shooting. Or they were
very far into preproduction."

Pileggi recalls De Niro visiting him and Scorsese while they
revised the script. "Marty was very excited, he said, 'I think we
got Bob to do it, he's coming by later.' And that was wonderful, I hadn't seen Bob in many, many years. And he showed up.
We went from there directly to Richard Bruno, the costume
designer on the picture. Bob started going through costumes,
and he wanted more of this and more of that, I mean, the attention to detail... I was just really so impressed."

Some accounts—ridiculous accounts, one would note from
this position—say De Niro's agreement to work on *Goodfellas*
secured $20 million over the original budget. Less dubious ac-
counts put the final budget at *Goodfellas* at somewhere between
$20 million and $25 million. Winkler's book has the budget,
pre–De Niro, at $16 million. Getting the picture made at any
of those prices would be a nearly monumental undertaking. But
Scorsese had the people who could do it. And he had his own
meticulousness.

Three:

THE PREP WORK

When I interviewed Robert De Niro for this book, he was friendly, welcoming, and willing to help. The actor is, however, by nature taciturn, particularly with people he's just met. He doesn't process his work the way critics and journalists and much of the rest of the world does; his idea of a milestone film in his career is more related to his life circumstances or frame of mind at the time than its critical reputation. A lot of the time when considering his work in the 1980s, his mind went back to 1986's *The Mission* rather than *The King of Comedy* or *Midnight Run*.

De Niro is not blessed with a prodigious memory. This has nothing to do with his being seventy-six. In an outtake from the 1995 *Casino* included in a reel screened at a tribute to Don Rickles, the insult comic is seen ribbing De Niro for not properly reading a cue card with his dialogue on it. "For the money you're making…go to your trailer and study!" This picture was made when De Niro was fifty-two. The challenges of memorization may be one reason he's favored screen acting over stage work; having to deliver lines piecemeal is less demanding in that respect than performing a whole drama over a few hours. And *Goodfellas* is now a film that he shot thirty years ago. So when I mentioned that I would be traveling to the Ransom Center at the University of Texas to look at an archive of his papers, he said, "You might find something there."

My friend and colleague Shawn Levy had gotten there first. In his 2014 biography of De Niro, Levy writes, "De Niro dove into preparing for the part of Jimmy the Gent with a vigor he hadn't demonstrated in years." He reproduces some of De Niro's notes on the character.

> *Lots of bets...he liked to laugh...when drunk a little loud... tried to be part of any situation...good at bullshitting people... bookmaker all the time...plays gin rummy...fabulous memory... dozen roses to mothers of guys in can...glide, little bounce... always shaking hands... Didn't like strangers... I'd go over in a restaurant if I knew them and say hello, buy drinks, send a bottle...big spender...likes to tell jokes, good company, a laugher... I created my own crew [...] I networked very well. I was always working, my mind was working. Anybody and anything... I made myself known and I made myself feared [...] Good dresser. A rebel but respectful [...] my mind was on making scores, not so much a woman...*

Several of De Niro's observations tend to be at least slightly contradicted by Jimmy's actual actions in the movie. "Respectful" certainly doesn't characterize Jimmy's ultimate approach to Billy Batts. But that's not the point. What De Niro is limning is Jimmy's self-image, who "Jimmy the Gent" envisions himself as. This is as much a product of creative imagination as it is research.

During my own time at the Ransom Center I also found a good deal, and it demonstrated something that I had only intuited when I wrote a critical account of his career (*Robert De Niro: Anatomy of an Actor*) that was published by Phaidon/ *Cahiers du Cinéma* in 2014. That is, De Niro's genius in building a character is reflective—of course—of the way the man himself seems to think. He is not interested in abstractions. Psychology for him is articulated via gesture and action, and is most vividly amplified through personal appearance/presentation. This has been the case for him since he began pursuing acting in the early 1960s.

While De Niro's dedication to craft is most famously associated with genuine feats of physical transformation—he infamously gained sixty pounds to play the middle-aged, gone-to-seed version of boxer Jake LaMotta in *Raging Bull*—the actor was never a pure naturalist. Levy writes of his early approach to headshots: he would concoct "a small library" of them—"single images and composites in the guises of various personae: cops, cabbies, beatniks, a hippie with a guitar, a Chekhovian man with glasses and a suit, an Italian gangster with cape and goatee, even some with hair apparently dyed blond, and beyond that a thick pile of photos of him in various suits, coats, and hats, with dark glasses, cigars, a pistol, and so on and so on [...] He was projecting an image of himself as a chameleonic sort of actor, not a leading man but somebody who could play a variety of offbeat types."

With Jimmy Burke, later to be renamed Conway, every scene meant a new outfit. The span of the movie meant that De Niro would play the character at several different ages. All of these things were opportunities for specific new presentations. Hence, De Niro's scripts contain, in blank pages at the end, or on the facing pages of scripts that have print on only one side, lists such as these:

Jimmy—clean shaven shiny on the forehead
Green suit
Snake skin belt
Black shoes
Watch on left hand
Black silk socks
Brown silver tie
No ring

V neck T-shirt
Chinos
No dungarees
Sneaker [incomprehensible; De Niro's handwriting tends to the scrawl] *shoes*
Also makes me look younger!

#52
Jimmy
1965
Summer
Tattoos, hair back, clean shave
White shirt with red stripe pants

Also in De Niro's files are pages from a reference book called *Fashions in Hair*, with illustrations depicting styles from year to year. There are plenty of photos of the actual Jimmy Burke at various ages, various newspaper clippings of stories recounting Burke's criminal trials, some of them moving past the point at which *Goodfellas* ends: for instance, the *New York Daily News*, September 5, 1984, headline: "Tampering Fear Sequesters Jury in Burke's Trial."

De Niro also had Jimmy Burke's Federal Bureau of Prisons Program terminal report from 1979. One passage therein reads:

"Although Mr. Burke did not avail himself to any of the self-improvement programs during his prolonged imprisonment, he nevertheless received outstanding performance ratings for his work in the Food Service Dept. and Ground Maint. Dept. His overall adjustment was above average and he was receiving earned good time and meritorious pay for his efforts."

In the margins of the scripts, De Niro gives himself not-quite stage directions, but instructions on small, specific gestures, or pauses. In the scene in which Jimmy is trying to decide whether or not to kill Morrie, a note in the margin reads: "long look + pause then 'What am I gonna do with you.'" For when Jimmy leads Morrie into the car where Morrie will die, the note is: "with head angle put arm around him."

His dialogue notes are mostly indicating emphasis, as in his spelling out of Jimmy's words to young Henry after he leaves the courtroom following his first "pinch": "NEVER rat on your friends and ALWAYS keep your fucking mouth shut."

De Niro would call on Henry Hill throughout the shoot. He also told me that early on he conferred with Jimmy Burke's daughter Catherine Burke ("The idea of meeting Jimmy Burke was complicated, as he was incarcerated," De Niro said), but that Burke cut off contact without explanation at a certain point. Apparently she tried to strong-arm the production into giving her $100,000 to use the Burke name. Rather than do that, almost all the names of the real-life characters in the picture were changed. These changes are listed on a script for the film dated January 12, 1989, but may have been appended at a later date to that extant script. In any event, it can be inferred that from the point of that refusal, Burke was no longer a friend to the production. (As we'll see later, Hill was irritated but not surprised by her actions.)

The first day of principal photography, May 1, 1989, De Niro was on the call sheet, that is, scheduled to do a scene. It was of his chat with Karen after Henry's arrest by the Nassau County narcs, where Jimmy gives Karen a wad of cash and instructs her to check out some dresses in a storefront up the way—the one in which Karen gets spooked, runs to her car, and drives off, thinking Jimmy was about to have her killed. (She's not wrong!)

First assistant director Joseph Reidy remembers that it was difficult to get De Niro out of his trailer. "So when we first started with De Niro, we started with the storefront, with Lorraine. I do remember that being the first day because he yelled at me in the trailer. Because he had not yet gotten his look right." Here he was playing Jimmy as an older man. "And because he had signed on to the movie so late, we had not been able to do tests with him the same way as we had with the other cast members. It was kind of unfair to him. And he hadn't finished his makeup, hadn't finished establishing his look. But we were running out of light, and it was the first day of shooting. So someone had to go in and move it along." I told Reidy about how vividly De Niro recollected his problems with respect to hair color and Reidy responded, "Yes, that's exactly the sort of thing he would get upset about."

Before she worked with Martin Scorsese, Barbara De Fina, after having been employed by comedian Alan King's production company, was a unit manager on Sidney Lumet's 1981 *The Prince of the City.* She did other uncredited jobs with the man who, before Scorsese took the unofficial title, was the quintessential New York movie director. "I worked with Sidney a lot, and he and Marty were similar in the way that they were both incredibly prepared when they would come on the set. Sidney maybe a little more so, to the point that he would know—in preproduction he would decide what lenses he was going to use. And Marty wasn't quite that, but he did make little storyboards for every scene. And I suppose he figured out a lot of the lenses he wanted, and more than that, camera movements, which were so important to him. I think he moved the camera much more than Sidney.

"Sidney, I think, was a little more—I don't want to use the word *assured*, but much more comfortable, I think. I think Marty, at the point I began working with him, thought he had a lot more to prove."

Joseph Reidy had worked on several films with Scorsese before getting to work with Lumet, on the 2006 *Find Me Guilty*. He agrees with De Fina's assessment of the two directors being unusually well-prepared. "In the time I worked with Marty, his preparation changed over time. But there's always one period, though, that's consistent, that he always did, and that is, he took time to himself, he cloistered himself for a few days and composed the film in his head, and put it down on paper, in the script. He told me what he really needed was just solitude and music, and maybe he would have reference films or something for him to look at—but he already had the reference films in his head. There was a period when I would prep with him, and he would disappear for a few days. Like eight weeks out into preproduction or something, at some point he would do that. For three or four days, and sometimes he would go to a hotel room, he'd be away from his office, away from distractions. And he would come back with a meticulously notated script that represented his 'composed' film." It always had to do with what he saw, and what he wanted to see. If there was a deviation from it on the locations they worked with—if a door was in a different position than what he had envisioned, for instance, he could roll with it, or adjust, but he was usually able to convey to the production designer, Kristi Zea, and the location staff, managed by De Fina and production manager Bruce Pustin, what he wanted with specificity.

Lumet, on the other hand, rehearsed almost as if for a theatrical production. "It's a two- to three-week rehearsal period, and traditionally he would be down at the Ukrainian National Home on Second Avenue, and then order sandwiches in from the Second Avenue Deli, he always had a habit of doing all these things, as he describes in his own book." The book is *Making Movies*, an indispensable volume for critic, filmmaker, and enthusiast. "And there would be, already, a set plan, but he would maybe alter the sets in this imaginary workspace, everything would be taped out on the floor and so on." Paul Newman worked with Lumet, who, like the star, had also spent time at New York's Actors Studio, on *The Verdict* a couple of years before doing *The Color of Money* with Scorsese. And Newman's Lumet-like approach to rehearsing threw Scorsese for a loop. "We did it the way he suggested, which was to take two complete weeks and just work it out with the actors in a loft. I was really nervous, because it was like the theater, which I'd never done before," Scorsese told Ian Christie and David Thompson. "So when [Newman] said, 'What you do is take a tape and mark out an area for a chair; then you tape out an area for a bed,' I could foresee those terrible theater things when people pretend a door is there, which I hate. I said, 'What if we use a real chair?' 'A chair is good,' he said, to my relief. So we used a chair, then we had a hospital bed brought in, and so on.

"Rehearsals are always aggravating. You are afraid that you are going to say ridiculous things, and the actors feel that way, too." In preparing with the actors for *Goodfellas*, Scorsese worked in personal spaces with small groups of actors, or one-on-one.

"He tended to meet with actors individually and in group," Reidy says. "That could be in his office or at his or their places. We did go to a few locations with some of the cast. They wouldn't be costumed, they wouldn't have everything together, and he would spend time with them, and that was important. After he had done the composition of the shots, and made notes, done location scouting and finding the places and continuing to cast, he'd work with the actors, and have Nick Pileggi come in for script revisions based on that." It was in one of these private meeting that Scorsese extracted the real-life "How am I funny?" anecdote from Joe Pesci.

"The shoot took sixty-eight days. And I predicted it was going to take sixty-eight days," Joseph Reidy recalls. "Marty was really good with me about this, because the schedule mattered to him at that point. I do not think it does as much to him these days, but it did matter on this movie. And I think he was given a budget of fifty-five days initially. But as we looked at what we had to do, I did a schedule that was around sixty-eight. It was toward the end of preproduction, and we were still aiming for a shorter schedule. And I still said, 'This is gonna be the number.' While budgeted for fifty-five, we went over that. But we went over to *exactly* where Marty and I thought it was going to be. To sixty-eight days."

I asked Reidy to explain to the layman what a first assistant director does: "An assistant director is really there to help the director, in any way they can, to achieve their vision. At the same time, they serve the producer's company in terms of moving the film along and trying to keep on schedule. But at least keep the production company running. So, stage management during the day, while maintaining a view, overall, of trying to accomplish the film within its scheduled time. How is the stage management done? I'm running this set, I'm orchestrating the day's work, working with the director of photography, and all of the crew members, to make things happen. And directing the background action. It encompasses, usually, much more. And with Marty I had a different relationship than with some other directors, in that he would have me sometimes orchestrate more extras, things like that. I often got a little more responsibility in terms of working with minor players, bringing them in and positioning them, giving them an idea of what is going on in the scene. I always had enough of an understanding that I could sketch out a scene for them. Especially when there were a lot of people in the scene—a lot of these wiseguys who are, you know, Number 28 on the call sheet, or something along those lines; Marty does not need to individually address all of them, and it takes up time that Marty needs to address the principals, so that would fall to me at times, too."

Scorsese was a crucial component of Reidy's early cinephilia, so working with the director became something of a dream job for Reidy. "I loved movies when I was a child and in high school. My mother would take me to films at Oberlin College, or I'd go into Cleveland to colleges or the art houses. Film school education was not widely known about then, particularly in Middle America. But I was reading film journals and books; I read about Coppola and people like that, and about little other things that were coming out by new directors. And I made my own short films. When I was a senior in high school I made my first trip to New York. There weren't college tours as such in those days, at least not that I knew about, but the idea of going to NYU had occurred to me. It's kind of shocking to think that I came to New York on my own at that time, but I went to the New York Film Festival during my visit. And *Mean Streets* was there. So I was thinking I should go into movies. My parents didn't quite understand that whole thing, 'cause it was not a common occupation, certainly no one they knew did it. I got into NYU, on a scholarship, and made movies there, and learned about living in New York and became a little more sophisticated than when I came in. I wanted to go on and write and direct myself, but when I got out of school, I realized I was broke! I had loans, I needed to do something, and I applied for jobs as a camera assistant, editor assistant, anything. And I took a test for the Directors Guild training program, and I had been working as a PA, a little bit of commercials and such. My first film job actually was working for a psychiatrist at Downstate Medical Center, shooting video of group therapy sessions. I got into the training program, and that put me on this track as assistant director. Two-year training program, became a second AD, I accelerated through that, and as soon as I got my experience as a second, it only took me a few years, I started working as a first. So I was twenty-nine when I started working as a first AD, and went a little slowly. It was a matter of time before I met Marty, and I met Marty twice, once for *After Hours*, because I'd worked with another producer, Robert Colesberry, and he brought me in to meet him for *After Hours*. I didn't get the job. But next was *Color of Money*. In the interim, I had worked on a television pilot for a TV series, *The Equalizer*. And Barbara De Fina was the line producer. So she had me meet Marty for *Color of Money*, I got the job, and I... I, like, fell in love with him. Working with someone I had admired for that long was really something." The relationship continued for twenty years, with Reidy acting as first assistant director on almost every Scorsese feature through 2010's *Shutter Island*.

After Hours, the picture that Reidy had not gotten a job on, was Scorsese's first with the German-born cinematographer Michael Ballhaus. Had Ballhaus, who died in 2017 at the age of eighty-one, never met Scorsese he would still count as one of cinema's towering figures by dint of his work with Rainer Werner Fassbinder. Between 1971 and 1981 he shot thirteen features for the prolific, volatile German director, all of them great or near-great; the best-known of them are *Beware of a Holy Whore*, *The Bitter Tears of Petra von Kant*, and *The Marriage of Maria Braun*. In addition to the ability to work quickly, Ballhaus was also able to do the seemingly impossible, and without seeming to break a sweat. There's one scene in Fassbinder's 1976 *Chinese Roulette* in which no matter where the camera turns, there's a reflective surface, but the camera manages to itself elude reflection, always.

Ballhaus began working in the US in the early '80s. His first English-language film, *Dear Mr. Wonderful*, directed by the German Peter Lilienthal, starred Joe Pesci—it's only the second film Pesci made after 1980's *Raging Bull*. And in it Pesci plays a particularly resonant role, that of a bowling alley lounge singer, something Pesci actually had been. (In 2019, writing about Pesci's return to acting after a long hiatus, for Scorsese's *The Irishman*, the critic Violet Lucca speaks of Pesci's underplaying in this picture: "He expresses [...] defeat without words or movements, without slouching or beating back tears. Instead, it all emanates from the haunted, crushed look in his eyes.") In 1983 Ballhaus shot *Baby It's You* for director John Sayles; the film's producers, Griffin Dunne and Amy Robinson, went on to produce *After Hours*, and in the process they put Ballhaus together with Scorsese.

In *Scorsese on Scorsese*, the director recalls: "The producers introduced me to a new cameraman, Michael Ballhaus, who had done many of Fassbinder's pictures. Michael is a gentleman. He smiles on the set, he is very pleasant and he's Max Ophüls' nephew. He also moves quickly." Years later, in a stage interview with Roger Ebert at the Wexner Center for the Arts in Ohio, Scorsese would detail just how quickly he could move, on *The Last Temptation of Christ*: "In the case of the crucifixion [...] we shot in two days, from sunup to sundown, and we did seventy-five setups [individual shots]." Ebert says, "A typical day of shooting on average by another director might get four." (It's worth noting here that they were shooting on film; digital technology has discombobulated production notions concerning setups, shooting duration, and a whole lot more.) Scorsese responds, "Six to ten. Ten's a good day [...] Michael Ballhaus, because he worked with Fassbinder, and he did a film with Fassbinder called *Beware of a Holy Whore*, which after three days of shooting, he needed another four days to finish. But [Fassbinder] didn't like the actor; he canceled the actor, he put himself in the part. He said they were going to reshoot everything in one day. So he did it this way. He said, Okay, at 7:52, we shoot by the window. At 8:01, we're up... And they literally did it that way. That's the way we did this crucifixion scene."

Barbara De Fina says of Ballhaus, "He was always friendly and happy; he was one of the happiest people I've ever met. And he had a great crew, so it worked really well." (Ballhaus's son, Florian, now a cinematographer himself, was the first assistant camera on *Goodfellas*.)

Reidy says, "Michael was very good at interpreting Marty's ideas, improving on them sometimes, in the shots, how the shots would be composed, how they would move. And he was very good with camera movement and, you know, would suggest things that maybe Marty hadn't thought of, to add to it. They worked very well together, because part of it was his personality; he was a gentleman"—Scorsese's word again—"and he had brought with him connections to European film history. Max Ophüls was an uncle of his, and he would talk about visiting the set of Ophüls' great film *Lola Montès*."

Max Ophüls' remarkable filmography includes both European and American masterpieces, and his work overall is known for elegant, complicated camera movements that influenced Stanley Kubrick and Scorsese, and more recently Paul Thomas Anderson. (James Mason, who starred in two of Ophüls' greats, 1949's *Caught* and *The Reckless Moment* from the same year, and who had great affection for the man, wrote this poem about Ophüls' cinematic practice: "A shot that does not call for tracks/Is agony for poor old Max,/Who, separated from his dolly,/Is wrapped in deepest melancholy./Once, when they took away his crane,/I thought he'd never smile again.")

"Marty and Michael could talk about cinema," Reidy says. "Marty is moody, and you've heard this from people, I'm sure; he's had his tantrums and can be difficult at times. And Michael had a way of dealing with him that took a lot of patience. He would listen to Marty and he would calm Marty if Marty would be upset. And this held, even if Marty was agitated about nothing that we were doing at the time, but anything else that was bothering him. And Michael had a way of smoothing it over so that Marty would get pleasure out of the work. Michael had brought joy to all of it, and together they would share the joy of the filmmaking. They really took pleasure in it. And that's what made that relationship really special."

I mentioned to Joseph Reidy that Barbara De Fina had talked about how reassuring Michael Ballhaus could be. "*Reassuring* is exactly the word. If Marty was insecure about something, really worried that something was not gonna work, and if Michael believed that something would work in that shot, he would take the time to make Marty understand that it would. He had a way with his language, his demeanor, while being entirely honest with Marty. With a shot that was difficult, that maybe would not be possible within Marty's idea of it, Michael could create an idea that would help, like something simple in restaging, like 'Can we just move the actors over here to this window?' They would discuss things at length, and sometimes Marty would not want to go along, because he was thinking about shot order, or considering whether the suggestion lined up with what he thought the character would do. And I think on *Goodfellas*, Marty would come away feeling satisfied. I don't think he was ever disappointed. On some movies, you'd think, Oh God, that's not working, but then, he's living with it. But on *Goodfellas* Michael and he were able to get what Marty wanted, almost always." (As it happens, though, Ballhaus was not able to see the entire film through. He was contracted to shoot the Frank Oz comedy *What About Bob?* and had to leave the production a little before its completion. Taking his place was Barry Sonnenfeld, the future director who had lensed several films for the Coen brothers. In a 1999 interview with the *Guardian* it's said that Sonnenfeld was on the shoot for a week; Barbara De Fina recollects it being more like two. As the picture went almost two weeks over its budgeted schedule, the latter seems likely. Another source remembers Sonnenfeld lensing all of the sequences featuring the teen Henry Hill. Sonnenfeld's recent memoir does not clear any of this up, but features an amusing anecdote in which the then-very-youthful-looking Sonnenfeld is razzed by Scorsese and De Niro for appearing to be twelve years old.)

As such, the high drama on the set was kept to a minimum. The authenticity of some of the actors became a minor concern for Reidy. Scorsese and Nick Pileggi, when dining at the legendary Harlem restaurant Rao's—a very exclusive joint in which mobsters would mingle with the landed gentry—would spot these memorable faces, many of which could provide perfect authentic atmosphere for the cinematic world of criminals they were building. With casting director Ellen Lewis, Reidy made sure to keep them under close watch, not just because several were active criminals or convicted felons themselves, but because they did not know how being an extra worked—factors as elemental as showing up on time and keeping quiet on the set. "They were different levels of extras from different eras and affiliations. Paulie would have a crew, but that would change, you know, there'd be, like, key guys—when you look at the movie, you'll see in a number of scenes in a given era, a lot of the same faces, then it would change for another era. I told the casting director, Ellen Lewis, 'We have to hire these people as principals, they can't be extras, we have to know who they are, we have to control them, because they all have to get dressed, they have to have lots of costumes, we have to know how to get ahold of them, we—you know, we have to deal with them like principals."

Property master Bob Griffon had a lot of fake money made for the Air France heist, but for the scene in which Jimmy "the Gent" is introduced, De Niro insisted on real money to throw around. Griffon withdrew $2,000 from his own savings and remembers gathering it back up quickly after each take, because there was a very real possibility one of these on-set characters would walk off with the uninsured cash. Keeping track of these guys became a project in and of itself. "Ellen and Marty took all these pictures of all these guys, and she'd remind him who this guy was and who this guy was, and she made a chart, and a board, and they put the photographs of this group, and then that group, and I would remind the members of each group of certain things, I'd say, 'We're gonna need them to do this next,' or 'They need to be around for this long,' and so on."

Despite the large number of locations and scenes to shoot, the principal photography was for the most part drama free, albeit labor intensive. Bob Griffon remembers spending a day at Long Island's Catalina Beach Club, shooting the scene in which Henry is introduced, briefly, to Karen's upper-middle-class world, where he tries to pay for an al fresco meal with cash and is told by Karen that here you "sign" for things. The shooting of Stacks Edwards was also on that day's shot list. The apartment where that would be shot was in Manhattan, well over an hour's drive from the beach club, and once there, Scorsese had decided to restage the murder, having Stacks propelled from his chair and bouncing off a bed, where the blood spatter from his shooting would end up. (He was originally to go up against a wall.) The sequence took six hours to restage and shoot.

Of the budget they worked with, De Fina says, "Well, we were comfortable. I mean, it's funny, budgets today are often smaller than some of the budgets were at that point. It was comfortable. We didn't have a lot of extra money, but it wasn't the kind of movie that needed a lot of expensive things. With so much of the dressing, for instance, there was a lot of just found material."

I asked Reidy if he was aware, at the time, of how singular a film *Goodfellas* would be. "I had a fantastic time on it," he said. "Every day was special in some way, either with acting, or we're doing some interesting shots, or we did great things with extras, or—you know, things like that, so it was, bit by bit, coming together. I thought: 'This could be pretty great.' And you know what, I had the benefit of this: I could sort of see where Marty was going, that he was making something really special, that was dear to him, that was close to him, and that really had his mark on it. You know, when he talked about his own upbringing, and what it was like living in Little Italy and seeing guys on the street—when he would relate that to young Henry looking out the window and seeing the guys...it's like that kind of thing he did, except that while Henry wanted to be like them, Marty was an observer of the action. He had to be, because he had asthma, was sickly, he would just be seeing these things. So there was his sense of what it was like for the real wiseguys, bringing to this story what he knew of it personally, that helped make it special. And he was bringing out great performances, that's something you couldn't deny. Joe Pesci or De Niro or Lorraine Bracco. Or how Paul Sorvino was in that, he has some really good scenes, but a lot of it was just his *pres-*

ence, and how he would sit and look and *be*, which came out of how Marty worked with him. So yes. I felt we were making something really special. And different."

Four:

A MARTIN SCORSESE PICTURE, SCENE BY SCENE

CREDITS BY SAUL AND ELAINE BASS

The disquieting opening scene is punctuated by two brief sets of credits, the white block type rolling like lane marks down a highway, horizontal rather than vertical (as they would be from the perspective of a driver). They've already been described a bit in a prior chapter. The first set announces "An Irwin Winkler Production" and "A Martin Scorsese Picture" (despite being a director whose films bear the distinct stamps of his personality and aesthetic, Scorsese does not use the more blatant possessory credit "A Film By"). Then the principal cast, Robert De Niro first.

In the second set of credits, after Henry closes the trunk, the film's title is revealed—in red-on-black type rather than white-on-black type. As if the blood of the murdered man in the trunk had seeped into the fabric of the film itself. The remaining credits, for executive producer Barbara De Fina, *Wiseguy* author Pileggi, screenwriters Pileggi and Scorsese, producer Winkler and director Scorsese, are in white.

Saul Bass was a graphic designer with a particular distinction: he was spectacularly good at designing specifically for film. And his images, in opening credits and on posters, always bolstered a film's theme: the hinged Capitol Dome in *Advise and Consent*, the trifurcated, shifting main title of *Psycho*. (Bass also storyboarded that film's infamous shower-murder scene.) From the mid-1950s on he collaborated closely with his wife, Elaine, and they began sharing credit on film work in 1960, beginning with *Spartacus*. It is no coincidence that the above-named films were made by directors of distinction: Otto Preminger, Alfred Hitchcock, and Stanley Kubrick.

Goodfellas was the first Scorsese film for which the Basses concocted the credits. One might wonder why, given Scorsese's taste. As it happened, Scorsese had believed that the Basses were dead, or no longer working.

In the book *Saul Bass: A Life in Film and Design*, Scorsese recalls: "I had a placement for the credit but I didn't have the right lettering. I had the right music cue but something wasn't right. I just didn't know what to do with it. I was watching a movie called *Big* and I see the end credits—Elaine and Saul Bass. I said, 'My God, this is great! They are working—they are still around. This is fantastic.' I said to my producer, 'Do you think we should venture to call and see if they would do it?'"

Bass is subsequently quoted as saying: "Were we interested in working with Martin Scorsese? You bet your ass we were." And in the same book Nicholas Pileggi reacts to their work: "You write a book of 300 to 400 pages and then you boil it down to a script of maybe 100 to 150 pages. Eventually you have the pleasure of seeing that the Basses have knocked you right out of the ballpark. They have boiled it down to four minutes flat."

The Basses maintained their relationship with Scorsese for

several years, doing the titles for the films *Cape Fear*, *The Age of Innocence*, and *Casino*. Saul died in 1996. Elaine did not carry on solo; *Casino* was the last picture they worked on.

YOUNG HENRY HILL

Like Holden Caulfield, *Goodfellas* doesn't want to bore you with any "David Copperfield kind of crap." Its account of Henry Hill's boyhood, while crucial, is also brisk. It takes up less than thirteen minutes of the movie's 145-minute run time. And it's more than just a warm reminiscence of a "glorious" misspent youth. It's a minitutorial on the Italian American gangster environment in New York neighborhoods in the 1950s.

Over the song "Rags to Riches," the medium close-up of a having-some-kind-of-second-thoughts adult Henry Hill cuts to the credit titles, and then to an extreme close-up of a green eye, transfixed. That's thirteen-year-old Henry, played by Christopher Serrone, and his eye is fixed on the cabstand across the street from his East New York house, and the sharp-dressed gangsters who roost there. "To me, being a gangster was better than being president of the United States." Young Henry is seen though the slats of his bedroom window; down below on the streets, wiseguys in sharp clothes driving big cars horse around. In voice-over Henry lists some of the things he saw them getting away with. "In the summer when they played cards all night, nobody ever called the cops."

The movie homes in on a portly man with slicked-back, receding black hair. Henry names him. "Tuddy Cicero." He pauses, and says the first name again, wistfully: "Tuddy." Because it's so early in the movie, one doesn't notice the anomaly. But this one-word evocation is perhaps the only moment of genuine tenderness in the entire movie. A yearning invocation of an entire world that's now lost to Henry, a recollection

of affection and loyalty that at the time felt real. By the end of
the movie, as the betrayals among thieves mount up, Tuddy is
largely absent, except in one crucial scene in which he's easy
to miss despite the fact that he's pulling the trigger on the gun
that kills one of the central characters. (Vito "Tuddy" Vario, the
real-life model for this gangster, was indeed present and active
in his brother's real-life operations to the end; he died in 1988,
the same year his brother Paul died in prison.)

Tuddy is played by Frank DiLeo, a music industry executive who at the time of the movie's shooting was severing ties
with Michael Jackson, whom he had been managing since 1984.
Scorsese had directed a short film that served as a music video
for the song "Bad," the leadoff single for the Jackson album of
the same name. (Scorsese's cameo in that picture is his face on a
"Wanted" poster in the subway, citing his crime as "Sacrilege.")
It was during the making of the short that Scorsese became acquainted with DiLeo.

A year later the peculiar Michael Jackson feature film *Moon-
walker* was released. One segment, showcasing the song "Smooth
Criminal" from the 1984 album *Thriller*, featured Jackson protecting three homeless children, played by Kellie Parker, Bran-
don Quintin Adams, and Sean Ono Lennon, from the drug
kingpin known as "Mr. Big," whose "real name" is Frank Lideo
(the last name is a not-at-all-obvious anagram for DiLeo) and
who is played with arguably overelaborate relish by Joe Pesci.
Jackson chose to portray his manager as a supervillain before
there was an actual falling-out between them. Such winking
inside jokes were not entirely uncommon in a music industry
that had been "mobbed up" since shortly after jukeboxes had
been invented; they weren't commonly made in public, though.
According to DiLeo, he and Jackson intended to resume their
business relationship with the 2009 "This Is It" concert tour,
but Jackson died during rehearsals for the shows.

In his portrayal of Tuddy, DiLeo plays down the larger-than-life profile he cultivated as Jackson's manager. Tuddy is not soft-spoken as such—listen to him berate Henry after the youngster tries to help out a shooting victim, clearly one of the guys, who makes the mistake of wandering over to the pizza place while bleeding profusely—but he knows his place. Which is subordinate to Tuddy's older brother Paulie Cicero, played by Paul Sorvino, who is soft-spoken when he speaks at all. Paulie is first seen breaking up some cabstand horseplay so mild it barely registers as such; the second his potbellied profile is seen, the guys break it up; after Paulie recedes they bicker about who "started it," whatever it even was.

Henry's narration describes Paulie's slow, deliberate, track-covering way of doing things, alternating with his home and school life. "I couldn't see over the wheel and I'm parking Cadillacs," he exults. As the frame freezes to show Henry's enraged father raising a belt to the kid, Liotta's voice-over notes that "Everybody takes a beating sometime." The wiseguys torment a mailman who had been imprudent enough to deliver a truant notice to Hill's house. After witnessing this thug justice, Hill asks, "How could I go to school after that and pledge allegiance to the flag and sit through good government bullshit?" Henry's education in how things work is brutal but not, obviously, an entirely inaccurate one.

He speaks of the robbers giving Paulie "tribute just like in the old country." The proximate causes of monetary crime, at least those not related to ephemeral notions of "human nature," often have to do with economic oppression/suppression. Italian Americans from Sicilian and Neapolitan backgrounds didn't just hew to the ways of their own country out of a perverse defiance of assimilation. Italian Americans were targets of bigoted scorn, denied opportunities in the land of opportunity. Their insulation was a form of self-governance and self-protection.

"That's what the FBI could never understand," Henry says. "What Paulie and the organization does is offer protection for people who can't go to the cops... They're like the police department for wiseguys." This of course is a skewed perspective on things, and mob-affiliated Italian Americans were not met with wholesale approval in Italian American neighborhoods. They were seen with disdain and scorn by many of what you'd call "law-abiding citizens," and the disapprobation was often bitter.

Edward McDonald, the prosecutor who got Henry and Karen Hill into the witness protection program and who plays himself in *Goodfellas*, reckons that the mob-as-neighborhood-protectorate model began crumbling in the early 1960s. But of course latter-day boss John Gotti kept the conceit going into the '80s and beyond with his elaborate Fourth of July celebrations in his home turf of Ozone Park, Queens. And to this day his "constituents" boast that he kept the neighborhood "safe," e.g., that his mooks would chase out any person of color who happened to step onto the wrong side of his neighborhood's "border."

For Hill, the mid-'50s represents the most unsullied of Edens. Over shots of him setting the parking lot of a rival taxi company on fire, he details the joys of his status as one of the boys: "I didn't have to wait in line at the bakery. Our neighbors didn't park in our driveway anymore, even though we didn't have a car." He tells of some neighborhood strangers carrying his mother's groceries for her: "It was outta respect." At this point the whole lot explodes as he runs away and the frame freezes. The implication could not be more direct, at least when described on the page: he earns respect by being a destroyer. But the image of flames is a beautiful one, the look on Henry's face beatific. The ins and outs of this way of life do not represent anything quite so simple as a double-edged sword.

"It was a glorious time. The wiseguys were all over the place. It was before Apalachin and before Crazy Joe decided to take on a boss and start a war." The names "Apalachin" and "Crazy Joe" drop quickly, and there are no footnotes. Scorsese and company realize they won't necessarily register with a large percentage of the viewership. For those who come to the movie conversant with mob history, they're added value. Apalachin, as I mentioned, was the burg in Upstate New York where, in 1957, mob boss Joseph Barbara, who owned a substantial estate there, convened a mob summit intended to quell internecine feuding that had been rising and falling since the early '50s. The meeting was raided by state police before it had even begun and over fifty mobsters were arrested. This was the beginning of sustained public scrutiny of what would be called "the Mafia." Prior to that it was practically a genuine secret society.

"Crazy Joe" was Joseph "Joey" Gallo, a mob hit man who (with future boss Carmine Persico) assassinated family head Albert Anastasia in the barbershop of the Sheraton Hotel in 1957, a couple of weeks before Joseph Barbara's abortive conference. Gallo and Persico's acts were never proven in a court of law, but Persico himself privately bragged of them in subsequent years. Gallo's nickname derived from his brazenness, which only increased over the years. In 1972, having been suspected by some of arranging a hit on Joseph Colombo at a rally for Colombo's Italian American Civil Rights Association (a group formed to, among other things, combat cinematic depictions of Mafia mobsters) the year before, Gallo was shot to death at Little Italy's Umberto's Clam House. This event is chronicled in Scorsese's 2019 *The Irishman*, in which the assassination is carried out by that film's narrator, the considerably less flamboyant (than Gallo or Henry Hill for that matter) killer Frank Sheeran. By bringing the criminal organizations further into the light, Hill's narration implies, Apalachin and Gallo helped destroy what was sometimes referred to as "our thing," that is, "Cosa Nostra."

Handing out sandwiches at a makeshift casino, Henry is

thrilled by the grown-ups drinking and throwing around large wads of cash. "It was when I met the world. It was when I first met Jimmy Conway." Robert De Niro, made up to look in his late twenties perhaps, walks in. The first sentence you clearly hear from him is "The Irishman is here to take all you guineas' money."

When Christopher Serrone played young Henry he was a thirteen-year-old child model—one of the agency Wilhelmina's "Wee Willies"—when the casting director Ellen Lewis (who had worked in the storied Juliet Taylor's office and was casting a movie solo for the first time) called Serrone's agent, while Serrone was in that agent's office.

"Apparently they'd been looking to cast young Henry for months and were getting nowhere. As she explains on the phone what they're looking for my agent says, 'I think I'm looking at him.'" Serrone did not get more specifics about the movie beyond its crime themes. "I was thinking about movies with tough kids in them and the only thing I could go off of was *The Outsiders*," he said. "My exposure to film at the time was limited. I ripped the sleeves off of one of my T-shirts, slicked my hair back, picked up some sides [script portions] for a cold read. I go in the room, I do the little spiel. And I get the 'Thank you!' Which I took for, 'Don't call us, we'll call you.' I thought I had bombed. But then my beeper's going off—I thought I was in trouble!" Serrone had heard that thousands had been turned down for the part, so he felt especially fortunate.

"The casting people gave me *Wiseguy* to read, said that would be a great resource. I also went back to my dad's old 'hood, went to Corona. I used to go to Gotti's Fourth of July party as a kid. And not to sound cliché but I was always a people watcher. And now I watched any gangster films my parents let me watch. My father, who was a working guy who liked movies, he wanted me to be aware of the magnitude of what was going on, who I would be working with. De Niro was the focus. We watched—without my mom's knowledge—*Taxi Driver, Mean Streets, Raging Bull, The Untouchables, Once Upon a Time in America.*"

Although Serrone would have no scenes with Joe Pesci—young Henry only interacts with young Tommy, who was played by Joseph D'Onofrio—they spent time on the set together, where Pesci invariably referred to him as "the kid."

"That's why when Paulie introduces me to Jimmy, he says, 'I want you to meet the kid, Henry.'"

Serrone recalls spending almost three months on the film; as almost all commercial pictures are, *Goodfellas* was shot out of sequence, and scenes were dictated by the availability and condition of locations. He remembers his first day of shooting as "devastating" for reasons having nothing to do with the movie. "My pet parakeet died! There it was, dead at the bottom of the cage. My mom and dad had contemplated not telling me, but my dad said, 'Well, he should know. It's his pet.'" The first scenes he shot were the first shots of Henry we see in the movie, the character looking wistfully at the cabstand and pizza parlor where Tuddy and company congregate.

The final minutes of the sequence after Jimmy meets "the kid" show Jimmy tutoring Henry and Tommy in selling bootlegged cigarettes from the trunk of a car, later the back of a truck. A typically fleet set of shots shows Jimmy tucking a bribe into a Pall Mall carton going to a couple of cops, one of whom responds to a how's-it-going query with "Jimmy, I'd complain but who'd listen." We break away briefly from Henry's POV to see how Jimmy—"What he loved to do was steal," Henry says—managed a truck hijacking. The comedian Margaret Smith shows up as a post office worker getting some cigs. Then on the rise at New York's comedy clubs, she was one of many up-

and-coming performers who leaped at a shot at appearing in a Scorsese picture.

After a couple of plainclothesmen take Henry in while he's selling smokes, Henry looks pretty rattled in front of the judge. He doesn't notice his lawyer's broad wink to "His Honor" or even register his nonsentence. He's bummed at getting caught. But heartened when he leaves the courtroom and sees Paulie, Tuddy, Jimmy, and a bunch of other wiseguys there to celebrate him. Paul Sorvino smiles for the first and very nearly last time in the movie, and delivers his only truly exuberant line reading as he opens his arms: "Oh ho, you broke your cherry!"

To this day Serrone, who lives in Denver with his wife and their child, has warm feelings about the crew he ran with as a thirteen-year-old. Scorsese encouraged him to improvise and try new things just as he did with the adult members of the cast. "He's the first guy to say: 'make it your own.' If the way it's worded in the script would never come out of your mouth, don't do it." The taxi lot explosion scene was an enjoyable bit of mischief and movie illusion. "What kid wouldn't want to do that, you know?" But the crew ensured Serrone's safety. "Everything about the explosion was very carefully calculated, and of course they cheated the camera to the nth degree. I was about ninety feet from the actual blast," he says. "But you'll notice when the movie goes to freeze-frame and the top part of my body is leaning forward? Then, at that moment, I could feel the heat from the explosion."

At the end of young Henry's education, he tells Jimmy, his new father figure, that he was afraid the older guy would be mad at him for getting pinched. No, Jimmy says, "I'm proud of you." Henry is happy but confused. Jimmy fills him in.

"You took your first pinch like a man, and you learned the two greatest things in life."

"What?"

"Look at me. Never rat on your friends and always keep your mouth shut."

Subsequently we'll see Tommy telling an elaborate story of getting beaten by cops and refusing to talk: "Are you still here? I thought I told you to go fuck your mother." But eventually Henry talks. Partially on account of how he's afraid he'll be killed. By Jimmy, or by Paulie.

But here we are still in Eden. The frame freezes on the exuberant men surrounding an exuberant boy, and a panoramic doowop version of the standard "Stardust" plays on the soundtrack.

IDLEWILD

The attraction/repulsion dynamic of the movie's perspective is at work all the time. The opening scene of Hill and company stabbing and shooting an already gravely wounded man to death should raise an eyebrow at least. But the look on Hill's face and the irony of the "wanted to be a gangster" line in contrast with it suggests extenuating circumstances for the character who is to serve as the audience's surrogate.

That said, the viewer gets asked to look the other way pretty frequently, despite how much Henry/Liotta's ingratiating narration lures them into an "a way of life, like any other" tolerance. Put it this way: the corrupt good times are very good times, provided you're in with the corrupt, where the movie puts you.

After the freeze-frame of mobsters celebrating young Henry, the movie cuts to a view of a passenger jet descending to its landing place. That place, a title says, is Idlewild Airport, in 1963, before the assassination of John F. Kennedy precipitated its rechristening as Kennedy Airport. The airport, tucked into a corner separating the New York boroughs of Queens and Brooklyn, was constructed in the 1940s to relieve congestion at LaGuardia Airport, then called LaGuardia Field, located in Queens proper.

The adult Henry, and the adult Tommy, are hanging out in the parking lot of the Airline Diner. The camera tilts up from Henry's tasseled brown loafers up his not-too-shiny sharkskin trousers and jacket, black sport shirt with white pinstripes, wide collar worn outside the jacket, two buttons unbuttoned showing the neck of a T-shirt later tastelessly dubbed a "wifebeater" in some colloquial usage, up to Henry's head; he's dragging on a cigarette. (While Scorsese is known for being a stickler about geographical accuracy in his New York–set films in particular, for period authenticity and logistical reasons, *Goodfellas* "cheats" a lot; the Airline Diner, still extant albeit converted to a Jackson Hole burger joint, is in the vicinity of LaGuardia, not Kennedy.)

"By the time I grew up there was thirty billion a year in cargo moving through Idlewild Airport, and believe me, we tried to steal every bit of it," Henry says. The airport was practically in East New York's backyard, so it "belonged to Paulie," Henry says. "We had friends and relatives who worked all over the place and they would tip us off about what was coming in and what was moving out." Henry and Tommy aren't just standing in the parking lot looking cool for no reason. A truck pulls in the lot, they exchange nods with the driver. "It was beautiful," Henry says of the arrangement. "Whenever we needed money, we'd rob the airport. To us it was better than Citibank." Henry and Tommy pay off the driver, hop in the truck, and drive away.

This is all very roguish and charming up to a point. But the spell may be broken when the driver rushes into the diner in fake indignation. "Did you see that? Two n———rs just stole my truck. Do you believe that?" A whole minihistory of New York City race relations is laid out in those sentences. Institutionalized racism against blacks was capable of doing sufficient damage without this sort of scapegoating, which fed, and feeds, into an endless blacks-as-criminals narrative.

In *Goodfellas*, the main characters spout off all kinds of bigoted language, against blacks, homosexuals, women, and so on. Italian Americans may have, in the early part of the twentieth century, seen themselves as up one or two mere rungs above blacks on the social hierarchy ladder (never considering, of course, that blacks had been literal slaves); for many individuals, that provided a pretext for kicking or punching down as hard as they were able, if not institutionally, then personally.

Scorsese's films have treated the situation frankly over the years. In *Mean Streets*, the protagonist, Charlie, a guy who's not as slick as he'd like to be but is often more glib than he ought to be, is attracted to one of the go-go dancers at his friend Tony's bar. "She is real good-looking," he notes in his interior monologue. "But she's black. Well, you can see that, right?" Forbidden fruit, to be sure. When he finally gets the nerve to ask her out—on a bullshit pretext, telling her he, too, might be opening a club and he'd like to maybe hire her—he stands her up.

The 1976 *Taxi Driver* is most often cited as being especially provocative. Travis Bickle, its protagonist, who makes a pretty short journey from neurotic to psychotic in the course of the movie, is not Italian American. But the idea of him as such tends to stick on account of his being portrayed by Robert De Niro. (If one is keeping score, not that one should, De Niro's lineage is not predominantly Italian; his mother, Virginia Admiral, was of Irish descent, while his father, the artist Robert De Niro, Sr., was of Irish and Italian ancestry.) The movie's "racial politics in particular remain problematic," Geoffrey Macnab wrote in the British newspaper the *Guardian* in 2006. While, exasperatingly, hardly anyone today seems to believe that depiction does not equal endorsement, just what the movie's "racial politics" are is not a question to be answered without some deliberation.

Yes, Paul Schrader's early draft of the screenplay had all of the victims of Bickle's rampages as persons of color. The screenplay was rewritten to change that, but not to drain all the racial hostility out of Bickle.

Bickle's racism is depicted in what prose writers might call the "close third person." The character is seen getting particularly uptight in the presence of black men; he stares down a presumed pimp in the Belmore Cafeteria who he thinks is looking at him. He seems genuinely perturbed when his fellow cabbie, Charlie T., a black man to whom he's just paid five bucks he had borrowed off of him, makes a gunshot gesture. His bigotry is mostly communicated in silent exchanges, glares. The only piece of racist language he uses is "spook." As in his voice-over pronouncement, "I go all over. I take people to the Bronx, Brooklyn. I take 'em to Harlem, I don't care. Don't make no difference to me. It does to some. Some won't even take spooks. Don't make no difference to me." This could be an excerpt from his journal. But like a lot of other white racists, he feels compelled to explain, even if only to himself, that he's not motivated by bigotry even though he is. (Beyond that, he tries to befriend—let's say—a woman of color, played by Diahnne Abbot, De Niro's real-life wife between 1976 and 1988, who works at the candy stand at the porn theater he visits early in the movie.)

In the scene in which Bickle shops for weapons, the ever-more-manic black market salesman Easy Andy (played by Stephen Prince, the future subject of the Scorsese documentary *American Boy*), raves to Travis: "I could sell those guns to some jungle bunny in Harlem. For 500 bucks. But I just deal high quality goods to the right people."

But the most provocative racial epithet in the book is spoken only once in the movie, by the director, in the role of a lunatic fare who's in a jealous rage concerning his wife, and aims to end it with a .44 Magnum, a gun model Bickle himself later purchases. (Scorsese was filling in for the actor George Memmoli, the "that guy is a mook" fellow in *Mean Streets*, who could not make it to the set on account of a back injury. De Niro encouraged Scorsese to take the role, which he plays with the staccato verbal rhythms of an insult comic while wearing a stiff suit. It's still an incredibly disturbing scene. As is the scene in which Bickle shoots a black would-be bodega robber, and the bodega's enraged owner, played by Puerto Rican actor Victor Argo, takes a club to the felled man.)

But there's nothing in *Taxi Driver* that programmatically encourages racism or bigotry. These characters of Scorsese's are deeply disturbed, and while their racial attitudes are symptoms of that, the movie doesn't ask that they be excused on those grounds. What's "problematic" with Scorsese's portrayals, one supposes, is that there's never a character who comes along and gives anyone a talking-to about how racism is bad. While Bickle gets uptight around people of color, the movie doesn't come close to making a statement that the viewer ought to be, too. (To give one contrasting example, the 1973 cop picture *Badge 373* comes off as pretty heavily invested in the idea that Puerto Ricans are generally bad news.) Neither, though, does it condescend to present a pleasant black character to counter Bickle's discomfort, although Charlie T. seems pretty chill. (In the follow-up to *Taxi Driver*, the musical *New York, New York*, De Niro's character, Jimmy Doyle, is a jazz saxophonist eager to play with African American musicians in Harlem. One of whom is played by Clarence Clemons, Bruce Springsteen's longtime sax player—here mimicking a trumpeter.)

In 1980's *Raging Bull* the Italian American characters routinely refer to blacks as "moulies" or "moulignans," meaning "eggplants." Boxer Jake LaMotta's grudge against his black opponent Sugar Ray Robinson is multifaceted and certainly contains a strong racist element. Which does not prevent Jake from calling Joe Louis, the heavyweight he can never fight, "the best there is." He's a very confused person.

Scorsese shows a noteworthy awareness to changing mores pertaining to what contemporary audiences will accept in his 2019 movie *The Irishman*, without making a big deal out of it. In that film, protagonist Frank Sheeran is called upon by his mob bosses to take out Joey Gallo after the shooting of Joseph Costello. Sheeran's boss, Russell Buffalino, discusses the matter with Sheeran. The characters are played by Pesci and De Niro. They discuss Gallo's associations with African Americans and never once drop a racial epithet, referring only to "blacks." One might not believe that an authentic conversation between these characters would go like that. By the same token, there's no real sacrifice of verisimilitude in the scene, and the attitudes are clearly the same, regardless of the words.

The brisk depiction of Henry and Tommy's repellent practice in thievery is not given much time to sink in. The shock of hearing the truck driver's word is like a slap to the face that, depending on where you sit—depending on who you are—fades fast. From Henry's perspective, these are the good times, and they're rolling, and you're invited along for the ride.

MEET THE GANG

The exterior of the Bamboo Lounge, the short-lived hangout for Henry and his crew (replaced, but not seen for long in the film, by The Suite, Hill's own club, which figures more prominently in *Wiseguy* than it does in this movie), was a dressed front, covering up the facade of what was then an Italian restaurant on Brooklyn's Coney Island Boulevard. (The website Movie-Locations says it's now a Nissan dealership.) Most of the interior shots were made at Hawaii Kai, a theme restaurant (guess the theme) that was inside Broadway's Winter Garden theater, a longtime home to the shows *Cats* (which was playing there at the time of shooting), *Mamma Mia*, *School of Rock*, and so on.

Production designer Kristi Zea recalls that, with their kitschy approximations of Polynesian and Hawaiian design motifs and tropes, the Hawaii Kai interiors did not need much dressing. "Going and finding locations is one of the things I love to do most," she says. "You'll find things you'll never be able to dream on any planet. I'll go to homes. Sometimes people just do their thing and you get hit over the head by it. In the Hawaii Kai, we added a few bits and pieces, but essentially it was as it was."

One of the things it was was going out of business. The restaurant was operational at the time of the shoot but would close later in 1989. A sign of its increasing decrepitude was, according to some, its flea infestation. Illeana Douglas recalls showing up at the site: "It was ancient, and inside everything was made of straw and glass. Marty said, 'Careful, this place has fleas'—and let me tell you, it did."

"Yes, I do remember the fleas," Kristi Zea says. Producer Barbara De Fina does not, but says, "Because we started setting up early in the morning I remember it, when all the lights were on, looking dingy and dirty and smelling of last night's booze."

"I don't remember fleas," Joseph Reidy says, "and had there been fleas I definitely would have been bitten. I do remember after seeing it with all the houselights on I did think I would never in a million years eat there."

Liotta's voice-over accompanies an involved Steadicam shot. There's an overtly theatrical feel somehow, as if a lighting designer is pointing spotlights to introduce characters. The point of view is meant to be Henry's, and the characters he names in voice-over look at the camera and say a greeting. It's a showy piece of work, with the "look what I can do" vibe common in the 1940s films made by Michael Powell and Emeric Pressburger. Powell, in his later years, became a great friend of Scorsese's, and married Thelma Schoonmaker. *Goodfellas* was a movie he particularly wanted to see made.

"There was Jimmy...and Tommy and me..." The lighting is deep red, as in the 1960s Italian horror movies Scorsese admired. "And there was..."

In the real-life world of cops, criminals, and "neighborhood" business owners plumbed by Pileggi, in the realm of real-world "consultants" who would give actors and directors tips on how to achieve authenticity for their projects, there's a lot of inter- and intradisciplinary give and take. Ex-mobsters and the guys who once busted them can meet up months or even years later working on some book or show business project. As we've seen, Frank DiLeo was not an actor, and his music industry connections were hardly free of mob associations, as indeed the entire American music industry of his day was largely "mobbed up." (Frederic Dannen's 1990 book *Hit Men* is both an exemplary primer on the topic and the tip of the iceberg.) In a 2010 oral history of *Goodfellas* complied by *GQ* magazine, Nick Pileggi says of the casting of the smaller mobster roles: "We'd put the word out [to the mob guys]: 'Anybody who wants to be in the movie, come.' He must have hired, like, half a dozen guys, maybe more, out of the joint."

The Bamboo Lounge crew was a mix of authentic guys and actors whose backgrounds gave them a veneer of authenticity. In the shot you can't tell the difference. "Jimmy...and Tommy and me..." and Anthony Stabile. He's the first "how you doin'?" and he's played by Frank Adonis. Who looks exactly like an Italian American guy born in Brooklyn in 1935, as he was. Adonis started doing bit parts in the early '70s, providing urban color for *The French Connection*, *The Gang That Couldn't Shoot Straight*, and other gritty fare. He appeared in an early biopic (heavily

fictionalized) of the frantic mobster Joey Gallo, 1974's *Crazy Joe*.
He is in Scorsese's 1980 *Raging Bull*, as Patsy, one of the mobbed-
up crew of boxer Jake LaMotta's brother Joey. In a scene early
in the movie, he comes with Salvy, played by Frank Vincent,
who plays Billy Batts in this film, to watch Joe Pesci's Joey spar
with Robert De Niro's Jake. Jake is enraged by their presence;
we're not quite sure why. Eventually we can infer that he doesn't
want these men, who represent mob interests that fix fights—
and also can make careers—involved with him at all; he's going
to do things his way. "You told them to come up here?" Jake
demands. "Yeah, why, can't I have my friends up here?"

"Don't ever bring him up here again, you hear me?" Near
the ring, Salvy and Patsy and Guido whisper disparagingly. "He
looks mad."

"I'd hit his fucking head with a pipe."

"They look like two f-gs up there." To make a point, Jake
pummels Joey for real. The three wiseguys, hair slicked back
and smirking, leave the gym.

Back at the Bamboo Lounge, to the left of Stabile is Frankie
Carbone, his amused face almost a caricature of an elastic-jawed,
prominent-proboscis Italian American; the jet-black oversize
Brillo pad atop his head is delightfully garish. He jabbers at
Henry in Italian. Actually, in French, with an Italian accent.
Or something. He says, "*Como sava*," which falls somewhere
between the French "*comment ça va*" and the Italian "*come va*,"
that is, "How's it going?" The actor is Frank Sivero, who played
the wingman of De Niro's Jimmy Doyle in Scorsese's 1977 *New
York, New York*. Sivero also had a small role in *The Godfather
Part II* in 1974, and after *New York, New York* did considerable
character work, including a 1989 bit on the sitcom *Mr. Belvedere*.

After these established pros, we have roles filled by some semi-
pros. The camera moves up to an alcove to present "Moe Black's
brother Fat Andy," a hefty guy with a mustache who says "How

you doin', buddy?" to the camera/Henry. He is played by Louis Eppolito, a former NYPD detective who was still with the force during the shooting of the movie. He retired in the winter of 1989. And became a mob hit man.

Behind the placid mook mug seen in the movie was a remorseless killer. He was known as a "Mafia Cop" because he had relatives in the mob (something he did not, it happens, mention when applying to become a cop), and then worked in the organized crime unit. But not too long after *Goodfellas* was released, he and a former partner in the force, Stephen Caracappa, reputedly took out Lucchese crime family made man Patrick Testa. He was "discovered" for this picture, so to speak, by Joe Pesci, at a nightclub. And after *Goodfellas* he continued to act in bit parts. He's in Woody Allen's 1994 *Bullets Over Broadway* as a comedic tough. After the team of Louis and Stephen moved to Las Vegas, he was closer to Hollywood geographically, and took a role as yes, a hood, in David Lynch's 1997 *Lost Highway*. He was plotting a New York comeback, not as an actor, but as a murderer; he was involved in a plot to take out Sammy "the Bull" Gravano, the Mafia soldier who sang on John Gotti. He also had the nerve to write and publish *Mafia Cop: The Story of an Honest Cop Whose Family Was Mob*. It is reputed that a relative of one of his victims saw him on TV promoting the book and contacted authorities, leading to his arrest. Eppolito died in November of 2019 while serving a sentence of life plus one hundred years, having been convicted in 2006 on eight counts of murder, as well as obstruction of justice, racketeering, and more.

Next to Fat Andy is Frankie the Wop, a noticeably older or at least more grizzled guy, who asks Henry, "Stayin' out of trouble?" The actor, Tony Vallelonga, played a nightclub patron in *Raging Bull* under the name Tony Lip. Nicknamed "Lip" as a kid for his ability to persuade his pals to participate in mischief, Vallelonga was a well-known bouncer-around-town who had played burly character extras in *The Godfather* and *Dog Day Afternoon*. His son Nick decided to follow in the old man's show-business footsteps, and for several frustrating years tried to make a movie of his father's experiences in the early 1960s chauffeuring a black pianist through the Deep South. Yes, that film was *Green Book* and the character played by Viggo Mortensen is the guy saying, "Stayin' out of trouble?" Tony died in 2010 and hence never saw the fruits of his son's efforts. In accepting a Best Picture Oscar for the movie, Nick said, "Dad, we did it."

Freddie No Nose's nickname is given no explanation, and it wants one, as the character, who's sitting at the bar behind the alcove, has an entire nose. This is Mikey Black's only film credit, so one can infer that this may be one of the performers who, as Nick Pileggi relates in the *GQ* oral history, got a little tongue-tied when asked to provide his Social Security number to the movie's casting director.

The camera swerves up and over the bar to say hey to "Pete the Killer, who was Sally Balls' brother." By this time the viewer is sufficiently caught up in the shot that they don't notice the camera is making moves that Henry can't, but this underscores, at least subliminally, the ornamentally beautiful unreality of the shot. Pete the Killer delivers one of the more memorable bits of wiseguy banter: "I took care of that thing for ya," a line that insinuates quite a lot in this context. Peter Cicale is the performer, and he's another one who did *Goodfellas* and disappeared from movies.

The camera makes a sharp right turn and swoops over the bar again, to a sharp-dressed guy with a lean jaw and dark-tinted glasses with a bored-looking young woman. This is Nickey Eyes—so named perhaps because you can't see those eyes—and he puts a finger up to Henry and says, "What's up, guy?" John Manca would write his own book about being a crooked cop and then trying to become a "half wiseguy," called *Tin for*

Sale, a little after working on this picture. He would go on to act in and serve as a consultant on Scorsese's 1995 *Casino*, also based on a Nick Pileggi true-crime book. (He can be glimpsed briefly in that film, too, playing a wiseguy.) Manca got the role because of his acquaintance with Pileggi. He'd been destitute, living in the Flushing YMCA, and in heavy debt to a mob guy. The work on *Goodfellas* as both an actor and consultant lifted him out of the gutter, but he was still scraping together money because he knew he'd be found. "Word got around that I was working on the picture, and it's not that hard to find a film crew shooting in New York, so one day I got a visit," he says in the book. He met the mobster, handed him twenty grand, and got a nod and a "No hard feelings, right?" in return. Of his life as of 1990, he wrote, "I get by. I do odd jobs, strictly legit. Thanks to the movie, I got a Screen Actors Guild card, and I look for roles in films and TV shows where they need a wiseguy."

With his slick-backed hair and intensely set eyes, Joseph Bono looks practically unchanged since playing Guido, the third guy in Salvy's crew in the sparring scene in *Raging Bull*. Here he plays Mikey Franzese, who shares a name with a real mob guy but doesn't do much more in this film than say, "I saw that guy, yeah, I wanna see him," during this shot, which takes the greeting/banter into the realm of non sequitur.

Finally there's "Jimmy Two Times, who got that nickname because he said everything twice, like——" And here Anthony Powers stands up, ostentatiously straightens his tie (it's a marvel he can actually find it, given it's covered by his freakishly long shirt collars, which look like giant fangs), and says, "I'm gonna go get the papers get the papers." Steadicam operator Larry Mc-Conkey recalls this shot as particularly fun, with the director by his side cueing all the gang members.

★ ★ ★

The shot continues into the back room of the place, as Henry pushes a rack of winter coats past the lounge's owner, Sonny Bunz, played by Tony Darrow. (The other actor pushing the coatrack is Vincent Pastore, later to play Big Pussy in *The Sopranos*.) "This is the middle of fuckin' summer, what am I gonna do with fur coats?"

"Ah, you don't want furs, I'll take 'em away."

"No, no, no, no, don't take 'em away, I want 'em. You know what we do, we'll hang 'em up, we'll hang 'em in the freezer, how's that?"

Taking up the apologia for the gangster ethos from his prior explanation of Paulie Cicero's function in the neighborhood, Henry waxes rhapsodic: "For us to live any other way was nuts. To us those goody-goody people who worked shit jobs for bum paychecks and took the subway to work every day and worried about bills were dead. They were suckers. They had no balls." It never occurs to Henry that he may have traded a leash for a noose.

"If we wanted something we just took it. If anyone complained twice they got hit so bad believe me they never complained again."

But what we saw just moments ago depicts the absurdity at the core of this venality. Presented with a rack full of women's fur coats, Sonny, the owner, bitches and moans about the uselessness of these stolen goods; being the middle of summer, they'll prove hard to move. Henry says he'll take them back. (To the truck from which they were stolen? Not likely.) No, no, no, no. Sonny still wants the goods. Anything they can grab, snatch, lay hands on, they will take. Even if it ends up as useless overstock taking up space in a freezer that serves your "legitimate" business. This is bad practice, wholesale or retail or what have you. But the boys can't help it.

★ ★ ★

An overhead shot of a crowded Bamboo Lounge table resolves on Henry looking at his watch; then Frenchy (Mike Starr, who bears a pronounced resemblance to character actor Danny Aiello, a Scorsese type who was forever irked to have never appeared in a Scorsese picture) shows up. The urgency is underscored when Henry summons Jimmy to the bar. The camera tracks in on Jimmy fast, and undercranking, to produce speeded-up motion, as Jimmy gets up from the table to join them. This is the wiseguy version of a staff meeting. "Too good to be true," Frenchy says as he lays it out: dollars that tourists and servicemen changed overseas into foreign currency is coming home via Air France cargo, and it's gonna be held until Tuesday on account of a Jewish holiday. What's the security? "You're looking at him!" Frenchy says with some hilarity. "I'm the midnight-to-eight man."

HOW AM I FUNNY

This is one of the film's most famous, most quoted scenes. And it defines the knife edge of comedy and mayhem (physical and/or moral) that much of the rest of the film balances on, almost always falling on the side of mayhem.

The Bamboo Lounge sequence kicks off as just another night with the boys. Scorsese and Schoonmaker make it bloom, so to speak, stretching it to advance the narrative (setting up the Air France heist) and to contain the movie's first great "set piece," one that defines Tommy, played now by Joe Pesci, as a human incendiary device.

After Frenchy says, "We're on," to Henry and Jimmy, the picture cuts to a table where Tommy holds court, flanked on the left side of the frame by Franzese; Henry and Nickey Eyes are to his right, in profile. The sequence was shot with two cameras, not a common occurrence in this picture, but since the comic timing needed to work as overt performance, having to stop and start to capture different angles would not be productive.

Tommy's story begins with him saying, "What's really funny is..." and he follows with his comedic "I thought I told you to go fuck your mother" tale of standing up to police interrogation.

"You're a pisser. Really funny," Henry says. Tommy then asks, approximately fifteen times, including the variations "Am I a clown?" and "Do I amuse you?" just how he is funny, or how *the fuck* he is funny. As his rage increases, his breath becomes shorter, until when he says, "What the fuck is so funny about me? Tell me. Tell me what's funny," he seems barely able to get the words out. Then, quiet. Almost endless quiet, it seems.

Henry breaks the deafening silence by saying, "Get the fuck out of here," raising his palm. The table erupts in laughter, varied repetitions of the opinion that Tommy is "funny," and more. "Sometimes I worry about you, Henry," Tommy jokes back. "You may fold under questioning." Tommy won't live to see that.

The conflict lasts for less than a minute, but seems a lifetime, and the relief that it does not end in gunfire is physically palpable, a release. The lifting of a potential curse. So much so that the impact of the violence that follows is ostensibly blunted.

In the hilarity's wake, Sonny, the owner of the lounge, mistakenly sees an opportunity. In a bowing and scraping posture, he leans into Tommy and entreats him to pay what he owes on his tab. Which is $7,000. Tommy breaks a glass over his head, threatens the waiter who brought up the subject in the first place, comments that just the week before Sonny had asked Tommy to christen his son, says his fee would have been $7,000, then the table breaks into "you're a funny guy" again, and Tommy fake-jumps on someone.

In his exchange with Henry, Tommy is arguably more fearsome than he is when he's actually in the act of killing. In two of four subsequent homicides he's shown committing, he's crassly efficient; in the other two, he's shown as blustery but also weak, in one instance practically sniveling, which of course reflects what's truly underneath all his psychotic bravado.

The scene was created by Pesci himself. Scorsese recalls, in the GQ oral history, that the actor was hesitant about taking the role, but interested in exploring what life he could bring to it, out of his own observations and experiences. "We went up to my apartment," Scorsese recalled, "and [Pesci] said, 'Let me tell you a couple of stories. If you could find a place for this sort of thing, then I think we could make it special.' […] Joe acted it out. Then we did a rehearsal with Ray and Joe and put it on audiotape, and I constructed the scene from the transcripts and gave it to them to hit those levels, the different levels of questioning and how the tone changes. It was never in the script."

Joe Pesci, born in Newark, New Jersey, in 1943, was already a show business veteran when Robert De Niro saw him in the 1976 low-budget crime picture *The Death Collector* and recommended that Scorsese check it out. Pesci was about ten years behind fellow Essex County products Tommy DeVito and Frankie Valli, founding members of the Four Seasons. But because Joe had a robust voice, including an impressive falsetto, and because his father wanted Joe to pursue the performing arts, Pesci ran in their circles. He introduced his friend and contemporary Bob Gaudio to DeVito and Valli. Gaudio's songwriting and arranging skills helped get the Seasons their hits. The association is commemorated in both the Broadway show *Jersey Boys* and its film adaptation, directed by Clint Eastwood. Both the book of the show and the film script were cowritten by Marshall Brickman, the waggish onetime Woody Allen collaborator; the interpolation of the line "funny how?" into the character Pesci's mouth in the Eastwood movie seems a Brickman touch.

In his early days, Pesci had also appeared on *Startime Kids*, a New York–based variety show produced by and aired on WNBC. Its emphasis was on child and teen acts; one of them, besides Joe, was Little Scott Engel, who would move to Hollywood, become a protégé of Eddie Fisher, make international hits from Great Britain as one of the Walker Brothers, and then pursue a solo career as Scott Walker, first making melodramatic Jacques Brel–inflected art pop and then full-on uncategorizable progressive music. Adult Bobby Darin also pitched in on *Startime* when he was in the neighborhood.

Pesci was acquainted with Joey Dee and the Starliters, who had a regional '50s hit with "Peppermint Twist," and during the 1960s he kicked around the New Jersey/New York nightclub/restaurant/lounge scene a lot, and, as depicted in *Jersey Boys*, he did work at a bowling alley. In 1968, he cut an album called *Little Joe Sure Can Sing*, and the disc demonstrated that he could, in a tenor and a falsetto that was very much in the mode of Valli's. But Pesci's interpretations of contemporary hits such as "To Love Somebody" lacked the interpretive oomph to put him across as a credible solo act, at least at the time. Issued by Brunswick, the label that launched Jackie Wilson among others, the record was a respectable effort that moved no needles. It was almost ten years following the LP, after he had formed a musical act with Frank Vincent, that both Pesci and Vincent appeared in supporting roles in the aforementioned low-budget, made-in-Jersey gangster picture *The Death Collector*, which also turns up under the title *Family Enforcer* on various video-on-demand services. While one couldn't call it a classic, the story of an ambitious mobster collections guy who oversteps a few too many boundaries (played by Joe Cortese, whose vibe falls somewhere between young De Niro and young Michael Douglas) has, despite its derivations, an almost docudrama feel. The barebones plywood-walled back rooms where the wiseguys play cards, the tacky dining rooms with the green upholstery on the chairs, all feel real, probably because they are. Into this milieu Pesci, as a short-tempered crook, and future Billy Batts portrayer Vincent, as an insolent debtor, fit in like they were to the manner born, so to speak.

The point is that Pesci got around, and in *The Death Collector* he played a character he knew well. (In *Scorsese on Scorsese*, the director actually says, "Joe Pesci comes from that world.") He had been steered into a performing career by his dad on the pretext that he felt his kids should have a better life than he did, and so on. But Pesci has said that he wasn't all that enthusiastic about performing. But he continued, within the Jersey-NY circuit, and in towns like Newark and Lodi and Union, boroughs like the Bronx, where you see a lot of things. "Stories," as Pesci put it to Scorsese, that could make the movie "special."

That Scorsese and Pileggi were not just willing but eager to accept such a contribution was not a matter of indulging a performer. They understood the value of Pesci's experience and how it dovetailed with Hill's experience. Today Pesci does not do interviews with the press, in part because of a reticence that was always there, but has only increased in age, and also because he doesn't like getting questions about certain aspects of his background.

The mob and show business have always been in the same bedroom, if not the same bed. Later in the movie Karen, Henry's wife, played by Lorraine Bracco, will remember the real-life singer Bobby Vinton (who's played in the movie by Vinton's namesake son) sending a bottle of champagne to Henry and Karen's table at the Copacabana. Garry Trudeau, in his comic strip *Doonesbury*, frequently lambasted Frank Sinatra for his ostensible connections to organized crime. What Trudeau willfully failed to understand was that any US entertainer working a nightclub circuit in post–World War II America rubbed up against wiseguys.

Nick Tosches' biography of Dean Martin, *Dino*, lays out how postprohibition mobsters like Frank Costello bought into legitimate liquor distribution and arranged for exclusives with networks of nightclubs, many of which fronted secret casinos (like Bill Miller's Riviera in Fort Lee): "Entertainers were like booze," Tosches writes, "[…] just another way for a joint to make money off the hustlers." Tosches goes on to recount a hair-raising tale in which Jerry Lewis, then Martin's partner in a nightclub act, razzed a mobster—a onetime bodyguard for Al Capone himself—from the stage, and lived to tell about it. Not only lived—Lewis befriended the guy and collected big checks from him every year for his muscular dystrophy telethon. Lewis recounted this in detail, and with pride, to Tosches.

The mob connections of the singing group the Four Seasons are recounted in detail in *Jersey Boys*. The Broadway show and movie were made with some cooperation from the real-life figures. Frank Vincent, Pesci's longtime friend, had a blithe attitude about knowing real mobsters.

Pesci himself is not playful about this kind of stuff, or forthcoming at all. In the late '90s, when *Premiere* magazine mentioned Pesci in an article about filmmakers and actors who had strong social ties with Mafia members, Pesci was sufficiently irked that he sent a letter to the editor that made his distaste for film journalists manifestly clear.

On the day the scene was shot, producer Irwin Winkler was on the flea-infested (or not) Hawaii Kai set. So was Terry Semel, the Warner Brothers studio executive who had, at one point early in preproduction, offered that Tom Cruise might make a good Henry Hill and Madonna might make a good Karen Hill. (In his 2018 memoir *Who Is Michael Ovitz?* the onetime CAA power broker Ovitz takes credit for talking Semel out of these ideas. Many others have, as well. It's an attractive thing to want to take credit for.)

In an interview, Winkler recalls, "Terry Semel came to visit that day, and he said, 'What is this scene, what are you shooting?' There was a young production assistant with him, named Billy Gerber, who has since become quite a producer himself. He just did Bradley Cooper's *A Star Is Born*. He was there, and he was watching what was going on, and he said to Terry, 'You know, this looks great, this scene is terrific.' And Semel shut him up and said, 'I don't remember okaying this and why should it be in?' And eventually he said, 'You're not going to Tampa for the zoo scene. It's gonna cost a million dollars, and I'm not going to approve that.' That was his punishment to us for the 'How am I funny?' scene."

Some punishment. Barbara De Fina, the credited executive producer of the film, did the kind of magic that made her an invaluable part of Scorsese's crew for over a decade; as Winkler puts it, "We ended up shooting it in Queens at night, and we had a sign that said Tampa Bay Zoo, and we put a lot of greenery around there, palm trees, we shot it there." (Other accounts place the fake Tampa zoo at Brooklyn's Prospect Park Zoo.)

Pesci spoke in depth about his approach to Tommy and other roles to Mary Pat Kelly, a longtime friend of Scorsese (they met at a convent where she was studying to become a nun, all the way back in the early '60s, when Scorsese himself was contemplating a monastic existence), for her 1991 book *Martin Scorsese: A Journey*. "The real Tommy was six-foot-something. I'm not tall. Marty and I were laughing about that the other day. Every time someone tells us something about these guys, they get bigger and bigger. [...] But acting has nothing to do with that kind of reality. People ask if I want to know about the real Tommy DeSimone. I know a lot about him. I read and I talked to people, but I don't take that stuff into the film with me. Now,

Bob De Niro will find out everything about his characters, and take those traits and little things with him, and let it start to feel like that for him. What I do is think of somebody that I know very well who is the same type, and play him. I do *my* Tommy DeSimone. I do Joe Pesci as if I were this killer, this crazy, funny, wisecracking person. [...]

"I believe the wiseguys justify what they do the way any soldier who goes to Vietnam, or Korea, or Germany, does. They fight people they don't know. How do they justify that? How do you justify killing someone you don't even know? Because a government says it's okay? They give you a gun and teach you how to shoot it. And if someone in Brooklyn or the Bronx that helps you feed your family and clothe them, but who, say, runs a bookmaking business or whatever, if they tell you there's a piece of garbage on the other side of town who is looking to take something that doesn't really belong to him... They kill their own, within their crime families. They don't go out on the street and kill ordinary people. Tommy goes overboard. I think he's a psychopathic killer. He just kills anybody. [...]

"I can draw on my temper because it's terrible. My father had a terrible one, and my brother and I have it, too. I have to calm myself down. I've learned as I've gotten older to control it or to walk away from people, to stay clear of somebody that I don't like, that will upset me in a way that would make me want to strangle them or beat them to a pulp. So, as Tommy, I use those urges to kill. It becomes nothing after a while. I did one of those murders like it was absolutely nothing."

THE FALL OF THE BAMBOO LOUNGE

It's an abrupt cut when Tommy disappears from the frame after his "jump" across the table, to a medium close-up of Sonny, the right top of his head now bandaged, saying breathlessly,

"But I'm worried, I'm hearing all kinds of fuckin' bad things. I mean, he's treating me like I'm a fuckin' half a f——t some— I'm gonna wind up a lam-ist, I gotta go on the lam from this guy..." The reverse shot is on Paulie, and it dollies in to a medium close-up as he sits and listens. He can't offer much help to Sonny.

"Tommy's a bad kid, he's a bad seed. What am I supposed to do, shoot him?"

"That wouldn't be a bad idea." Sonny shrugs. Paulie is not amused and in fact looks affronted. It's not a look one wants to elicit from Paulie. Sonny immediately, furiously, backpedals. "I'm sorry I said that. I didn't mean to say that. I just mean that he's scaring me."

Paulie may be offended now, but near the end of the movie, it will be his own brother, Tuddy, who puts a bullet in the back of Tommy's head and then (as we learn from Henry) shoots him in the face to deny Tommy's mother the luxury of an open-casket funeral service. An act that would not be committed unless Paulie gave his approval or direct order. So things change.

While making his complaints about Tommy, Sonny, with some backup from Henry, proposes a more general solution to his Bamboo Lounge problem: Could Paulie buy into the place and then have Henry oversee it, bearing Paulie's interests in mind? The buy-in would, we presume, ameliorate Tommy's debt—not that he can be counted on to settle any new tab he would naturally start running up—and possibly usher in a new era of prosperity for the joint, which, as we have seen, is already operating as at least an adjunct to crime: Sonny is in business with Henry, selling stolen goods. (Sonny's portrayer, Tony Darrow, born Anthony Borghese, was not nearly as hapless as his character. He went on to work as an actor in the De Niro film *Analyze This* and the entire run of *The Sopranos*. But he was indicted in 2009, at the age of seventy, for extortion. In a case that showed he was a longtime personal associate of the Gambino crime family, he had tried to get a debt paid by means of a strong-arm collector. In 2013 he was sentenced to six months of house arrest and had to make a don't-be-a-wiseguy PSA.)

Paulie demurs at first, but after reassurance from Henry gives in. (Referring to Henry, Sonny says, "He's in the joint twenty-four hours a day. Another few minutes, he could be a stool," which is a funny bit of foreshadowing if you consider the gangland meaning of "stool.") What follows is a little lesson in capitalism, mob style. And it's not too much different from the legitimate version, just faster. Henry, in voice-over: "Now the guy's got Paulie as a partner. Any problems, he goes to Paulie."

Paulie, however, has to be paid his weekly protection fee. In legit capitalism this is called maximizing shareholder return. And it has to be done "no matter what. 'Business is bad? Fuck you, pay me.' 'Oh, you had a fire? Fuck you, pay me.' 'The place got hit by lightning, huh? Fuck you, pay me.'" In addition to getting paid without fail, Paulie runs the business into the ground by borrowing on it. Less than a minute after Paulie nods, and after a brisk montage of loading and unloading goods, Sonny is signing the bankruptcy papers and saying, "Fuckin' shame." While the torching of the Bamboo Lounge is one of the movie's very few out-and-out fabrications—that is, it does not occur in the book—in *Wiseguy* Henry implies the ways in which mob business and so-called legit business don't mix. Henry buys a lounge in Queens called The Suite, which in the film will be the scene of Billy Batts' murder. Henry: "Before I thought about taking over The Suite I talked it over with Paulie. He liked the idea. He liked it so much that he ordered the place off-limits for the crew. He said we had to keep the place clean." They did not manage to keep it clean, and the place did become a mob hangout, to Henry's consternation; and once Henry was on his way to prison he had to take, as we'll see, extreme measures with the place.

Scorsese and Pileggi's script is a model of narrative resourcefulness. The Bamboo Lounge is now to be torched for an insurance scam, and Henry and Tommy are tasked with the setting of the fire. While they sit in the car waiting to make sure the joint is lit, Tommy complains about his love life. "The Jew broad," Diana, won't put out for him. "I been trying to bang this broad for a fuckin' month now. The only thing is that she won't go out with me alone, you know?" Henry knows what is up, and turns to Tommy and says, "No."

But Tommy is a hard man to say no to, and before he even knows it, Henry is on a double date and enjoying it not at all.

KAREN

In pictures such as this one and *Casino*, Scorsese is apt to shift perspectives with no warning and little regard for conventional linear verisimilitude. Joe Pesci's Nicky in 1995's *Casino* is practically the co-narrator of the film, and it isn't until the very end that the viewer learns that, unlike De Niro's Ace Rothstein, Nicky is speaking from beyond the grave. Sure, there's plenty of precedent for that (see *Sunset Boulevard*), but pairing a living narrator with a dead one is a bit unusual.

The kind of French New Wave–derived license used in these cases constitutes a kind of dare Scorsese gives himself: How often can he remind the viewer that they're watching a movie and still keep them emotionally invested in the happenings on-screen? This is, in a sense, the inversion of what Scorsese's early mentor John Cassavetes practiced, which was an attempt to immerse the viewer in an unbroken circumscribed reality.

In the first double-date scene, Henry is fidgety, and he says in voice-over, as the camera makes an elegant arc to isolate Karen and Henry at the table, "I couldn't wait to get away." A medium shot of Tommy and Diane tracks in on that couple steadily, as Tommy insists that the party not leave "like a buncha hoboes, staggering out one at a time," which amuses Diane. There's a cut to a medium close-up of Lorraine Bracco's Karen. The white stripe running across the slightly scooped top of her navy blue dress accentuates her tasteful pearl necklace. As the camera pulls back, she takes the voice-over: "I couldn't stand him." As much as this shift in linear perspective/continuity is a Scorsese hallmark, Pileggi's *Wiseguy* also yields some portions of the narrative to Karen's telling.

Many of Karen's observations come practically verbatim from *Wiseguy*, as it happens. The narrative sees Henry, after standing her up for their second "date," eventually amused by Karen's feistiness when she confronts him in front of his boys, and struck by her beauty. There's a small but noteworthy difference between descriptions in *Wiseguy* and in the scripted voice-over of the film. Book: "She had violet eyes, just like Elizabeth Taylor—or that's what everybody said." Movie: "She had these great eyes, just like Liz Taylor's. At least that's what I thought." Real-life Henry doesn't know from Liz Taylor! But Movie Henry does. (And because of the actual color of Lorraine Bracco's eyes, they can't be called "violet," by the way.) He has a something like a *sensibility*.

Otherwise, though, *Goodfellas* doesn't give Henry much of an inner life. He hasn't much in the way of a personal ethos, obviously. But neither is he neurotic. He hasn't many anxieties or fears. He's a walking appetite whom we're rarely made to see as aggressively sociopathic (although the way he laughs a bit in the presence of physical violence is revealing). So his semi-delighted reaction to being dressed down in front of his male buddies, including surrogate uncle (at least) Tuddy, by Karen is intriguing. He digs her nerve. Maybe she reminds him of himself. As their relationship deepens into an alliance, it's one that's increasingly defined by very definite affinities. She will become a literal partner in crime.

Their courtship contains the movie's most famous single shot, one that encapsulates and epitomizes the glamour of Henry's wiseguy lifestyle: the couple's entry via the kitchen of the famed New York nightclub the Copacabana. The scene was staged and shot at the actual Copa, which despite having mobster Frank Costello as an ostensible silent partner, was a legit joint, but as we see here, its wheels were greased by wiseguy money—it's doubtful that a Tommy DeVito could run up and run out on a tab here.

As the Ronettes' classic "And Then He Kissed Me" plays on the soundtrack, the three-minute shot begins with a close-up of Henry's hand, giving his car keys to a valet. Film buffs will remember the epic crane shot in Alfred Hitchcock's *Notorious*, which begins from the top of a staircase and swoops down to a close-up of Ingrid Bergman's hand, clutching a key she is not supposed to have. This beginning is an homage in reverse, so to speak. As Henry leads Karen away from the line at the front entrance of the club, he says, "I like going in this way. It's better than waiting in line."

Scorsese's conception of the shot was not quite as elaborate as the vision that ended up in the film. He had seen a straight line—across the street, down into the rear entrance corridor, straight into the club where the table would be rushed out to almost the lip of the stage and put in front of the couple. Kristi Zea recalls that cinematographer Michael Ballhaus was captivated by the dim lighting of the hallway's contrast with the harsh bright fluorescents of the kitchen, and felt he could make something of it. Scorsese himself, via his office, says that this opinion wasn't presented to him in his recollection, and that the reasons for the shot's expansion were multiple. In any case, Barbara De Fina's observation holds here: "Michael was one of those cinematographers who was always engaged, always excited, always ready to try new things. He was very good at keeping Marty engaged, too. He had this way of convincing a director that yes, the shot had been gotten, or that the shot was gettable, even when the director was skeptical. And he always had fresh ideas."

So they would go through the kitchen. Which created two challenges: what Henry and Karen would do in the kitchen, and how to camouflage the fact that they had no real reason to go through the kitchen at all—the ballroom was at their right at the end of the corridor, the kitchen entrance to the left. They'd be coming out of it the same way they came in.

Steadicam operator Larry McConkey mapped out the specifics with the help of first assistant director Joseph Reidy and with Ray Liotta. One of only a handful of skilled Steadicam operators in the US at the time, he had, and has, a philosophy of how a good Steadicam shot should work. "When you're doing a take that's this long in duration, you have to make edits within the shot to keep it interesting. If you just have a shot following Henry and Karen and nothing's happening, it's not very dynamic. So you pick points where a little bit of business occurs and the action has to be just so. For instance, we begin on a close-up of Henry's hand giving the 'valet' a tip, and then the camera recedes, and lets Henry and Karen get some distance away as they cross the street. Once that action is completed, you want to get the camera closer to them, so you contrive a reason to make them stop. In this case, it's a doorman at the back door, who Henry stops to give a tip to. This came out of talking to Ray, and of his understanding of what Henry would do in this situation.

"Whenever I needed a 'cut,' we would engineer something new to look at. We decided to have a couple making out, and

Henry sassing them a little. There were so many extras around that Joe was just able to grab a couple. When you're constructing shots on this level, that's when it feels most like directing. When we come into the kitchen, there was a tight turn where the cooks were; I had one of the cooks look at Henry. We gave him a line, but I think for the last take Joe told him not to say it, because the extra would have had to have gotten a pay raise and we didn't want to have the shot go over budget."

As for the potential leaving-through-the-same-way-as-they-came-in problem, McConkey wasn't too worried. "One of the basic things about film is that it's a two-dimensional medium. The camera moves, but the screen does not. The difference in turning 360 degrees in the actual world, and the effect of watching a 360 movement shot on film, is therefore considerable. The flattening of the 2D image means that you will reach a full 360 degrees in a shot well before the audience's eye expects it. So in the restaurant kitchen, the audience would not think the camera had actually panned a full 360. It will only look like a 180, or less, under most circumstances." Nevertheless, the production design team was tasked to enhance the illusion that the couple was going from point A to point B rather than from A back to A.

"It was quite a feat," says production designer Zea. "We had to assemble a wall, place it in front of the opening of the ballroom, and then as Ray and Karen were going through the kitchen we had to move the wall out of the way." It's most likely the curtained wall had rollers at its bottom, which you don't see in the shot. To add to the illusion, prop placers put stacks of empty plastic crates against the wall that was bare when the actors first entered the kitchen.

"I rehearsed every little bit once I knew what mattered and what didn't," McConkey says. "Prerehearsed everyone in front of the lens; I dealt with every single person on matters of just how fast to move, just how high to hold the tray." The crew did a test shot with a Video 8 assist.

"We showed Marty the take and I was a little nervous. He was liking it fine and then at a certain point he said, 'No, no, no.'" It was the movement of the waiter who brings Henry and Karen their table. Scorsese remembered seeing how this was done from when he went to the Copa as a teenager, and he wanted it reproduced exactly. He said to McConkey, "You have to understand when the table comes, it should fly into the lens and you should fly after it." They rehearsed the adjustment and were ready. McConkey remembers Scorsese's agitation. "He had asthma, and there was smoke in the air on the set, and I was a little scared for him because he was feeling it."

Once the shot was finished, though, there was enough time in the day to do more setups. And as memorable as the Copa shot is, McConkey is even fonder of the Bamboo Lounge introduction. "That's an even better shot for me. It's more precise and complicated in terms of timing. It's a real Steadicam shot. Marty would read what would end up being voice-over as we walked through it. It was all about the rhythm. Whatever visual ideas I had, I don't know if he ever disagreed."

Once seated, the dazzled Karen asks Henry, "What do you do?" and without batting an eye he responds, "I'm in construction." Almost as quickly Karen, no dummy, observes that Henry doesn't have the hands of a construction worker. And Henry has a fast comeback there, too. "I'm a union delegate."

In Hollywood crime films in which cops infiltrate the mob, the undercover cop wife is almost invariably a whiny worrywart, a thankless role even when entrusted to the most talented actor (see Anne Heche in *Donnie Brasco* for a paradigmatic version). In *Goodfellas*, the wiseguy wife has more fun, at least for a

while. She still lives under the thumb of three distinct patriar-
chies: that of society itself, that of her husband, and that of the
organization. As we'll see, the organization will come down on
her side, for pragmatism's sake, when one of Henry's affairs gets
a little too semipublicly messy. The portions of the movie that
give themselves over to Karen's perspective depict her making
the best of each discrete alienating situation she finds herself in.

Karen has several opportunities to walk away but she chooses
to follow her particular bliss, so to speak. As we'll see, she found
Henry's renegade side a turn-on. In real life, after going into
witness protection, the thrill was gone. (Aside from getting a
verbal reprimand from a prosecutor in the final twenty minutes, Karen doesn't figure heavily in the film's post-arrest aftermath.) In addition to having to live like "schnooks," Henry's
alcoholism accelerated, as did his abuse of Karen. The movie
plays down Henry's physical abuse of Karen (although its extent during his years as a wiseguy is not as well-documented as
it is in the witness protection period). He slaps her around after
she has trained a loaded revolver at him while straddling him,
and he shakes her violently after learning she's dumped all the
cocaine he had in the house after his bust—his idea was that it
was insurance, to be sold to secure his bail.

In Scorsese's early features *Who's That Knocking at My Door*
(1967) and *Mean Streets* (1973), we have Italian American male
protagonists of differing religious convictions who are both
confounded by women. In *Knocking*, Harvey Keitel's J.R. can't
handle the revelation that his "nice" girlfriend played by Zina
Bethune (her character is sufficiently archetypal that she's not
even given a name) is a rape victim. But he has trouble even
before he finds out; he cuts off a makeout session with the
woman for no real reason, possibly due to a fear of impotence.
J.R. ultimately attempts a reconciliation in which he verbally

brutalizes her, and that is the end of that, but not before J.R. imagines them reunited in a room with a crucifix above the bed and the sound of church bells ringing. In *Mean Streets*, Charlie, also played by Keitel, is dating Amy Robinson's Theresa, a cousin of his lunatic hellion pal Johnny Boy (De Niro). Charlie tries to keep the relationship under wraps, but he's in Little Italy, everybody knows everybody, and his mobster uncle disapproves of her because she's got epilepsy and is therefore wrong in the head. All this gets mixed in with his roiling Catholic guilt and confusion, his attraction to the black go-go dancer Diane (Jeannie Bell), and more. A shooting leaves their lives and fates in awful suspension at the end.

The protagonist of 1976's *Taxi Driver*, Travis Bickle, has no religion. And, despite his addiction to pornographic movies, he has seemingly little in the way of a sex drive. In 1980's *Raging Bull* Jake LaMotta is a devout, or at least churchgoing, Catholic, driven into insanity by sexual jealousy once he marries his erotic ideal, Vicky.

Henry Hill is not an obsessive; sex, like everything else in his world, is there for the taking, and when he's not taking it he's got other business to look after. In this respect the prior Scorsese character he most resembles (although the resemblance can't be said to be inordinately pronounced) is Jimmy Doyle, the musician played by De Niro in 1977's *New York, New York*. At first avid in his pursuit of Liza Minnelli's Francine (he did just get out of the army; the movie opens at the end of World War II), he loses a good deal of interest upon their marriage. He cheats without compunction, and the further the singer Francine drifts from Jimmy's own realm of creativity, the worse things get. At a certain point Henry is fine with being a "family man," and until confronted by Paulie and Jimmy about it, barely considers how his extracurricular activities have any impact on that. He gives up his girlfriend—who one suspects

he only cultivated because it was the thing that wiseguys do—
but picks up another, one who can help with his drug business. Pursuit of the opposite sex is never even near the top of
his mind, one infers.

AIR FRANCE MADE ME

Henny Youngman's Copa schtick continues on the soundtrack
after a hard cut to Henry and Tommy purposefully striding
across shiny wet tarmac toward a storage warehouse at Idlewild.
("Dr. Welser was here. Wonderful doctor. Gave a guy six months
to live, couldn't pay his bill, so he gave him another six months.")

The robbery goes very smoothly. In and out, brisk, no winks
to Frenchy. *Professional.* (In *Wiseguy* Hill relates a very picaresque
episode about getting the back room key, which was under the
jurisdiction of one of Frenchy's coworkers, copied: Frenchy and
Hill set the key keeper up with a call girl of their acquaintance,
and while she kept him occupied, Hill absconded with his key
ring and had almost every key on it copied at a hardware store.
He repeats the tale in *The Lufthansa Heist*, a post-*Goodfellas* book
he authored with Daniel Simone.)

"We walked out with four hundred and twenty thousand
dollars without using a gun," Liotta/Henry says with pride in
the voice-over. "And we did the right thing. We gave Paulie his
tribute." Just so we understand what it means to "do the right
thing" in this world.

The fellows are seen counting out $60,000 for Cicero, a sev-
enth of their total. "It's gonna be a good summer," Jimmy says.
Paulie advises Henry to tell those curious about his new cash
flow that he won big in Vegas.

The next few bits show Henry's naivete, and his power. Taking Karen out to what's presumably a country club where her
family is known, he attempts to settle a check with cash, and

Karen tells him he has to "sign" for it, which briefly flummoxes him. Here we meet Bruce, in tennis whites. This immediately smarmy across-the-street neighbor arouses suspicion in Henry right away. Actor Mark Jacobs resourcefully imbues the young man with the entitled softness of a guy who knows he's so protected within his class that he'll never need to defend himself. He doesn't walk away from their table so much as he oozes.

Another night at the Copa features Bobby Vinton, Jr., playing his '50s heartthrob ballad-singer father (still alive when the film was made; alas, digital de-aging technology was not available at the time), singing "Roses Are Red," and Karen's recollection, "One night Bobby Vinton sent us champagne. There was nothing like it." Henry "was an exciting guy."

The introduction of Morris, who's mostly referred to as "Morrie" (really, only his wife calls him by his proper name), is another bit of clever narrative cross-hatching from Scorsese and Pileggi. Morris, the wig man and degenerate gambler who will put together the Lufthansa heist, is first seen in one of the cheesy TV commercials he runs on local channels late at night, and on the set in his store nonstop. "Don't buy wigs that come off at the wrong time!" he announces ebulliently. He is then shown jumping into a swimming pool with one of his stay-put toupees on. Scorsese wanted a piece of film as goofy as the real thing, and one night he came upon an ad for a window replacement company that had the feel he was looking for. First assistant director Joseph Reidy and cinematographer Michael Ballhaus worked with the man, the actual head of the window company, on putting it together. And of course Chuck Low, as Morrie, added his own accents. Initially it's kind of amusing that the spot was shot two weeks prior to principal photography of *Goodfellas* itself. But, of course, it would have to be ready to roll for this scene.

As Jimmy glares at the set in the front of the shop, Henry tries to reason with Morrie about a debt. The voluble Morrie, who likes to show off his vocabulary, refers to Jimmy as an "unconscionable ball-breaker." He further complains that he "didn't agree to three points above the vig," that is, three percent more interest on the money he owes Jimmy. Soon Jimmy is so fed up he comes back, wraps a phone cord around Morrie's neck (knocking the man's own wig back, showing the double-sided tape on his forehead that held it in place), and bellows, "He's got money for the fucking commercial!"

The specifics of this interaction are all based on not unamusing fact. The real-life Morris, Marty Krugman, did own a wig store called For Men Only and did have a commercial that ran on late-night local TV. Jimmy Burke suspected that Marty "was booking out of his store and paying nothing in tribute or protection," according to Pileggi. "The situation was exacerbated by the fact that Jimmy was a part-time insomniac, and when he couldn't sleep he turned on the television. Whenever he saw Marty's wig commercial at four in the morning he felt duped. 'That fuck has the money to go on television,' he complained to Henry. 'But no money for anybody else?' Eventually, Jimmy had Tommy DeSimone and Danny Rizzo work over one of Marty's employees as a warning, but instead of giving in, Marty threatened to call the DEA." According to Hill, "Jimmy never trusted Marty after that."

Henry laughs at Jimmy's anger but his amusement is short-lived. Morrie's phone rings; it's Karen, calling from a booth. Bruce, that across-the-street neighbor, has tried to sexually assault her. (The moment is so charged that one never thinks to ask how it is that Karen knows the location where Henry is doing a shakedown; it's like she's calling him at the office or something.) Henry rushes to her rescue and deposits her at her house, where she lives with her parents. Across the street, Bruce and his buddies are working on a car.

Henry sits in the car and considers his move. He tucks a revolver into the front waistband of his pants.

His action is seen in an unbroken handheld camera shot, brief (forty seconds) but dense and shudder-worthy and shamefully rousing all at once. He crosses the street, his face drained of color, a white kabuki mask of cold rage. Still smarmy, but now defiant, Bruce says, as two of his friends look on, "What do you want, fucko, you want something?"

Here the staging of the action uses an old trick from the theater. As Henry bangs the butt of his revolver into Bruce's forehead, seemingly very hard, Jacobs raises his left hand to his forehead, and releases some fake blood onto his forehead and around his nose. It's a very effective trick, even if latter-day know-something-ish film "buffs" characterize it as a "gaffe." Henry continues hammering until he gets his point across, sputtering about how "if you ever touch her again so help me God," and when he gets up from the crouch he's in now that Bruce is on the ground, he just randomly points the revolver at one of Bruce's friends, who puts his hands up and begs, "Don't shoot." You are a better person than most if you don't feel, at least a little bit, that Bruce had it coming; here, more than anywhere else in the picture, *Goodfellas* is wishing you to cheer Henry on.

Breathless, Henry walks back to Karen's house; there's a close-up of his bloody hand placing the gun in Karen's hand: "Here, hide this."

And so Karen's heart is definitively won: "I know there are women like my best friends who would have gotten out of there the minute their boyfriend gave them a gun to hide. But I didn't. I gotta admit the truth: it turned me on."

THE WEDDING AND MARRIED LIFE

Henry and Karen's wedding and subsequent reception are the only sequences in which almost the entire ensemble appears. It was practically overwhelming for Kevin Corrigan, the then twenty-year-old actor who played the adult incarnation of Henry's wheelchair-bound younger brother Michael. Corrigan, whose agent had done some back-and-forth with Ellen Lewis, first met Scorsese in the Brill Building. He did not know what part he was auditioning for. "I had a scene prepared, Ellen gave me the pages, it was Henry and Paulie, when he gets out of prison. Later I read that Paul Sorvino improvised the slap in the scene, it wasn't in the pages I had. I rehearsed the scene with my father.

"I dressed like a gangster, like when Elaine Kagan, Henry's mother, opens the door in the movie! I was wearing a jacket and tie and cuff links. That's how I found out I was up for the part of Ray Liotta's brother. I didn't think I looked like him, I convinced myself that I did. I guess Marty thought that I did. We made small talk. He saw on my résumé that I had been in *The Lemon Sisters* and he mentioned that it was being edited downstairs. I couldn't help myself, I blurted to him, 'I love your films and I'm a huge fan!' I was very emotional. He could see the state I was in. He took it in stride: 'I could use that, it's early in the day!' he said. I got the call that I got the part later that day."

Once on the set, Corrigan says, "*Exhilaration* is an apt term. I was so excited it took me out of the story, I felt like a bat boy on the Yankees during the World Series, just being allowed to walk out on the field, it was vivid on the set. When I watch the movie now and I see all the colors in the movie, all those dark red hues, I remember walking through those colors and being in it and being aware I was in it, and walking through the looking glass, into *Alice in Wonderland*, it was Scorsese Wonderland."

This is a busy, almost hurried sequence. It begins with the crushing of a glass, a crucial component of a Jewish wedding ceremony. On introducing Henry to her mother on their first date,

Karen hurriedly covers up the cross that Henry wears around his neck. When Karen's mother tells him that Karen has told her he is half-Jewish, he picks up the ball without a blink and says, "Only the good half." Pileggi's book details how Hill underwent a full conversion to Judaism before marrying Karen, and underwent circumcision as an adult, a rather painful undertaking. (In the book, Linda, a postmarriage girlfriend of Henry's, says of Karen: "[She] was a very strong, demanding person. She put a lot of pressure on him. When they got married, for instance, she had him convert. He was twenty or twenty-one at the time, and she made him get circumcised. It was horrible. He was walking around with a diaper for a month.")

The snapping of the wedding photo features a whiteout in one shot, recalling the disconcerting flashbulbs of *Raging Bull* and the later film *The Aviator*. Scorsese himself projects his own loathing of flashbulbs onto his characters as much as opportunity allows him to. The wedding photo minimontage features a whip pan that resolves very briefly on Henry's side of the family, and the still extremely disgruntled look on the face of Henry's father (Beau Starr), from whose influence and belt Henry presumably escaped some time ago, is potent.

The most honored guests are seen in a horizontal tracking shot that begins with a swivel at the table where the more serious wiseguys sit: Paulie, Tuddy from the back, and then in profile, Jimmy. Vinnie (Charles Scorsese, the director's father), who will be heard from more decisively in the prison scene and after, is seen from the back; he's wearing a hearing aid. Tommy is being harangued by his mother (Scorsese's own mother, Catherine) about getting married; she, too, will figure more strongly soon. There's Morrie and wife, Belle, some mob wives, Frank Carbone, Frenchy.

"It was like we had two families," Karen says in voice-over; the play on words with respect to "family" is not emphasized.

"There must have been two dozen Peters and Pauls at the wedding, plus they were all married to girls named Marie." There are no boxed wedding presents: just envelopes stuffed with cash, the friendly face of Ben Franklin looking through the plastic window, and in cut after cut after cut, hand after hand after hand gives an envelope to Karen. Prop master Bob Griffon recalls that such envelopes, another detail Scorsese was particularly concerned about getting right as far as his memory of them was concerned, were particularly difficult to conjure: "They're very ornate on the outside and you can see the cash inside them. Marty was adamant that that's how they used to do it in Little Italy. I went to several stationeries and gift shops—keep in mind, this is thirty years ago. Nobody ever really remembered it like that. So we ended up—at the time, I used to use a graphic artist at *Saturday Night Live*, and he just made them. He printed them in gold foil somehow and die-cut the envelopes and it worked. So many people have asked me about them. I wish I still had a few of them."

As Karen and Henry dance, she worries that the bag in which she put all the envelopes will be stolen, and Henry laughs. Here, among thieves, is the safest place for them. Karen, for the first of two times in less than ten minutes, speaks of finding life in Henry's world as disorienting, intoxicating.

Corrigan was raised in the Bronx, and he says that while watching the construction of the ornate wedding scene, "It was interesting, too, how it seemed to intersect with my notions of my parents' generation." As, too, with the emphasis on particular details of the Copa in a prior scene, Scorsese was putting on a mini-memory-play.

As it happens, an old childhood friend of Corrigan's dad had gone to Cardinal Hays High School with Scorsese. "He made copies of yearbook pages, and I brought them to the set one day to show Marty and Marty got a real kick out of them. But when I started showing them to the other actors, he asked me to please stop."

The honeymoon period for Henry and Karen is brief. On a night he doesn't come home—they're still living with Henry's in-laws, and they're up and worrying with Karen—we are miles away from the feral chivalry of the Henry who pistol-whipped Bruce. He laughs with real disdain at the very idea of being told what to do as he gets back into the car with Tommy.

JEW HEAVEN

Forty-five minutes into the movie, after Henry walks from the front door of his in-laws' house and back into the car with Tommy, chortling his hearty "fuck you" laugh, the movie gives us ten minutes or so of Karen's world.

Karen picks up the voice-over.

"Well, we weren't married to nine-to-five guys. But the first time I realized how different was when Mickey had a hostess party." The motorcycle crash from the song "Leader of the Pack" accompanies a backward dolly of a crowded dining room, with a cardboard cutout of a Jackie Kennedy–style woman presiding over the festivities. The gathering was initially conceived as a Tupperware party (housewife entrepreneurs of the era would host events to sell the kitchen storage supplies), but the company did not want to be associated with a gangster picture; then the idea was a Mary Kay party (same, but with cosmetics). The cardboard standee indicates the gathering has some sales function, but that's the end of it. A close-up of Karen, alone in the frame, looking dumbstruck, underscores a sense of isolation and alienation. Into the frame, from the right side, enters the smiling profile of Rosie, played by Illeana Douglas.

"Karen, where you from?"

"Lawrence."

A reverse shot shows Rosie, full face, saying Lawrence, on the island, is nice. A medium shot of the two characters shows that Rosie is rubbing hand cream on Karen, demonstrating a product.

"I'm from Miami. You ever been there?"

"No." It's the softest voice we've heard from Karen.

"It's okay, but it's like you died and went to Jew heaven."

The phrase "Jew heaven" is emblematic of suburban American anti-Semitism: casual, "humorous" in intent, compressed in its venom. But the venom is there. (When I was a teen in New Jersey I was rather stunned to hear one of my mother's friends, in every other respect a very "nice lady," and also a genuinely kind person in general, refer to a higher learning institution as "En Why Jew.")

Illeana Douglas is the paternal granddaughter of Golden Age Hollywood icon Melvyn Douglas, the guy who made Garbo laugh in the 1939 comedy *Ninotchka*. That connection did not do much to facilitate her career as a movie actor. She recounts her eccentric East Coast upbringing and New York acting-school dues-paying in her funny and engaging memoir *I Blame Dennis Hopper.*

She met Scorsese when they were both working in the Brill Building. Douglas, while taking acting courses and pursuing auditions in film and theater in New York, made ends meet in the office of the powerful film publicist Peggy Siegal.

One of her more unpleasant tasks was to call prominent critics to get their reactions to a movie Siegal was representing. In her book she recounts having David Denby hang up on her when she contacted him to get a prereview reaction to *Beverly Hills Cop II.* The same David Denby who Nick Pileggi believed was prank-calling him, pretending to be Martin Scorsese. Following this mortification, though, came an encounter with the director Frank Perry, whose past work Douglas, a lifelong movie nut, revered. ("My show business knowledge, which not everyone who gets into the publicity business has, was considered a skill," Douglas says. "To know that songwriter Adolph Green was married to actress Phyllis Newman, but that his professional partner was Betty Comden. That made me invaluable in the office, because I knew who everyone was; Peggy or someone else would flash a headshot at me or something, and I'd say 'That's So-and-So, and he's on Broadway in This-or-That.'")

Now, Perry is helming a Shelley Long–starring reincarnation comedy, *Hello Again*, and has neglected to cast a small speaking part. He pulls Douglas out of her office, into his, has her read two monologues, then takes her directly to the set from there to shoot the scene, in Douglas' telling.

"The story, which sounded as if a famous publicist like Peggy Siegal had made it up, immediately made its way through the halls of the Brill Building. I was excited because people finally started identifying me as an actress. One of these people was Martin Scorsese's assistant, who asked for my résumé," Douglas writes. A little later, she recounts: "I was at work and I got a call from Marty's assistant. It sounded very conspiratorial: 'Hey, I was reading your résumé. Do you really have a blood-curdling scream?'"

The director was looping dialogue for *Last Temptation* and needed some screams. (Shades of the 1981 Brian De Palma thriller *Blow Out*, in which the sound man played by John Travolta is tasked with finding a credible scream for a cheap horror movie, which drops him into a web of murder and conspiracy and so on.) A brief and loud scream demonstration clinched the gig, and the next day she was in the "loop group."

The actor and the director bonded over comedy. Douglas dropped a line from the classic comedy character "The 2,000 Year Old Man," created by Mel Brooks and Carl Reiner. Brooks and Reiner were television comedy writers in the 1950s, not yet known as performers and also a good deal removed from becoming filmmakers; they created the bit to amuse friends at parties, initially. The premise has straight man Reiner interview Brooks, as a guy claiming to be 2,000 years old, about the historical figures he had met over the course of his epochal life. ("Jesus? He was a nice boy. Wore sandals. Thin. He came into the store but he never bought anything.") Douglas' reference perked Scorsese right up. "How do you know that?" he asked.

As Douglas points out elsewhere in her book, the image of a comedy-loving Scorsese doesn't square with, say, the fast-talking lunatic that he plays in the back seat of Travis Bickle's cab in *Taxi Driver*. But his films, particularly the contemporary ones, are steeped in humor derived from stage and cinema and television. You don't have to be conversant with Abbott and Costello, the '40s comedy superstars, to laugh at the back room exchange, full of self-conscious buddy-buddy schtick, between Charlie and Johnny Boy early in *Mean Streets*. But if you know Abbott and Costello, knowing where these guys picked up their double-talk from is an insight into their characters.

Scorsese subsequently cast Douglas in *Life Lessons*, a segment in the 1989 anthology movie *New York Stories*. Douglas plays the cynical best friend of Rosanna Arquette's Paulette. It's a short but meaty role in the tradition of Eve Arden or Glenda Farrell, two old-school performers prominent in Douglas and Scorsese's philosophy.

Douglas and Scorsese became romantically involved. The director and Barbara De Fina were married at the time; they were officially separated around the time of *Goodfellas'* release. Scorsese seems to have attempted to keep the strands of his professional/personal involvements segregated. In interviews, neither De Fina nor Douglas recounts any unpleasant interactions with the other. For Douglas' part, she said that Scorsese had given her to believe, at the relationship's outset, that he and De Fina were living apart. De Fina's response when I mentioned this to her was an eye roll.

In any event, Douglas was caught up in *Goodfellas* fever before it was clear that she'd be involved in the movie. "The casting of *Goodfellas* was top-secret stuff," she writes. "I was privy to hearing about and sometimes even seeing every actor or actress that was even in consideration, but I was sworn to secrecy. Listen, I knew that I was in consideration, and Marty wouldn't confirm or deny if I was going to be in the movie, and we were in a relationship."

Once production started, she writes, in an account echoing the recollections of supporting players such as Michael Imperioli and Kevin Corrigan: "Word was spreading about *Goodfellas*, and actors, mobsters, you name it, were requesting if they, too, could come down just to get a glimpse of Robert De Niro. In some neighborhoods a carnival-like atmosphere developed and folks were having cookouts and sitting in lawn chairs outside places where they were shooting. It was like they were part of the atmosphere and Marty harnessed that energy and put it into the film."

Douglas was visiting the set well before she was cast. Scorsese had given her the book *Wiseguy* before the shoot began, and he would ask her to visit the set for certain scenes: "Why don't you come down, it's gonna be fun." When she read the book, and then the script, she told Scorsese she was interested in the role of Sandy, the hard-bitten friend of Henry Hill's mistress, Janice, who becomes a love interest of sorts to Henry after he enlists her in his drug-dealing business. She recalls saying to Scorsese, "That's the good part," to which he responded, "Nah, nah, you're not ready for that."

As it happens, the unclear-product retail party for which Douglas got the role of Rosie was Douglas' own idea. "Marty would talk to me about what was going on in the run-up to shooting. The actors were coming in and doing character-based improvs every day, recording the improvs, and then typing them up, incorporating them into the shooting script. He really had his hands full with that. And he said, 'I haven't given much thought to the scenes with Karen.' Particularly with the way she got drawn into Henry's world and the world of the other mob wives." In *Wiseguy*, the event Karen Hill describes wherein she first finds out "how different [Henry's] friends were from the way I was raised" was a hostess party where one of the mob wives was selling copper-and-wood wall decorations. "I suggested, what if I stage a Mary Kay party at my apartment, and we invite all the women in the movie, have the production designer and the art people photograph it, as we do improvs. That became the basis of what went into the movie."

It's quite a whirlwind of activity. Women making each other up and sassing each other—"Angie, stop picking at that!"

"I'd like to smack his face"—a quick shot of a giant beehive hairdo—"You think you got problems, what about Jeannie's kid," "Well, you know Jeannie drinks," and so on, and on to the sad tale of one absent wife whose husband is off to prison.

"They had bad skin and wore too much makeup," Bracco's Karen says in voice-over. "They looked beat up." And indeed, many of them probably were. In *Wiseguy*, Karen goes further: "They had missing teeth. You never saw mouths like that where I grew up. Also, they weren't very well-dressed. The stuff they wore was unfashionable and cheap. A lot of polyester and double-knit pantsuits. And later, when I met their kids, I was amazed at how much trouble their kids gave them. Their kids were always in trouble. They were always in fights. They wouldn't go to school. They'd disappear from home. The women would beat their kids blue with broom handles and leather belts, but the kids didn't pay any attention. The women seemed to be on the edge of just making it. They were all very nervous and tense. Their younger kids looked dirty all the time. It was that thing some kids have of looking dirty even after their baths. That was the look."

In contrast to this near-Dickensian evocation of deprivation, Scorsese plays the scene for dark, disorienting humor. "When Henry picked me up I was dizzy," Karen says of the party. (The wedding had made her feel "drunk.") The sequence's bluntness and slam-bang pacing create a similar alienating effect on the viewer.

As for "Jew heaven"?

Having set the scene in an improvisation, Douglas asked Scorsese whether she'd be in the shoot. "He goes, 'We'll come up with something, we'll come up with something.' At that point I just was, you know, an excited participant. When it came to actual lines, I didn't have any idea when the shoot began. I re- member being a young actor thinking, 'When the camera is on you, just talk.' My grandmother was Italian, so I came up with a name, Rosie, that was my grandmother's sister and, I told myself, I'm gonna be my grandmother and say anything that my grand- mother might say—but within the logic of the scene. You can't improvise willy-nilly. But yes, 'Jew heaven' was something that my grandmother always said about going to Florida." (Douglas would use the phrase again on the HBO series *Six Feet Under*, playing a blunt mortician.)

"The atmosphere on set was really fun, almost carnival-like. And Marty again was such a great audience. I mainly just wanted to make Marty laugh. If I heard him laughing…you know, that's a good sign."

Like almost all narrative movies, *Goodfellas* was shot out of sequence, and Douglas had a harder time with her very first scene in the film, the celebration of the Lufthansa heist, which is discussed later. But the party scene made up for her earlier confidence-shaking experience, and clinched several things for Douglas. "We just all bonded in the scene. Melissa Prophet, who plays Angie in the scene, soon left acting to form a management firm, and ended up becoming my manager. Lorraine came and took me under her wing. The part got me an agent."

In subsequent years, Douglas would act in Scorsese's *Cape Fear*; getting her cheek bitten off by De Niro is a particularly brutal sexual assault scene. Her relationship with Scorsese continued into the '90s. When she collaborated with the director Allison Anders on the ambitious 1996 *Grace of My Heart*, about a female songwriter of the Brill Building ilk in the '60s, Scorsese executive produced and Thelma Schoonmaker edited. In Douglas' book she writes about how, despite the many fulfilling aspects of their relationship (watching her speak about movies on TCM, you can see one significant way in which they got along: they are both eloquent movie lovers with encyclopedic knowledge), she felt, as time went on, overshadowed by the director. "I loved Marty, of course, but my identity was becoming overshadowed under his, and part of me was becoming lost." Nevertheless, when I interviewed her, she said she felt "blindsided" by the way the relationship ended.

"How so?" I asked her.

"He got married."

She drops the line like the excellent comedic actress she is. Still.

Like several people I have spoken with who thrived in Scorsese's orbit but are now out of it, she is slightly rueful and a bit resigned. Her current interactions with Scorsese are minimal but cordial. She herself married—"mistakenly," she says—shortly after the breakup.

One nasty story Douglas did not tell in her book was about how the former CBS head Les Moonves sabotaged a 1997 show she was working on, and allegedly sexually assaulted her; this came out in a *New Yorker* story by Ronan Farrow in 2018. She confided in Scorsese at the time of the incident (they were no longer romantically involved), and he provided her with what she considered good advice: the lawyer he steered her to was able to reach a decent financial settlement for her. Nevertheless, Moonves had "torpedoed" her career with his actions.

When the *New Yorker* story came out, Douglas was told by some parties that she should not expect corroboration from Scorsese. "His people that I knew—agents and Hollywood people— would say to me, 'He's not gonna come forward.' And I was like, 'You don't know Marty.' We had retained a respect for each other. And I remember when the whole thing happened, it was so traumatic, because things had just ended with Marty, and I was a little bit like a babe in the woods in LA, going out there on my own…like a babe in the woods, out of protective custody, so to speak, and boom, this happens. One thing Marty and I were always in sync on was the importance of the work, and that's one reason he was incensed to hear about this. And then yes, he did corroborate. Without my asking. So that was important. It confirmed the thing about him that I already knew."

AFTER A WHILE IT ALL GOT TO BE NORMAL

Karen returns from her Mafia Girl Party in a state of panic. Telling Henry of an account of a jailed husband and his wife's depressed/alcoholic plight at home, she asks, "God forbid, what would happen if you had to go to prison?"

"Lemme tell you something," Henry says, applying what he doesn't yet know to be a delusional argument. "Nobody goes to jail unless they want to. Unless they make themselves get caught."

Henry, and his fellow wiseguys, have things organized.

Karen, sitting on the bed wearing cream-orange sleepwear, buys Henry's schtick.

"You know who goes to jail? N———r stick-up men, that's who. You know why they get caught? Because they fall asleep in the getaway car, Karen."

This declaration is shocking in its crassness just on the face of it. It's even more so when remembering the way that Henry and Tommy and whatever trucker they bribed would arrange their heists, paying off the trucker who would then say his rig was stolen by, say, "two n———rs."

Gregg Hill, Henry's real-life son, writes in a book he coauthored with his sister, Gina: "I was never afraid of my father's friends. If anyone ever scared me, it was my father—not because I thought he'd do anything to intentionally hurt me, but that his belligerence would get us into some kind of trouble. Like we'd be driving to visit Stacks Edwards in Harlem on a summer day with the windows rolled down. Stacks was a big black man who hung out at The Suite, a really nice guy whom I liked a lot. But on the way, my father would start talking loudly about 'these fuckin' n———rs.' I'd say, 'Dad, shut up.' He'd just laugh. 'Are you fucking out of your mind?' he'd say. 'These fucking n———rs aren't going to touch us.' Then if some black guys looked over, he would slow down and stare back at them. 'Daaaad! Just go,' I'd say. It was weird because, for all his many flaws, my father wasn't a racist. He was just crazy."

Gregg is not depicted in the movie because of certain stipulations made by the production. The movie went forward while Hill and family were presumed to be still under witness protection program safeguarding. The names, ages, and genders of the Hill children had to be changed. In the movie Karen and Henry have two daughters who don't age entirely realistically; in real life, Gregg Hill and Gina Hill were thirteen and eleven, respectively, when Hill entered witness protection.

★ ★ ★

After his racist digression, Henry further assuages Karen with lovemaking. Sex scenes are rare in Scorsese films, and he telegraphs this one with two horizontal pans down the couple's bodies as Henry seduces his bride. "After a while it got to be all normal," Karen says. "None of it seemed like crime. It was more like Henry was enterprising and that he and the guys were making a few bucks hustling, while the other guys were sitting on their asses waiting for handouts. Our husbands weren't brain surgeons. They were blue-collar guys. The only way they could make extra money, real extra money, was to go out and cut a few corners."

As if to illustrate this, the film cuts away from the lovemaking to show a particularly rough truck hijacking committed by Henry, Tommy, Jimmy (who, as we recall from Henry, likes stealing pretty much more than anything), and Frankie Carbone. As Henry puts the truck in gear, Tommy points his shotgun out the window and up in the air and blasts, whooping. Cutting corners, of course.

The contrast is there so viewers won't buy Karen's rationalizations. What the wiseguys do certainly doesn't look like any kind of work. Still, many prosecutors and crime novel writers will tell you that in terms of risk versus reward, not to mention expenditure of effort, the life of a full-time thief is such that often one might as well just get a gig in the straight world. Scorsese told Mary Pat Kelly, "I've tried to point out in my movies that they work more hours a day than if they had a nine-to-five job." Everyone makes their own excuses and rationalizations for whatever morally aberrant actions they're "compelled" to carry out for the sake of a living. And these arguments conveniently ignore moral agency, which so much of the other dialogue in the movie at least hints at, as in Henry's assertion that Jimmy "loved" to steal.

Karen lays out the ways she was magnanimous to the cops who'd occasionally show up with a search warrant. "You boys want some coffee?" she asks of two detectives she shows into her house. She says in voice-over that most of them were just looking for their own bribes, a "handout." Their own cut corners. As the detectives look around, perfunctorily, Karen and her new daughter sit on the lounger before the TV. *The Jazz Singer*, widely touted as the first sound picture, is on the box.

The use of the clip from this 1928 musical melodrama, starring the biggest pop singer of the early twentieth century, Al Jolson, is a touch obscure. Yes, Jolson is singing "Toot Toot Tootsie," which contains the lyric "Watch for the mail/I'll never fail/if you don't get a letter then you know I'm in jail," and yes, Henry will be just that—in jail—in not too very long. But ascribing significance to that is a bit of a stretch even so. It could just be there because *Singer* was a staple of local television movie programming in New York in the '60s, something Scorsese remembers being on in that period. Whatever the reason, Scorsese cuts twice to ever-closer screen-filling shots of the television, Jolson's manic eyes looking a little panicked as he whistles through an instrumental break. The reverse shot dollies in on Karen, looking hypnotized by the performance. (A different clip from *The Jazz Singer*, in which Jolson's character explains his hopped-up music to his mother, is seen in Scorsese's 2004 *The Aviator*, and shown to more direct narrative effect, as the introduction of sound movies compels its protagonist, Howard Hughes, to reshoot his film *Hell's Angels*.)

"We always did everything together," Karen says over one live-action children's birthday party and a series of vacation-with-Jimmy-the-Gent still photos, as Dean Martin's "Ain't That a Kick in the Head" plays on the soundtrack.

The living is very easy: Henry's suits receive a panning shot through the closet, as do Karen's dresses, and in front of the closet, Henry stands, pulling rubber-banded stacks of hundred-dollar bills from the waistband of his pants.

As he goes to leave, Karen tells him, from the kitchen, that she'd like to do some shopping today. Henry asks, "How much do you need," and she gestures with her fingers the height of the wad she requires. (This detail comes from the book.) "How much?" he asks again, approaching her, and she answers, "That much." There's a playful flatness in the delivery that suggests this is a game they regularly play, as they kiss and he hands her half of one of the banded group of bills, and she goes to her knees. "Oh, all right," he says, handing her the rest of the cash and no longer in such a rush.

Frisky newlyweds still hot for each other; you love to see it. With this kind of money and these kinds of good looks, the pornography of everyday life is not a fantasy. A more expansive/expensive iteration of this theme is seen in Scorsese's 2014 *The Wolf of Wall Street*, with Leonardo DiCaprio and Margot Robbie as the even more monied and movie-star attractive couple.

A SERIOUS PROBLEM WITH BILLY BATTS

"June 11, 1970/Queens, New York" reads the on-screen title over the establishing shot—which holds just long enough to show that the diner-like structure we'll occupy on this night is called "The Suite Lounge." The movie doesn't delve into it, but this is the bar Henry Hill bought and was advised by Paul Vario to keep "clean." And he did make an effort. This incident could be seen to undercut that to an extent.

The bouncy, infectious song is "He's Sure the Boy I Love," a Phil Spector–produced girl-group classic from 1962. There are balloons on the walls of the bar inside and the men at the bar are middle-aged. It's a wiseguy celebration and the music fits. To a superficial extent at least. Its use here subtly underlines the implied self-delusion of "And Then He Kissed Me" in the Copa scene, its innocent exhilaration being just a mask over the corruption enabling Henry's ability to sweep Karen off her feet.

"Hey, Batts," exclaims a guy in a leisure suit and turtleneck as he approaches the bar.

Batts, a guy with stiff hair, a raspy voice, and a dark mustache, orders more booze, saying, "Give those Irish hoodlums a drink down there," indicating the far side of the bar where two men stand.

"There's only one Irishman here," Jimmy Burke, drinking with Henry, says.

"It's a celebration, fellas. *Salud.*"

Joe Pesci wasn't the only actor in *The Death Collector* who impressed Robert De Niro. Frank Vincent is also in that picture, in the role of Bernie Feldshuh, a deadbeat "businessman" whose refusal to pay a debt results in heavy consequences for him but heavier ones for the obstreperous "collector" played by Joseph Cortese. Much is made of Bernie's Jewishness in the dialogue, but Vincent, his ostentatious large hair (sometimes referred to as, if you'll excuse the term, a "Jewfro") notwithstanding, mainly plays him as Extreme Jersey, expectorating lots of couldn't-give-a-fuck "ay"s.

Born Frank Vincent Galluso, Jr., in 1938, Vincent played trumpet, piano, and drums; in a latter-day interview he claimed to have drummed on sessions with pop great Del Shannon, Vegas staples Paul Anka and Trini Lopez, and jazz bandleader Don Costa. He cited argumentative jazz drummer Buddy Rich and soul/R&B innovator Bernard Purdie as influences. Did he actually play on Shannon's classic "Runaway" as he claims? The song was originally cut in New York in January 1961; Vincent was twenty-three at the time. The credited drummer was a "Joe Marshall." Shannon recut the song in 1967 and released it again as a single; if Vincent recorded with Shannon, this seems the more plausible session.

Prior to landing their roles in *Collector*, he and Pesci were in the trio Vincent, Pesci, and Capri. After Capri bailed, they cropped their publicity shot and billed themselves as Vincent and Pesci. Under this handle they recorded a novelty Christmas single about a kid who wants Santa to make him stop stuttering, with Pesci doing a tape-speed-enhanced Porky Pig impression. (One thinks, unavoidably, of Tommy's epithet "ya stuttering prick ya" in the Bamboo Lounge scene.) They also cut an instrumental side, "Little People Blues." There's 1990 footage on YouTube of Pesci, with saxist "Muzzy" and singer Arlene Carol, performing "This Can't Be Love" with Vincent laying a steady carpet on drums behind them, in an unnamed nightclub.

Their characters in Scorsese films consistently antagonize each other, to say the least. (In *The Death Collector* they have no scenes together.) The scenes hit home for the actors personally. In their nightclub days, scraping to survive, as close as they were, there were disagreements, feelings of rivalry, genuine enmity. "It is the supreme irony of Mr. Vincent's life that he owes his film career to Mr. Pesci but that it is the tension between them that makes their performances work. The two can conjure up a feeling of bad blood that is palpable," wrote Edward Lewine in a 1996 profile of Vincent for the *New York Times*. "'It's a friendship,' said Mr. Pesci. 'And when you know someone that well you know where all the buttons are. It's easy for him to drive me crazy.'" In *Raging Bull* Vincent plays Salvy, a mobbed-up friend of Jake LaMotta's firecracker brother, Joey. Their banter is typically mookish. "Hey, Salvy," Joey says as they part ways on the block. "What?" Salvy says. Joey silently mouths, "GO FUCK YOURSELF." When relations sour for real, Joey attacks the much larger Salvy, crushing the upper half of his body repeatedly with a car door. Later, compelled by mob boss Tommy (the great Nick Colasanto) to make up, Joey hugs Salvy just a little too ardently, hurting Salvy's broken arm. In this *Goodfellas* scene, Pesci's Tommy pistol-whips, beats, kicks, and eventually stabs Vincent's Batts. Vincent got a bit of payback in 2004's *Casino*, in which his character, Frank Marino, brutalizes Pesci's freewheeling sadist Nicky with an aluminum baseball bat before burying his bloodied body alive.

After going the tough-guy-player-journeyman route through the '80s and '90s, Vincent settled into a primo gig on *The Sopranos* for a few years in the early '00s. Unlike Pesci, Vincent seemed to enjoy fame as a screen actor. While not as ubiquitous as the actress Sylvia Miles, whose omnipresence in New York's showbiz social whirl earned her the reputation as someone who would show up for the opening of an envelope, Vincent became a genial, approachable figure at various and sundry premieres and semiexclusive after-parties, always happy to say hello and/or tell you about the line of cigars he was putting his name on. (He was regularly featured in *Cigar Aficionado* magazine.) With Stephen Priggé, in 2007, he penned a jocular advice book called *A Guy's Guide to Being a Man's Man*. Vincent died in September 2017 after suffering a heart attack; he was eighty.

"Good to be home," his Billy Batts says during the glass-raising. That feeling won't last. Vincent's big line here, after some squirrely back-and-forth and a feint at smoothing things over, is "Now go home and get your fucking shine box." In many accounts of the shooting of the film, the actors and crew have said that the words spoken by the actors in this film were almost never their lines as scripted. This is not entirely true, and indeed, you can't make a narrative film such as this one using that method; the scene's beginning, middle, and end, its ability to be properly "cut into" the larger work, depends on the actors following the specific scripted action, which is often spurred by dialogue. As is the case here, when Batts' harping on Tommy's childhood career in shoeshining—"busting [his] balls"—culminates in Tommy's murderous rage.

What Scorsese does, in this scene and with almost all his actors, is give them their way with the dialogue. In Pileggi and Scorsese's script, Batts' line is "Now get the hell home and get your shine box." A good line, yes. But Vincent polished it with a certain authentic street vehemence. "Get the hell home" expends more syllables than it needs to say to Tommy: get out. "Go home" is even more direct. And of course "fucking shine box": Vincent makes the four syllables ring like pistol shots. The rhythm there, missing from the scripted line, is crucial, and lands just in the right place for Pesci to scream back, "MOTHER-FUCKING MUTT!!!"

The volley of words is matched in cutting and camera movement; Scorsese never does a static shot-reverse-shot pattern when he can be dollying in on a character before they land a verbal death blow. When Batts beckons, "Come on, you feel strong," to Tommy, the viewer feels the camera responding to the goading. "Keep him here," Tommy yells. Batts pays that no mind, and he should have. Jimmy, after mildly scolding Batts—"Nah nah nah nah nah, you insulted him a little bit" is a comedic high point of his work as Jimmy—is the one that keeps him there. (In actual life, Batts insulted Tommy at Robert's Lounge, and Tommy took his revenge several weeks after, coming upon Batts drinking in The Suite.)

When Tommy returns and he and Jimmy get to beating Batts, the song playing on the jukebox is Donovan's "Atlantis," a non-wiseguy, hippie-dippie tune if there ever was one, all about a lost civilization and the poet, the physician, the magician, all taking off in a boat to bless the world we know. (Scorsese has said he homed in on the song's twilight of the gods theme, hearing a consonance between it and the fall that these characters are semi-unwittingly setting themselves up for.) "Way down/below the ocean" goes the hard-rocking chorus/outro; in a Batts POV shot the shoes of Jimmy and Tommy are stomping.

Robert De Niro, while anecdotally known to have, or have had, a temper, does not identify as a tough guy. His father, Robert De Niro, Sr., was an artist, a well-known and well-respected one among his peers, if a somewhat publicly obscure one relative to those peers, who included Mark Rothko and Robert Motherwell. His mother, Virginia Admiral, was also a painter and a poet. He was raised in an atmosphere of aesthetic refinement, albeit of the New York bohemian variety.

Viewers both inside and outside of the business nevertheless look at this scene and ask, "Where did De Niro learn to kick like that?" In the GQ oral history, Pileggi says, "De Niro has mastered the art of kicking people. I suspect that happened growing up. He didn't get that from the Actors Studio." In the next bit, De Niro is quoted: "I don't know if I can say that. Anyway. [laughs] Whatever." And Peter Bucossi, a stuntman, sums up: "De Niro was kicking the hell out of me that night. I had pads on, but I recall being quite bruised a few days later. I mean, he tried to hit the pads, but in the midst of their fury they're not worried about making sure." In an interview, De Niro said to me, "You're doing a film. It's not, you know, not to be taken literally, though some people do." It could be taken as a compliment, he continued, "they think you're doing well and so, that's okay, you know. But it's just part of the job."

There is more unforgettable imagery here. The demolished revolver, bullets askew, sliding across the floor like a sputtering hockey puck. The overhead shot of the men bringing a tablecloth they will make into a winding sheet to wrap Batts in. Speaking of sputtering, Tommy continues to, his anger still unsatisfied despite killing Batts: "Fuckin' mutt did to my shoes." He then looks over at Henry, with tears in his eyes, and bleats, "I didn't wanna get blood on your floor."

De Niro laughed a little when I brought up that line. "Everybody has their moments of politesse."

Liotta's reaction shot, and the later reaction shots when they're at the dining room table with Tommy's mother, are interesting. He's put off by Tommy's hysteria, and he can barely believe that Tommy and Jimmy can laugh and eat while the body of a guy they've brutally murdered is in the trunk of a car they've parked in the driveway. But these aren't so much twinges of conscience as expressions of *cognitive* dissonance relative to certain social mores. This is not anything Henry would leave the life over. He will only leave it to save his own skin.

Then the burial. "We'll pick up a shovel at my mother's house," Tommy says. In *Wiseguy*, Hill recounts: "His mother was already up and made us come in for coffee. She wouldn't let us leave. We have to have breakfast—with a body parked outside."

A whole scene is extrapolated from these three sentences. "Look who's here," Catherine Scorsese, the director's mother, as the character known only as "Tommy's Mother" says almost the second Tommy enters the house.

Catherine Scorsese was involved with her son's work from very early on. In Scorsese's 1966 short, made at NYU, *It's Not Just You, Murray!*, a pretty eccentric effort by almost any student film standard, she is Murray's mother, who feeds him spaghetti through a prison gate. In his first feature, *Who's That Knocking at My Door*, she looks severe in the opening scene, baking prosciutto bread. She is the tenement neighbor in *Mean Streets* who drops her groceries when Charlie's girlfriend, Theresa, goes into an epileptic seizure on the stairs.

For *It's Not Just You, Murray!* Catherine not only had a small role, she was the de facto caterer. She told Mary Pat Kelly: "Now don't forget. I started to work with him when he was in college. Especially when we made that movie in the swamp. When we made that, I had to get up at five o'clock in the morning and make spaghetti. [...] Charlie was in bed. And it was so cold and he said to me, 'You know, Katie, you and your son are both crazy.'

"My name is Catherine, they call me Katie, I don't know why," Mrs. Scorsese says in *Italianamerican*, the documentary Scorsese made about his parents in 1974. By all available accounts beloved by all who met her, Catherine sparkles in *Italianamerican* just as she does in *Goodfellas*. Teasing her reticent husband, Charles, to sit closer to her on the sofa in its opening minutes, she says, "They say as you get older, your love grows stronger... he's bashful."

When talking of Scorsese's mother, Barbara De Fina, at the time of the movie Catherine's daughter-in-law, still refers to her as Katie, and invariably speaks of her with both respect and affection. "She was what you would now call a 'Tiger Mom,' in a way," De Fina says. "Throughout my association with Marty people would ask me, 'Oh, but how do you get along with *Katie?*' but I never had any problem with her. I spent some time with her in the kitchen and picked up a lot of things. The person you see in *Italianamerican* and in *Goodfellas*, that really is who she was."

Over the years, even as Scorsese brought his parents more and more into the filmmaker fold (Charles would make his on-screen debut in *Raging Bull*, as a confederate of mobster Tommy Como), he maintained a protective attitude. Larry McConkey first worked with Scorsese on the 1985 black comedy *After Hours*, filming the Steadicam shot of Paul Hackett's office that runs under the end credits. He says that Scorsese's parents were on set that day to witness the filming—because that was the only scene in the movie he felt comfortable having them watch.

★ ★ ★

For this scene, Nick Pileggi provided a painting from his mother, and Scorsese explained to his mom what he needed. To Mary Pat Kelly, Catherine explained: "In my scene, Tommy brings his friends home and his mother cooks for them. I play his mother, so I said to Marty, 'What am I going to make for them?' And he said, 'Make pasta and beans, just like you used to make for me—or scrambled eggs.' If he'd come home late from a date or from being over at NYU, I'd get up and make him something to eat, and then I'd go back to sleep. And, you know, it was the middle of the night so I'd make him something like scrambled eggs or pasta and beans. He said, 'If it was good enough for me, it's good enough for them.'"

From the looks of the scene, it's pasta and beans, which Jimmy the sacrilegious Irishman, in his most unforgivable act in the movie, slathers with Heinz's ketchup as Tommy tells his mom that he's been "working nights." The mordant comedy here is kind of irresistible, as Tommy concocts a cock-and-bull story about hitting a deer and needing one of the kitchen knives to remove its "hoof" from the car's grille, or something. "It's a sin," Tommy says. It's funny enough one doesn't necessarily think to shudder, especially with De Niro pointing his cutlery at the dish and saying, "Delicious, delicious."

The hilarity and the creepiness run about neck-and-neck, as Tommy's mother picks up the thread from Henry's wedding and asks why her son doesn't settle down, and he ends his answer with, "I wanna be with *you*, Ma."

Tommy's mom tracks Henry's alienation and asks why he's so quiet.

"I'm just listening," Henry responds. The Quiet Italian joke Tommy's mother tells, with the punchline, "What do you want me to say? That my wife two-times me?" is another bit that emerged out of recorded improvisations; Mrs. Scorsese could just as well have told it in *Italianamerican*. Mrs. Scorsese and Pesci do some back-and-forth in Italian, and at the end Tommy delivers an indirect insult to Henry: "It means he's content to be a jerk."

Henry lets it slide. He's got heavier things on his mind. "Did Tommy ever tell you about my painting?" the mother asks, and then seems to pick up the canvas from the floor. (Such is the current cult of the movie that Pileggi's mother's work, an image of a man with white hair and beard sitting in a small boat with two dogs, is now both an internet meme and a T-shirt. The image, incidentally, is not original: Pileggi's mother painted it from a photograph in the November 1978 issue of *National Geographic* magazine, illustrating a story about Ireland's River Shannon.) Tommy's befuddled account of its allegorical content—"I like this one. One dog goes one way, and the other dog goes the other way. And this guy's saying, 'Whaddya want from me?'"— is funny, and then Jimmy chimes in saying, "Looks like somebody we know." The man in the painting doesn't really look like Batts, but Tommy cracks up, anyway, and Henry gives a tight-lipped, tolerant smile. The camera pushes past a laughing Tommy to gaze at the back of the car, considering the faint sound of the still-alive Batts kicking at the inside of the trunk.

The burial of Batts is bathed in red, from the back lights of the car; the image could be from Mario Bava's *Hercules and the Haunted World*, if that haunted world contained cars. In voice-over, Henry, for really the first time, weighs in on the downside of gangsterdom:

"Murder was the only way everybody stayed in line [...] shooting people was a normal thing. It was no big deal." Unless you shot the wrong guy.

"We had a serious problem with Billy Batts. This was really a touchy thing." Batts was, in Italian mob parlance, a made man. "Considered untouchable."

This is where the movie first hints at it—that the rules, the supposed ethos or code of the wiseguys, weren't worth the paper they were, well, never actually printed on. Billy Batts, the untouchable, got whacked. Ultimately, this aggression would not stand, as we will see. But the eventual avenging of Batts is of small value to Batts himself. Dead is dead.

FRIDAY NIGHT AT THE COPA

As grim as the culmination of the Batts business will prove to be, it won't hit our gang for some time yet. After Henry's account of what it means to be a made man, accompanied by a snapshot and slow-motion reprise of Batts' homicide highlights, we see another airborne Copacabana table making a furious transit, in slow motion.

"Saturday night was for wives, but Friday night at the Copa was always for girlfriends." Gina Mastrogiacomo plays Janice, Henry's girlfriend. Janice is younger, looser, more vulgar than Karen—she's a smoker but you get the impression that she'd just as soon be chewing gum—with a big bouffant hairdo. Mastrogiacomo is vivid and immediate in the role. The reason she does not turn up in retrospectives or oral histories of the movie is terribly sad: she died in 2001 of a bacterial heart infection.

There's something pro forma about Henry keeping a mistress. The movie depicts his sex life with Karen as more than merely satisfactory. As with several other aspects of the wiseguy lifestyle, Henry seems to be following his friends' leads. Girlfriends are the done thing. Part of the social conformity/ unofficial regimentation of mob life. Pileggi states as much in *Wiseguy*: "For most wiseguys, having a steady girl was not unusual. Almost all of [Hill's] friends had them. You didn't leave a wife or abandon a family for one, but you did swank them around, rent them apartments, lease them cars, and feed them regularly with racks of swag clothes and paper bags of stolen jewelry. Having a steady girl was considered a sign of success, like a thoroughbred or a powerboat but better: a girlfriend was the ultimate luxury purchase."

Janice's rhapsodizing over Sammy Davis, Jr.'s talent gets the other girlfriends in Henry's party going, and soon Tommy's hackles are mildly raised, which still represents pretty thin ice for others, by Tommy standards. "You could see how a white girl can fall for him," Tommy's date says. "Wha?" Tommy asks. The date alludes to Mae Britt, Davis' Swedish wife, and Tommy says, "In other words you condone that stuff."

"EASY!" Henry exclaims, cackling a little, cocktail straw in his mouth, the same impish look on his face that he had on when he semitaunted Tommy after the "How am I funny?" confrontation. "I just wanna make sure I don't wind up kissing fucking Nat King Cole over here," Tommy spits.

This makes zero sense. He is just, as many racists do, being racist for the sake of being racist. (In real life, Joe Pesci's singing testifies to his reverence for black artists; on the Joey De-Francesco "featuring Joe Doggs" album *Falling in Love Again*, Pesci's timbre and idiosyncratic but thoughtful phrasing often bring to mind, believe it or not, Nina Simone. There are also hints of Little Jimmy Scott, to whom Pesci pays explicit homage on the more recent record *Still Singing*.)

A horizontal tracking shot sees Henry, Janice, Tommy and his date, and Frankie Carbone and his date gazing, rapt, at the Copa stage. We finally learn the one thing that can make Tommy shut the fuck up: Jerry Vale singing "Pretend You Don't See Her."

"Pretend you don't love her," Vale sings in a plaintive tenor, instructing his heart.

The segue, as the song plays out, is to a shot of Janice's apartment building with Henry's car parked outside it. Night turns to morning in a dissolve. The inauthenticity of the relationship notwithstanding, this is an odd, short submersion into a kind of lyricism, a pause from the frenetic and increasingly reckless and amoral action. While Henry has not asked for this moment of respite, it's possible that the viewer could use it.

It's a *brief* respite. Henry's double life reveals itself as increasingly unmanageable. The Hills pay a visit to "Uncle Paulie." Tuddy is there, as is the mysterious Vinnie, played by Charles Scorsese, Marty's father. As befitted his reserved personality, the onetime garment district worker Charles Scorsese did not relish performing in his son's films, and tended to feel more comfortable in roles that had a more or less contemporary setting, as this one did. "He did not like getting into costume for *The Age of Innocence*," Barbara De Fina recalls. The whole gathering has an undercurrent of unease.

Paulie pulls Henry aside and asks him if he knows anything about Billy Batts, a made man who has vanished. Associates of Batts' crime family have inquiring minds. "These people are driving everybody crazy," Paulie says. Henry tells Paulie he knows nothing about it.

This is the first time Henry lies to Paulie, and it seems to come easily to him. There won't be any immediate, direct consequences for this. When Tommy is ultimately dealt with, his accomplices in Batts' death won't figure at all. But Hill's subsequent lies to Paulie will cost him.

Another horizontal track from behind the bar of a hangout that is not The Suite shows a more raucous evening. The loudest voice is Morrie's; he's relating an anecdote in which someone is repeating, "I want my money." Henry and Janice are sharing a semitender moment when Jimmy calls to him. Wearing the most vivid plaid in which he'll be seen, Jimmy pulls Henry over and tells him they've got to relocate Batts' body—the ground in which he is laid is soon to be dug up for condo-building. In a cut they are back in the red-lit haunted world, shovels blazing. Henry can't stand the stench, he's about to puke, and Tommy and Jimmy bust his balls. "My mother's gonna make some fresh peppers and sausage," Tommy yells. "Hey, Henry, here's an arm, here's a leg!" says Jimmy. "You go for the hearts and lungs," Tommy asks, and Henry finally loses whatever he last ate.

Say what you will about "those goody-goody people who worked shit jobs for bum paychecks and took the subway to work every day and worried about bills," they generally don't have to deal with stuff like this. Henry finds that he can't hose the Batts-corpse stench out of his trunk; Karen is repelled but not curious.

And Henry rolls with it all. Nothing is catching up with him yet. He procures a new apartment for Janice ("all Maurice Vallencia," she brags of her furniture, mispronouncing Maurice Villency, a popular Manhattan-based designer), brings Tommy and Jimmy on a little ass-kicking job when Janice's boss at a dress shop hassles her about showing up late, and even flirts with one of Janice's friends, Sandy (Debi Mazar, the New York actor then known outside of work for her hip retro stylings and friendship with Madonna). Sandy digs how Henry's keeping Janice: taking a whiff from a bottle on Janice's perfume table, she says, "French," and raises approving eyebrows.

First assistant director Joseph Reidy recalls the shooting of this scene as being a little tough on Liotta, as were the confrontation scenes between Henry and Karen. "Everybody was at a different rhythm; each character was playing it differently," referring to the differences in emotional temperature between the killers Jimmy and Tommy and the less homicidally experienced Henry. "I felt that the most emotional scenes or the hardest scenes were the scenes between Henry and Karen in the house when they're battling, those were hard for all concerned. People were unhappy, they brought a lot of anger into the room. And the scenes among the wiseguys, you know, they were still having some fun, you know, but always with an edge. Joe Pesci was always wound up, and he was both fun and difficult to be around. He didn't want to mess with anybody, or be messed with. The scene where they're burying Billy Batts, that may have been a little tough for Ray. But I think his toughest scenes were with Karen, and those moments when he was coke-addled toward the end there. That was rough stuff."

THE KILLING OF SPIDER

The seductiveness of the gangster lifestyle is shown as dubious throughout *Goodfellas*, but for most viewers of moral sentience there's a specific point at which the penny drops and you're obliged to see these fun-loving criminals as the largely irredeemable thugs they are. For many it's the especially senseless killing of Billy Batts. But even this murder will be let slide by ride-or-die romanticizers of criminality. After all, Batts was busting Tommy's balls a little bit, as Jimmy notes before helping Tommy kick Billy's skull in.

If you are not off the bus after Tommy kills the hapless bartender Spider, though, you may have a problem in that moral sentience department.

The scene is a poker game in what could be somebody's basement, but given the presence of a jukebox is more likely the back room of a bar. Poker is the game and the players are Henry, Tommy, Jimmy, Frankie Carbone, Anthony Stabile, and Mikey Franzese. Tending the bar is a young guy in a blue pullover shirt, halting in manner, called "Spider."

"Hey, Spider, on your way over here bring me a Cutty and water, huh?" Tommy asks, before announcing to the table that he's gonna play the cards he's holding. But Spider's already on the way, slowly, without the Cutty and water, and soon Tommy's asking if Spider's got him on the "pay-no-mind list." Spider's having trouble following Tommy. The guys find Tommy's truculent abuse funny, as they will.

"You walk like fuckin' Stepin Fetchit," Tommy bellows as Spider hastens back to the bar. Stepin Fetchit was a Hollywood actor, ostensibly comedic, who was born Lincoln Theodore Monroe Andrew Perry in 1902. He invented a persona from the play-on-words name up, playing a nasty racist caricature: a droopy-eyed, slow-walking, "laziest man in the world" African American. Wildly successful in its time, his film work is rarely screened today. (In the three films he made with John Ford he got a slightly more dignified treatment than usual; two of these costarred white comic performer and legend-in-his-own-time Will Rogers, who was a close friend of Perry's.) "Anybody else you fuckin' run. Run for me, you little prick! Dance the fuckin' drink back here."

Continuing in a vintage pop-culture vein, Tommy asks, "Hey, what's the movie that Bogart made?"

"Which one?"

"The one where he played a cowboy, the only one."

Someone says, "*Shane?*" which Tommy would disdain further than he does but someone else offers *The Oklahoma Kid.*

"I'm the Oklahoma Kid!" Tommy exults, waving his gun in the air. And then he shoots Spider in the foot.

In 1939's *The Oklahoma Kid*, directed by Lloyd Bacon, the title role is played by James Cagney, who did a bunch of Westerns; Bogart plays the Kid's nemesis, Whip McCord. Neither the Kid nor McCord compel anyone to do any bullet dancing. There's a scene early on in a bar in which Cagney gets the saloon piano player to accompany his singing of "I Don't Want to Play in Your Yard," which is rudely interrupted by Ward Bond as one of McCord's men. Eventually the Kid is able to hold McCord and his men at gunpoint and he instructs the pianist, "Play, Professor," as he backs out of the bar and makes his escape.

This is the only movie talk in *Goodfellas*. While Scorsese's pictures teem with nods to other films, it's only in his first feature, *Who's That Knocking at My Door*, in which the protagonist is any kind of cinephile; Harvey Keitel's J.R. prattles at length about John Wayne and Lee Marvin to his very tolerant girlfriend.

At the next game, the players are one fewer: Franzese is no longer in the mix. Positions at the table are different; Tommy is sitting farther from the bar than he had been. As Spider limps over with a cast on his foot, Tommy mocks him: "Hey, Spider, that bandage on your fucking foot is bigger than your fucking head, you know that?" And so the goading begins, with Jimmy asking Spider if he's gonna take that from Tommy. (In De Niro's script notes: "What do I do here that lets Tom get like this? It will be more evident when we prepare to do [the scene]."

"The only line that was consistent was 'Go fuck yourself, Tommy,'" says Michael Imperioli, who plays Spider. Those four words compel Tommy to shoot Spider four times in the chest, point-blank, killing him. "Every take was different. But it had to get to 'Go fuck yourself, Tommy.'"

Imperioli had only been working in film for about a year when he landed the part in *Goodfellas*. He can be seen in an auditorium scene in the unorthodox pedagogy drama *Lean on Me*, a March 1989 release, as one of the many no-good Eastside High School students expelled by Morgan Freeman's principal Joe Clark.

"When I heard about the auditions [for *Goodfellas*], I thought, well, as an Italian American actor living in New York, I should definitely be involved." Most of the young actors who went to Ellen Lewis' office were given Tommy's lines to read. "I really thought I was trying out for Pesci's role," Imperioli laughs. "Ellen said, 'Great job, I want you to come back and meet Marty.' Which made me nervous, because I'd heard accounts of him 'sitting in judgment,' so to speak. But he could not have been more cordial. 'You got the part of Spider,' he told me, which both elated and disappointed me a little—I really thought I was going to get Tommy, that's how deluded I was."

While Imperioli's subsequent character on the television series *The Sopranos*, clueless wannabe filmmaker Christopher, is ostentatiously starstruck—"*Kundun*! I liked it!" he shouts to a Scorsese look-alike while on a nightclub queue in the second episode of the first season—the young actor Imperioli knew better than to gush to his scene partners once he got to the set. As recently as in press accounts of the 2019 movie *Joker*, anecdotes abound about how Robert De Niro comes to a set to work and has little patience for small talk. Imperioli had an intuitive sense of this, and how to approach the work in general once he got to the set. "I asked the prop master to let me reset the card table after each take. And before the scene was ready, I played as Spider. I would sweep the floor, as if waiting for the wiseguys to arrive." On one day, De Niro was the first to take a seat at the table. Imperioli didn't introduce himself. Instead, he said to De Niro, "What are you having?"

It was a moment before De Niro fully understood, and asked for a Scotch and club soda. "Sometimes on the set, if it's with guys you already know, you could have some kind of banter because people want to get loose," De Niro says. "But at the end of the day, you're shooting the scenes." He found Imperioli's approach commendable.

"When I first rehearsed the scenes, I played Spider more like a wiseass, a younger version of those guys," Imperioli says.

"Marty came after the rehearsal and said to me, 'I think this kid's a little slow.' That was it, that guided my performance from that point on. That makes it more twisted when he's killed. Marty's genius is to balance a scene's elements for a real unexpected impact." Spider isn't given any specific characterization in *Wiseguy*—he's not the after-hours poker game bartender, he's just a "kid," hanging around, that Tommy decided to torture by making him bullet dance. After actually shooting Spider in the foot, the wiseguys put Spider up at their hangout, Robert's, for a spell, and then one evening Spider refuses to dance and Tommy kills him.

Pesci's ad lib after killing Spider—"Whadya want, I'm still a good shot"—adds arguable mordant levity to the shocking scene. There ensues some shouting over who's going to dig Spider's makeshift grave ("What is it, the first hole I dug?" Tommy shrugs), and muttering about how Spider is from a family of rats, anyway.

In *Wiseguy*, Henry Hill says, "Jimmy just made Tommy dig the hole right there in the cellar [of Robert's], and all the while Tommy was grousing and pissed off that he had to dig the hole. He was like a kid who had been bad and had to clean all the erasers after school." With guys like Tommy and Jimmy in your crew, corpse burial became a near-constant concern. (I could find no account of this victim's body ever being found.)

As recently as 2013 bodies killed by this crew were being discovered. In June of that year, the skeletal remains of Paul Katz were dug up in a cellar in Ozone Park, Queens. He had disappeared in 1969. The Ozone Park house was registered to Catherine Burke, the daughter of Jimmy "the Gent" Burke and the only Burke family member consulted by Robert De Niro when he was researching Jimmy "the Gent" Conway for *Goodfellas*. Katz was a trucker whom Burke believed might have been an informant. So he allegedly strangled him and buried him in a property that he had registered to his daughter. Albeit perhaps not at the time of the murder, which occurred when Catherine was a child.

The shooting of Spider was on Imperioli's second day. "Wardrobe put me in a white shirt and tie, and Scorsese changed it to another pullover shirt, like the one in the prior scene. I had squibs on my chest underneath. Things were very well-rehearsed, and I was going to do my own stunt, the fall backward after Tommy shoots me," Imperioli says.

Only one thing went wrong. "The prop person didn't give me a breakaway glass; instead, I was holding an actual drinking glass. And when I fell, my hand clenched around it and broke it, and I cut my palm open. The location was in Queens; they rushed me to the hospital there.

"The emergency room people took one look at me and put me on a stretcher." This is something that never happens. Except everyone forgot, in the rush to get Imperioli taken care of, that he has also just had three explosive squibs full of fake blood blow up and through his shirt. "They think I have three bullet holes in my chest." Once in the ER itself, the doctors tore his shirt open and saw...wires. "I said to the hospital people, 'I told you I'm in a movie, I just cut my hand.'"

They were not amused. Imperioli was sent back out into the waiting room and processed and stitched up a little while later. "We did a couple more takes with my stitched-up hand, but I think the first take is what ended up in the movie. Having not seen the entire script, and having shot only two days, I really did not have any idea how crucial that scene was. It really stood out.

"Which was great for me. A scene like that puts you on the map. 'I'm in *Goodfellas*, I'm in this scene,' and people know exactly what you're talking about. Spike Lee saw it, and he was casting *Jungle Fever,* and a lot of *Goodfellas* people got cast in that movie." Imperioli is not exaggerating: in addition to himself, Frank Vincent, Illeana Douglas, Debi Mazar, Joseph D'Onofrio, and Samuel L. Jackson worked on *Jungle Fever,* Lee's film about an African American/Italian American romantic relationship. Douglas' scenes were cut, and Jackson's relationship with Lee predates his appearance in *Goodfellas,* but the point still stands. "I now have a six-film relationship with Spike Lee," Imperioli continues—which includes coscripting Lee's superb 1999 *Summer of Sam.* Imperioli directed *The Hungry Ghosts* from his own script in 2009, and recently published an idiosyncratic novel *The Perfume Burned His Eyes,* about an outer-borough kid in the '70s who befriends Lou Reed and the musician's real-life transgender companion of the '70s, Rachel Humphreys. (Known for many years, and in the book, solely as "Rachel.") Imperioli remains best known as Spider and as Christopher in *The Sopranos.*

KAREN ON THE RAMPAGE

The two shootings of Spider are punctuated by Karen Hill's reaction to learning that Henry has a girlfriend, whose way of life Henry is heavily subsidizing, so to speak. The reaction is not good. We see a set of keys going out the bedroom window.

"Karen, will you grow up? Stop, I'm still gonna go out!" In the ensuing argument Henry throws a dresser lamp over Karen's head and storms out. As Karen screams, "Get out of my life, I can't stand you!" the movie cuts to a shot of one of the young Hill daughters, befuddled, standing outside her bedroom door. The screaming continues—and the cut is to Henry's scream of laughter at the poker game where Spider will be shot to death. He was not even going out to see what Karen calls his "ready-made whores."

Karen turns up at Janice's apartment and starts banging on her buzzer. "You keep away from my husband," she yells into the buzzer panel's screened microphone. Bracco's own daughters, Margaux and Stella, playing the two fictional Hill children, stand there looking confused, trying to attach themselves to Bracco's skirt hem.

Inside her apartment, Janice, who read in prior scenes as what one might have called "a tough cookie," is scrunched up on her sofa, terrified.

"Rossi, Janice Rossi, do you hear me?" Karen punches apartment buzzers with the flat of her palm. One, two, three, four, a series of shots of the white plastic buttons and her hand hitting them. This presages the flash-montage of the prison visitor logbook that sets Karen off in a later scene. This affair is driving her nuts.

How nuts? A shot from Henry's POV of a gun in his face, held by Karen.

"There's no live ammo on the set, ever," property master Bob Griffon says. "And it's all about making sure the actor is comfortable. If the actor has doubts, the prop master can bring in a full-time armorer." Griffon himself is practically that; "I have pretty much every firearms license imaginable," he says. For Karen's gun, he loaded it with dummy ammunition. That is, bullets specially prepared to not go off. "It's a spent shell and a slug, put together, with no primer and no gunpowder," Griffon says. "You could fire the revolver all day and get nothing." Still, the loaded shells help make Karen's gun a formidable, terrifying sight. On the anniversary edition Blu-ray/DVD of the film, Lorraine Bracco recalls in an audio commentary: "Michael [Ballhaus] had the camera lying down on the bed and if I remember correctly I straddled his knees. And the gun and everything is literally right into the camera. I remember seeing my reflection, and aaaugh, once an actor sees itself, it's a very strange thing." She, too, was intimidated by the fire-arm: "I remember asking a hundred times, 'Promise me there's nothing in there, show me that there was nothing in the gun,' because it was horrifying." A couple of close-ups, one of the trigger with Karen's finger on it, the other of the gun barrel (which, in letters raised on the metal, reads ".38 S&W. SPL." for .38 Smith & Wesson Special), heighten the dread.

The exchange between Karen and Henry loses none of its suspense value despite Karen saying in voice-over that she could never bring herself to physically harm Henry. In *Wiseguy* she tells Pileggi, "The truth was no matter how bad I felt, I was still very, very attracted to him." That line is reproduced almost verbatim in the voice-over.

Henry coos, "Karen, take it easy," but once he neutralizes her it's his turn to go nuts. He throws her off the bed, puts a hand around her throat, points the gun at her, pulls her hair, repeats, "How does it feel?" It's brutal, the yelling and the physical abuse, but this Henry, the movie version of Henry, is self-aware enough, or whatever it is, to hold back. Rather than hit Karen he punches the night table and tosses the weapon.

"One time the gun went flying and hit Michael Ballhaus in the head," a mortified Bracco says on the commentary. A cheerful response from Ballhaus is spliced in: "That happens, it's no problem at all." Bracco continues: "I remember I bought him a pith helmet."

Henry moves in with Janice. The visit there from Paulie and Jimmy is another scene expanded from something only barely mentioned in the book. In this case, a sentence: "Karen called Paulie and Jimmy, and they came by and said it was time for me to go home."

Everyone's friends here. Paulie says to Janice, "Hi, honey, how are ya." Henry sends her out: "Why don't you go get some cigarettes."

There's no hint of moral disapprobation in Paulie and Jimmy's complaint to Henry. Karen's frantic behavior is proving inconvenient for the both of them, is the thing.

"She's wild," Paulie says of Karen. "And you, you gotta take it easy. You got children. I'm not saying you gotta go back there this minute. But you gotta go back. It's the only way. You gotta keep up appearances." At this point Henry might as well be a company man. But he acts like a sullen but smart teen who knows he's going to have to take his punishment: he looks down, eyes closed, interlacing his fingers. He doesn't want to hear it and still is going to do Paulie's bidding.

Jimmy expresses himself with more self-centeredness, which does not surprise. "I can't have it," Jimmy says of Karen's visits, where she commiserates with Jimmy's rarely glimpsed wife, Mickey. "This is what it is. You know what it is."

The two are going to make it easy for him. Jimmy and another wiseguy were gonna head for Tampa, take care of something. Now Henry's going with Jimmy. Take a few days off, get some sun. And then, come home. And come home to Karen. Paulie will smooth it all over: "I know how to talk to her, especially to her."

It's the only way. "You're not gonna get a divorce," Paulie says. "You're not *animale*." Of all the things in the world that could possibly make a human being an animal, Paulie believes that divorce is close to the top. He really *is* Sicilian. (The line, as it happens, was a Sorvino improvisation.)

"She'll never divorce him," Jimmy says, with some De Niro mugging. "She'll kill him but she'll never divorce him." This observation lightens the mood.

Pileggi interviewed the real-life Janice; in *Wiseguy* she is referred to only by her first name, Linda. She speaks freely, and somewhat disparagingly, of Karen, and affectionately of the wiseguys. She describes her adjustment to her situation and in the book it is she, not Karen, who pronounces, "After a while everything began to feel almost normal." Henry says of the situation, "My life was a constant battle but I couldn't bring myself to leave either one. I couldn't leave Linda and I couldn't leave Karen. I felt like I needed them both." In *Gangsters and Goodfellas: The Mob, Witness Protection, and Life on the Run*, a 2004 "as told to" book by Hill and Gus Russo, Henry refers to Linda by her full name, Linda Rotondi, and tells of breaking off with her in 1974 right before he goes to prison. "I was supposed to turn myself in at nine a.m.; by the time I left Maxwell Plum's [sic; the Manhattan nightclub was Maxwell's Plum], it was eleven. The bondsman was going nuts; he was calling Paulie. I was out on a quarter-million-dollar bail, so he was close to losing the farm. He called my wife and asked, 'Where the fuck is he?' What happened was that on my way to West Street, which was where the Manhattan Correctional Center (MCC) was located at the time, I stopped at the Empire State Building, where Linda worked. I went to Linda's office and took her up to the observation desk. And I just told her, 'Listen, honey, I got ten years to do, sweetheart. I love you. I'll always love you.' [...] I broke up with Linda at the top of the Empire State Building just before I went to turn myself in, but we stayed great friends from then on."

Hill tried to catch up with her when he embarked on the project with Russo. "My old girlfriend Linda died on February 28, 2003. The poor thing had cancer. I didn't even know she was sick. I had started calling her again because I wanted her to say something for this book, and I kept getting the answering machine. She wasn't picking up. I thought, 'What the hell? Are you mad at me?' She wasn't calling back because she was in a big cancer hospital and didn't want me to know. She had gotten married years ago, but it only lasted three months. I was blown away when I found out about her death. It was weirder because her phone was still on and you get her voice on the machine even though she's dead."

TAMPA

"Tampa Florida,/Two Days Later," a dispassionate title card reads, and Jimmy slams the face of the Florida bookie into the front seat of the car they're in, repeating, "You gonna pay it?" The man is pretty badly bloodied, and gurgling incoherently. The car is in gear, and some signage says "Tampa City Zoo." Jimmy says to the guy, "We're gonna throw you to the lions!" and one of the most amusing shots in the movie comes as they upend the guy to toss him into the lion's enclosure headfirst: a tilt motion revealing an upside-down male lion. A female lion is also seen, seemingly free of gravity.

"They must really feed each other to the lions down there because the guy gave the money right up," Henry observes. Such, one supposes, is the perspective of the hardened criminal. For most law-abiding citizens, crying uncle while being held above a lion pit after having one's nose broken through repeated contact with an immovable object does not exactly constitute "giving the money right up."

The Florida bookie is played by Peter Onorati, whose face is so bloodied up throughout most of his short scene that you can barely read it. A couple of years after this he'd be one of the leads in a network dramatic comedy, *Civil Wars*, along with Debi Mazar, who plays Sandy in this picture.

The Tampa twist of fate is conveyed at an almost breakneck pace. "I couldn't believe what happened." Jimmy and Henry are "all over the newspapers" when they get home. In a carefully choreographed dolly shot, a sea of men in jackets, ties, and shirtsleeves parts as the camera moves in on a crying woman, the sister of the Florida bookie, an FBI typist whose concern for her brother reached fever pitch when she saw his busted nose. "She gave everybody up." A series of five black-and-white stills— "Jimmy, me, even her brother"—show the criminals cuffed; on the last shot of the Florida bookie, her sobs are mixed higher on the soundtrack and she's heard saying, "These friends of his."

When editing *Goodfellas*, Scorsese cited the fictional drama series *The Untouchables* and the television crime docudrama in general as influences. In the latter, still-photo imagery abounds. (But it also abounds in the work of Jean-Luc Godard and Chris Marker, two early and persistent influences on Scorsese.) The use of imagery not in motion, both in freeze-frames that pause the action and still photos in montage that convey a series of visual beats or hits, is crucial to this picture. Scorsese frequently interpolated simulated "home movie" footage into his pictures. *Mean Streets* opens with an 8mm introduction to its milieu, and *Raging Bull* gets its own interlude of respite in 16mm amateur-style footage (in color, contrasting with the diegesis' own black-and-white) of Jake and Vicky LaMotta's wedding celebration.

But the use of stills was relatively new to Scorsese, and from here on in it was integrated into his toolbox, a frequent vehicle for dramatic irony. In 2013's *The Wolf of Wall Street*, another fact-based crime story, it counters the glib narration of title character Jordan Belfort (Leonardo DiCaprio), as in a montage in which Belfort crassly recounts his interoffice sexual conquests. "One of our brokers, Ben Jenner, christened the elevator by getting a blow job from a sales assistant." This is shown in motion and real time so to speak. "Her name was Pam, and to her credit, she did have this wild technique with this…wild twist and jerk motion. About a month later, Donnie and I decided to double team her on a Saturday afternoon while our wives were out shopping for Christmas dresses." This, too, is in a quick cutting full motion montage, DiCaprio and costar Jonah Hill grinning like school-boys and Carla Corvo's Pam looking what they call "game." Then come the stills, three in all, boxed inside the movie's wide-screen frame. "Eventually Ben married her, which was amazing considering she blew every single guy in the office." This observation is a kind of record-scratch given the posed, "nicely" lit wedding pictures presented, with the couple (Ben is played by Dustin Kerns) smiling in a dignified fashion appropriate to the holy sacrament of marriage and all that. Pam's bridal gown is sleeved, with a high scoop top. Ben's tuxedo is similarly traditional. Jordan continues with an audible shrug: "Then he got depressed and killed himself three years later." And here is the third still, in color but highly desaturated—like the massacre scene at the end of *Taxi Driver*—of a bathtub, seemingly filled with blood, with a man inside. You only see his arm from his elbow down, and the very top of his chest. The side of the bath-tub is splattered in blood, the man's wrist and hand are similarly splattered, and on the floor, bright red around the edges, is a large splotch of blood. Details such as these flew very high over the heads of critics who were determined to condemn Scorsese for somehow endorsing Belfort's idea of the bacchanal.

Discussing *Goodfellas* in Ian Christie and David Thompson's *Scorsese on Scorsese*, the director expounds: "The real trick, of course, was the voice-over. I showed Nick the opening of *Jules et Jim* to explain what I was aiming for. So he understood when I started pulling lines out from here and there and mixing voice-over and using stills—really all the basic tricks of the New Wave from around 1961. What I loved about these Truffaut and Go-dard techniques from the early '60s was that the narrative was not that important. You could stop the picture and say: 'Listen, this is what we're going to do right now—oh, by the way, that guy got killed—and we'll see you later.' Ernie Kovacs did the same kind of thing on TV in the early '50s. He would stop and talk to the camera, doing crazy, surreal things. I learned a lot from watching him destroy what you were used to thinking was the form of the television comedy show." (Arguably, the animated shorts directors Tex Avery and Frank Tashlin, the latter of whom would become a live-action filmmaker, and who corresponded with Jean-Luc Godard when Godard wrote for *Cahiers du Cinéma*, broke ground with similar anarchic disruptions of form.) This mode is present in Scorsese's latest picture, *The Irishman*, which will pause in the middle of a random scene to freeze a character and insert a title card describing his usually grisly cause of death.

In the Tampa sequence the stills are there for speed: Henry has been riding high and now he has to go to jail before he even knows it. Here, too, is an example of the narrative compression Scorsese and Pileggi brought to bear on the story. "It always struck Henry as grossly unfair that after a lifetime of major crimes and petty punishments his longest stretch—a ten-year sentence in a federal penitentiary—came about because he got into a barroom brawl with a man whose sister was a typist for the FBI," Pileggi recounts. As he sets it down, and as Hill himself elaborated in his subsequent book *Gangsters and Goodfellas*, a shakedown wasn't even the purpose of the Tampa "vacation."

"In 1972 it was decided that I was going to become a union delegate—a business agent—for Disney World in Florida. Since I was the only one in the crew who didn't have a felony conviction, I had the best chance of avoiding attention," Hill wrote in *Gangsters*. A "Cuban wiseguy pal," Casey Rosado, was to be Henry and Jimmy's docent on the trip. It was he who had a money beef with the bookie, named here and in *Wiseguy* as John Ciaccio. The meet was initially to be a peaceful one, in a bar, despite Casey's cousin handing Henry an "antique" .38 that "was bound to explode if you tried to use it" before they entered the establishment. Before Henry knew it, "I felt like I was in the middle of some hotheaded family feud." Beatings were administered and Ciaccio's sister took notice of her brother's condition and called in the authorities.

This resulted in two trials, a state one in which all the parties were acquitted, and a federal one in which all were convicted— in Henry's estimation on account of the key defense witness in the state trial dropping dead before the start of the federal. The movie's voice-over line: "The judge gave us ten years like he was giving away candy."

As recounted earlier, on the day the "How am I funny?" scene was shot, Warner Brothers chief operating officer Terry Semel was on the set, and he was incensed that Scorsese and company were, right before his eyes, burning up his budget shooting a scene that wasn't even in the script. He would punish the production by withholding money for a scene that was in the script: the trip to Tampa, and the threat of throwing the Florida bookie to the lions.

"Semel was not around the set that much, so we didn't have any more confrontations like that," recalls Barbara De Fina. De Fina is credited as executive producer on the picture, but it was she who drew up the initial budget for the picture, was on the set regularly, and handled problems such as this one as they emerged. Her relationship with Semel was less than ideal, but on this shoot she could largely shrug it off because of her cordial relationship with Semel's boss. "Terry was difficult to some extent, and that was one example, but the Warner executives never really bothered us when we were shooting," De Fina says. "And Bob Daly [Warner's chairman and CEO; Semel was president and COO] was wonderful. Bob Daly was the greatest, he was like an Irish uncle. You know, he was terrific, and then Terry was, you know, the opposite. Terry was never nice to me, and he frequently spoke to me in a way he'd never speak to a male producer. But Bob was terrific. This helped."

Rejiggering the Tampa scene so it could be shot in New York required making up some signage for the "Tampa City Zoo" (inaccurate, as it happens—at the time of the events depicted, the zoo in Tampa was called the Lowry Park Zoo) and renting a palm tree or two for that Florida feel. And even if that could have been done, the fate of the Florida bookie could have been handled another way, because in fact the wiseguys never threatened or attempted to throw the guy to the lions. They fought in the bar, then took him away in a car, and beat him up around Busch Gardens. But the throwing-to-the-lions fabrication became such a part of the Henry Hill mythos that Hill at one point in the aftermath of this movie took to auctioning autographed tickets to the Tampa Zoo.

At the sentencing, Henry looks to his immediate right to Jimmy, who's looking at nothing. Then he looks over his left shoulder to Karen, in the spectator section. She appears lost, and the attentive viewer will remember her plaints on how she would not be able to handle things if Henry went to prison, and Henry's boast that he's too well-organized to ever get caught. Prison will find Henry in a tightly knit mob unit, but also completely unmoored from his customary way of making his living.

NOW TAKE ME TO JAIL

Green liqueur is poured into three cordial glasses; daylight begins to pour into whatever bar this is. It's Henry's going-away party, and Morrie is pouring on the sentimentality: "Sweet Henry," he calls him. "Good trip, Henry." A view of Karen in tears implies that certain domestic issues have been forced, and quickly. In real life that was at least partially the case—unseen here is Henry's side trip to the Empire State Building to break it off with Linda Rotondi. But it was actually almost two years between the beating of John Ciaccio and Hill's time at Lewisburg. (During that time, Pileggi writes, Hill "hustled like he had never hustled before." He did some time he owed on a Nassau County misdemeanor, did some trucking work, "borrowed money from loan sharks he never intended to pay back," and, as his term got closer, "busted out The Suite." He ransacked his own club and sold off its contents, down to the last ashtray, according to Pileggi.)

"Now take me to jail," Henry says, tired but arrogant, to an unseen driver after swallowing a handful of pills.

The sense of an idyll is announced by the breezy Bobby Darin tune "Beyond the Sea" and the image of...a razor blade slicing a clove of garlic. The "cooking in prison" scene is another of *Goodfellas'* most celebrated set pieces. Its sense of simultaneously exuberant and low-key bonhomie expands with the counterpoint of Henry's voice-over and the spoken dialogue of the older wiseguys with whom Henry's sharing his bunk. The guy quietly running things, and slicing the garlic, is Paulie Cicero, in on a contempt of court charge.

"It was a very good system," Henry says of Paulie's thin-sliced garlic prep work. In other areas there is dissent. Charles Scorsese, the director's father, as Vinnie, is "in charge of the meat" and he expounds on the three different types he uses for the meatballs. "Ya gotta have the pork," an off-screen voice says, and Vinnie agrees: "That's the flavor." As for Vinnie's sauce, though, Henry says, "I felt he used too many onions." Cut to Paulie, who is still slicing. Without looking up, he says, "Vinnie. Don't put too many onions in the sauce." The audio pingpong continues, with Johnny Dio's aside on someone's steak order: "Medium rare, hmm, an aristocrat." (Johnny Dio, portrayed here by Frank Pellegrino, was not quite so amiable on the outside; he was long implicated in the 1950's acid attack that permanently blinded the investigative journalist Victor Reisel. Pellegrino, on the other hand, was the universally beloved co-owner of Rao's.)

"We owned the joint," Henry reflects on the wiseguys' privileges. "Even the hacks we couldn't bribe would never rat on the guys that we did," he says as the camera pans across the room, where Paulie, now through with his prep, sits at a table by himself and pours a glass of whiskey from a bottle that has a cardboard sign hanging on it that reads "Paulie." Okay, then.

The real-life situation for Hill was even cozier for a while. For some time he, Paulie Vario, Johnny Dio, and a Connecticut boss, Joe Pine, were put up in an "honor dorm." Hill told Pileggi: "The dorm was a separate three-story building outside the wall which looked more like a Holiday Inn than a prison." The movie also elides all the rehabilitation options offered to the fellas. Hill considered getting an associate degree in hotel management. "Paulie and Johnny Dio used to push me to go to school," Hill said. "They wanted me to become an ophthalmologist. I don't know why but that's what they invited me to be."

The ins and outs of Henry's time—which in real life did include him taking classes, and at one point featured a cameo from Watergate supervillain G. Gordon Liddy—are compressed into a desperate survival-of-the-fittest scenario that sets the stage for Henry's drug-dealing troubles on the outside. At the end of the dinner prep depiction, after Henry presents a new load of smuggled food, including a fresh bottle of Scotch for Paulie, and they all eat, he goes over to his bunk and quietly removes a stash of drugs from his gym bag.

Drug dealing in the joint with the cooperation of guards and officials is shown as a down-low enterprise, something that needs to be kept from his old-school cellmates. After some deals are done, there's a horizontal sweep of a row in the prison's visiting room—seven seconds in hell, or something like it. A guy with a shaved head presumably receiving fellatio, another guy delivering what appears to be a pained apology, a woman changing a diaper, noise, chatter, noise. Upstairs, as Karen and the Hill daughters are waved ahead of the crowded line to come in, it's not much more pleasant.

While Henry is not a creature of jealousy, Karen is, as we've seen. Scorsese treats hers with the same acuity as he did Jake LaMotta's, creating visual correlatives to the agonized pangs of obsession. Here it's Karen's discovery of Janice's name in the prison's visitor log. Twelve shots in eleven seconds. The first is a single overhead shot of the open log, turning on its revolving stand to face the visitor who is signing in. The camera, positioned above Karen and looking down so you can see the visitor's room behind her, shows her holding a pen. There's a quick close-up of the ledger, listing visitors between the times 7:04 and 7:20. Three extreme close-ups of lists of names. The first, from Steven Shea to John Ford (very funny, although not the inside joke you'd immediately take it for; John Ford is also the name of one of the film's assistant property masters). The second, from William Stratford to Georgia Riddle and including an all-caps Casey Ford. Three, from FT Long (also very funny, and this time actually a joke) to Henry Hill. There we go. In the next shot visitors and visitees are included. Mrs. Handel saw Mr. Handel, Mrs. Young saw Mr. Young, the Sabats sat together, as did the Fortunados.

Property master Bob Griffon glommed very quickly on Scorsese's tendencies. Faced with a scene featuring a document, he is likely to shoot that document in great detail, so it had better be ready to shoot. He explains: "Crew names are always technically cleared. You could use them, right? But the other thing was we wanted lots of different handwritings, you know, because that ledger book was just pages and pages. So it was literally us going around constantly to anybody who passed through the show and getting them to sign a name and a time as in and out in order to make the book look right. Because Marty, the thing about Marty is, you have to be prepared that almost anything can get inserted. He loves inserts and he will do them to death, so you have to be ready for all that."

In the middle of the list is Henry's name, and who saw him? It's Janice Rossi. Then a close-up, boxed in shadows, of Henry's name. There's a close-up of Karen's eyes; like the ledger pages, they are marked by shadows of a gate that throw multiple X's on them.

Scorsese and Schoonmaker cut back to the shadowed close-up of Henry's name and the camera tilts to the left to highlight Janice's name the same way. There's a close-up of Karen at eye level and Bracco looks almost directly into the camera lens. And downstairs, in medium close-up, holding one of his daughters and looking a little worn out, Liotta's Henry asks, "What are you talking about?"

Talking about his films in general and *Raging Bull* in particular, Scorsese has remarked that he wants the viewer to see as he sees. Here he's putting his camera eye in the service of Karen Hill, in a context of anger and possessiveness that's usually the domain of his male characters.

Their argument shifts to the issue of Karen's survival. "Nobody's helping me. I'm all alone." Paulie is now out—and indifferent to Karen's plight. And so Henry's independence is further established. And Karen has to become his accomplice. "All I need is for you to keep bringing me the stuff." And here we first hear of "the guy from Pittsburgh," who will become the guys from Pittsburgh, "such creeps" as a future accomplice will put it.

Karen already knows Paulie won't be pleased. Henry insists that she forget Paulie:

"Don't worry about him. He is not helping us out. Is he putting any food on the table?" In less than seven minutes we've gone from *Big Night* to *Desperate Living*.

"We gotta help each other—we just gotta, listen, we gotta be really, really careful while we do it," Henry concludes. And there's a long pause.

Karen has found her hook. She doesn't even necessarily fully understand the risk that Henry is taking. But she knows that his need here is real. She takes a deep breath before saying, "I don't wanna hear a word about her anymore, Henry."

"NEVER," he responds instantaneously. One is reminded, perhaps, of the question Alec Baldwin asks of the hapless salesmen in 1992's *Glengarry Glen Ross*: "HAVE YOU MADE YOUR DECISION FOR CHRIST?" Here, Henry has.

FOUR YEARS LATER

The extreme marriage therapy undergone by the Hills seems to have done some good. As Henry comes out of the steel door, barbed wire above his head, he strides forward with a smile as the camera, on a crane, swoops down and in to meet him. He's got a cocky half smile as he looks to his left. The camera pans, almost a whip, to an equally nonchalant Karen leaning against the car.

Henry is ready for a new life. In a POV shot, the current residence is viewed and assessed and found wanting. "Karen, get packed, we're moving out of here." She asks with what. Well, among other things, the guys in Pittsburgh owe him fifteen grand.

The revitalized marriage will find its sense of twisted teamwork; right now Henry is all "don't worry about it." The subsequent visit to "Uncle Paulie's" will do nothing to deflate him.

An overhead shot of a plate of meat and sauce says the feast is back on. But Paulie would like a word. Taking Henry out to the backyard they walk placidly past the patio furniture. There's a shrine to the blessed Virgin in the left side of the frame. Paulie is very direct, even in front of Mary: "I don't want any more of that shit." Henry feigns ignorance, and Paulie says: "Just stay away from the garbage, you know what I mean."

The authority in his voice suggests that he's taking a strong moral stand. He continues: "I'm not talking about what you did inside. You did what you had to do. I'm talking about now. From now. Here and now."

Henry can now lie to Paulie without even thinking, knowing that Paulie probably knows he's lying. "Paulie, why would I wanna get into that?" Henry knows that's a weak one, and so does Paulie: "Don't make a jerk out of me. Just don't do it." And soon we get to the gist of Paulie's objection. There's not even a pretext of "moral" consideration, it's all self-interest: "I ain't gonna get fucked like Gribbs. You understand. Gribbs is seventy years old. The fucking guy's gonna die in prison. I don't need that. So I'm warning everybody. Everybody. Could be my son, could be anybody. Gribbs got twenty years just for saying hello to some fuck who was sneaking behind his back, selling junk. I don't need that. Ain't gonna happen to me, understand?"

Goodfellas is frequently cited as a scruffy grandson to, and maybe outright deconstruction of, Francis Ford Coppola's 1972 *The Godfather*. Because of that film's 1940s time frame, the autumnal warmth of many of its settings, and so on, many have misperceived it as a portrait of a "noble" crime family. But the early central figure of the film, Don Corleone, while not inclined to gloat about the malfeasance he rules over, is a clear-eyed pragmatist rather than a moralist when it comes to defining limits.

It's not upstanding of him to deny the undertaker Bonasera's request for murder in the movie's opening scene. He's just using logic and enacting a variant on Old Testament vengeance.

Bonasera's daughter still lives, so her assaulters will still live. But an eye will be taken for an eye.

When "the Turk," Sollazzo, approaches Corleone with a sweet deal in exchange for financing a narcotics operation, Don Vito drolly asks, after finding out his projected cut, "Why do I deserve this generosity?" Well, he will earn it by going to the cops and politicians he has in his power and asking them to clear the way for Sollazzo. And there's the rub. Marlon Brando's words are perfectly clear as his Corleone lays it out to Sollazzo: "I must say no to you. And I'll give you my reason. It's true, I have a lot of friends in politics. But they wouldn't be friendly very long if they knew my business was drugs instead of gambling, which they regard as a harmless vice, but drugs is a dirty business. It doesn't make any difference to me what a man does for a living, you understand. But your business is a little dangerous."

There's no moral consideration here. Corleone will eventually capitulate. But only after his son Michael, for whom he had a legitimate career planned, kills Sollazzo in retaliation for an attempt on the don's life. Michael goes into exile; Corleone's second son Sonny is assassinated. Corleone's still recovering from being shot when, back against the wall, he attends a meeting of the "five families."

Corleone is eloquent on this occasion, too: "I believe this drug business is going to destroy us in the years to come. I mean, it's not like gambling or liquor or even women. Which is something most people want nowadays and is forbidden to them by the pezzonovante of the church. Even the police departments that have helped us in the past with gambling and other things are gonna refuse to help us when it comes to narcotics. And I believe that. Then. And I believe that now." (*Pezzonovante*, a dialect compound word with a literal meaning along the lines of "ninety-cent piece," is slang for "big shots.")

You can still feel a seething resentment in the room over Corleone's withholding. Playing mediator, Richard Conte's Barzini glibly assures the don he'll be remunerated for his minimal participation. "After all, we are not communists."

The Detroit don, Joseph Zaluchi, played by Louis Guss, is the one to make *something* like a point of morality: "I don't want it near schools, and I don't want it sold to children. That's an *infamia*." His touching concern is undercut severely in his next declaration: "In my city we'd keep it to the dark people, the coloreds. They're animals, anyway, so let them lose their souls."

The cultural critic Greil Marcus cites this scene, with a couple of inaccuracies (forgiven, since he was writing without benefit of home video, and because he can often be some kind of genius even when he's wrong) in his 1975 book *Mystery Train*, discussing the revenge modes in low-budget movies known as "blaxploitation," which thrived at the time of his writing. He considers "the reality behind one very carefully thrown-away line from *The Godfather* (a movie, it is worth remembering, that attracted millions of black Americans, even though it had no black characters, let alone any black heroes). 'They're animals, anyway,' says an off-camera voice, as the dons make the crucial decision to dump all their heroin into the ghettos. 'Let them lose their souls.'"

In *Goodfellas* we'll hear Paulie say that divorce is not possible because "we're not *animale*." Marcus continues: "The Mafia may have missed the contradiction in that line, but Francis Coppola certainly did not; neither did the black men and women in the theaters. They suffered it; in *Lady Sings the Blues*, Diana Ross was stalking screens all over the country showing just what it meant." *Lady Sings the Blues* was a film biography of Billie Holiday in which Ross depicted the ravages of heroin addiction. Zaluchi understands he will consign whole communities to that hell, because selling it near his people's schools is "*infamia*."

"That audience had a right to revenge," Marcus concludes,

summoning up the black avenger of song, Stagger Lee, and dozens of '70s blaxploitation movies such as *Trouble Man*.

In contrast to the crass moral feints and dodges of the "noble" 1940s gangsters, Paulie's objections play more like blatantly enlightened self-interest. Corleone's prediction that "this drug business is going to destroy us in the years to come" is arguably vindicated in *Goodfellas*, even if Paulie's downfall is not ultimately predicated on an association with Henry as *a drug dealer*.

But Henry shrugs it all off. Now using Janice's friend Sandy as an accomplice for cocaine-cutting ("All I had to do was every once in a while tell Sandy that I loved her"), he discovers "a really good business." Sandy apparently snorts more than she mixes, and given the amount of cocaine they're seen chopping up with a playing card, that's a lot of cocaine. (The "equipment" they're using, which also includes a lot of kitchen utensils, speaks of an operation that's something less than pro-am.) The real-life Sandy was Robin Cooperman, who had no relation to Janice/Linda; rather, she worked at an air-freight company. In *Wiseguy* Henry complains to Pileggi that on his visits to Robin she would always want to "have a talk about their relationship," which sounds much less interesting than the frisky mode they're seen in at first in the movie.

As they snort and canoodle, the Rolling Stones' "Gimme Shelter" plays, ragged and raw. Scorsese, a committed Stones person (he has used tracks by individual Beatles on his soundtracks, but never a song by the full group), finds room for the Stones in almost every period-appropriate picture he can, and pulled out "Shelter" several times after this. In 1995's *Casino* a live version of the song is used, while 2006's *The Departed* practically makes a leitmotif of the tune.

The fact that his supplier is in Pittsburgh makes it easy for Henry to sneak around Paulie, and soon Jimmy and Tommy, whom Paulie had also warned Henry away from—Tommy is "crazy, he's a cowboy, he's got too much to prove"—are in on the action, strategizing from Jimmy's appointment at the Department of Probation, very cheeky.

One amusing real-life detail in *Wiseguy* that didn't make it into the movie was a member of Henry's 1978 drug crew named "Bobby Germaine, a stick-up man who was on the lam and was pretending to be a freelance writer." *Wiseguy* also goes into substantial detail about Hill's other criminal enterprises at the time, including jewelry fencing. And the big one, one entirely unrelated to drugs: a scheme to rig college sports betting by getting the Boston College basketball team to shave points off their games. The team was not obliged to lose, which as Pileggi notes made the corrupt players feel like they were saving their honor; they only had to not go over the point spread. (For those readers out there who are not inveterate gamblers, understand that sports gamblers don't just bet on wins and losses but on point differentials and God knows how many other things depending on what innovations the bookmakers come up with.)

The main reason Hill was not a physical participant in the Lufthansa heist was because he was in Boston, lining things up for a game and its incoming bets. "Some people might not know it," Hill told Pileggi, "but betting lots of money on college basketball is a very difficult thing to do." When prosecutor Ed McDonald took charge of Henry in 1980, the Boston College alum was so affronted by these crimes that he insisted on trying the case himself. As it happens, the first publishing event in Henry Hill's life was not Pileggi's *Wiseguy* but a February 16, 1981, article in *Sports Illustrated* titled "How I Put the Fix In."

Morrie stands, hands on hips, as his wife, Belle (Margo Winkler, wife of producer Irwin; she is in several Scorsese films, perhaps most memorably as a receptionist who variously calls

Rupert Pupkin "Mr. Pumpkin," "Mr. Pipkin," etc., in *The King of Comedy*) almost reels in awe of the black-and-gold patterned wallpaper in the Hills' new house. The Stones are replaced by smooth tenor Jack Jones and "Wives and Lovers," whose opening lyric is "Hey/little girl/comb your hair/and fix your makeup."

"Four and a half months of DIRT!" Karen exclaims as the camera pans to the white sofa with faux leopard skin draped over the back, the two framed arrangements of fanned Asian cards, a real fan hung above that. Karen's hand comes into the frame holding a very clunky remote control to reveal the interior design's pièce de résistance. What once might have been a chintzy fireplace alcove is now a mosaiced wall of fragmented gray rectangles, in which rest colored triangles (for the most part). The remote makes the wall separate at the center to reveal shelves for liquor and pictures and what then was a full audio/video system, including a reel-to-reel tape deck.

This is all pretty chortlesome. The movie is having a laugh at the Hills' taste and inviting us to, as well. But one also recalls Vladimir Nabokov's pronouncement that "nothing is more exhilarating than philistine vulgarity." In any event, production designer Kristi Zea considered putting in the wall and the A/V system "one of the most satisfying things I did on the movie. That whole wall, I don't know what made me do it, but I said while putting it together, 'It's like *The Flintstones*, there's a beyond-retro garish thing about it. We got many items from an absolutely incredible furniture store on Grand Street called Roma Furniture with extraordinary lacquered, high-gloss stuff. I wanted that kind of texture because this is the beginning of the descent into hell for these characters." In searching for accurate looks, for this film and elsewhere, Zea found that the usual suspects of vintage shelter magazines wouldn't necessarily do. "Those were too high-end." Even if the Hills had the money, it wasn't their taste. "In the standard magazines of the period, there's not as much documentation of what kind of furniture Long Island mobsters would have. So you have to dig deep into photo-journalism, certain kinds of art photography. Amy Arbus on suburbia, say. Portraits of people in living rooms."

Morrie, being a guy's guy, isn't so excited by the new house. He's hatched up a new scheme and wants to make sure Henry has conveyed the information to Jimmy. "Do you understand? There's millions in there. And I've been bleeding for this caper," Morrie says. He will bleed more.

THE LUFTHANSA HEIST

It takes a certain amount of professional brass to introduce the crew that's about to pull off "what turned out to be the biggest heist in American history: the Lufthansa heist" and then not show the heist.

In what will be the movie's penultimate tracking-to-the-right-from-behind-a-bar shot, Jimmy, his hair now streaked with silver, sits with Henry looking at an above-the-bar TV showing a basketball game, about which stray comments are heard: "if they fuck this up," of course that's Tommy, and later "it's a lock." Moving down the bar, there's mastermind Morrie. Tommy and Carbone are the guys who will "grab the outside guard and make him get us in the front door." Cut to the pool table: Frenchy and Joe Buddha "had to round up the workers." There's a new face, "Johnny Roastbeef."

"He had to keep them all tied up and away from the alarms." And another new face, an African American one, and today, because he's played by Samuel L. Jackson, a very familiar one. "Even Stacks Edwards got in on it," Henry says. "He used to hang around the lounge and play guitar. Everybody loved Stacks.

What he was supposed to do was steal the panel truck and afterward compact it by a friend of ours out in Jersey."

"Only Morrie was driving us nuts," Hill says as Chuck Low's rug man sidles up to De Niro's Jimmy. Just as in the scene in the Hills' new house in which he needles Henry about whether Jimmy's going to do it and when he's going to do it and how this will be the culmination of everything Morrie has ever worked for, now that he can get Jimmy's ear he's bringing the droning directly to him. "He didn't mean anything by it, it's just, it's just the way he was," Henry says.

After a check-in with the cocaine crew—Henry and Karen prepping babysitter/drug mule Lois, Henry doing a little snorting, mixing, weighing, and scolding with/of Sandy ("Take it easy […] it's like a pigpen…look at all this powder"), and succumbing to her sexual solicitation—we join Henry in the shower, as the famed New York news radio station WINS ("You give us twenty-two minutes, we'll give you the world" was once its slogan) reports that "nobody knows for sure just how much was taken in the daring predawn raid at the Lufthansa Cargo Terminal at Kennedy Airport. The FBI says two million dollars. Port Authority says four million dollars…" Henry goes nuts, banging the shower tiles with his palms, screaming and laughing. Several shots in this montage have become internet memes connoting high exhilaration levels. (So, too, of course, have the shots of Henry's uproarious laughter in the "How am I funny?" scene.)

One book about the Lufthansa heist was published in 1980, five years before Pileggi's *Wiseguy*. *The Ten Million Dollar Getaway: The Inside Story of the Lufthansa Heist*, by Doug Feiden, a crime reporter for the *Wall Street Journal*. It is a solid narrative, dense and packed with dates and facts and transcriptions of interrogations and prose that often feels like the narration of a television true-crime documentary. To wit: "While a coup like Lufthansa attracts the most attention, gets the biggest headlines, contains the greatest drama, produces the most bodies, provides the quickest gratification for greedy mob schemers, and profoundly rattles the very foundations of the Mafia itself, there are other airport scams than cargo theft, and some of them present a larger threat, with consequences far more significant for law-abiding citizens." It is rather intriguing, and perhaps a thorn in Feiden's side, that his book originated the line "Now take me to jail," uttered here by Jimmy Burke, not Henry Hill. Henry Hill was still a free man when Feiden wrote the account, and doesn't figure in it.

The Heist: How a Gang Stole $8,000,000 at Kennedy Airport and Lived to Regret It, by Ernest Volkman and John Cummings, was published a year after *Wiseguy,* in 1986. Hill is here, as is Ed McDonald, the prosecutor. The book, which is not bad at all, draws heavily on what Hill spilled to McDonald, and paints some very different portraits from the ones that would appear in *Wiseguy* and be distilled into *Goodfellas.* "Not noted for mental organization, Hill rambled all over the place, flitting from one topic to another. But there were plenty of nuggets of gold among the worthless pebbles: stories about the fallout among members of the Robert's Lounge gang; beatings of several men who had run afoul of the Mafia; the killing of Tommy DeSimone; the intricate pattern of betrayal among those involved in the Lufthansa heist; and for good measure, an incredible (and, given the accounts of others, probably completely untrue) story about Theresa Ferrara. Paul Vario, Sr., had been smitten by her beauty, Hill claimed, and the aging don's infatuation led him to use her as a courier to move $3 million of the Lufthansa proceeds to Florida. Later, after discovering she was an FBI informant, Vario had her gruesomely murdered, destroying her body so that he would never again have to think of the physical beauty that had so nearly unhinged him." It is difficult, in any event, to imagine the taciturn man-mountain Paulie Cicero of this film in thrall to sexual obsession.

After *Goodfellas*, both books were adapted into made-for-television movies. The film of *The Ten Million Dollar Getaway*, made for the USA Network in 1991, opens with a crooned "Wrap Your Troubles in Dreams" accompanying shots of outer-borough locations. Here, the distinguished British-born actor John Mahoney, of *Frasier* fame, plays Jimmy Burke. He seems to be grappling with the anxiety of influence here, his New York accent marked by distinctly De Niro–like inflections. His dark pompadoured hair (probably a wig) is jarring.

Burke is the narrator here, and his voice-over, scripted by Christopher Canaan, is just...well. The Lufthansa heist was "bigger than the Great Train Robbery. Bigger than Brinks. To put that much money in your pocket normally you'd have to be a senator." Burke introduces his crew right away. "Stacks Edwards. Sang the blues like nobody's business and always had a story to tell." Tommy DeSimone? "A good family man and a great shot." As we've seen.

In a bit of a jaw-dropper, Mike Starr, who plays the robbery-happy "midnight-to-eight man" Frenchy in *Goodfellas*, appears here as...Frenchy. Nevertheless, the whole thing plays like an SCTV parody.

Volkman and Cummings' book didn't get made into a TV movie for the Ovation Network until 2001. *The Big Heist* opens with yes, voice-over, only the Michael Zager Band disco hit "Let's All Chant" is playing under it as a bunch of very broad character actors enacts a truck hijacking. "That's Louis the Whale, belly-up to the steering wheel there. He used to be a stick-up artist but he had to give it up. Everybody knew it was him!" Stacks is with us one more time: "Stacks Edwards. He thinks the girls love him for his singing. But in the morning they always ask him for money. He thinks it's a loan." Oh dear. The narrator continues: "Believe it or not these are the guys who would pull off," etc., etc. Further setting the scene, he notes, "Disco was big and the streets of New York were dangerous."

The familiar (at least for some American film buffs) voice belongs to John Heard, who plays a detective named Wood who's a composite largely drawn from prosecutor Edward McDonald (at the end of this movie, Henry lets slip to Wood about the Boston College point-shaving scheme, which the real-life Henry did to McDonald). Donald Sutherland plays Jimmy Burke, with a magnanimous bearing and a ridiculous leonine hairpiece, slipping in and out of an Irish accent. (While of Irish extraction, Burke was born and raised in New York.) While Mahoney allows himself to be pinned by De Niro, Sutherland aims a flamethrower at the idea that a movie called *Goodfellas* ever existed in the first place. The performance is no less impressive for being utterly ghastly.

The movie itself also portrays Burke in a completely different light than the Scorsese picture: here, because of concerns about "earning" and the criminal incompetence of his son Frank, Burke is backed into masterminding and directing the heist, and then further pressured to kill his accomplices. Poor guy.

The heist itself is scored to the Ami Stewart disco version of the R&B classic "Knock on Wood" and the dialogue is replete with gems like "I never met a dead guy yet who made a good witness" and "You bring that rat bastard to me." Instead of "Layla" accompanying the discoveries of criminal corpses, John Paul Young's "Love Is in the Air" plays as the tortured Jimmy is forced to preside over the murders of his beloved crew. Henry Hill, played by Nick Sandow (later of the series *Orange Is the New Black*; I once took Mr. Sandow's son to the movies, it's a longish story), is portrayed as a cocaine-addled mook who at one point is discovered in bed with a man. Because, presumably, that's what being a cocaine-addled mook will do to a guy. This detail does not appear in Volkman and Cumming's book, or any other book I know of, in case you were at all concerned.

My wife, catching a few minutes of *The Big Heist* while I was looking at it for this chapter, spoke for many who for whatever reason have sat through the movie, I think, when she said, "I'm starting to feel embarrassed."

A PINK CADILLAC CHRISTMAS

The bar is decorated in tinsel and Christmas lights and Jimmy the Gent welcomes Henry and Karen with open arms as the Phil Spector "Frosty the Snowman" plays on the jukebox. Tommy looks on proudly in the background. "Look at this genius," Jimmy says, kissing Henry. Jimmy's exuberance is tamped down when the next couple walks in. Johnny Roastbeef and his tall blonde wife exchange kisses and then Johnny commits a fatal mistake. He brings Jimmy to the door and shows him a pink Cadillac coupe, the sticker still in the passenger side window, and says, "Ain't she gorgeous? I bought it for my wife. It's a coupe. I love that car." Jimmy pulls Johnny inside, and begins to re-instruct him as to the importance of not throwing around the heist money, which will attract the attention of cops.

It's easy to miss just how quickly these guys will lie their asses off to each other: Johnny almost immediately changes his story to mollify Jimmy: "It's a wedding gift, Jimmy. It's from my mother. It's under her name. I just got married." Johnny gestures to his wife. In a flat "how dare you" tone that suggests she really hasn't heard much about Jimmy, Mrs. Roastbeef (Fran McGee) protests, "I love that car."

Jimmy's simmering, then boiling, annoyance at this infraction, puts Johnny at a severe disadvantage. Johnny Williams,

Roastbeef's portrayer, was a deli owner who was part of the regular crew at Rao's, the ultraexclusive East Harlem Italian restaurant where Scorsese and Pileggi commanded a table. "I had no résumé to speak of and didn't even consider myself an actor," Williams recalls on his website. Scorsese was eventually so taken with Williams that he changed the character's name; in the script this wiseguy was supposed to be Angelo Sepe, the real name of a real-life heist participant; sometime before shooting, he was rechristened with Williams' deli-world nickname, Johnny Roastbeef.

In the GQ oral history of the film, Williams discussed having to play to, and off of, De Niro. "Here's a guy who's done 200 films, and here I am. I owned a deli up in Harlem. I don't act. I can't act for shit. But he needed a fuse, he needed a light, and he says, 'Johnny, somewhere—I don't care where it is—just tell me not to get excited.' If you watch that scene, when I said, 'What're you getting excited for, Jimmy?' that was liftoff. I gave him what he wanted. This is Robert De Niro. The line wasn't in the script." De Niro said in the same article, "I would hope that anything that I was doing was helping him. And he was helping me. He was very good [...]just reacting. I was the more kind of dominant, aggressive person in the scene because I was chewing him out. So all he had to do was just react, and the best thing is to do nothing and just sort of take it. And that's how those things happen in life, you know, usually."

"Of course we relished holding on [his face] because he was just falling apart as he was being abused," editor Thelma Schoonmaker added to that account. "It was wonderful. This guy was real: he was exactly what Marty needed for the part. Johnny Roastbeef, oh my God."

Illeana Douglas was particularly interested in observing De Niro, and in making a good impression on him. Speaking to GQ, she conveys the awesome impact he makes on his fellow performers who watch him in action: "You see his face, it's like, 'Whoa, I thought I was going to do a *scene*, but I didn't know...' And I think Bob likes to utilize something that is really happening in you. He kind of waits like an animal and sees what you're going to do, and then it triggers something in him that is so ferocious that you're just hanging on for dear life."

Williams concluded: "He's relentless. You ever pull a thread on a sweater and found that it's taken off the whole fucking sleeve? That's what he did. He felt that these guys spending this money was pulling apart the whole affair. In his head, he was figuring out how he was going to get most of the money. Then you start seeing the bodies come up. That's how nuts he was." Williams segues from talking about De Niro to discussing Jimmy himself. Jimmy hammers into Roastbeef until the whole room is stunned into silence. Even Tommy is impressed. Jimmy barely bothers to lay into Frankie Carbone; he just strips his wife's fur coat off and sends them into the cold.

De Niro, in his script notes, took care to underscore Jimmy's defensive and paranoid view of the crew members—he will next go up against Morrie, who is insisting, "I need the money."

Low's performing ebullience got the better of him at times, according to Joseph Reidy. "In the scene with Chuck Low as Morrie, hassling Jimmy and Henry, saying, 'I want my money, I want my money,' Chuck overdid it with a gesture and he hit Ray. Chuck wasn't a trained actor, and that's the kind of thing that happens in such a situation, he was not controlling himself and he went too far. And he hit Ray and cut him, and Ray had to go to the hospital, and we had to wait for Ray to come back from the hospital. I think Ray was okay, but a bit pissed off that that had happened, and it was kind of a tense set from then on, for that scene. It should be different now, maybe; in this day and age, it shouldn't happen. And I have a feeling that subsequently a lot of the actors sort of treated Chuck like they treated his character."

Jimmy retreats into a back room, with Henry following. Once Jimmy's away from Morrie, he's beaming, with a wad of cash in hand. He's giving Henry "just a little taste" of his "share," wetting the beak so to speak. In his notes to the script, De Niro wrote, "I'm really happy to give it to him!" As delighted as he is, he gives Henry a friendlier version of the "don't spend it" lecture. There's then a pointed cut to Henry bursting into his home saying, "Karen! Judy! Ruth! C'mere! I bought the most expensive tree they had!"

This scene was Illeana Douglas' first day on the picture. She's at this celebration as Tommy's date, and in the movie's final tracking shot down a bar, which starts in tight on the two glasses in which Stacks is doing some liquor magic—"This drink here is better than sex, babe," he says as he pours two shots into two almost-already-full cordial glasses—she's instructed by Tommy, who's going to join Stacks, to "look straight ahead or I'll fucking kill you." But he walks away smiling, so who knows.

Here's Douglas' account of her first takes, recounted in her memoir (in an email exchange about the quote, Douglas made a few changes to it—"always the writer," she said—and I've kept those): "I had a front-row seat watching Robert De Niro. Enough time to get pretty nervous because my first line in *Goodfellas* was coming up. We had been shooting in the bar a few days, and there was going to be this very long, complicated tracking shot, and I had a line during it to Julie Garfield, referring to my relationship with Joe Pesci, which was, 'If I even look at anyone else, he'll kill me.' The camera then holds for our reaction, and then moves on to De Niro and Joe Pesci, and the scene continues. It was like an eight-minute shot. We rehearsed it all day. And this is on film, remember. Finally Marty said they were ready to shoot. And even though I had told myself, Don't screw this shot up. Don't do anything phony. Don't do anything that makes Robert De Niro go over to Marty and say, 'How did that bad actor get in my movie?' The first thing I did was try to get a laugh. I thought, Let me goose my one line in the scene like a bad actor. So the camera starts on Sam Jackson, it's tracking along, there are twenty people in the frame, all these actions. Out of the corner of my eye I see the camera getting to me, and all of a sudden I become Eve Arden. 'If he catches me with *anyone* he'll *kill* me!' then I downed a glass of wine to button it. It was dreadful, of course, awful and hammy. I knew it immediately, and so did Marty. He yelled out, 'Cut. Cut. Technical difficulties.' Everyone started groaning. Marty came over to me and whispered into my ear so that no one could hear it but me: 'Don't do that again.' Then he laughed, 'Sorry, everyone, sorry,' running back to the camera. 'Our fault. Our fault. Technical problems.' Twenty-thousand-dollar mistake, Marty later told me. He never let anyone know but me, but he cared enough that he wanted every actor in the frame to be perfect."

The exchange with Julie Garfield is all the more mordantly funny because of Garfield's response: Douglas' Rosie says, "He's so jealous. I mean, if I even look at anyone else, he'll kill me," and Garfield, as Mickey Conway, Jimmy's wife (who is never introduced as such in the film), says, "Great!" The camera doesn't move to Pesci—who's talking to Stacks—but tracks De Niro and Liotta, walking behind them, and then finding some space at the bar, where they are accosted by Morrie, who ends his demands by repeating, "Poison my eyes," such is his frustration. The origins of this evocative phrase are unclear.

After bringing in that most expensive tree, Henry gives Karen a jewelry box wrapped in gold paper, and a passionate kiss. (One recalls her holding a gun on Henry while admitting in voice-over, "I still found him very attractive.") Henry then hands her a thick wad of hundreds and adds, "Happy Hanukkah," which gets a raucous laugh from her. There's a nicely centered shot of the kids sitting at the foot of the Christmas tree. It's a faux tree, all white, with purple orbs the sole ornaments. The camera tracks in until only a few branches and a single purple ball are in the frame. In voice-over Henry reflects on the caper: "Lufthansa should have been the ultimate score. The heist of a lifetime. Six million in cash. More than enough to go around." On the soundtrack is the song "The Bells of St. Mary's," a doo-wop version by the Drifters, the B-side to their 1954 single "White Christmas." Written in 1917, the song was subsequently featured, and repopularized, in the 1945 film of the same name, directed by Leo McCarey and starring Bing Crosby and Ingrid Bergman. That movie was a nostalgic touchstone for many directors of Scorsese's generation. Not just that—Scorsese, and his contemporaries, hold director McCarey in high regard, as did the old French master Jean Renoir, who said, "Leo McCarey understood people better than any other director in Hollywood." Michael (Al Pacino) and Kay (Diane Keaton) see the movie at Radio City Music Hall in *The Godfather*. The semiotics of this music choice in this *Goodfellas* scene are practically fraught.

The plaintive vocals of the Drifters continue as Stacks Edwards is roused from his slumber by Tommy DeSimone's insistent knocking and squawking. Stacks is haggard and nonchalant as he gets the door.

CUTTING EVERY LINK

The weary Stacks receives Tommy and Frankie, and Tommy barks at Frankie to start some coffee as he follows Stacks into his bedroom.

"I thought you had one of your bitches in here." Tommy,

always with a pleasant word. Too tired to register the vitriol, Stacks says, "I thought I did, too, where is she?"

Using an automatic with a long silencer attached, Tommy shoots Stacks through the back of the neck after telling him, "You'll be late for your own funeral."

The staging here is not realistic. After the blood and brain spatters on the mattress, Jackson actually throws himself off the chair, left arm outstretched, upper part of his torso bouncing off the bed, landing on the floor. Carbone, hearing the first shot, comes into the doorway and watches Tommy shoot Stacks three more times.

In a very sour reiteration of the "take the cannoli" bit in *The Godfather*, Tommy, noticing the pot in Frankie's hand, says, "Make that coffee to go," and when Frankie makes to follow Tommy out of the apartment holding the pot, Tommy tells him, "It's a joke!" They leave the apartment. The cut is to black.

The film does something odd at this point. Scorsese made the audience watch the stabbing and shooting death of Billy Batts twice. Now he reiterates the appallingly cold-blooded murder of Stacks, but in a way that contradicts the prior account. The Drifters' tender religious-themed song fades back in on the soundtrack.

The black field moves. It's the back of Tommy's coat. (Alfred Hitchcock similarly used fields of black that were revealed as characters' clothing in his experimental 1948 feature *Rope*, in which he attempted to simulate a single long shot without any cuts; technology at the time allowed only for ten-minute takes so such trickery was necessary to create an idea, at least, of seamlessness.) Light comes in from the right side of the frame and the room swims into view. There are speckles of blood on a wall behind Tommy. It's a low-angle shot, you see the gun in his hand. In slow motion he turns to the right. His face is impassive. He raises his right arm. He fires the gun. The slow motion lets you see the fire coming out of the silencer, and the shots have a thudding percussive echo. And Tommy fires five times, not the three that Carbone observes. And he walks away.

About eight minutes prior, Henry told us that, "Everybody loved Stacks." Now, in voice-over again, he says, "Stacks was always crazy. Instead of getting rid of the truck like he was supposed to, he got stoned, went to his girlfriend's, and by the time he woke up, the cops had found the truck." Gregg Hill, Henry's son, described the real-life Stacks with affection; Hill's daughter, Gina, recollected her father being especially affected by Stack's death: "My dad spent Christmas Day at the funeral parlor."

There's a nearly overhead shot of Stacks on the floor in a near-fetal position. Blood runs down his left shoulder and over his back. The bed is washed with blood that looks to have splattered in a circular motion from the right-hand side. The shot is held for nearly ten seconds. It is a little reminiscent of Scorsese's treatment of the bloodbath following Travis Bickle's massacre of Iris's traffickers at the climax of *Taxi Driver*. That chronicle of human devastation is stomach-churning. This is, too, and it's meant to prick the conscience more. Henry offers a "Stacks had to die" narrative. The movie comments that his death was... well, this disgusting, this detached, this grotesque. There's no human dimension to it. "Everybody loved Stacks." But here's Tommy, abusive, insulting, finally murderous, and acting like a robot, like this is nothing. As the shot holds, the song seems to get louder: "The bells/of St. Mary's/I hear they are calling..."

The shooting is also a culmination of the racist loathing expressed in prior scenes by Henry and Tommy and others. And while one doesn't want to read too much into it, the fact that the film's next African American character is a doctor, played by Isiah Whitlock, Jr., assists in ushering into the movie a world apart from Henry's, a world into which he will be forced to assimilate at the end.

"I gotta talk to you" about Stacks, Henry says on meeting Jimmy in the bar.

"Don't worry about that." Jimmy and Tommy are drinking because "Everything is beautiful. There's nothing to worry about," according to Tommy. "Didn't you tell him yet?"

Jimmy to Henry: "No, I didn't tell him yet. Guess what?" Henry: "What?" Jimmy: "They're gonna make him."

Henry looks at Tommy: "Paulie's gonna make you? Tommy!"

"They opened up the books," Jimmy says. "Paulie got the okay. You believe that? This little guinea bastard?" Here we are circling around the tenderness with which Henry evoked Tuddy at the movie's beginning. Jimmy's twinkly eyes and grin bring more of the genuine exuberance De Niro was so determined to put across when he gave Henry a "taste" of his Lufthansa share. "Motherfuckers, we got 'em now," Tommy says.

We should pause here. Not once, but twice, it is stated that Paulie has given the okay for Tommy to be made. As we know, Tommy will not be made, but killed. Ergo, it is Paulie who pulls the switch on Tommy's execution. Tommy, who he's known, like Henry, since he was a kid. Tommy, who he stood up for, without even saying a word, in front of the Bamboo Lounge owner Sonny. Tommy, the guy Paulie came to see as a "crazy cowboy" with "something to prove," sure. And now he's going to have Tommy killed. "I just can't have it," Paulie complained to Henry about Karen's bitching and moaning about Henry's abandonment of her and the kids. That idea has finally come to apply to Tommy. And so he's going to die.

Then Morrie barges in on the three ebullient wiseguys to kill their buzz. "Fuck him, I want my money!" he practically screeches to Henry. The "him" is Jimmy. "Good, go tell him," Henry says. This shuts Morrie up. Morrie knows that Jimmy will not have Morrie in his face. So he yells at Henry, who will listen. Up to a point. Morrie's impotence is epic. In the face of it he can only become the affable high-vocabulary schmuck he ever was, singing "Danny Boy," changing it to "Oh Henry boy." (Behind him, at a table outside the back room, one can see Vincent Gallo, then one of the other lot of young New York actors who scrambled for just about any role in this movie.)

Cut to De Niro smoking. He hears the singing. He looks vaguely disgusted with Morrie's schtick. Cut to Morrie entering the front room. Striding to the bar. He steps out of frame. Cut back to the bar. The Cream song "Sunshine of Your Love" comes on the soundtrack, loud. Is it the jukebox or is it the score, so to speak? Scorsese, in *Mean Streets*, brought the Rolling Stones' "Jumping Jack Flash" out of the jukebox at Tony's bar when De Niro's Johnny Boy entered the joint in slow motion, then he put it back in/on the jukebox, letting it settle into the ambient noise when Johnny Boy and Harvey Keitel's Charlie began to talk. Here, the distinction doesn't matter: it's the insistence of the drums, of the tensile guitar riff. The words don't matter. It's the way the music constitutes a kind of incantation in itself. (Of course, this is the "cream" that Scorsese had Sinatra lover Nick Pileggi type into their script.)

Jimmy continues to regard Morrie, to size him up, not that he hasn't sized him up before. What he could do to that guy. What he should do to that guy. It's a slow dolly in to Jimmy at the bar. Jimmy looks left, right, left, then gives a little grin to nobody but himself. He takes a long drag on his cigarette. A look flashes on his face, pure hatred. Then another, of resolution. His eyes almost meet the camera lens at the end of the shot.

A film actor is often required to ignore the presence of a camera. Because De Niro's work so often has an emotional immediacy that implies "naturalism," the amount of time, especially in Scorsese's films, in which he's required to almost directly interact with the camera isn't much noted. The scenes in which Travis Bickle talks to his mirror in *Taxi Driver* are pertinent examples. This shot in *Goodfellas* is one of several in which the actor has to be almost synchronized to the movements of the shot. De Niro describes the process with standard straightforwardness: "Marty just had a shot, and then he explained what he wanted to do, and that's pretty much what it was, you know, he's gonna come in slow, and...that's it." Producer Barbara De Fina says, "Well, yes, that is pretty much how it works. But with a lot of takes."

Given the intensity of the "Sunshine" shot, Henry's subsequent voice-over—"I could see for the first time that Jimmy was a nervous wreck"—is a bit of a "no duh" moment. With a freeze-frame and a return to the gang's social life, we get this peculiar ping-ponging between "That's when I knew Jimmy was gonna whack Morrie" and then an exhalation over Jimmy not whacking Morrie, underscored by Henry's self-serving voice-over insistence "I was just stalling for time."

This is at a card game at the bar where the gang has been hanging out, never named in the movie, but mostly the interior of the real-life Neir's Tavern in Queens, standing in for what was Robert's. On the wall behind Henry is a reproduction of the 1924 George Bellows painting *Dempsey and Firpo*, the one showing a fighter being literally knocked out of the ring. A great work of art but a near-egregious cliché of old-school New York bar decoration. "Sunshine" is playing in the background, softly this time—it's definitely the jukebox—and the camera pulls back to show Jimmy next to Henry, laughing as Tommy tells another one of his stories. Cut to, of course, Tommy telling one of his stories. Morrie's laughing, Frankie Carbone is laughing. It's the Bamboo Lounge and "I thought I told you to go fuck your mother" again. Except it's not. The laughter is rote, forced. Tommy is maybe kind of a bore when you come down to it.

But Tommy's tale does have Jimmy feeling the bonhomie. "Forget about tonight," Jimmy says to Henry. "Poor bastard, he never knew how close he was to getting killed," Henry says in voice-over.

And THEN THEY KILL HIM. Morrie follows Jimmy, Tommy, and Carbone to the car, and from the back seat behind the passenger seat, Tommy sticks an icepick in the back of Morrie's head.

Morrie's last words: "You hear about the points we were shaving up in Boston?"

"No, I didn't," says Carbone. "Oh, it's terrific. Yeah. Nunzio up in the—" Then there's an "ugh!" and a crack and that's it for Morrie. Grunting himself, Tommy puts the icepick in the back of Morrie's neck, pushing it in to the hilt; pulling it out, he says, "I thought he'd never shut the fuck up," and looks at Jimmy, who says, "What a pain in the ass." Tommy seems to have absorbed Jimmy's own hatred of Morrie.

Morrie's mention of the Boston College basketball point-shaving scheme is a useful shoehorning in of the real-life caper that had substantial consequences for Hill, but which is not depicted in detail in the movie.

After Tommy and Carbone are instructed by Jimmy to "chop him up," Carbone gets out of the car, which prompts Tommy to call him a "dizzy motherfucker." Because they're not going to do the chopping in the *bar parking lot*. First the thing with the coffee, now this.

In fairness to Jimmy, it's clear throughout the picture that he never much liked Morrie. Still, the way he shrugs off Henry's concerns about what to tell Belle is brutal. Morrie, for all his flaws, was a devoted husband. Before bringing up Boston College he announced to the guys his intention to pick up some Danish pastries for his wife, a gesture about which Jimmy, Tommy, and Frankie Carbone could scarcely give half a fuck. When a frantic Belle comes to Henry and Karen's house in a panic, she says that Morrie's "never been away all night without calling."

With Jimmy at a diner, Henry is at a loss. "What the fuck you want me to tell Belle." The showing-off of the house to Morrie and Belle earlier indicate that the Hills had been constructing a simulacrum of normal suburban life, and indicates the social awkwardness of having a friend in that life get whacked. Jimmy's life as depicted in the movie is more isolated, which enables his arguably nihilistic indifference. His answer to Henry's question is "Who gives a fuck?" In fact, he's a little puzzled. "What do you care about her?

"Watch this," Jimmy says, pointing out some sleeping plain-clothesmen in an unmarked car. He goes over and taps on their window while Henry pleads he not give the cops the satisfaction.

"Come on, fuckos, let's go for a ride," he says to the now-awake cops. "Keep 'em up all night," he laughs to Henry. De Niro's note in the script: "This guy is tough!"

The pink Cadillac, its sticker still in the passenger side window—sharp-eyed viewers will detect it has a big blood patch on it—is parked next to an overpass archway. Two young boys—the one in the lead, holding a piece of wood that looks like a broken slat from a fence, is particularly angelic looking—approach the car. They stop and stand together in a nearly noble composition practically out of Sergei Eisenstein.

Cut to the grille of the car practically filling the frame as the camera begins to move up. Then the piano comes in. Those block chords from the coda to Derek and the Dominoes' "Layla."

The song was famously written by Eric Clapton as a lament for the woman he wanted but it seemed he could never have, Patti Harrison, originally the spouse of Clapton's great friend George Harrison. (In 2011 Scorsese would create a lengthy documentary about the former Beatle.) To use its final, mournful but eventually soaring postscript as the accompaniment to a series of death tableaus is arguably counterintuitive. But there's also something undeniably cinematic about its pacing, the way it uses the markedly Beatles-esque device of starting with a single instrument and having the other pieces in the ensemble come in gradually, as with "Ticket to Ride." In the *Cahiers du Cinéma* book entitled *Scorsese on Scorsese* (not to be confused with the Faber and Faber book entitled *Scorsese on Scorsese*), the director told Michael Henry Wilson that yes, this was, like "Sunshine of Your Love," a song that Scorsese heard for the sequence from the start: "The scene was even shot to fit the song. I had 'Layla' running in playback. The pink Cadillac, the refrigerator truck, all the executions Jimmy ordered, were shot with 'Layla' in playback. Why? Because it's a tragedy, a tragic procession passing before our eyes. It has a certain majesty, even if our actors are no princes. They're called common criminals but they're human beings who don't deserve to die. The music conveys the tragedy; its sadness should arouse sympathy." The sight of Johnny Roastbeef and his wife, who loved the car, stiff in place hours after breathing their final and perhaps terrified breaths, is too shudder-worthy at first to register as sad. But it is.

This section of "Layla" was credited to Jim Gordon, the drummer for Derek and the Dominoes. Gordon was a prodigy who made his recording debut backing the Everly Brothers when he was just seventeen. He came into Clapton's orbit via Delaney and Bonnie, the American roots rock act to whom Clapton was drawn while recuperating from what he came to see as the psychedelic excesses of his prior group, Cream. The singer Rita Coolidge was Gordon's girlfriend (she, too, had been affiliated with Delaney and Bonnie, and also the Joe Cocker/ Leon Russell aggregation called Mad Dogs and Englishmen, for which Gordon drummed). In her 2016 memoir, *Delta Lady*, she writes of a day in California when Gordon came to visit. "He sat down at my piano, and played for me a chord progression he'd just composed." The virtuoso drummer was also, per Coolidge, "a capable pianist." The progression, in C-sharp, was one Coolidge found "haunting [...] especially when the bright major chords suddenly dipped to B-flat 7th for the refrain." The progression wasn't a whole song, and in Coolidge's account, she took over and added a countermelody and wrote some lyrics. The composition was called "Time (Don't Let the World Get in Our Way)." Coolidge writes that she and Gordon demoed it (the year was 1970), played it for Eric Clapton, got a noncommittal reaction, and then forgot about it. "But our song, with Jim's wistful melody and my sweet countermelody, would come to haunt me the rest of my life." She does not mention *Goodfellas* in the book, but one can be reasonably sure that it has played a part in the haunting.

As the bodies tumble—literally, in the case of Frenchy and Joe Buddha coming out of the garbage truck—Henry speaks of Jimmy "cutting every link" to the Lufthansa heist. "But it had nothing to do with me," he says, maybe trying to explain to himself how he lived through this slaughter. "Anyway, what did I care?"

Still, Henry says: "Months after the robbery they were finding bodies all over." And here is possibly the most dangerous shot in the movie, the discovery of Frankie Carbone's frozen-solid corpse in the back of a refrigerated meat truck.

It begins far behind the truck, at the height of almost three stories. The camera moves toward the truck and as its doors open, the camera descends, and goes deep into the truck, and moves in to a medium close-up of the frozen Carbone, hanging from a meat hook.

The original idea, according to Larry McConkey, was to do it all from a crane, a small crane. But the crane did not have sufficient maneuverability to get deep enough into the truck, which, besides frozen Carbone (the actual actor, Frank Sivero, in effects makeup and strapped in a harness), was stuffed with sides of beef.

One morning, possibly a Saturday, very early, Michael Ballhaus called Steadicam operator McConkey. Can McConkey suit up and get to the meat-packing district in Manhattan to do a "step-off?" A move in which an operator goes to handheld, or Steadicam, from a moving crane by stepping off said crane and continuing the movement. "What crane do you have?" McConkey asks.

"Usually for a step-off they'll be using a Chapman-Titan crane," says McConkey. This sturdy piece of equipment has a sizable platform.

To avoid a potential corporate defamation action, I will not repeat the name of the crane actually being used, and merely record that McConkey's reaction on being told. "That's like a death trap."

Death trap or not, McConkey decided to accept the challenge. Major film productions are generally insured to the hilt, but every now and then a technician will assess a situation and, having considered its considerable risk, go for it, anyway, without going to the trouble of getting an okay or checking on whether or not they're protected in this case. Also, the set is prepped and ready and the actors are there and time is money. (For the record, Joseph Reidy's recollection is that the Steadicam shot was always part of the plan for this scene.)

"I got my gear together, went to the set, I was shown the shot, worked it out." The choreography, so to speak, and the timing were precisely calculated. When the truck door was opened, the viewer should not be able to see the floor of the truck, because there was a crate there that McConkey had to step onto from the platform of the crane. There also had to be someone out of frame on the crate to keep it steady for McConkey to step onto it. "We did not completely nail it; there's a little wobble when I'm stepping off the crane." (It's barely noticeable but it does in fact occur about twenty-six seconds into the shot, a slight jar to the left.)

THIS WAS THE DAY THAT TOMMY WAS BEING MADE

"Still, I never saw Jimmy so happy." A dolly tracks in from outside the diner, where Jimmy enthusiastically chows down with Henry. The Pittsburgh thing is bringing money in for him, he presumably has gotten to keep all the money he hasn't given to the Lufthansa crew, and the heat from the cops on that matter is going down. "But the thing that made Jimmy so happy that morning was that this was the day that Tommy was being made."

Henry and Jimmy are not just dining; they're anticipating news that the ceremony that accompanies being "made" has come to its rightful conclusion. Henry speaks of Jimmy having a "signal" worked out.

At Tommy's home, the wiseguy is dressed to, um, be killed. Jacket in a tight plaid pattern, the white shirt with the vampire fangs collar, a black tie wide enough to make it look as if the shirt is black with a white collar, black pocket square. He walks into the living room and greets his mother like they're about to start a Burns and Allen routine. Their exchange—how he looks wonderful, and how he should "be careful," and God be with him—raises the question of what Mom knows about Tommy's life, work, his "being made" and all. She seems very relaxed about having a criminal son.

"Just don't paint any more religious pictures, please," Tommy says as he goes out the front door. A funny line, but more a thing that would be said by someone going away for more than just the afternoon. How long are these "being made" ceremonies supposed to take, anyway?

The camera swerves, we see Tommy's white Caddy in the driveway; in a more nondescript Buick sits Vinnie; waiting for Tommy at the rear of the four-door is Tuddy, dressed more formally than usual, so much so it's easy not to immediately make him.

And here in voice-over Henry waxes most eloquent about how special it was to be a part of *this* band of brothers, even as the "Layla" coda still plays faintly under all the other sounds: "You know, we always called each other 'good fellas.' Like you'd say to somebody, 'you're gonna like this guy, he's all right, he's a good fella, he's one of us? You understand? We were good fellas. Wiseguys. But Jimmy and I could never be made."

No: "The Irishman," Jimmy Conway, and the half-Irishman, Henry Hill, by dint of not being pure Sicilian, could never be full members of the crew. You had to be able to trace "all your relatives back to the old country." There's some awe in Henry's voice as he says this. "It's the highest honor they can give you. It means you belong to a family and a crew. It means that nobody can fuck around with you."

But this assertion has already been disproven. Billy Batts was not just fucked around with, he was killed, and rather ignominiously at that. If you're in a room with the right psychopath, being "made" means nothing. "Hey, I known you all my life." Batts shrugs off Tommy. Billy Batts thought he was just having a night out with friends. And now Tommy thinks he's being made.

"How many years ago was it you were made?" Tommy asks Vinnie after the Buick parks. The camera, on a crane, backs up and rises, a magisterial move that reveals a sizable but banal outer-boroughs suburban structure, a wide garage with a patio/garden on top of it, leading into a large house of brick and stucco exterior. Thirty years, Vinnie says, and Tommy notes, "Pikes Peak was a fucking pimple then, wasn't it?"

At the diner an anxious Jimmy heads to a phone booth. Henry muses on Jimmy's fallacious reasoning: "We were all being made."

When Tommy turns a knob, pushes open the door, and walks into the room he's been led to, he's moving slowly. He stands and looks to his left, then to his right, then to his left. A fast cut reveals the room: looks like something you order out of a catalog, model "Long Island Sportsman's Den." There's a marlin mounted on the wall. The thing is, it *looks* pretty much exactly like a catalog shot, because the room is empty. Which it should not be. The shot lasts maybe a second and a half and right before it ends Tommy says, "Oh."

Cut back to a tight shot of Tommy saying, "No," exactly as a bullet fires into the back of his head. There's a quick cut to a wider view of the shooting, so you can see Tuddy's impassive expression as he fires. He holds Tommy's shoulder as he pulls the trigger. An exit wound forms at the top of Tommy's hairline and blood runs down his right cheek. Vinnie looks on like a statue. Tommy hits a tile floor that looks like it could be from one of David Lynch's alternate-dimension rooms. He falls with a force that is, as with Stacks' fall, unrealistic, except for the possibility that Tuddy threw him down.

Let's take a moment here to consider, once more, what's happened. Paulie Cicero has ordered his brother Tuddy to kill a man they've known since that man's childhood. Tuddy, who was not just the cabstand guy but the pizzeria guy. Remember *Do the Right Thing*, when Sal says to Pino about the Bed–Stuy kids, "They grew up eating my food?" Did not Tommy and Henry grow up eating Tuddy's pizza? The point is that this community of good fellas, wiseguys, what have you, is absolutely depraved. As Tommy himself was. These people betray themselves and each other constantly and then shrug it off over braciole.

Jimmy is on the pay phone, agitated. "This is Vinnie," says Vinnie on the other end. Jimmy asks if everything's been straightened out, and Vinnie says, "Well, we had a problem. We tried to do everything we could."

We have not been made privy to the trying-to-do-everything-they-could part. We just see them take him into a room and kill him.

"He's gone," Vinnie says, "and we couldn't do nothing about it."

In 1957's *The Brothers Rico* (a 1957 Mafia picture, based on an American-set story by Georges Simenon, directed by Phil Karlson, and much admired by Scorsese), Harry Bellaver's West Coast enforcer Mike LaMotta listens to Richard Conte's Eddie Rico plead that the organization spare his younger brother's life. Expansive in sympathy, LaMotta replies, "That's the way you shoulda talked at the beginning. Not that it would've done any good."

Before he's made to pay with his life for betraying the Corleones, Tessio, in *The Godfather*, says to Tom Hagen, "Tell Mike it was only business. I always liked him." In a rather extraordinary display of mercy, for him, Hagen replies, "He understands that." Seeing a possible lifeline, Tessio asks, "Tom, can you get me off the hook? For old times' sake?"

"Can't do it, Sally."

In *The Irishman* the planned, then impending, murder of Jimmy Hoffa is discussed thusly: "It is what it is." The orders come from nameless "higher-ups." Hoffa himself is a "higher-up," notes his future assassin, Frank Sheeran. No, there are higher up higher-ups. "If they can takes out the president, they can take out the president of a union."

In Cosa Nostra fictions internecine murder is always referred to in fatalistic terms; it's inevitable, inexorable, it cannot be helped. With few exceptions it is always done at the behest of an unnamed "they." This is arguably the most Kafkaesque convention in the genre. Years before in this movie's world, we will recall, Paulie asked an indignant Sonny Bunz about the even then out-of-control Tommy, "What am I supposed to do, shoot him?" One can imagine a conversation between Paulie and a figure who has real power over him, in which the answer to the same question is a "Yes" that cannot be responded to except by performing the action.

"The fact that Tommy gets killed that way is very important," Scorsese told Ian Christie and David Thompson. "Neither Henry nor Jimmy could have done anything about it, because it was among Italians. It was my father on the phone telling Jimmy, 'He's gone.' Bob De Niro asked my father not to tell him directly what had happened, but to talk around it. I suggested my father should say he had done 'everything he could.' In fact, the mob had been shielding [Tommy] for years, but he was out of control, causing a lot of trouble and angering everyone. Finally they decided he had gone too far. Even Jimmy and Henry are not part of the big organization, though Jimmy was a *professore* type, in charge of the young kids. I especially liked the way Bob held down the emotion after he comes out of the phone booth. He's just standing there with his hands on his hips. Henry doesn't even know yet. The body language is great between the two of them."

Here Scorsese misremembers things a bit. De Niro's Jimmy, in tears, takes to destroying the phone's receiver as soon as he processes the full import of Vinnie's "He's gone." He then com-poses himself, leaves the booth, stands before Henry, and says, "They fucking whacked him." He kicks, then knocks over, the booth. De Niro told *GQ*: "One of the hard scenes for me was when I heard that Joe's character was killed—to be crying and emotionally really upset. I tried my best. I might have wanted to get even further than I did in it—not expressing just the anger but the emotional distraughtness, if you will. For my charac-ter, for him, because they were close. It takes a lot out of you emotionally, the things that you're trying to...it takes so much effort and energy. Either you're there or you're trying to get there, but both of those processes take a lot out of you." In *GQ* Michael Ballhaus said: "I think we shot that scene only once. He was so much into it that you couldn't do it again." Ten years after being interviewed for the *GQ* piece, and thirty years after shooting the scene, all De Niro could say to me about Jimmy and Tommy was, "They were good friends."

Just as we were served doubles on the deaths of Batts and Stacks, now, too, we are again shown, from overhead, Tommy dead on that floor, the only thing in motion the blood coming out of his skull. "It was revenge for Billy Batts." You then hear the shrug in Henry/Liotta's voice: "And a lot of other things." Vinnie moves into the shot from the right side, Tuddy from the left. "And that's that," Vinnie says. "And there was nothing that we could do about it."

Henry, who has just been lauding the ways of this organization and the high honor of becoming a made man, now dismisses it all, disgustedly: "It was among the Italians, it was real greaseball shit." As Jimmy weeps Henry can only shake his head. They're gonna show those motherfuckers now, all right. This was sup-posed to have been a new beginning. Instead, as Scorsese ob-served to Christie and Thompson, the killing of Tommy "puts them all in their place, and it's the beginning of the real end."

MAY 11: THE TO-DO LIST

It's a Sunday. Not to put too fine a point on it, but it's not the actual date this all went down, which was in late April of 1980.

It's not even seven in the morning. Herbie Flowers plonks the pickups on his electric bass and then launches into the tense but bouncy riff of "Jump into the Fire," the hardest, loudest song on the pop singer Harry Nilsson's 1971 album *Nilsson Schmilsson*.

Henry's doing coke off the linoleum of his kitchen table. In the left of the frame a gun barrel points out. Once you've stopped doing cocaine to get high, or "high," and begin using it as a general everyday stimulant, you've developed a dependence. For years, decades, maybe, perhaps because of its long periods of relative scarcity from the US and European narcotics market, cocaine had established a reputation as a nonaddictive substance. The great jazz pianist Bill Evans, a hopeless addict for all his adult life, managed to provisionally kick heroin in the 1970s and rejoiced in his discovery of cocaine, which was invigorating and, as far as he knew, would not get you hooked. Of course it did, and he died at the age of fifty-one. On the other hand, there are, even today, hundreds and perhaps thousands of people who will go through periods of recreational use and then walk away. Whether they are ingesting cocaine of the quality that Henry Hill and Bill Evans were able to obtain probably has something to do with that, but it's not really the purview of this text.

The pinpoint clarity, or illusion thereof, that the drug is said to produce when you are first introduced to it, is in this sequence undercut by Henry's overall sloppiness as he goes about his errands, and in one shot by the sight of Henry's raw, red nostrils. (Frank Zappa's late song "Cocaine Decisions" nails an end product of the drug: "You make expensive ugliness/how do you do it/let me guess:/cocaine decisions.") One thing cocaine does is empower denial. As does heroin, but the drugs do it in inverse ways. Heroin denial is "It doesn't matter," cocaine denial is "Actually, I've got this!" Henry keeps boosting all day to keep up the lie that he is handling his shit.

He carries a paper bag out of the house and goes to his car, a brown Cadillac Coupe de Ville. He lays out his to-do list in voice-over: "I was gonna be busy all day. I had to drop off some guns at Jimmy's to match some silencers he had gotten. I had to pick up my brother at the hospital and drive him back to the house for dinner that night and then I had to pick up some new Pittsburgh stuff for Lois to fly down to some customers I had near Atlanta."

In the book Hill remembers: "On the day I finally got arrested my friends and family were driving me crazy." There's even more to do in that chapter than in the movie, including a meetup with Bobby Germaine, the stick-up guy whose cover story was that he was a freelance writer.

Another thing cocaine does is engender paranoia. Here's a helicopter, flying at a diagonal through the frame, seen through tree branches. First, Henry finds it curious. Soon he will determine that it's following him. It is. But that doesn't mean he's not paranoid.

Jimmy's wearing a blue bathrobe when Henry shows up at his house. Here is the oldest we will see the character, and one of De Niro's most vivid memories, looking back at the movie today, is how difficult it was to get his hair right. "I remember going out to Queens Boulevard where they were shooting, we were trying to get my hair as white and as light as possible, with a woman I worked with, the hair and makeup person at that time. I'd worked with her a long time, quite a few years. And we kept going back to the hair place on Madison Avenue, because stripping my hair was harder than we thought it would be. When we did it for a test, it wouldn't look as white or light as we wanted it to. So we did it a few times, more than a few times."

Jimmy rejects the guns. He demonstrates to Henry how they're not right, trying to screw one of his dingy-looking silencers to one of Henry's dingy-looking automatics. "What the fuck are these things?" he grouses, cigarette in mouth. "None of them fit."

In the 1976 *Taxi Driver*, in the scene in which De Niro's Travis Bickle buys several firearms from the motormouthed dealer Easy Andy, there are a number of close-up shots of the pieces that practically caress them. Gun fetishization wasn't an *overwhelming* characteristic of the filmmakers of Scorsese's generation/circle, but it was a characteristic, and an unappetizing one. A photograph from the 1970s included among the illustrations in Peter Biskind's *Easy Riders, Raging Bulls* showing *Taxi Driver* screenwriter Paul Schrader smiling with a small revolver in hand doesn't seem as cute today as it might have. And while Scorsese is playing a character in *Taxi Driver*, that character's ruminations on the destructive powers of a Magnum have been contributing to inaccurate impressions of the man for decades. (The director's cameo as an actual gunman in *Mean Streets*—an associate of wannabe wiseguy Michael, who's referred to as "Shorty" by Harvey Keitel's Charlie in an earlier scene—who shoots and probably kills Johnny Boy is more immediately recognizable as a metafiction character bit.)

In *Goodfellas*, guns are deadly but they're also garbage. When Tommy is hitting Billy Batts with his revolver, the gun slips from his hand and slides across the floor, lubricated with blood, its chamber smashed loose from its body; it's defunct. For his May Sunday, Henry's carrying a bunch of them in a supermarket brown bag. A far cry from the "elegant" leather holster Easy Andy tacks on to his firearms sale to Bickle.

"Jimmy was so pissed off he didn't even say goodbye." What he says is "Stop with those fuckin' drugs, they're making your mind into mush. You hear me?"

Henry is reflected in the rear bumper of the Cadillac. He tosses the bag into the trunk, and the camera swerves to the left and up for a medium close-up of Henry in his Ray-Bans, his mouth slightly agape. Because he's played by Ray Liotta, he still looks pretty cool. But not nearly as cool as he did at the diner by Idlewild.

Ry Cooder's slide guitar kicks off "Memo from Turner," a song first sung by Mick Jagger in *Performance*, a film whose grab-you-by-the-back-of-the-head style was surely an influence on this one, although it's scarcely been cited as such. If you know the song, its lyrics, while not yet heard here, will carry some thematic resonance—not just "weren't you at the Coke convention back in 1965," but the final line, "Gentlemen, you all work for me." It's 8:05 in the morning and Henry would like to enjoy a cigarette. He can shrug off Jimmy's rejection of the guns. He's seeing the guys from Pittsburgh that day and they are always in the market for guns so "I was pretty sure I'd get my money back." He's on top of it! He looks up his windshield for the helicopter.

"Turner" segues into the middle of the Who's "Magic Bus" with singer Roger Daltrey repeating, "I want it I want it I want it." Henry looks up again. Cut to outside the car, through the windshield at Henry, looking up.

Here occurs a nifty bit of breakneck montage. After Henry looks up, he looks straight ahead again, straightens out his steering arm, thrusts his torso into the seat, and screams. Cut to what he sees: a collision stopping traffic, cop car on the other side of the thruway. Cut to one side view of Henry in the car, swerving his torso and turning the steering wheel left; cut to a closer version of the same perspective; cut to his foot coming off the gas pedal and hitting the brake.

In a return to the outside-the-car view, Henry, holding tight to the wheel, grimaces. He's not gonna make it. He looks down to his left and has a eureka moment. Cut to him putting his foot now on the emergency brake. Cut to his perspective: the car is still dead aimed at the rear of a stopped Mustang. A view of the Cadillac skidding to a halt over a yellow line at the side of the asphalt. From the opposite angle, the front of the Cadillac stops just short of the Mustang's bumper. Ten shots in less than seven seconds, resolving on Henry exhaling with no little relief. "Oh my God," he says. In a sober state this near-collision would be bad enough; the montage gets the heightened coked-up panic Henry feels.

"When I finally got there at the hospital to pick up Michael, his doctor wanted to put me in bed." Kevin Corrigan's Michael is sitting in his wheelchair waving his left hand, a goofy look on his face. He's either oblivious to Henry's state or completely used to it.

Kevin Corrigan interacts with Liotta's Henry more here than in any other sequence. This, too, was a prize for the young actor. "I just loved *Something Wild*, I wanted to be that kind of actor. I loved his volatility, and also that he was just so precise in his choices, so driven and charismatic. Working with him was like being in a cage with a tiger. I was thinking, 'Goddamn, this is the big leagues, it's fucking amazing.' There was a giddiness with that, too.

"He was fun to be around, and supportive, and took the job very seriously. He was very much in the world of the film, and that extended to me; he treated me like a brother. He was very preoccupied. Of course he's preoccupied. He's the lead in a Scorsese movie. And he's also playing Henry Hill, a guy who thinks he's gonna get...whacked."

MAY 11: COME ON, GET OVER HERE

It's 8:45 a.m. on that Sunday, and nearly two hours into the movie. Michael's doctor takes one look at Henry and wants to admit him. Henry makes the "I was partying last night" mutter, and the doctor, a warm smile on his face, insists: "Come on, get over here," and gives him an impromptu checkup.

Isiah Whitlock, Jr., later to be a familiar and welcome screen presence, is in *Goodfellas* for only a short period of time, but he makes a strong impression. Whitlock is one of only a few African American actors in the film, and hence he portrays one of the few African American characters, so there's that.

But it's also who the character is and what he does. Michael's doctor, out of genuine kindness and concern, and without an agenda, tries to look after Henry. He's under no obligation. What he does is representative of his values, values of giving rather than taking, an inversion of the wiseguy ethos. He's one of the "suckers" Henry and his crew disdains.

He is not a criminal.

In fact, it would be only slightly inaccurate to say that up until this point in the movie, he's the only adult character who is not a criminal.

Whitlock, who had moved to New York to pursue acting in 1983, had been in Scorsese's orbit before. "I was doing work at the Actors Studio, and Paul Newman had come and enlisted a group of students to come over to his house in Connecticut and do a table reading of the script for *The Color of Money*." There's a part in that script for a black pool player, Amos, who quite cleverly hustles Newman's Fast Eddie Felson, which is what Whitlock read. "I wanted to get that and they ended up getting Forrest Whitaker, rightly, because he was great."

A few years later Whitlock was netted into a group audition. "Frank Sivero, who pays Frankie Carbone, was helping Ellen Lewis, wrangling young actors into the auditions. It was off, because I was the only African American in the whole outfit. And I read for the part of Sonny, the owner of the Bamboo Lounge, who was not a black character." Sonny is Italian American, of the clan if not the wiseguy tribe. "I was a little confused; I remember thinking, 'I don't know, I don't think I would be cast for something like this.' But who am I to say; that is not going to prevent me from doing the reading.

"But I was surprised. I got a callback, and I got it fairly quickly. To see Martin Scorsese. I spent some time thinking how I was going to successfully act like this was a routine thing for me to do! When I saw him, he acknowledged the fact that Sonny was not going to be a viable role. He asked me where he had seen me before, and I reminded him that I was one of the actors at the reading Paul Newman arranged. And he said, 'Right,' and told me that he had liked me in the role.

"'I got a small part,' Scorsese explained, 'of a doctor.' He took me through the setup, the fact that it's related to Henry's brother Michael, and so on. And then he said, 'This is happening at a moment where you're the only guy Henry trusts.' And I'll never forget what Marty said after that: 'Do you think you can do this for me?'"

Whitlock was working as a waiter at a restaurant on Manhattan's 10th Avenue at the time. "I mentioned what had happened to another waiter/actor, and he said, 'You got a part? I'm going in.' Which was funny, as if he thought that if I got in, then they were just handing out parts. He didn't get one. But that production really was the talk of the town among young and struggling actors at the time, and if you got in it was like hitting Lotto. It was one of the first movies I did.

"And it was interesting, because of what Marty told me about the trust issue. Especially at that point in the movie, the way people are so scared of one another and of getting whacked, you're sort of taken aback by it. You almost don't believe it as a viewer: 'What's going on here, what's the connection?' It's something you haven't seen much of in the film.

"And it's funny to me, too, because when I see the movie I

look like I'm about twelve. People to this day are always kind of very surprised to see me turn up in it. It tells you how long I've been around. It has always been great, having been a part of it. I had this favorite Italian restaurant in the Village at that time, and I walked in one day and the owner said, 'I just saw you in a movie!' which was odd because it hadn't yet been released. But he had seen it, and for the next month he bought me dinner and Sambuca whenever I stopped in."

The shoot itself was exciting for Whitlock, having not spent a lot of time on any film sets, let alone one as dynamic as this. "They were shooting at an old hospital on the Lower East Side, one that was out of use. And this was late '80s New York, so the Lower East Side then was a 'what the hell am I doing here?' kind of place to go to work. When Martin Scorsese came out to where we were, and told us what he wanted to do, he was very specific about the shots he wanted to get. I had been speaking to Kevin Corrigan a little during the prep time and we'd gotten to know each other a little bit. I hadn't met Ray Liotta and didn't know much about his work—you couldn't Google your potential colleagues in those days—so it was a little interesting when he showed up looking very raggedy, as if he had actually been up all night. And he had been! Not partying or anything; he knew he needed to look sleep-deprived, so he had deprived himself of sleep."

The checkup ends with a reprieve for the busy Henry: "He took mercy on me. He gave me ten milligrams of Valium and sent me home." In the car, his pack of Winstons handily resting over the dashboard, Henry points out the helicopter to Michael, who at first doesn't get it. "Get the fuck outta here, what are you nuts?" He then at least has to acknowledge the existence of *a* helicopter.

What does Michael know and when did he know it? What would you say to an older brother who told you a helicopter was following him? After chastising Corrigan for sharing the old high school pictures of the director a little too freely on the set, Scorsese spoke with the actor at length on the subject of Michael's ostensible complicity. "I remember conversations with Marty, and I'd ask, 'How much did I know about him? Did I KNOW he was in the mob?' He kind of threw a curveball in those scenes when the helicopter's following Henry around. I had this theory about why Michael wouldn't know, and finally Marty just came out and said, 'No no no. He would know.'"

MAY 11: I WAS COOKING DINNER THAT NIGHT

Henry Hill took a lot of pleasure in cooking, and in telling people how good a cook he was. After his arrest, while working with federal agents, he used his expertise to charm them. This is a passage from Volkman and Cummings' *The Heist*:

"There were some compensations for the agents, however, chief among them the meals. Accustomed to a diet of fast food, especially in the midst of a major investigation, the FBI men had little opportunity to eat decent meals. Hill, it turned out, had an even greater distaste for take-out cuisine, for he was a trained cook with great culinary talent.

"He demonstrated it one day after announcing that he would prepare a grand dinner for 'us.' While [FBI supervisor Stephen] Carbone and his agents waited, Hill bustled around the kitchen, frenetically preparing what he promised would be a multicourse masterpiece." The meal for the agents was a reportedly "exquisite" lobster fra diavolo.

When Henry gets home from his first jaunt that Sunday, he explains. "See, I was cooking dinner that night. And had to start braising the beef, pork butt, and veal shanks for the tomato sauce."

The recipe for the meal, his disabled brother's favorite, is in Hill's 2002 *The Wiseguy Cookbook: My Favorite Recipes from My Life as a Goodfella to Cooking on the Run*, perhaps the best and certainly the most useful of Hill's post-*Wiseguy* publishing ventures. I reproduce it, slightly condensed, below.

MICHAEL'S FAVORITE
ZITI WITH MEAT SAUCE

This was my brother Michael's favorite pasta recipe. He'd sit in his wheelchair and stir the sauce lovingly all day to make sure it didn't stick. It uses some meats which are hard to find now. If you can't find them, substitute a version of them and it'll still be fine.

¼ cup olive oil

1 pound pork butt (or shoulder), in one piece

1 pound veal shanks

6-8 cloves of garlic, minced or thinly sliced
    (about 2 tablespoons)

Two 28-ounce cans peeled plum tomatoes with basil,
    drained, reserving juice

12 large basil leaves, torn in large pieces,
    or 1 tablespoon dried

¼ cup finely chopped Italian parsley
    or 2 teaspoons, or 1 tablespoon dried parsley

¼ to ½ teaspoon each salt and pepper (to taste)

Six to eight meatballs

1 pound cooked and drained ziti

In a large pot, heat oil over medium heat. Add pork butt and veal shanks and brown on all sides. Remove meat from pan.

In the same pan, cook garlic over medium heat until soft (do not brown) and add tomatoes, basil, parsley, salt, and black pepper to taste. Bring tomatoes to a boil, breaking them up, and stir once thoroughly, then reduce heat to a low simmer. As the acid from the tomatoes flows to the top, skim it off (after 10-15 minutes).

Remove bones from veal shanks and coarsely chop meat.

After 15-20 minutes of cooking, return meat to tomato sauce. Continue cooking at a low simmer, skimming when necessary and stirring briefly right after skimming for four hours (this was my brother Michael's job). One half hour before serving, add the six prepared meatballs and continue cooking.

When ziti is cooked al dente, place in a large bowl and toss with the meat sauce. Serve immediately with Parmesan or Romano cheese on the side.

This may look a little excessive to some, particularly in the meat department. It is, and it's intentional. I shared the recipe with Missy Robbins, the owner of the acclaimed New York Italian restaurants Lilia and Misi. She said of putting multiple meats in the sauce, "Well, it simply adds depth and different flavor profiles to the sauce, but I'm also guessing in the context of this scene and in general it was a bit of a way to show off how abundant you can be. I do a pork sugo at Misi that has six different kinds of salumi/cured meat plus pork shoulder. It actually started as a way to use all the scraps of meat we had (that happened to make sense to be in the same pot)."

Some time after corresponding with Robbins, I tried this recipe myself, with a few modifications. (I found that with only two cans of tomatoes, what you were working with was more a stew than a sauce, so I threw in another can.) I have to say it turned out great. If you don't mind a case of the meat sweats, it's an incredible meal.

"I'm gonna make all this meat," Henry says, looking at the goods. Such is his hurry that he rolls meatballs with a lit cigarette hanging from his mouth. The sauce is not all he's concocting. There are green beans that he'll cook in olive oil, and, he says, "I had some beautiful cutlets that were cut just right," which he would serve "just as an appetizer." You don't have time to think about it, but if you think about it, it is touching that he's going to all this trouble to create such an elaborate meal for his little brother even though it also involves more or less chaining said little brother to a stove for four hours.

Henry's plan is to "start dinner early so we could unload the guns." That's something you don't hear every day. What follows also goes by too fast for the viewer to really consider just how absurd is the quandary Henry has backed himself into. Telling Karen "we're going to your mother's," they are off again, to stash the brown paper bag full of guns in a garbage pail inside

INT. NIGHT - Biller Date - Camera moving in
ON JUKEBOX - pan or track to see B.B. in long shot - REAR
See Decorators.
See Hood regular greet
High Treasures to b3
JUNE 11, 1970: QUEENS, NEW YORK.

INT: THE SUITE - NIGHT

A smoky, overdecorated cocktail lounge and nightclub on
Queens Boulevard. Sergio Franchi is in full voice on
the jukebox. It is after midnight. It has been a long
night. Balloons and empty glasses litter the place.
BILLY BATTS, a 50-year-old hood in an out-of-date suit,
holding court at the bar. WE SEE a younger, more sharply-
dressed HOOD walk in with a BEEHIVE GIRLFRIEND and hug
BATTS.

                    HOOD
          Billy. You look beautiful.
          Welcome home.

                    BATTS
               (laughing and turning
                to the bartender)
          What are you having? Give 'em
          what they're drinking.

WE SEE FOUR OTHER MEN, including HENRY HILL and JIMMY
BURKE, standing near BILLY BATTS at the bar, raise their
glasses in salute. TOMMY DESIMONE and ANOTHER BEEHIVE
BLONDE enter. BILLY BATTS looks up and sees TOMMY.

                    BILLY
          Hey, look at him. Tommy. You
          grew up.

                    TOMMY
               (preening a little)
          Billy, how are you?

                    BILLY
               (smiling broadly at
                Tommy and the girl)
          Son of a bitch. Get over here.

TOMMY walks over and BILLY, too aggressively, grabs
TOMMY around the neck. TOMMY doesn't like it.

                    TOMMY
               (forcing a laugh)
          Hey, Billy. Watch the suit.

                    BILLY
               (squeezing Tommy's cheek,
                a little too hard)
          Listen to him. "Watch the suit,"
          he says. A little pisser I've known
          all my life. Hey, Tommy, don't go
          get too big.

                    TOMMY
          Don't go busting my balls. Okay?

                    BILLY
               (laughing, to the
                crowd at the bar)
          Busting his balls?
               (to Tommy)
          If I was busting your balls, I'd
          send you home for your shine box.

TOMMY's smile turns to a glare as he realizes BILLY is
making fun of him. The MEN at the bar are roaring with
laughter. His GIRL is looking glumly at her shoes.

                    BILLY (contd)
               (to the hoods at
                the bar)
          You remember Tommy's shines?
          The kid was great. He made
          mirrors.

                    TOMMY
               (almost a threat)
          No more shines, Billy.

                    BILLY
          Come ooonnn. Tommeeee. We're
          only kidding. You can't take a
          joke? Come ooonn.

WE SEE that TOMMY is still angry, but begins to relax
with BILLY's apparent apology, but as soon as BILLY sees
that TOMMY is beginning to relax, he contemptuously
turns his back on TOMMY.

                    BILLY (contd)
               (facing the bar)
          Now get the hell home and get
          your shine box.

HENRY quickly steps in front of TOMMY who is about to
explode. BATTS is facing the bar and does not see just
how furious TOMMY has become.

                    HENRY
               (gently wrestling Tommy
                away from the bar)
          Come on, relax. He's drunk.
          He's been locked up for six
          years.

Scorsese's annotated script;
the movie's original opening
had the killing of Billy Batts
as the starting point; the
completed film begins with
Henry, Tommy, and Jimmy
driving out to bury Batts.

Photo credit: Martin Scorsese
Collection, NY

The "meet the wiseguys" scene in Scorsese's annotated script.

21

25   CONTD
     POLICE CAR
     pulling onto the sidewalk where HENRY, TOMMY and JIMMY
     are standing. The COPS recognize JIMMY.

                    COP #1
          Anything good?

     HENRY watches JIMMY smile and toss a couple of cartons of
     cigarettes into their radio car.

     The COPS wave and drive off.

26   EXT: FACTORY GATE - QUITTING TIME

     WE SEE HENRY busily selling cartons to WORKERS. TOMMY is
     getting cartons out of the trunk of a car parked nearby.
     HENRY is so busy he can hardly keep the money and cash
     straight. Instead of the neat roll we saw on JIMMY,
     HENRY's cash is a wrinkled mess. Some of it is rolled,
     some folded, some in different pockets. WE SEE HENRY
     approached by TWO CITY DETECTIVES.

                    DETECTIVE #1
          What do you think you're doing?

                    DETECTIVE #2
          Where did you get these cigarettes?

                    HENRY
               (offering them cartons)
          It's okay.

     DETECTIVE #1 roughly grabs HENRY's arm. DETECTIVE #2
     grabs HENRY's cigarette cartons. WE SEE HENRY pull his
     arm away and ONE of the DETECTIVES slaps him across the
     face.

     WE SEE that TOMMY is about to say something, but runs away
     instead.

27   INT: CABSTAND - DAY

     WE SEE TOMMY talking to TUDDY and ASSORTED HOODS at the
     cabstand.

28   INT: COURTROOM - "AR-1" (ARRAIGNMENT PART 1)

     HENRY is waiting along with DOZENS OF HOOKERS, nodding
     JUNKIES, MUGGERS and SHOPLIFTERS. When HENRY's case is
     called, WE PAN to a well-dressed MOB LAWYER,
     who has never seen the LAWYER before, walks to the

22

28   CONTD

     PROSECUTOR's, rather than the DEFENDANT's table. A COURT
     CLERK nods him over toward his own LAWYER.

     Without acknowledging HENRY, the LAWYER nods and smiles
     at the JUDGE, who smiles and nods back.

                    JUDGE
          Counsellor, proceed.

                                        CUT TO:

29   INT: COURTROOM - CENTER AISLE

     HENRY is walking out of the court. HENRY sees JIMMY
     BURKE smiling and waiting for him in the rear of the
     courtroom. JIMMY puts his arm around HENRY like a
     father, and tucks a one-hundred dollar bill into HENRY's
     chest pocket. They walk out into the court corridor in
     silence together and then, suddenly, HENRY sees PAUL
     VARIO, TOMMY, TUDDY, and the WHOLE CREW from the cabstand
     waiting for him. They start clapping and whistling and
     slapping his back and cheering. VARIO, TUDDY and BURKE
     embrace him.

     While bewildered COPS and LAWYERS watch:

                    CHORUS OF HOODS
          You broke your cherry! You broke
          your cherry!

     LAST FREEZE.

     TITLE UP - IDLEWILD AIRPORT: 1955

30   EXT: WIDE SHOT - IDLEWILD CARGO AREA

                    HENRY (VO)
          By the time I grew up, there was
          thirty billion a year in cargo
          moving through Idlewild Airport
          and we tried to steal every bit
          of it.

31   EXT: AIRPORT DINER - PARKING LOT - DAY
     ANGLE - GREY LIZARD SHOES AND SHARP GREY PANTS

     and UP TO SEE HENRY standing in parking lot, when a large
     truck pulls up. WE SEE TOMMY DESIMONE standing with him.

                    HENRY (VO)
          You've got to understand, we grew
          up near the airport. It belonged
               (MORE)

23

31   CONTD

                    HENRY (VO contd)
          to Paulie. We had friends and
          relatives who worked all over the
          place and they tipped us off about
          what was coming in and what was
          going out.

     WE SEE DRIVER get out of truck with engine still running
     and leave door open. He nods to HENRY who does not
     respond and the DRIVER casually walks toward the diner.

                    HENRY (VO contd)
          If any of the truckers or airlines
          gave us trouble, Paulie had his
          union people scare them with a
          little strike. It was beautiful.
          It was an even bigger money-maker
          than numbers, and Jimmy was in
          charge. Whenever we needed money,
          we'd rob the airport. To us, it
          was better than Citibank.

32   INT: TABLE IN DINER

     WE SEE DRIVER rise from debris of breakfast dishes, leave
     a tip and pay the CASHIER. He walks out the door toward
     his truck in the parking lot.

     HOLD ON the door.

     DRIVER rushes back in through the door toward the CASHIER.

                    DRIVER
               (flushed and agitated)
          Hurry, gimme the phone. Two niggers
          just stole my truck.

33   INT: SONNY'S BAMBOO LOUNGE - DUSK

     A cavernous room within earshot of the airport that looks
     like a movie nightclub. No matter when you walk into the
     Bamboo Lounge it's always the middle of the night.

     CAMERA TRACKS past the zebra-striped banquettes and bar
     stools, past sharpy BUSINESSMEN, BOOKMAKERS and HOODS.

                    HENRY (VO)
          There was Jimmy and Tommy and me.
          And there was Anthony Stabile,
          Angelo Sepe, Fat Andy, Frankie
          the Wop, Freddy No Nose, Pete
          the Killer, Nicky Blanda, Mikey
               (MORE)

He's got the money, and he's not giving it back: Scorsese with the prop cash from the Air France heist.

Scorsese with cinematographer Michael Ballhaus, an ingenious, fast shooter and a source of constant reassurance for the director.

Scorsese on the set with
his father, Charles Scorsese.

Scorsese confers with Robert De Niro.

De Niro: "Marty just had a shot, and then he explained what he wanted to do, and that's pretty much what it was, you know, he's gonna come in slow, and...that's it."

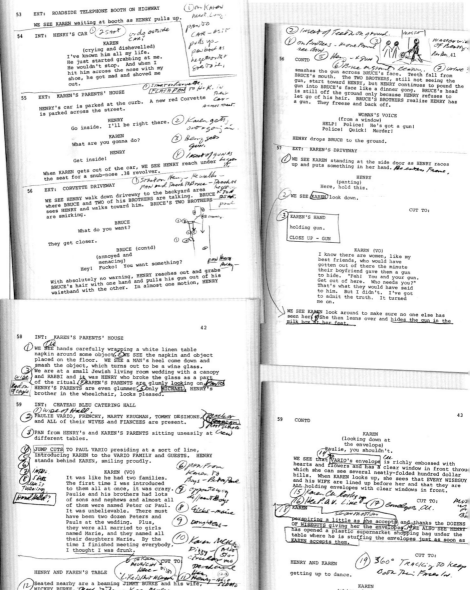

From Scorsese's annotated script, the complexities of the wedding scene and more.

Photo credit: Martin Scorsese Collection, NY

Scorsese with first assistant
director Joseph Reidy, shooting
the wedding scene.

Scorsese's handwritten song suggestions, including one that fell by the wayside, Billy Joel's "Only the Good Die Young."

Photo credit: Martin Scorsese Collection, NY

Karen's mother's garage. "Oh God, I can see it," Karen says of the chopper. The car swerves and into the sound of the skid, it seems, we get a segue into the Rolling Stones' feral "Monkey Man." Hiding guns in your mother-in-law's trash can until you can sell them: hardly the move of a *master* criminal.

Their goal accomplished, the couple look up at the blue sky. The movie has up until now mostly been set in the night, the early morning, or indoors. It's unusual to see Henry in broad daylight. And right now this daylight does not illuminate a helicopter. In a frame full of blue with a couple of fluffy clouds dotting it, Muddy Waters sings, "Everything gon' be all right this morning." Henry says, "Let's go shopping," and the song changes again, to George Harrison's catchy, grandiose "What Is Life."

But Henry is seesawing. At a strip mall, the camera fast-dollies to him on a pay phone saying, "I'm not nuts." At a motel, Karen says to one of the unctuous Pittsburgh guys, "I need a hit," and the unctuous Pittsburgh guy asks her if she wants to see helicopters. Who should call during the guns-and-drugs exchange but Henry's cocaine-mixing girlfriend, Sandy. Following that, Henry makes a call to drug mule *cum* babysitter Lois.

When her airline tickets are freeze-framed during the call, the airline logo is blacked out, in the manner of old tabloid photos of "anonymous" subjects. It's a mildly startling effect, done because of a practical problem. The production did not get clearance from American Airlines (which one can guess as the airline given the colors red, white, and blue on the papers) to use their logo. Given the purpose of Lois' air travel, the airline might not have extended permission, anyway. David Leonard of the movie's editorial department recalls Scorsese making a snap decision: "Just put a black bar over it. We're making a documentary here."

Henry's detailed instructions to Lois and Michael continue

after he and Karen arrive at the house. They include: "Don't let Karen touch the sauce!" He kisses his brother on the top of the head before going out again.

At Sandy's place, a line of cocaine goes up Henry's nostril and his head reels back. The camera follows and then recedes, showing his face in full close-up, wide eyes and red inflammation around the lower part of his nose. Muddy Waters' "Mannish Boy" starts up again.

Scorsese told Christie and Thompson: "I wanted to create for the audience—people who have never been under the influence of anything like cocaine or amphetamines—the state of anxiety and the way the mind races when on drugs. So when Henry takes a hit of coke, the camera comes flying into his eyes and he doesn't know where he is for a split second. It's impossible for Henry to recognize what's important and what's not."

Here Scorsese was drawing on very painful, and eventually life-threatening, experience. The director's public persona around the time of *Taxi Driver* was that of a fast-talking, manic ball of cineaste energy, and many still presume that he was doing cocaine in this period. Scorsese, however, says his use of the drug began around the period of *New York, New York* and *The Last Waltz*. In *The Andy Warhol Diaries*, Warhol recounts a summer 1977 meeting with Julia Cameron, the future creativity guru who at the time was married to Scorsese (and from whom Warhol got Valerie Solanas vibes—Solanas being the woman who shot Warhol in 1968) at which she told him, "Marty has coke problems and he's got blood poisoning and now he takes medicine to clean himself out." Warhol's diaries also include another lurid tale involving Scorsese and Liza Minnelli recounted to him by the fashion designer Halston. Scorsese himself rarely if ever discusses Cameron or Minnelli in interviews.

Scorsese himself wrote about his problems in *Projections*, a film journal edited by director John Boorman and Walter Donahue.

The dependence arose out of a deep despair. Looking at *The Last Waltz*, the concert film he made with the Band as he was wrapping *New York, New York*, he says, "I knew it was probably the best film I had made up to that point—I thought—and I still wasn't happy. Not that you have to be happy every minute of your life, but there was no sense of creative satisfaction. And then I knew I was in trouble because there was a void, there was nothing anymore. So I took more drugs. And finally I collapsed."

In this period he met actor Isabella Rossellini (also a daughter of a director Scorsese revered, Roberto Rossellini; her mother was screen icon Ingrid Bergman, of *The Bells of St. Mary's* and *Notorious* among other pictures); although they would marry in 1979, in the timeline of this essay, with the collapse occurring in late 1978, Scorsese admits "it was too late." The collapse happened at the Telluride Film Festival (the high altitude there likely did not help matters physically): "I remember [...] not being able to sit through a wonderful Wim Wenders film. Wim was there, and I had to tell him; I had to get up and leave because I couldn't stay in the room, I couldn't function, I didn't know what was happening to me. Basically, I was dying; I was bleeding internally all over and I didn't know it. My eyes were bleeding, my hands, everything except my brain and my liver. I was coughing up blood, there was blood all over the place. It was Labor Day weekend of 1978 [...] I made it back to New York; they put me in bed, and the next thing I knew I was in the emergency ward at New York Hospital. The doctors took care of me for ten days.

"I stopped taking drugs. During that period I remember talking with Robbie Robertson. He got up and went to the bathroom a few times, and I said to him, 'You don't need to go to the bathroom, you can take drugs in front of me.' And Robbie said, 'Marty, I'm not taking drugs. I don't want any. Why should you want me to take them? You did them all! You did every one of them.' I said, 'I know, I know.' He was exaggerating, but it was such a waste of time and energy."

At Sandy's, Henry is relieved, and riding high on a wave of artificial energy. Against all odds, he's completed his to-do list. One thing not on it was staying any longer than he had to with Sandy on the drug preparation, which inspires some fresh indignation on her part: "You think you can come over here and fuck me and leave?" Henry sweet-talks her and practically goads her: "Do you believe me? Do you believe me?" Then he jumps back and goes out the door with a wicked laugh.

Was dinner delicious? The camera cranes out from a close-up of a serving dish containing a still-substantial portion of ziti and meat and it looks pretty good. But poor Henry looks exhausted.

MAY 11: MY LUCKY HAT

We had seen the drug mule Lois in a previous scene, introduced by Henry thusly: "I had everybody working for me. Even our old babysitter, Lois Byrd." Our first look at Lois is an hour and a half into the movie, in a POV shot from the perspective of a baby. Henry and Karen are cooing at the baby with apparent sincerity; Lois, wearing a beige bucket hat, and looking like she could be the salty cousin of a character played by Lisa Gerritsen on a '70s sitcom, has a more cynical bearing that's immediately evident. She is not a happy worker. "I hate Pittsburgh," she sniffs to Henry. "Where did you find such creeps?" While no couple are heroes to their babysitter, Lois finds Henry's business associates creepier than Henry himself.

The baby is a prop that Lois brings on a plane with her to escape detection by airport security as she shuttles drugs and money between Long Island and Pittsburgh. This is well before the age of the enhanced TSA. (Detection dogs for drugs came into use in the US in the early '70s, but weren't ubiquitous and largely were not, to speak to our immediate point, directed at white women who were carrying infants.) The Hills and Lois are amused by their ruse. "Is this the same baby you used last week?" asks Karen. "No, that was my sister's. This one's Deirdre's," says Lois.

Lois' attachment to the aforementioned beige floppy hat will lead to Henry being arrested several minutes, at least, earlier than he might have been. In the May 11, 1980, scene, Henry decries Lois' sloppiness. He's arranging to send her off on a deal on the same day as he's making the epic dinner for his brother Michael. Lois is at the Hills' home.

Henry calls her from the motel where he and Karen meet his "Pittsburgh guys." Back at the Hill house, Lois eye-rolls almost before she's got the receiver fully to her face.

"Tell Michael not to let the sauce stick," he insists. "I'm stirring it," Michael insists back. "Jesus, you must think I'm dumb," Lois says after Henry tells her to call Atlanta from an outside line. On hanging up, he says, "Un-fucking-believable. All of them. Every fucking girl in my life." It's one of the last really funny lines in the movie.

"So what does she do after she hangs up on me? After everything I told her, after all her yeah yeah yeah bullshit? She picks up the phone and calls from the house." During these shots is where occurs the docudrama visual—the blacked-out airline logo on the ticket Lois holds with one hand (a lit joint is in the other).

Once Henry returns home he gets the dinner back in order as Lois sits at the kitchen table, paging through an issue of the black-and-white Marvel "adult" comic *Tales of the Zombie* (these comics were printed in a magazine format and not subject to Comics Code oversight/censorship due to that distinction from smaller-size books). After dinner, it's almost airport time...and

Lois announces, "I gotta go home." Henry protests that they don't have time to drive to Rockaway; they need to tape the drug packages to Lois' legs (one presumes it's Karen doing the manual labor here) and that takes a bit. Lois is not moved: "I need it. I gotta have it. It's my lucky hat. I never fly without it."

There are no bit players in *Goodfellas*, just as there are no bit players in *Casablanca*. In both pictures everyone with a speaking role has a little something extra. As Lois, Welker White is particularly vivid. It's also, one supposes, because it's she who puts Henry in the driver's seat right before he has a gun pointed to his head.

"I went in to read for Ellen Lewis," White recalls, "who's remained a good friend since. I think it was the first movie of Marty's that she cast, and she's cast for him ever since. And Marty was there! Those were the days. Today, when you audition for anything, you just go on tape and you never meet anybody. In the late '80s you met with the director, you sat down with him, you said hello, and you talked first, and you got to know each other a little bit. My recollection of my state is that I was so young, and not afraid of anything."

White, who'd trained for the stage, auditioned specifically for Lois and had gotten her scenes in the script. Her read on the character lined up with what Scorsese was looking for, particularly in the May 11 scene. "He said to Ellen, 'Yeah, Lois is kinda stoned—everybody else is like all wired up, and she's kinda the other way.' And that was sort of my take on it, was that she's, like, a pothead."

The actor also saw the power Lois had over Henry. "She didn't really care what happened to these people, she wasn't invested one way or the other, and she felt some power from them, in being this important cog in their trafficking business. And that there was something titillating about that."

The house that was used for the Hills' residence was in Fort

Lee, New Jersey. "And the kitchen was very, very small," White says. "We were all kind of cramped in. You might know that, famously, Catherine Scorsese made the sauce" that Henry had such concern about. "It really did smell great, but we didn't eat it because it had to be there, visible in the various parts of the scene, which took several days to shoot."

The components of the interactions, White recalls, were detailed and specific. She was given free rein to add little details to her characterization—the comic book was one she picked out. "I searched for weeks for the right comic book, I went to all these comic book stores all throughout the city, you know, back when they were all over the place, and I rifled through them, and I came upon that one." While the scene is set in 1980, the *Tales of the Zombie* issue was published in 1973. "I brought it, and Marty loved it, he said, 'Oh, that's perfect, that's so exciting.'" White says she's still got the comic in her basement.

"Kevin Corrigan was wonderful, all the actors were wonderful, very generous. The interactions between my character and Henry's include that key phone call, and Marty and Ray made sure that we could have Ray on the other end of the phone for the shooting of that. Which is not so common. And this was one of my first films, and I had no idea that that's uncommon until I worked for thirty more years and discovered how little that's accommodated."

White has worked for Scorsese twice since, after a long interim: she plays a waitress in *The Wolf of Wall Street* and Jimmy Hoffa's wife in *The Irishman*. "Yes, thirty years later I'm working on *The Irishman* with Marty, and again, there is at least one key scene with a phone call." If you've seen *The Irishman* you know the scene to which White refers; to call it "key" is almost an understatement. "It's funny to come back to it, but I remember that phone call very vividly, because they put him in his location. The level of detail that Marty's fostering, and supporting and asking everybody to contribute to. I didn't learn until much later that that's—that's…somewhat rare. My memory is that it was in a highly detailed environment, a highly specific environment, that allowed all of us to really just kind of play, and that was a very exciting experience."

When Lois and Henry go outside and get into the car, Henry is confronted by the local narcs, led by a cop played by Bo Dietl, the real-life detective who had auditioned for the role of Edward McDonald, which McDonald ultimately ended up playing himself. Dietl screams at a volume just a notch or two up from what he once whipped out as a Fox News commentator. (A couple of years back I was having breakfast with a friend at New York's very upscale Four Seasons Hotel, and coincidentally, Dietl was seated at a nearby table; I was almost shocked to discover that he has an actual, quiet "inside voice.") The staging and filming of the arrest was engrossing to White. "I come from a theater training background. I'd shot on sets, but I hadn't really shot on a location like that before. To be in the car, and to have the whole thing unfold as if it was really happening—which sounds so obvious on the face of it, but until you experience that as an actor…it's really incredible, because it's infused with the realness of the thing." The realness only extends so far—the gun Dietl points at Liotta's head is a prop, after all. But it's enough like the real thing that it can register as such, especially in the kind of charged moment White speaks of.

"Your head starts to spin," White says, "because you kind of don't know what you're meant to do. Because you spent all this time training how to manufacture the experience, right? And all of a sudden it's just seeming to actually happen in real time! There's really a car here, and I'm really sitting in a seat, and this guy is really here, and he's really holding a gun, and there is no audience, there's no one I have to get this to, there's a windshield and there's nobody beyond the windshield. And I do remember having my head kind of explode with excitement about working in that form, about really just being with those two other people, and allowing the experience to come through me."

White's experience in acting for films has given her a profound appreciation for how that kind of work differs from stage performing. "I now do an MFA course in screen acting; my husband"—Damian Young, a wonderful actor who got started working with the independent director Hal Hartley—"and I developed a program that we take all over the world. We start with teaching actors the grammar language of film. We'll screen movies and we take out all dialogue; we work with no dialogue, and then we start to teach the actors what camera coverage is and why the frame and the image moves, why the camera tells the story the way it does, and how the performer can use that knowledge and awareness to craft a performance that specifically addresses the camera."

The entirety of the May 11 scene took several days to shoot. Joseph Reidy remembers: "The interior of that house, that—the kitchen and all that, was several hours. The driving was done on a different day. The shots of the helicopter itself and that kind of stuff was second unit, which I did; that is, I directed the second unit. That didn't take a day to shoot, it took a couple of days. I think between the driving and all that it was several days, but even so, those scenes were not the only thing done during that time. We didn't stop everything else and shoot those scenes continually."

THE MUSIC STOPS

The film's final fifteen minutes constitute a grinding downshift. They encompass twelve individual scenes, and it's not quite so schematic that each one is a little longer and a little slower than the last, but it's close. No more pop songs—not even from a jukebox in the diner where Henry has his final sit-down with Jimmy. Only one freeze-frame. And a gradual descent into a new reality. *Goodfellas* deliberately becomes a relatively pedestrian film, the better to pull off two stunning pieces of formal gymnastics at the very end.

At the station house, Bo Dietl's obnoxious arresting officer continues to needle Henry, calling him a fuckhead. A former New York City detective and another Rao's regular, Dietl went on to play himself, from the period when he was a detective in private practice (which he still advertises himself as being), in *The Wolf of Wall Street*. And there he is funny and uninhibited about portraying himself as a sleazeball, more or less. In *The Irishman* he is very funny as an AFL/CIO crony who instructs Robert De Niro's Frank Sheeran how to surreptitiously imbibe alcohol in the presence of the teetotaling Jimmy Hoffa (Al Pacino). The secret is to pour a bottle of vodka into a hollowed-out watermelon, a fruit Hoffa also abjures. Again, the performance works.

No one else in the station house affords Henry any respect, either. Lois is paraded by him in cuffs, and she sticks her tongue out at him. Sandy is hustled in, petulant as usual. Another detective samples the white powder caked to one of the strainers found in Sandy's apartment, and nods with a smirk, the camera closing in on his face. "Bye bye, dickhead," Dietl's cop taunts.

Stuck in jail for a bit, Henry has been doing the math. "Don't make a jerk of me," Paulie had said to him earlier. Now he's gone and done just that. In the wake of Tommy's fate, Henry's got an even clearer picture of what happens to people who make a jerk out of Paulie. His reaction when Karen tells him, "I spoke to Jimmy," is rightfully panicky. As he leaves the jail—his mother-in-law has put up her house to get cash for his bail—Henry in voice-over sketches out scenarios. "Paulie would whack Jimmy before he would whack me," he calculates matter-of-factly. "This is the bad time."

It gets worse when Henry is home and discovers Karen has flushed all the cocaine. Despite being busted seven ways to Sunday on a narcotics charge (albeit a local, not a federal, one), Henry had planned to raise cash by selling the rest of the drugs he had in stock. Karen had considered them insufficiently hidden, and so disposed of them (in the montage prior, featuring the starkly memorable shot of her stashing a revolver in her panties). Here Henry once again comes close to hitting Karen, and they scream at each other and collapse into hopelessness, Henry half sleeping with a gun in his hand.

Henry then visits Paulie at what looks like a small restaurant where Paulie is cooking sausages. Here is a more or less standard two-minute scene of reversed medium close-ups and dialogue. It's still dynamic, because Scorsese and Ballhaus are constitutionally incapable of creating nondynamic shots. But the quality of the scene is in its culmination of a years-long association crumbling in betrayal, and it's carried by the acting. "I'm really sorry" is the best Henry has to offer Paulie. Paulie's silences add to his enigma. Is there a way he didn't know this was going on, or that he genuinely expected that it wouldn't? It ultimately doesn't matter, because he's still in charge. He hands Henry a wad of cash and says, "Now I gotta turn my back." Paulie meant it when he told Henry, "I don't need that."

Henry is bitter nevertheless. "Thirty-two hundred bucks for a lifetime." What did he expect? Besides a bullet in the back of his head.

Back at home Henry and Karen continue their "We're dead/ You're paranoid" dispute. This will be resolved when Karen goes to meet Jimmy in Brooklyn. In a small warehouse, holding a clipboard and wearing tortoiseshell glasses, Jimmy looks like a bland manager type. He needles Karen with questions and demands ("Tell him he's gotta call me, okay?"), gives her some cash, and then directs her up the street; there's a storefront where he's got some "beautiful Dior dresses," she should go pick some out. Moving down the street (Scorsese and Schoonmaker toggle between two tracking shots, one focused on Karen, the other on the buildings she's looking at, resolving with a slow-motion shot of Karen looking back at Jimmy), Jimmy directing her from behind, she arrives at a storefront. There's a shot of Jimmy himself looking behind, down the street. Inside, two men, shadowed so their features are not visible, speak, one's moving a crate; seeing Karen in the doorway, they stop what they're doing and wait. Panicked, she backs off, over to her car, and drives away.

I still encounter people who ask peculiar questions about this scene. "What are those two silhouetted men doing in there? Are they supposed to kill Karen?" Well, I doubt they're supposed to make her a flat white. But what about the illogic of Jimmy having Karen killed before killing Henry? Why would Jimmy kill Karen *now*? As if Jimmy has only ever acted logically. The fact that the cops haven't yet caught up with his murders does not mean he's a mastermind of homicide. And it is peculiar that people are so invested in the competence of these fact-based but nevertheless fictional criminals.

In any event: yes, it is highly likely that those men would have killed Karen had she entered the storefront. As Karen rushes away yelling to Jimmy that her mom's watching the kids and she doesn't want to keep her waiting, the camera rises to show the cross-signs of the streets: Smith and Ninth, Brooklyn, the southern edge of the Italian American neighborhood Carroll Gardens, near the area now referred to as Gowanus because of its proximity to the ecologically messy Gowanus Canal. There used to be a bar on Court Street, which runs parallel to Smith, a few blocks north of Ninth, where whenever someone would bring up *Goodfellas,* one of the regulars would say, "Hey, you know Billy Batts used to live around the block." It was only in March of 2019 that Carmine Persico, the mob boss whose territory included Carroll Gardens, died at age eighty-five after having spent much of his adult life in prison. Carroll Gardens is a pleasant neighborhood. Don't move here, please.

"If you're part of a crew"—Liotta's pause here is exquisite—"nobody ever tells you that they're going to kill you." Another diner, a tracking shot in the counter area moves toward a booth in the back where Jimmy sits, his nervous enquiring head visible through a window in the right part of the frame. "There weren't any arguments or curses like in the movies," Hill continues. The voice-over is perfectly synchronized, emotionally, to the camera movement that ends on Jimmy, getting up to give Henry a hug. Your murderers "come with smiles, they come as your friends. The people who have cared for you all of your life." The steer into Jimmy comes on the words "a time when you're at your weakest and most in need of their help." The reverse shot of Henry in the hug shows he still looks like hell, pale and hollow-cheeked and coated in a thin veil of sweat.

Once Jimmy and Henry are seated, in a booth with a window facing outside, Scorsese and Ballhaus do a variation of the disorienting zoom/dolly combination that Alfred Hitchcock concocted to create a vertigo effect in guess which film. The camera dollies backward while the lens zooms forward, creating a visual tug-of-war within the shot, a move to get away that's countered by a force that insists there's no escape. Eventually the shot tightens in on the two as Jimmy prepares to offer Henry a job of the sort he'd never approached him for before. He puts on a different pair of glasses, wire-rimmed, to make his pitch. When he slides a piece of paper across the table, the close-up of Jimmy freezes, the only point in this sequence where the technique occurs. "Now he's asking me to go down to Florida and do a hit with Anthony. That's when I knew that I would never come back from Florida alive."

The cut now is to the same view of Henry and Jimmy seated, with the camera dollying back. No zoom-in this time. The camera is making an exit. The situation is what it is.

The cops in the movie's station house are such creepy obnoxious assholes that they might as well be criminals. By comparison, Edward McDonald, tall, buttoned-down, nicely dressed, and tough as nails in a laconic kind of way, is a law enforcement representative who doesn't gloat at Henry and Karen. He doesn't have to.

McDonald plays himself in the film. Although *Goodfellas* was shot almost ten years after McDonald got Hill and his family into witness protection, McDonald retained his youthful looks. He's also markedly more healthy-looking than his bedraggled charges.

In real life McDonald had been an assistant federal DA, assigned to the Lufthansa heist. So in a sense Hill was in his life before he ever met the criminal. He told Pileggi: "Hill's arrest was the first real break we'd had in the Lufthansa case in over a year. [...] Henry was one of the crew's only survivors, and he was finally caught in a position where he might be persuaded to talk. He was facing twenty-five years to life on the Nassau County narcotics conspiracy. His girlfriend and even his wife could also be tied into the drug conspiracy and life could be made very unpleasant for him. He knew this. [...] Henry was too vulnerable."

Henry also managed to inspire some peripheral indignation in McDonald, as has been mentioned earlier. In *Wiseguy*, Pileggi writes: "One day [...] while being asked about the Lufthansa robbery, Henry said he had been in Boston. It was the third or fourth time he had mentioned Boston, so McDonald finally asked what Henry was doing there. Henry answered matter-of-factly that he had been bribing Boston College basketball players in a point-shaving scheme at the time and had to keep everyone in line. 'I played for the Boston College freshman team,' said McDonald. 'I had been to a few of the games Henry had fixed. It was my school. I almost went across the table at him, but then I realized that to guys like Hill it was just a part of doing business. To Henry shaving points on college basketball wasn't even illegal. He had never even thought to mention it. I came to realize Henry didn't have too much school spirit. He had never rooted for anything outside of a point spread in his life.'"

McDonald got the role because he asked for it. "There was a researcher who came to my office, who was working also with props and set decoration, I think," he says. "She was looking at the photographs on my office wall and desk, asking, 'Can I take some pictures, can I take those photographs of your children? And can I take your diplomas and, you know, other things?' And I'm saying, 'Sure,' but I'm nervous about getting them back. She said, 'No, Nick Pileggi'll vouch for it, you don't worry, I'll give you a receipt.' And she was asking a lot of questions, as well. After a while, I said, 'Look, I'm doing all this shit for you, I'm sitting here for two hours with you, telling you all this stuff about the, you know, how things should look, so let me ask you, who's playing me in the movie? Because in the book, I have a bigger role.' And she mentioned the possibility of Brian Dennehy playing me. You know—big Irish guy.

"I said, 'Holy shit, that'll be great, Brian Dennehy's gonna play me in the movie!' But she said, 'We haven't really cast your part yet.' And I said, 'I'll do it.' As a joke. Or half joke. And then, Pileggi called me, like an hour and a half later, after she got back to the office, and said, 'Are you interested, and Marty is sort of intrigued with the idea of making a cinema vérité move, and having you play yourself,' and I say, 'Yeah!' So I went over and, you know, they gave me a script to look at. It was a day they were casting smaller roles, all of the waiters and background wiseguys, all doing their screen tests. And there were, like, you know, sixty wiseguys there, and guys who looked like wiseguys."

It was lucky for McDonald that he was three weeks into private law practice when that happened. Were he still working for the government at the time, he would have been enjoined from appearing in the movie.

For his audition, and on into the actual shooting, McDonald wasn't asked to read lines. While McDonald had experience performing, so to speak, for juries, this was a different kind of acting. It was his sudden access to sense memory of his actual early meetings with Henry and Karen that gave him the key.

"I had a vivid memory of my reaction to Karen, my exasperation with her when she tried to portray herself as an innocent who had just gotten swept up in her husband's misdeeds. We had wiretaps on the Hill home, and we had tapes where, in conversation after conversation, she's talking about cocaine and the deals. There was plenty to charge her on. So I remembered saying to her not to give me a babe in the woods routine. And I pulled that back up."

McDonald makes clear not merely that he is trying to help the Hills, but that he is their only source of salvation, their only deliverance from certain mob death. He does this with equanimity but also a barely concealed contempt, making clear that he doesn't care about Henry or Karen's comfort as such; he is only interested in playing Pygmalion with them and their circumstances to the extent that it will make them valuable witnesses for the feds.

"In playing out the scene with Ray and Lorraine, it did click with me: 'I'm listening to the same bullshit that I heard from her then.' And that was my genuine attitude at the time: 'I don't give a shit whether you go or not, you think I care about you?' With the Rockefeller drug laws at the time Karen could have been facing two lifetime sentences. And they're bothering me about wanting to live someplace warm? I didn't have a whole lot of patience to deal with that crap. What else is he going to do? Go to jail? He's gonna get killed in jail."

In the years ahead, McDonald would befriend the entire Hill family. At the end of his life, in fact, Hill told McDonald that Ed was, when it came down to it, his closest friend. It's likely that Hill made that statement to more than one person. But not too many more.

On the set McDonald got as good as he gave, if not better, from Lorraine Bracco. "She was really hostile. Which was confusing for me at the time, because we had had a couple of phone conversations prior to doing the scene in which she was so nice to me. We had spoken once while I was at my mother-in-law's house in Boston, and my mother-in-law was so excited that a movie actress was calling! And then we are on the set and she's giving me this death-ray stare, even between takes. After the scene wrapped, she put her arms around me and kissed me. She just needed to keep being in that mode to maintain her consistency."

McDonald had a slight impact on the movie's mise-en-scène. In the scene, the Hills sit on a couch opposite McDonald; on Karen's end of the couch there's a small table, on which is a photograph of McDonald's children, one of the office pictures borrowed for the movie.

"Before we started, Lorraine put a coffee cup right in front of the picture, and I'm sitting across from her, and I get up, and I say a little something about my bad back, I'm stretching, you know, and I sort of walk around to the coffee table, and I get her coffee cup and I put it around behind the picture, and Lorraine's in her hostile mode, total hatred, so she's like, 'What the fuck?'"

The film's director understood exactly what was happening.

"Scorsese emerges from out of nowhere, and says, 'Lorraine, Ed doesn't want to deprive his children of their immortality!' And here it is. Thirty years later. And they're still there. When they were in college, they told everybody in college, 'Hey, I was in *Goodfellas.*' Their classmates would say, 'Get the fuck out of here,' they're watching it in the dorm, and they point out that picture. They had a lot of fun with it growing up."

At this point in *Goodfellas* the pace has slowed to the extent that McDonald's terse laying out of witness protection protocol does play like a conventional procedural or investigative journalism drama, the two-minute expository scene of shot, reverse shot, and so on. Cutaways to Jimmy and Paulie being led, in handcuffs, by cops, provide jolts: these are the people who will kill Henry if they are able.

So Henry testifies. McDonald is doing the questioning in the courtroom, a genuine one on New York's Centre Street. McDonald remembers being the fly in the ointment there— he kept referring to Paul Vario and Jimmy Burke rather than Paul Cicero and Jimmy Conway and hence fluffing a couple of takes. He also remembers De Niro as cold and distant—saving up his death-ray stare for Liotta as Henry Hill sings on his two former friends. Various crew members had asked him whether everything looked right, and he said yes, except the actor appearing as the judge was way too young. Scorsese put that actor in a different place—standing outside the courtroom door— and shut things down for a considerable period searching for an older African American actor to don the judge's robes. One was found among the courtroom's janitorial staff.

And here the film breaks out of the staid mode it has deliberately settled into. In voice-over Henry once more extols the lifestyle virtues of being a wiseguy while one of the attorneys for Conway and Vario drones, "People call them rats because a rat will do anything to survive, isn't that right, Mr. Hill." And soon, instead of speaking back to a lawyer, instead of looking at Paulie and Jimmy, Henry is looking at the camera and speaking to us. Addressing his gambling losses and how he would make up for them, he says, "It didn't matter. It didn't mean anything. When I was broke I would go out and rob some more." He practically leaps out of the witness box and strides to the camera, which backs up to make way for him as he walks down the center aisle of the courtroom. "We ran everything. We paid off cops. We paid off lawyers"—he's ticking them off on is fingers now—"we paid off judges. Everybody had their hand out. Everything was for the taking." He stops, and the camera that had been backing away approaches, with a little tentativeness, for a nicely framed medium close-up.

"And now it's all over."

Henry continues, after the cut to a tractor digging up dirt in a suburban housing development. A pan and dissolve resolves on Henry's bland front stoop—a station wagon is parked outside the garage—and a bathrobe-wearing Henry comes out the front door to get the paper. Here is the famous bit about his inability to get "decent food" out in the sticks: "Right after I got here I ordered some spaghetti with marinara sauce and I got egg noodles with ketchup." This is the third iteration of a joke that Nora Ephron used twice before, once in *Cookie*, with Peter Falk's mob boss complaining about his inability to get good eggplant in prison, and again in *My Blue Heaven*, with Steve Martin's witness protection fish out of water bemoaning the lack of arugula in his California supermarket. Here the cri de coeur returns to its originator, the gourmand Henry Hill. The camera pans up and Liotta gives a little "what are you looking at" glare, but then smiles faintly. "I get to live the rest of my life like a schnook."

Cut to Pesci, in a costume he hasn't worn in any other scene in the movie. Shiny gray jacket, white black-dotted tie, black shirt, well-blocked fedora. (In a truck hijacking scene earlier in the movie, his hat was floppier, his jacket blue.) He lowers a hand in which he holds a gun, and shoots at the camera six times as the music fades in.

This nightmare vision is a nod to *The Great Train Robbery*, a short Western made in 1904. There's nothing inordinately modern or postmodern about most of it: criminals take out a telegraph office, rob a train, make a getaway, are chased. But the last shot! Gilbert Adair breaks it down in his 1995 book *Flickers*: "Most amazingly, it concludes with a point-of-view shot worthy of Hitchcock (who actually reemployed it in *Spellbound*) and of Sam Peckinpah (who would employ it yet again in one of the very best and most complex Westerns of recent years, *Bring Me the Head of Alfredo Garcia*)—a shot in which an outlaw draws a bead on the camera itself and fires point-blank at the spectator. [...] That, truly, is a first for *The Great Train Robbery*. For it was the first filmic narrative to establish what was to be the enduring link between the cinema (not only the Hollywood cinema) and the gun."

This link, Adair eventually concludes, is "the blessing—as also the curse—of the American cinema."

"MY WAY"

Henry turns around and walks back in the door. The song on the soundtrack is "My Way," but not the Sinatra version. It's a cover done in electric-guitar-drenched punk-rock style by a group still named the Sex Pistols, but missing its once-central figure, snarling front man Johnny Rotten, nee John Lydon. The singer is instead the group's ostensible bass player, Sid Vicious. (Lydon had left the band in early 1978, at the end of a calamitous US tour; the remaining members hobbled on for some months after.) Sinatra sings, "Regrets, I've had a few," in a pensive, reflective style; Vicious contemptuously drawls the words out, exaggerating his prole British accent. One may not immediately put this together as the depraved, Dorian Gray mirror image of the Tony Bennett and big band number with which the film opened, but there it is. Some on-screen texts wrap up the loose ends. The first: "Henry Hill is still in the witness protection program. In 1987 he was arrested in Seattle, Washington, for narcotics conspiracy and he received five years probation. Since 1987 he has been clean." (Several arguable inaccuracies here. According to Gregg Hill his father gave up witness protection in 1984.) The second: "In 1989, Henry and Karen Hill separated after twenty-five years of marriage." The third: "Paul Cicero died in 1988 in Fort Worth federal prison of respiratory illness. He was seventy-three." The fourth: "Jimmy Conway is currently serving a twenty-years-to-life sentence for murder in a New York State prison. He will not be eligible for parole until 2004 when he will be seventy-eight years old." Then begin the end credits proper, starting with "Director of Photography MICHAEL BALLHAUS, ASC."

Five:

ALL THE SONGS

"For me, it's very, very serious," Scorsese said in a 2019 interview with the *New York Times*. "Probably the most enjoyable part of making movies is to select these songs."

As well-versed as Scorsese is in conventional film music—that is, the composed score, most frequently orchestral, that accompanies and heightens the on-screen action—the practice in his own films for which he is most cited is to score with songs, mostly pop and rock songs.

He's acknowledged that his primary influence in this respect is the Kenneth Anger underground movie *Scorpio Rising*. Anger's early-'60s-shot picture is an impressionistic, homoerotic, not infrequently threatening portrait of motorcycle gangs the filmmaker hung out with in Brooklyn. Over lovingly lingering shots of, say, a biker's dresser drawer and its various photos and emblems and totemic objects, montages of drunken revels, and interpolated clips from old silent pictures, Anger laid rock 'n' roll songs. Most pointedly, he intercut clips from the by-this-time cheesy Cecil

B. DeMille silent film *King of Kings* with shots of his bikers; in a particularly faux-sacrilegious segment, he accompanied views of H. B. Warner's Jesus leading his apostles with the Crystals' song "He's a Rebel." ("See the way he walks down the street/watch the way he shuffles his feet" and more of the lyrics have a markedly sarcastic if not deeply ironic resonance.) Later, as one of the biker parties turns explicitly S&M-ish, and one of the bikers is pantsed, the lugubrious Kris Jensen song "Torture" plays.

In Scorsese's 1967 short *The Big Shave*, a violent metaphor for not just the Vietnam War but what would become a near-compulsive theme for Scorsese's subsequent work, that of the man who cannot stop hurting himself, the accompaniment to the nameless protagonist's endless unintended self-laceration by safety razor is the 1937 recording of Bunny Berigan performing "I Can't Get Started."

Scorsese exercised the Anger influence more expansively in 1973's *Mean Streets*, *Goodfellas'* most explicit and significant precursor in the director's filmography. The story of four male friends in Little Italy in the early '70s, much of the action takes place in a bar owned by one of the group. It's a place where the jukebox is always on. The Rolling Stones' "Tell Me" plays as one of the bar's go-go dancers, Diane, puts Harvey Keitel's Charlie in a semitrance. "She is real good-looking," he muses in voice-over. (In this film the voice-over conveys this character's thoughts in the present moment, unlike *Goodfellas'* recollected storytelling. Sometimes Scorsese himself dubs in the character's inner voice.) "But she's black. I don't need to tell you that." The movie's Scorsese surrogate, Charlie is something of a coward. It's worth laying out his situation again here: he can't stand up to his uncle about the girlfriend he already has, Theresa. She has epilepsy, which Charlie's low-level gangster relative takes to mean she's "not right in the head," and Charlie keeps the relationship on the down-low to tamp down his kin's disapprobation. As for Diane, Charlie will make a date with her later on in the picture, and stand her up. In the meantime, he's got baby loan shark Michael all over him about the debts owed by De Niro's largely crazed Johnny Boy.

As the jukebox music continues—Derek and the Dominoes' "I Looked Away"—Charlie deals with this and that, and soon Johnny Boy himself makes an entrance, flanked by two young women; he entertains them by clownishly trying to check his pants at the bar's coat check. "Thanks a lot, Lord, for opening my eyes," says Scorsese as Charlie in voice-over, and then the Stones' 1967 hit single "Jumpin' Jack Flash" begins. As Johnny Boy strolls down the bar in slow motion, the music goes outside the diegesis. The volume goes up, and it's no longer a jukebox song, it's a soundtrack song. It leaps outside of its function as bar music and serves as a processional theme for Johnny Boy, whose arrogance—he's Jumpin' Jack Flash, he's a gas gas gas—makes him a ruler of this environment, at least in this moment, at least in his own mind. But the movie doesn't disagree, hence the song's new place in the sound mix. Once Johnny Boy lands, with his strange new girls, at the end of the bar where Charlie stands, the music comes down in the mix again.

George Lucas' *American Graffiti*, another 1973 picture from a director who would prove a galvanic force in American cinema, also has a pop-song soundtrack. Its main function is as a toe-tapping nostalgia-inducing accompaniment to a coming-of-age story set in the ostensibly halcyon days prior to the Kennedy assassination. It's a deftly assembled soundtrack of oldies that's largely attuned to the cutting rhythms and overall dynamics of the individual scenes (Del Shannon's speedy heartbreak song "Runaway" backs the first depiction of the kids with their fast cars cruising the main drag of the "turkey town" at least one of them can't wait to leave). The songs it uses to comment upon characters' states are sometimes on the nose in a way that's amusing rather than overtly groan-worthy: when Richard Dreyfus' character spies Suzanne Somers' "vision" in a white Thunderbird, "Why Do Fools Fall in Love" by Frankie Lymon and the Teenagers plays. But there's not much in the way of consistent, purposeful interweaving of music with the characters' states of mind.

While both acknowledged as classics today, neither *Mean Streets* nor *American Graffiti* were box-office blockbusters. But, along with 1969's *Easy Rider*, whose rock-song soundtrack did a lot of heavy lifting in the verisimilitude and mood-setting departments, they were influential to an extent that even took Scorsese aback. By the time he made the 1986 *The Color of Money* he viewed the song-soundtrack practice with skepticism. He told Christie and Thompson: "These days every damn movie in America, and I guess all around the world, is using recorded music like Jerry Lee Lewis, the Ronettes, and all these people I grew up with as nostalgic soundtracks. So, to go a different way, I said, 'Why don't we shape the movie first and then actually get the artists we like?' Touchstone made a deal with MCA, so that Robbie [Robertson] could talk to their artists like Don Henley and Eric Clapton. We told Eric Clapton that he could do an actual guitar solo for about one and a half minutes where there was no dialogue, when Carmen walks down the aisle with all these guys looking at her before Eddie tells her to leave. So when the song begins exactly at the beginning of the scene, it's no accident. I remember Eric's original lyric—'He's getting ready to use you'—was a little too on the nose, so Robbie and he conferred on the phone and they came up with 'It's in the way that you use it,' which is slightly to one side and much better. It felt like heaven because I was able to mix separate tracks as if I was playing the guitar myself." For all that, though, the most memorable musical moment in *The Color of Money* is when pool cue demon Tom Cruise mimes to Warren Zevon's 1977 song "Werewolves of London" while destroying an opponent.

Scorsese also remarked on how soundtrack scores were turning into a cottage industry that had advantages for neglected musicians: "Robert Palmer did a little song called 'My Baby's in Love with Another Guy,' recorded by Little Willie John, who only made about five singles and no album. His fifth record had not been a hit and this song, which we thought was just great, was the 'B' side. When the company finally found him in Brooklyn, his wife answered the phone and they said, 'This is Disney and we're going to give you $2,000 to use that song in a film.' She screamed, 'It's a miracle!' Then she woke up her husband to tell him."

In *Goodfellas* Scorsese moves freely between songs coming from jukeboxes and live performers and songs that are just in the air, so to speak. There's never a scene, as in *Mean Streets*, in which a song *explicitly* disconnects from an in-scene source and then goes back to functioning as background—the closest we get, in my estimation, is the much-cited use of Cream's "Sunshine of Your Love," playing as Jimmy muses on murdering Morrie. What Scorsese does in the mix, generally, is more subtle: songs playing in one scene will segue, or bleed, so to speak, into the next. He doesn't just do this with songs. After Henry and Karen's first time at the Copacabana, the film cuts to Tommy and Henry carrying out the Air France heist, and the soundtrack stays *in the club*, with comedian Henny Youngman continuing his litany of one-liners: "Dr. Wellser is here," et cetera. And then the song "Look in My Eyes," a dreamy girl-group number introduced by starlight-evoking strings, begins.

In the movie's early scenes, doo-wop alternates between popular ballads from the old country. The opening song, of course, is sung by Italian American Tony Bennett, born Anthony Dominick Benedetto in Queens, New York, in 1926. Bennett was nearly thirty and signed to Columbia Records when he recorded the song in 1953. The label's A&R (artists and repertoire) head at the time was Mitch Miller, who'd become famous as a performer of sorts with popular "Sing Along with Mitch" television appearances and LPs. In Bennett's autobiography, he speaks of Miller's proficiency at finding novelty tunes that turned into hits—"Come On-a My House" by Rosemary Clooney is cited— and Bennett's own preference for more mature material. He sought Clooney's counsel, and was advised by her that as far as Miller was concerned, it was best to go along and get along, and besides, he was usually right about the commercial potential of such tunes. Bennett continues: "Mitch and I came to an understanding. We were still doing four tunes per recording session at that time, so we worked out a deal. He picked two songs and I picked two songs. [...] I'm not saying that I was always right. I absolutely hated 'Rags to Riches' the first time I heard it in 1953. They really had to tie me down on that one." It doesn't show in Bennett's performance, which is full-throated, almost lusty, and embellished with playful trills. He lives up to the blare of the horn section in Percy Faith's arrangement. "I had another colossal hit and a gold record," Bennett writes. The song indeed went to number one on the Billboard charts and stayed there for eight weeks. "More importantly, I grew to like the song and enjoy singing it." The inclusion in *Goodfellas* is not its first use as a pop-culture reference; its opening line was frequently sung by an Italian American character on the '70s sitcom *Laverne and Shirley*, a creation of Bronx-born Garry Marshall, whose father's birth name was Masciarelli.

Lou Reed, a rock innovator whose guitar-driven music emphasized unusual, drone-enabling tunings and high volume, gave the induction speech for Frank Zappa's entry into the Rock and Roll Hall of Fame. Zappa, an occasional (and possibly even then reluctant) proponent of free improvisation, composed music for rock and orchestral instruments that was knotty to say the least. There's substantial evidence that the two men disliked each other personally, which made the Hall of Fame induction thing raise a few eyebrows. There is one thing, though, that the two iconoclastic musicians had in common: a love of doo-wop music. It can be argued that doo-wop is a great, unequivocal uniter of white men of a certain age and temperament. It is a mostly black form in which a song is performed in polyphonic harmony that emphasizes blue notes and embraces potential dissonance but is mostly intended to create a lush, romantic atmosphere.

The doo-wop accompanying young Henry's adventures is all East Coast stuff. The music was developed in the 1940s, inspired by black vocal groups such as the Ink Spots, on the East Coast. But California developed a strong doo-wop culture, including such groups as the Penguins, who made "Earth Angel." (And perhaps this is where the doo-wop affinities of lifelong New Yorker Reed and Angeleno Zappa diverged.)

"Can't We Be Sweethearts," by the Cleftones, is a bouncy number opening with, as was doo-wop custom, the bass voice going "bom bom." Infectious and a trifle generic, and only ironic when you're hearing it under Henry's father giving him the belt.

"Hearts made of stone/will never break," jauntily sung by Otis Williams and his group, the Charms, accompanies the unfortunate fate of Henry's neighborhood mailman. The Moonglows' "Sincerely" and "Speedo," by the Cadillacs, play in the wiseguy barbecue scene and the introduction of Jimmy to Henry, respectively. These songs have faded back into obscurity in the post-rock-'n'-roll era of popular music. Substantial hits in the '50s (and for some reason "Speedo" was sometimes cited by certain pop-culture historians as the first rock 'n' roll song, which it absolutely was not), they enjoyed a new vogue in the 1970s largely thanks to not so much *American Graffiti* (neither song appears in the film) but a whole 1950s nostalgia wave buttressed by *Happy Days*, a sitcom largely derived from *Graffiti* and starring its lead actor Ron Howard. (And created by Garry Marshall.)

The Italian songs in this section of the movie, "*Firenze sogna*" and "*Parlami d'amore Mariù*" are both sung by Giuseppe Di Stefano, a Sicilian-born tenor who was a major influence on Pavarotti and was as beloved for his pop renditions as his classical work. "*Parlami*" comes from a 1932 Italian film *Gli uomini, che mascalzoni* (*What Scoundrels Men Are*), in which it was sung by Vittorio De Sica, who would become a key director in the era of Italian Neorealism, a substantial influence on Scorsese's work. (Among his most distinguished films are *Bicycle Thieves*, *Umberto D*, and in the 1970s, *The Garden of the Finzi-Continis*.) The song had a long life after De Sica's performance (which is maybe the most difficult to hear today) and was covered, eventually, by Pavarotti.

The viewer's reintroduction to Henry as an adult, standing outside the Airline Diner with Tommy, looking cool while he waits to steal a truck, is scored to Billy Ward and His Dominoes' stately, impassioned doo-wop version of the Hoagie Carmichael standard "Stardust." Scorsese lops off the song's twenty-four-bar prelude (which takes over a minute to spin out) and begins with Ward's grandiose "SOME… TIMES… I WONDER" lead vocal, into the song proper. With the Dominoes oohing in the background and the piano bashing out high triplets, the effect combined with Henry's suavity is elevating to an extent that it can't be immediately undercut by the actions Henry and Tommy take next. Scorsese lets nostalgia have its way with us, or at least what *was* us, back in 1990. (Nick Tosches called the Dominoes "the

most brilliant, and the classiest, of the rock 'n' roll vocal groups";
while the writer was skeptical about making definitive assertions
about who did what first—as all good historians ought to be—he
admiringly describes, in his *Unsung Heroes of Rock 'n' Roll*, their
ribald 1951 "Sixty Minute Man" as "the first record by a black
rock 'n' roll group to become a pop hit.")

Several subsequent songs nestle comfortably in the atmosphere
of each scene, with small notes of ironic counterpoint. "*Il cielo in
una stanza*," an Italian pop hit for the singer Mina in 1960, plays
at the Bamboo Lounge; "Playboy," a 1962 girl-group number
by the Marvelettes, plays as Henry and Tommy shut down the
Bamboo Lounge. The song is a warning to women to stay away
from its title character; the minor joke is that Tommy's complaining to Henry about striking out with this "broad" he's been
trying to "bang." The Marvelettes were a Motown group; their
prior single "Please Mr. Postman" had been a big hit in 1961. (It
was covered by the Beatles early on.) This was a little bit before
Motown really began to dominate the pop charts.

"It's Not for Me to Say," a better-than-average pop ballad
raised to near-exquisite heights by Johnny Mathis, accompanies
the disastrous double date where Henry first meets Karen. When
Karen confronts Henry in front of his buddies, you may recognize the melody of the song playing from a jukebox: "I Will
Follow Him," by Little Peggy March, which had been used to
optimum Anger effect in *Scorpio Rising*. But this version has Italian lyrics. The recording is by Betty Curtis (an Italian singer in
spite of her Anglo-sounding stage name; she was born Roberta
Corti) under the song's original title, "Chariot." The composition was first an instrumental co-composed by Paul Mauriat,
the French musician who later in the '60s would have a huge
hit with his arrangement of "Love Is Blue."

"Chariot" proved infectious enough to gain lyrics in at least
two languages; "I Will Follow Him" is, true to its title, a pop

hymn to obeisance, while "Chariot" promises that after taking a ride on the title vehicle, *"tu vivrai con me/in un'isola fantastica,"* that is, "you'll live with me on a fantastic island."

"And Then He Kissed Me," a Phil Spector production sung by the Crystals, is the next foregrounded song in the picture, playing over the Copacabana Steadicam shot, its lyrics "I felt so happy I almost cried/and then he kissed me" strengthening the heady rush of Karen's entrance into the glamorous part of Henry's world, its own fantastic island.

While nobody mentions the assassination of John F. Kennedy in *Goodfellas*, viewers who lived through the period, or who have a sharp historical sense, will intuit the event's existence in the periphery of the film's narrative. The fact, say, that the New York airport is called "Idlewild" when Henry and Tommy begin to raid it over and over again. From that point on it is referred to as "the airport," although its name was changed to John F. Kennedy a mere month and two days after the thirty-fifth president was killed.

"Then He Kissed Me" was written by Spector with Jeff Barry and Ellie Greenwich, New York–based songwriters associated with the post–Tin Pan Alley songwriters clustered around Times Square's Brill Building. By the early '60s Spector himself had relocated to Los Angeles, and he recorded the song using his "wall of sound" technique. Working with arranger Jack Nitzsche, Spector filled his studio with large ensembles and doubled-up key instruments such as guitar and piano. Strings and choruses put things over the top. The sound was as far removed from Chuck Berry or Buddy Holly (unornamented guitar and piano with rhythm section chugging out riffs and melodies) to the extent that it was more "rock" than "rock 'n' roll," except it wasn't "rock," either. (The fact that most of the singers Spector used were African American did lend some R&B inflections to the songs.) It was pop, grandiose pop; "teenage symphonies,"

Spector called his singles. "Then He Kissed Me" was released in the summer of 1963 and peaked at #6 on the Billboard singles chart. If the Kennedy Administration was "Camelot," Spector's songs were regal entertainments for its children. So, the use of the song in this position, at this point in time, reflects that idealized state, as well.

After "Look in My Eyes" comes the treacly "Roses Are Red" (sung by Bobby Vinton, who, as Karen recalls, sends a bottle of champagne to her and Henry's Copa table; Vinton is doubled in the scene by his son, Bobby Vinton, Jr.), and with the apropos Harptones' doo-wop number "Life Is But a Dream" in the wedding scene, Scorsese then has some fun mixing the sounds of a revving motorcycle amid the profane prattle at the cosmetics party where Karen meets the wiseguy wives and girlfriends for the first time.

"The Leader of the Pack," a story-song again by Greenwich and Barry and the single's producer, in this case one George "Shadow" Morton, is voiced by the Shangri-Las, white teens from Queens who toggled between being a trio and a quartet; in either configuration, they adopted a tough-girl collective personae. Producer Morton had some affinities with Spector, but less grandiosity, less money, and a more pronounced New York sensibility. This song is right at home with these outer-borough gum-snappers Karen has been thrown in with.

The film comes back to Spector, after contributions from Al Jolson (singing "Toot Toot Tootsie" on the Hill TV set) and Dean Martin (the blithe, upbeat "Ain't That a Kick in the Head," giving song to Karen's voice-over apologia for her husband's way of "making a living"). Another Crystals song, "He's Sure the Boy I Love," opens the Billy Batts scene. It's now 1970; the song is almost but not quite what they'd start calling an "oldie but goodie." Kennedy's assassination coincided with the release of *A Christmas Gift to You from Phil Spector*, an album of guess what kind of songs, featuring the Crystals, Darlene Love, the Ronettes, and more, a terribly expensive labor of love that ended with a spoken-word message from Spector himself, in which he thanks his fans for allowing him to express his "feelings" about the Christmas season. The album, of course, flopped given the circumstances. The failure of the record was possibly the most morbid note in pop-culture history, at least until the soundtrack to Mariah Carey's movie debut *Glitter* came out on September 11, 2001. While Spector remained a rich man and successful producer, the Kennedy assassination certainly ended not just "Camelot" but, arguably, Spector's reign as a titan of teen. But his sounds still galvanized in certain corners, and Henry Hill's nightclub The Suite, where Billy Batts celebrates his release from prison, was one of those. The song's spoken introduction—"I always dreamed the boy I loved would come along/and he'd be tall and handsome, rich and strong/now that boy I love has come to me/but he sure ain't the way I thought he'd be"—sets up a sense of occasion and anticipation, and sure enough, we meet a wiseguy we have not seen or heard of before.

Who is subsequently stomped nearly to death while a more current pop hit, Donovan's "Atlantis," plays, again ostensibly from a jukebox. The song begins with strummed acoustic guitar while the singer/songwriter Donovan Leitch tells the story of the ancient/mythic continent of Atlantis and how awesome it was, what with all the components of our current civilization in attendance, but BETTER. "The antediluvian kings colonized the world/All the gods who play in the mythological drama/In all legends from all lands were from fair Atlantis…" the singer instructs us as a piano joins in and plays a pretty countermelody over the guitar chords.

"Knowing her fate"—that is, she's going to sink—"Atlantis sent out ships to all corners of the Earth/on board were the twelve/the poet, the physician, the farmer, the scientist, the magician/and the other so-called gods of our legends/though gods they were."

In the *GQ* oral history, Illeana Douglas recollects that Scorsese was particularly keen on getting "though gods they were" heard, as the whacking of Batts was the onset of this crew's Götterdämmerung. But more crucial to the scene is the portion of the song after the recitation, when it rocks out to the chanted refrain of "Way down/below the ocean/where I wanna be/she may be" sung by Donovan and backup singers with the lead man vamping and comping and keening in the bars between those words. "The repetition of the phrase 'Way down below the ocean where I want to be' [conveyed] the hypnotic nature of what they were doing, that they couldn't stop themselves," Scorsese told *GQ*. As will be the case with the Cream song later in the picture, it's a perfect juxtaposition, a thoroughly successful counterintuitive placement.

When Henry takes a mistress, he and the gang see Jerry Vale at the Copa. As a 2019 piece about Scorsese's use of Jerry Vale in *The Irishman* detailed, the singer looms large in the director's consciousness. Genaro Louis Vitaliano was a Bronx-born first-generation American, the child of Italian immigrants, only twelve years Scorsese's senior. But the singer was the biggest one in Scorsese's childhood. "Aside from Sinatra, Tony Bennett was the authority," Scorsese told the *New York Times*. "He had such an extraordinary range and was top of the line. And of course, Dean Martin and his coolness. But it was Jerry Vale who we listened to pretty much all the time." Of these men, only Dean Martin was not a Columbia recording artist in the '50s; Vale differed from labelmates Sinatra and Bennett in several respects. While Frank and Tony styled themselves as worldly saloon singers with sensitive sides, Vale was all sincerity, all heartbreak, and a lot of Italian songs. His tenor was both more "widescreen" and more lugubrious than his chief competition; his delivery was often so infused with heartbreak that it bordered on schmaltz. This is particularly evident on "Pretend You Don't See Her," the song that hypnotizes Henry, Janice, and even Tommy when Vale croons it at the Copa.

The style has an aspect that's *paisan*-like, as well. Scorsese said to the *Times*, "He sounded like as if my uncle sang, or the way my brother could sing. Of course Jerry is a hundred times better, but he felt like that person in the room who would break into song. It was like a family member in a way; that voice was so familiar and comforting."

That comfort descends like a blanket as the sun comes up outside Janice's apartment building. It's a unique moment in the film.

Another #6 on the Billboard charts, Bobby Darin's 1959 recording of the Charles Trenet song "*La mer*," transformed in English translation (by Jack Lawrence) to "Beyond the Sea," conveys the relative breeziness of Henry's prison life as his cellmates prepare a lavish dinner. (Preceding this are Aretha Franklin's "Baby I Love You," an entirely different song than the one made famous by Phil Spector's girl group the Ronettes, and "Remember (Walking in the Sand)," another near-hysterical minimelodrama from the Shangri-Las and Shadow Morton.) In 2002 the critic and historian Will Friedwald wrote at length about the song for *Vanity Fair* (the Darin song was and remains an especial favorite of the magazine's then editor-in-chief, Graydon Carter, with whom Scorsese would work on *Public Speaking*, a 2010 documentary about their friend the writer Fran Lebowitz).

"'Beyond the Sea' is one of the few works of world culture that have held entirely different meanings for different groups of people," Friedwald explained. "In France the song is known as '*La mer*,' and it is significantly different from the better-known 'Beyond the Sea.' In stark contrast to Darin's impudent version, '*La mer*' is, for the French, an ongoing source of Gallic pride—the best-known work by a beloved son of France, one of the country's most celebrated singer-songwriters, Charles Trenet. Far from background for lindy-hopping teenagers, '*La mer*' is generally performed with all the solemnity of a national anthem. In America, the song has become an anthem of another sort, a call to arms for retro swingers (such as the Royal Crown Revue) who may be conscious that, by summoning up the ghost of Darin, they are bringing together two generations and two genres—the Sinatra thing and the Elvis thang—but remain unaware that they're also uniting two countries and two cultures." The ostensible impudence is no doubt what made it ring for Hollywood music supervisors of this time—the song appears on the soundtracks of two other films in close release-date proximity to *Goodfellas*, the fish-out-of-water crime picture *Black Rain* and *The Adventures of Ford Fairlane*, a pastiche comedy starring the then-novelty "blue" standup Andrew "Dice" Clay.

Once Henry gets out of prison, the songs come at you almost nonstop, and they're always, always pointed, not just atmospheric. Tony Bennett returns with "Boulevard of Broken Dreams," a standard whose title may be taken as a foreshadowing despite its playing at the celebratory scene of Henry's welcome-home dinner (of sorts) at Paulie's house. "Boulevard" was one of the songs Bennett used for a demo tape for Columbia Records, and Bennett writes in his autobiography that Mitch Miller was sufficiently impressed by his singing that Miller signed Bennett to the label "sight unseen." It was Bennett's first single.

After Henry lies to Paulie's face about dealing drugs, the movie cuts to him at Sandy's place, where "Gimme Shelter," the apocalyptic leadoff track from the Rolling Stones' 1969 album *Let It Bleed*, blares. We whip-pan, aurally, again when Henry shows off his new respectable home with his actual wife, and Jack Jones sings his counsel to the ladies, reminding them that "wives should always be lovers, too/run to his arms the moment he comes home to you."

"Wives and Lovers" was written by Burt Bacharach and Hal David as a tie-in for the 1963 romantic comedy film of the same name, but isn't heard in that movie. (The songwriting duo did the same deal for the 1962 John Ford picture *The Man Who Shot Liberty Valance*.) The only reason that the "this was the crew that Jimmy put together" scene has no song is because said crew is in a bar watching a basketball game, which they've probably all got bets on.

After which we are back to the Stones with another *Let It Bleed* cut, "Monkey Man." Scorsese told Christie and Thompson, "Sometimes we put the lyrics of songs between lines of dialogue so they commented on the action; for example, when the baby is put in the pram for the drug smuggling, you hear the Rolling Stones' 'Monkey Man,' and the first lyric is 'I'm a flea-bit peanut monkey and all my friends are junkies.'"

Scorsese has been accused of overrelying on the Stones; as has been noted in the last chapter, "Gimme Shelter" is a song he frequently turns to. It does not register quite as strongly in *Goodfellas* as it does in *The Departed*. "Monkey Man," though, is a tune this movie gets the most of, in part because of what Scorsese says. The actors preparing the infant to be a distraction from cocaine trafficking are "adorable," fresh-faced as they wax smug about their masquerade. The line in "Monkey Man" that follows "all my friends are junkies" is "that's not really true." The song is a burlesque, singer/lyricist Mick Jagger taking his band's reputation for self-destructive behavior for a spin, having a laugh while trying to deflate some myths. But then again, founding member Brian Jones was fired from the band and then died, drowned in his own swimming pool.

In these scenes Henry talks about how his cocaine business is a very lucrative one; and for him and Lois and Karen and sometimes Sandy it's kind of fun, too. "I am just a monkey man/I hope you are a monkey woman, too." Here monkey Henry has three monkey women.

The Christmas party where Jimmy chastises his heist crew for imprudent spending gives us a double hit of Phil Spector's Christmas album; by this time the record has had a renaissance thanks in part to a rerelease by Apple Records, a label owned by the Beatles. (Who allied with Spector for a salvage job on the unsatisfactory 1968 *Let It Be* sessions; John Lennon and George Harrison had Spector produce their early solo albums, as well.) The songs are the Ronettes' "Frosty the Snowman" and "Christmas (Baby Please Come Home)" from Darlene Love, their good cheer providing seasonal indifference for Jimmy's burgeoning homicidal resentments.

The killing of Stacks is gruesome, and made more eerie by the strains of the Drifters' cover of "The Bells of St. Mary's." When Henry confronts Jimmy and Tommy about Stacks' whereabouts, the jukebox plays "Unchained Melody," another very-often-covered ballad. This version is by Vito and the Salutations, a white doo-wop group that had its not particularly distinguished heyday in the mid-'60s. Positioning these two songs back-to-back, Scorsese notes a distinction that might be lost on the lay viewer/listener. "Even the music becomes decadent. When Stacks gets killed and Henry comes running into the bar, Jimmy and Tommy tell him to drink up and not worry. What you hear at this moment is an incredible version of 'Unchained Melody' by Vito and the Salutations. It's degenerated from the pure Drifters of Clyde McPhatter singing 'The Bells of St. Mary's' to the Italian doo-wop of Vito and the Salutations," he told Christie and Thompson.

In the same section of Christie and Thompson's book, Scorsese elaborated on his philosophy of using songs in his films, and the rules he set for this one. "A lot of music is used in movies today just to establish a time and a place and I think this is lazy. Ever since *Who's That Knocking* and *Mean Streets* I wanted to take advantage of the emotional impact of the music. Some of it even comes from the '40s. The point is that a lot of places had jukeboxes which were still carrying Benny Goodman and the old Italian stuff when the Beatles came in. On *Goodfellas* the only rule was to use music which could only have been heard at that time. If a scene took place in 1973, I could use any music that was current or older."

"Sunshine of Your Love" was a critical tune for Cream. The British trio formed in 1966 and allegedly took its name from the phrase "cream of the crop." The guitarist Eric Clapton had become a sensation with the Stones-ish Yardbirds, but quit that group because he objected to its Top-of-the-Pops direction. His cachet increased with John Mayall's Bluesbreakers. His soloing had a fluid facility and expressiveness *and* a real grounding in American blues music. Bassist Jack Bruce was also a blues guy, albeit one with jazz and classical influences, while Ginger Baker had been for a time a pure jazz drummer, albeit a very busy and idiosyncratic one. Baker and Bruce had played together in the Graham Bond Organization, a quartet fronted by singer/organist Bond and featuring John McLaughlin, who would go on to play with Miles Davis and help invent electric jazz fusion, for better or worse (his Mahavishnu Orchestra was for a time a shining example of "better"). Cream went heavy on the blues jams, and their original songs leaned heavily on older licks ("Strange Brew" was derived from "Hey Lawdy Mama," by Chicago bluesmen Junior Wells and Buddy Guy). But swinging London and its lysergic experimentations demanded more "far out" material. Working with beatnik poet turned lyricist Pete Brown, Bruce, consciously or not, took up the challenge. Bruce biographer Harry Shapiro wrote of this song's composition: "After one particularly difficult night when nothing was happening, Jack started playing a riff of syncopated eighth notes all on the offbeats, almost in a fit of desperation. Pete was looking out the window at the time, and muttered: 'It's getting near dawn/When lights close their tired eyes.' Jack had composed 'Sunshine of Your Love,' one of the most recognizable rock riffs of all time." The origins of Baker's unique beat are in contention; Tom Dowd, the American recording engineer of *Disraeli Gears*, the album on which "Sunshine" appears, recalled giving the drummer a suggestion to "play as Indians in American Westerns did."

The song was not universally well-received. There was building hostility within the band and from their record label about Bruce's knotty, sometimes dissonant compositions. When Felix Pappalardi, the musician who produced *Gears*, played "Sunshine" and "Tales of Brave Ulysses" for Atlantic label executive Jerry Wexler, he dismissed both songs as "psychedelic hogwash." (Himself an admirer of Bruce's songs, Pappalardi would lead his own band, Mountain, in covering Bruce and Brown's "Theme from an Imaginary Western," a Cream reject that, in this version, yielded some of protean guitarist Leslie West's best soloing.) The single nevertheless stayed on the US charts for twenty-six weeks, peaking at #5. And it did become a jukebox classic, so there you have it.

The use of the piano coda from "Layla" over the discovery of Jimmy's murderous handiwork can be heard as the opening of a suite titled "Henry's End." An end not in death, but in a stopping of the music, a burial and rebirth as a schnook.

In her book, *Delta Lady*, Rita Coolidge writes that after she and Jim Gordon cowrote the piano chords and countermelody that would become the final portion of "Layla," she and Gordon played the song for Eric Clapton and left a demo cassette with him. This was in early 1970. *Layla and Other Assorted Love*

Songs was recorded from August until October of that year, and released in November. "I was infuriated," Coolidge writes. "What they'd clearly done was take the song Jim and I had written, and tacked it on to the end of Eric's song. It was almost the same arrangement."

Still. "I had to admit it sounded stunning." She sought ways to get songwriting credit, but was stifled at every turn. The song as she completed it was eventually recorded by Booker T. Jones (onetime bandleader of Booker T. and the MGs and an early vetter of "Sunshine of Your Love"—he and Otis Redding gave it more of a thumbs-up than Jack Bruce's bandmates did) and Coolidge's sister Priscilla on the 1973 album *Chronicles*.

Could it be possible that Gordon, in the fevered atmosphere of the *Layla* sessions, pulled the tune out of a back pocket, forgetting its origins? Coolidge does not think so, and there's no real evidence that this was the case. But Gordon was a volatile guy who at the time was suffering in a way that nobody around him fully understood. Gordon beat Coolidge one night on tour—"that's not something that should happen even once," she writes—and she recalls the "empty look" on his face before hitting her. "There was no light, it was pure darkness." Gordon, like everyone else at the time, was doing a lot of cocaine. Coolidge tried to put it down to that. "What nobody knew at the time about Jim, however, was that he was an undiagnosed paranoid schizophrenic, and the symptoms of his disease, probably exacerbated by the drugs he was taking, were becoming very hard to conceal. He was hearing voices. And gradually, he just went away—the golden boy with the twinkle in his eyes was gone. Five years later, those same voices that had likely told him he should hit me as hard as he could commanded him to enter his mother's house and bludgeon her with a hammer; when the hammer failed to kill her, he switched to a carving knife. He was convicted of murder and is serving a life sentence at a psychiatric prison in Vacaville, California. In 2013, his attorney's more recent request for parole was denied—in part because Jim resists taking his antipsychotic medication, according to the parole board's decision—and he won't be eligible again until 2018." As of this writing, Gordon is still in prison.

"If I sound bitter, I'm not," Coolidge writes. "'Layla' has generated hundreds of thousands in songwriting royalties—maybe millions—over the years for Eric. But I know that part of Jim's share actually went to his daughter, Amy. And that, finally, was how I was able to deal with it, just knowing she had something from her dad."

Gordon is the drummer on Harry Nilsson's "Jump into the Fire," the nervous rocker that kicks off the May 11 sequence. He is hence tied with Eric Clapton for the Most Frequently Heard Musician on the *Goodfellas* soundtrack. Gordon and Clapton both play on "Layla," of course; Clapton is on "Sunshine," Gordon is on "Jump," and they reunite on another song in this sequence, George Harrison's "What Is Life." The star player on "Jump," however, isn't Gordon but bassist Herbie Flowers. His appropriately jumpy bass line opens the song; by the end of the orgiastic rave-up he's detuned his instrument. That portion's not heard distinctly in the sections of the movie in which the song is used, but is arguably a spectral presence in Henry's fall.

The music is increasingly used in fragments here. Mick Jagger's indolent "Memo from Turner," here heard in its *Performance* soundtrack version, features a backing band with Ry Cooder on slide guitar and Randy Newman on piano (a version featuring some of the Stones, or possibly—and in fact more probably—members of Traffic, is on the Stones' compilation *Metamorphosis*). The standout aural feature in the seconds-long portion is the greasy slide guitar, signaling a kind of heedlessness. But Henry has to snap to attention when he almost slams into a car ahead of him. The Who's "Magic Bus," from *Live at Leeds*, yammers "I want it" over and over again, Henry slamming the brakes as drummer Keith Moon goes ballistic. A vision of clear blue sky occasions Muddy Waters' observation "everything gon' be all right this morning" from a recording of the classic "Mannish Boy" made with a band fronted by albino Texas blues-rock guitar phenom Johnny Winter, then, just like that, the song is jettisoned in favor of George Harrison's "What Is Life."

Clapton's on guitar, Gordon's on drums...and Phil Spector's producing. This is a variant on his "wall of sound" technique, this time using orchestral overdubs and pushing the rock band up front. There are also a lot of tambourines and the people playing them are highly energetic. It is, on examination, an absurd setting for a sincere declaration from the "quiet Beatle":

"Tell me what is my life/without your love/Tell me who am I/without you/by my side." But the fuzzy guitar hook, the momentum of the rhythm section, the lift of the chorus, make it irresistible, and it adds great momentum to the feeling of relief that comes to Henry and Karen when they don't see that chopper.

"All these years later," Harrison wrote in the liner notes for a 2000 remaster and rerelease of his album *All Things Must Pass*, from which this song derives (it was an international hit single, as well, peaking on Billboard's chart at #10), "I would like to liberate some of the songs from the big production that seemed appropriate at the time, but now seem a bit over the top with the reverb in the wall of sound." Later in these notes, he thanks, sort of, "the amazing Mr. Phil Spector, who produced so many fantastic records in the '60s. He helped me so much to get this record made. In his company I came to realize the true value of the Hare Krishna mantra. God bless you, Phil."

One of the ostensible benefits of chanting the Hare Krishna mantra is "peace of mind." Which Spector was not a purveyor of by this stage in his career. A substance-abusing and spouse-abusing gun nut, Spector was the subject of countless bad-behavior anecdotes from the 1970s well into this century. You've probably heard a few of them—like the time he held a gun to Leonard Cohen's head and told the poet and songwriter that he loved him, to which the mordant Cohen replied, "I hope you do." He killed the actress Lana Clarkson in 2003; now eighty, he will most likely die in prison. For a nondocumentary, this movie certainly does feature a large number of convicted criminals.

Waters' "Mannish Boy," featuring the appreciative whooping of Winters, plays out some more at Sandy's place, as Henry mixes the coke with her, then skedaddles. As if to close a parenthesis, the mini–drum solo from "Jump into the Fire" plays as Henry and Lois fight it out about the lucky hat, and walk out to the driveway to meet their captors.

What is there to say about Sid Vicious and the Sex Pistols' version of "My Way"? The song, like "Beyond the Sea," was composed and first recorded in France. *"Comme d'habitude,"* which sort of translates to "my way"—it's literally "as is my practice" or "as usual"—written by Jacques Revaux with lyrics by François and Gilles Thibault, was recorded by Claude François in 1968. It caught the ear, at different times and in different ways, of Paul Anka and David Bowie. In the late '60s Bowie, still trying to make it, was flirting with the idea of selling himself as a near-Continental pop chanteur, and tried to transform the melody into a song he called "Even a Fool Learns to Love." In the meantime, the Canadian-born Anka, after a dinner with Frank Sinatra during which the Chairman of the Board talked about quitting this rotten business, put himself in Sinatra's shoes and reworked the François rendition into the self-congratulatory ballad we all know, and many love. The frustrated Bowie went on to write "Life on Mars," which stealthily confounds some of the chordings of Revaux's tune.

Sinatra's song was a hit that became a kind of kitsch sacrament. The blithe sophistication, barely camouflaging a subtext of obsession and heartache, of Cole Porter; the understated devastation of an "Angel Eyes"; this is replaced in Sinatra's testament by macho preening. People ate it up. They still do.

Famously raucous, Vicious joined Sex Pistols after charter member Glen Matlock quit, or was fired—the early punk-rock scene was genuinely tumultuous at a multivalent level, and even today its myths have yet to be definitively sorted out. The lore of the time had it that Matlock was not sufficiently "punk." Vicious, born John Richie, was. He didn't bring instrumental prowess to the group. He brought sneers, safety pins, mucous. An untamable persona whose fall has been documented in a great many articles, books, and films (including Alex Cox's estimable 1986 *Sid and Nancy,* starring Gary Oldman as Sid, in a breakout role), Vicious was also highly prone to substance abuse (his mother had been, and became again, an active heroin addict, and at some point the two began to share a habit). When asked, he could actually sing pleasantly enough: the Pistols' covers of good-old-rock-'n'-roller Eddie Cochran's songs "C'mon Everybody" and "Somethin' Else" are genuinely fun and charming and enlivened by Vicious' vocals.

But that bad attitude of his made him the perfect person to take the piss out of "My Way." His version was indeed considered sacrilegious when it came out as a single in the summer of 1978, when Vicious had well less than a year to live. Paul Anka deemed it "sincere."

As is the case when, say, eating the fried chicken from the Kansas City restaurant Stroud's for the first time, when *Goodfellas* brings up the Vicious "My Way" it is one of those moments you wish you could experience unspoiled over and over again.

It's a shock, because Scorsese, while certainly a rock 'n' roll person, is not (his fondness for the Clash notwithstanding) a punk person, so there's some surprise that he pulled it out. But it's one of those things that feels so right—the tossing of this self-aggrandizing procession into the trash. Anka is right—Vicious is sincere, in a sense. When he sings, "Regrets, I've had a few/ But then again/too few to mention," he means it, man (as his Sex Pistols bandmate John Lydon/Johnny Rotten would put it), but he divests the words of the pompous solemnity Sinatra's version relies on. Burn it all down. Throw the egg noodles and ketchup at the wall. Fuck it.

Six:

THE SCHOONMAKER
TREATMENT

Thelma Schoonmaker is the most consistent and stalwart collaborator Martin Scorsese has had, in a career distinguished by several collaborations that could be so characterized. Her first picture in his filmography is 1980's *Raging Bull*, for which she won a Best Editing Academy Award. But the two had met and worked with each other well before that, in the 1960s, when Scorsese was at New York University.

Schoonmaker recounted her meeting Scorsese—born in 1940, she is three years older than the director—to Mary Patrick Kelly: "I went to Columbia University for a year of graduate work in primitive art. And then I see an ad in the *New York Times*. First and last time it ever happened. Someone wanted to train an assistant film editor. I got the job and worked for a terrible old hack who was butchering the great foreign films for late-night television. [...] I learned enough to realize that maybe it was something I wanted to do."

With that in mind, she enrolled in an NYU summer course, and here she met Scorsese, Jim McBride (who would make the underground-to-mainstream-bridging *David Holzman's Diary* in 1968, and go on to direct *The Big Easy* and a remake of Godard's *Breathless*), and Michael Wadleigh. The head of the department, Haig Manoogian, one of Scorsese's earliest and most important mentors, asked Schoonmaker to help Scorsese cut a negative on a project, even though she wasn't in any class sections with her fellow student.

Here began their working method, evolving from the basis that Scorsese himself was already a trained and somewhat accomplished editor. "I would go over to him and say, 'We have to lose six frames here, do you want to do them at the tail or the head?' He would decide and I would make the correction."

Schoonmaker was impressed with Scorsese's energy and dedication. "He had much more drive and focus than any of the other people I met at NYU. Marty was burning up with wanting to get there." (One is reminded of this anecdote recounted by Roger Ebert: "After *Mean Streets* was released, I wrote a review saying that Scorsese had a chance to become the American Fellini in ten years or so. The next time we met after the review appeared, Marty looked serious and concerned: 'Do you really think it's going to take ten years?'")

In the summer of 1969, Michael Wadleigh enlisted the duo to join him in shooting a documentary about what was then called the "Woodstock Music and Art Fair" and additionally "An Aquarian Exposition." This morphed into, well, Woodstock, and then the film *Woodstock*. Schoonmaker described the shoot to Kelly as "an incredible nightmare." In the summer of 2019 I moderated a Q&A about the movie with Schoonmaker and one of its producers, and she was able to laugh about it. She described how nobody really knew what they were getting into—Scorsese packed a pair of nice cuff links in the event

that he would maybe go to a high-end restaurant on the trip—
and then ended up under the stage for three days. Scorsese was
both an editor on the project and an assistant director. (The sequence in *Woodstock* featuring Sha-Na-Na, a '50s tribute group
that stuck out like a sore thumb at the flower-children-friendly
concert, was cut entirely by Scorsese.) During the college-and-
after years of honing his craft, Scorsese seems to have done a
little bit of everything, and tackled it all with equal enthusiasm. Alfred Hitchcock famously did not like shooting; Sidney
Lumet, in his largely exemplary book *Making Movies*, is frank
in revealing that he considers sound mixing an utter bore. (His
chapter on it is subtitled "The Only Dull Part of Moviemaking.") Scorsese always gives the impression of being equally absorbed in all aspects of filmmaking, and accords to each of those
aspects a special weight.

There's a famous picture of Wadleigh, Scorsese, and Schoonmaker during the editing of the great documentary. Scorsese has
on a dress shirt with a neckerchief, Schoonmaker wears what
looks like a gray pullover, while Wadleigh is shirtless. At the
Q&A I asked Schoonmaker what the deal was with that—I'm
all about the important questions—and she said, "Yeah, he just
walked around with his shirt off a lot." Ah, the '60s.

"*Raging Bull* was my first feature!" Schoonmaker told Kelly.
"When I came to work with Marty, I said, 'You know, I've never
cut a feature before.' And he said, 'Don't worry, we'll do it together, it'll be okay.' It was my assistant, Sonya Polonsky, who
taught me how to organize a room for a theatrical film. Marty
had called me several times for other movies but I hadn't gotten into the union when I was younger. Now they said I would
have to work as an assistant for eight years before I could be an
editor. I said no. But on *Raging Bull*, through Irwin Winkler,
[consulting with] lawyers and standby editors [...] I got into

the union. We were working all night. I'm not a night person. I've never adjusted to working all night. But in that solitude we found an incredible ability to concentrate."

That concentration became crucial to their work process, and they worked to make sure they could always achieve it. As such, the editing room is a closed shop, so to speak. David Leonard, who was part of the Scorsese editorial department from *Last Temptation* through *Goodfellas*, recalls, "Thelma did everything. Yeah. I mean, there wasn't a lot of mentoring. That wasn't the way they worked. The door was shut. There wasn't a lot of 'what'd you think of this, look at this.' There was a whole editing lineage that went back to Dede Allen, who was very conscious about training assistants to the edit. So she always had an assistant who stood by her, and she would edit out loud and talk. Mostly Thelma didn't really at that time cut until Marty was in the room. Dailies would come in, and there was a very elaborate system of organizing the footage so that when Marty came in there were takes set up in reels, because it was film and he could see his preferences from the notes of dailies back-to-back-to-back. So there were very elaborate assemblies but not really cut.

"What she would do is she would run through the dailies and she'd mark them up with grease pencils, ins and outs, give it to us. We would have to then pull the sections out and rebuild them into new reels and there were two logbooks. There was the log of the main roll of dailies and then there was a select log so you knew where the trims went. So it was very organizationally intensive for the assistants."

One hallmark of Schoonmaker's editing philosophy is that dynamic discrete moments matter more than issues of continuity. "Performance, performance, performance," Leonard recalls as her motto. In a 2014 interview in *Film Comment* with the critic Nick Pinkerton, Schoonmaker elaborates. "I don't understand why people get so hung up on these issues, because if you look at films throughout history, you will see enormous continuity errors everywhere, particularly when you're talking about the [practically square] Academy aspect ratio where you see more in the frame. Even in *The Red Shoes*, a film that nobody ever has complaints about, there are enormous continuity bumps, and it doesn't matter. You know why? Because you're being carried along by the power of the film. So throughout our history of improvisational cutting, we have decided to go with the performance, or in this case particularly with the humor of a line, as opposed to trying to make sure a coffee cup is in the right place."

Schoonmaker then cites a pertinent example: "I remember that when I was nominated for an Academy Award for *Goodfellas* and we lost to *Dances with Wolves* for editing, the editor of that movie said to me: 'Why did you make that bad continuity cut?' And I said, 'Which cut? Which continuity error? We have tons of them.' He was talking about a scene with Paul Sorvino and another actor who was an amateur, but wonderful, though he didn't know about matching. It was much more important for us to get this beautiful performance by this untrained actor than to worry about where the cigar is in Paul Sorvino's hand. One doesn't want to do that, one would hope not to do that, but if the choice comes between a beautiful, clean line and a laugh, we would always go for the laugh."

Here Schoonmaker's recollection is not entirely precise: it's not the cigar in the hand, which stays in continuity, but the cigar in the mouth. It's the scene with Tony Darrow as the Bamboo Lounge owner begging Paulie to rein in Tommy, or take a business interest in the restaurant. It occurs about twenty-six minutes into the movie. There's a behind-the-head shot of Paulie, with the cigar is in his mouth, in the cutaway to a reverse angle there's no cigar in his mouth. Like so: "What the fuck you think I'm talking about, Paulie, please, come on." Paulie says, "It's not even fair," then cut, cigar is out of his mouth, and he finishes saying, "No." Yes, it is a "bad" cut, and I never noticed it until I read that interview and looked it up.

David Leonard is a professional film editor to this day, and he says, "Yeah, I never got over that cut. As I watched the movie again, I was thinking I couldn't remember what was so good about it or what the other takes were of Paulie in there that they had to have that moment."

The moments of feedback or active participation he was allowed are still special to Leonard. "During *Last Temptation* there's that very long slow-motion shot of Jesus walking with the cross. It's a very long shot. At one point I remember Thelma came out when we were eating dinner late and said, 'Do you think that shot's too long?' And it was one of the few times I can remember that. For me as an assistant where I got Marty time was the mixing of *Goodfellas*, the scratch mixing, because especially at that point [Schoonmaker's husband] Michael Powell wasn't well"—the director, in his eighties, had cancer—"and Thelma was going home early. So I would generally go do a scratch mix with the mixer and then Marty would come and tweak it. So that was where I sort of had some one-on-one time with Marty. I remember once after a screening I went up to do something on the ninth floor and Marty was like, 'Sounded great, David.' There wasn't a lot of that. Don't get me wrong. He's warm as shit. He's great."

At one point Scorsese's need to stay in the editing room uninterrupted for as long as possible became such that he had a soundproof phone booth installed in the room, so he could receive or make calls privately without leaving. As they were constructing it, Scorsese remarked to Leonard that it was like the isolation booth on the 1950s television quiz show *The $64,000 Question*, so Leonard rigged a device that would play that show's "question time" theme music whenever Scorsese closed the door. Scorsese got a huge kick out of it. The director's moodiness waxed and waned: "It depends whether he's not happy with what he did that day on set and it's three months later, or whether his agent said this person's not going to do this. And I remember Thelma would sort of say he never knows if they're going to let him make another movie." He was past the point of, as rumor had it, destroying editing rooms à la Charles Foster Kane raging in his soon-to-be-ex-wife's bedroom at the end of *Citizen Kane*. But he could still be volatile. "If you walked in the editing room without warning, Marty would jump up and say, 'How the FUCK am I supposed to get any work done,' or some such thing."

One of Leonard's responsibilities was rounding up sources for the song soundtrack. "I always think about this. He handed me a list of music to have prepared for the cutting room and, like, ninety percent of what's in the movie was on the list. And this was while he was shooting. It was, like, you know, have this stuff ready. That was always an amazing thing to me, all that stuff, and then it was in his shooting script. You know, 'Jump into the Fire' crosses with 'Magic Bus.'

"And there weren't many CDs around in 1989. So we had to go find stuff and at that point you would transfer a 45 or a cut from vinyl onto a quarter-inch tape so you could constantly reprint magnetic stock of it, but we would have to go find this stuff and fortunately we were upstairs from Colony Records. So you could run downstairs and for fifty dollars get a copy of a Dean Martin record with 'Ain't That a Kick in the Head' on it."

Schoonmaker's husband, Michael Powell, died at age eighty-four in February of 1990, while editing of *Goodfellas* was still underway. "So Thelma disappeared," Leonard recalls. "She had to go to England. She was away for about two, three weeks. Michael's devotion to Marty was wonderful. After a screening of

Last Temptation Michael got up. There were death threats against Marty over the movie at that point and Mike was, like, 'Marty, I'll take a bullet for you.' I got to have lunch with him a lot because Barbara had an assistant who had this dog, Elvis, a basset hound, and Thelma would say, 'Why don't you take Elvis to go see Michael,' because they lived around the corner on 51st and 8th. So I would walk Elvis over, and then Mike would show up and Mike would have a plate and a teacup set up for me. And he would run and, like, jump on the carpet to play with Elvis. I'm thinking, 'Great, Michael's going to fall and break a hip. I'm going to get Michael Powell killed.' He hadn't a care. He would be playing with the dog.

"He dictated his autobiography, I think both volumes, because he had macular degeneration. So he couldn't read. I mean, that's the thing about Thelma. She would spend all day with that nut in the cutting room, and she'd go home and she would type out what Michael had dictated, and then she would read it back into a recorder so he could listen to it and edit it and keep going. That's Thelma."

I had asked Schoonmaker about sitting for an interview when I saw her in the summer of 2019, and she seemed willing. But after finishing work on *The Irishman*, and working with Scorsese on its promotion, she went to England, to once again perform an act of devotion to Michael Powell: she is editing his diaries.

Scorsese said this about Schoonmaker to Richard Schickel: "Thelma knows who I am, the best and the worst of it."

He described how she, at that time, tended to stay away from sets, because watching the activity there could conceivably predispose a way of looking at footage: "She doesn't know that during a particular take somebody got sick, or somebody got angry. She simply writes down all the takes, in great detail, then types it all up. It's a long process. She knows my preferred takes, second preferred, third preferred, the possibility of a whole other way to go. Come back to the fifth take and she'll remember it. Then she edits it all together so that you just punch up the takes, they're all there. That takes a little longer, but when we're looking for something, she can always find it easily. And her comments are so helpful. She might say, 'Look at his eyes here. We need some more emotional impact, we need some more warmth. There was another take where he seemed a little more that way.' Things like that. And I'll look at what she is referring to and maybe say, 'I don't know if that's any different.' She might look doubtful. And then I'll say, 'We'll put it in. Let's see.' She's very good with keeping the heart of the picture foremost, in terms of emotion."

He concluded: "Sometimes Thelma and I are laughing, sometimes we get depressed. I might say, 'We lost the entire dramatic thread of this. They should shoot the director.' That's why I don't want people to be there. It's for me. I want to be able to say what I feel about the actors, what they're doing in the frame, uninhibited by anybody. Thelma is the woman I trust."

Seven:

THE AFTERMATH

To this day, some detractors of *Goodfellas* insist that it glamorizes violence and the mobster mode of living. One can credibly point out all of the ways that it doesn't do this and still leave them unmoved.

In a sense this can't be helped. Scorsese himself has recounted his fascination, as a cinephile, with movie gangsters. What he did with *Goodfellas* was relatively unprecedented. As Michael Powell pointed out when praising its script, no other movie—no other American movie at least—had shown the gangster life with this kind of detail. In his groundbreaking 1948 essay "The Gangster as Tragic Hero," Robert Warshow, thinking, one infers, mostly of Howard Hawks' *Scarface*, wrote: "The gangster's activity is actually a form of rational enterprise, involving fairly definite goals and various techniques for achieving them. But this rationality is usually no more than a vague background; we know, perhaps, that the gangster sells liquor or that he operates a numbers racket; often we are not given even that much information. So his activity becomes a kind of pure criminality: he hurts people. Certainly our response to the gangster film is most consistently and most universally a response to sadism; we gain the double satisfaction of participating vicariously in the gangster's sadism and then seeing it turned against the gangster itself."

Goodfellas gives us the "information" in detail: cigarette bootlegging, truck hijacking, airport cargo heists, restaurant mismanagement, and so on. This is the sort of thing that Michael Powell was talking about. These crimes, then, would be reenacted not by men who genuinely resembled the criminals they were portraying but by actors who were either well-established or just coming up in the Hollywood system. When Robert De Niro and Al Pacino were approaching mainstream stardom in the 1970s, much was made by some observers that these actors didn't have "movie star looks," but then again, Humphrey Bogart, John Garfield, and James Cagney didn't, either. By a more generous and sensible metric they *did* have movie star looks, and movie star charisma, and so does Ray Liotta.

Henry Hill, Jimmy Burke, and Paul Vario—these were guys who really, really, really didn't have movie star looks, and likely didn't have movie star charisma, either. Which brings us to the other part of the problem, which was most vehemently articulated by Manny Farber and Patricia Patterson in "The Power and the Gory," an essay on *Taxi Driver* that originally appeared in the May/June 1976 issue of *Film Comment*.

"The character of the Loner, which dominates American films from Philip Marlowe to Will Penny to Dirty Harry Callahan, has seldom been given such a double-sell treatment," they wrote. "The intense De Niro is sold as a misfit psychotic and, at the same time, a charismatic star who centers every shot and is given a prismatic detailing by a director who moves like crazy multiplying the effects of mythic glamour and down-to-earth feistiness in his star."

While future histories of '70s Hollywood, most prominently Peter Biskind's *Easy Riders, Raging Bulls*, would depict Scorsese and other filmmakers in his circle as daringly anticommercial, Farber and Patterson, in their contemporary account of *Taxi Driver*, assumed mercenary motives as only natural: "*Taxi Driver* is always asserting the power of playing both sides of the box-office dollar: obeisance to the box-office provens, such as concluding on a ten-minute massacre, a sex motive, good-guys vs. bad-guys violence, and casting the obviously charismatic De Niro to play a psychotic, racist nobody." They continued: "Many of the new demons in Hollywood are flourishing inside a Bastardism. They are still deep within the Industry and its Star-Genre hypocrisies, and at the same time they have been indelibly touched by the process-oriented innovations which began with *Breathless*."

This is a complicated issue, especially with regard to Scorsese. Irwin Winkler, the producer of *Goodfellas* and a continuing collaborator with the director, has called him a great independent filmmaker who's never made a film independently. His combativeness with regard to the entity referred to as Hollywood continues to this day, as his unenthusiastic and controversial (to some at least) remarks about "Marvel Cinematic Universe" show.

I should clarify my point, or points, here. *Goodfellas* is a Hollywood film, a Hollywood studio film, and as such, and for other reasons I've touched on above, can be perceived as almost automatically or reflexively "glamorizing" gangsterism, even if a more careful study of the picture demonstrates that not to be the case. What I'm getting to is, that when the movie had its first previews in Redondo Beach and another outer–Los Angeles burg no one seems to remember, the unwitting audiences for the movie did *not* see a picture that glamorized gangsters.

They saw a movie they found almost immediately repulsive in every respect.

Editor Thelma Schoonmaker has often remarked that it's important to play a movie before an audience to get a sense about how its rhythms work on viewers. But she's talking about a select, sympathetic audience familiar with the work and with the aims of the filmmaker. *Goodfellas* was the first Scorsese picture that was "sneak previewed" for unwitting audiences. In this practice, a picture is sometimes advertised as a special screening, or the picture is tacked on to a feature that the audience has already paid to see. Neither preview site was exactly Scorsese territory, nor places that had a special affinity for New York–set gangster pictures.

"The studio knew what the movie was, but nevertheless I think Warner's was kind of shocked at what a bad reaction it got, and kept getting," says Barbara De Fina. "After the first preview, it was pretty funny, you could accurately predict the point when all the women would get up and leave."

De Fina recalls one preview during which objections to the content were exacerbated by technical problems. "They had problems with the projector, the sound and image weren't syncing, and this made the audience even more hostile. At a certain point we all got up and ran and hid in a bowling alley next door, because the audience was really, really angry. I always read the cards, you know, there were 300 cards, and there were cards where a viewer had either scrawled incoherently all over it or had written 'fuck you' in big letters all over it—they were real angry. It had really aroused some sort of, you know, reaction."

Irwin Winkler also remembers the Redondo Beach retreat to the bowling alley. "We were next door, and when we walked back into the theater after the repair had been made and the movie was in sync, and the film started again, some guy or some guys started yelling, 'Get Scorsese!' Well, how could you have a preview when people wanted to kill the director? I *think* it was Encino, where we had the next preview, and we had forty-two people walk out in the first scene, the killing of Billy Batts, with Joe stabbing him, and Bob shooting at him. People were running out of the theater like it was on fire, for Christ's sake.

"When it was over, and then Marty came out, and he wouldn't talk with Warner Brothers people, he said to Margo and I, 'I'll be at the bar at the Beverly Wilshire Hotel.' I guess Barbara was there, I don't remember, and we all met there and said, 'What are we gonna do, because we know tomorrow they're gonna kill us,' and the next day we went to a postmortem at Bob Daly's office. I don't know if Semel was there, I know Bob Daly was, as were other executives. They were really, really upset, and wanted the film reshot, recut and everything else, and Marty was very calm. He listened to their suggestions. And then he did what Marty does. That is, what he wants."

While the director had not been promised final cut, the decision to allow Scorsese what he wanted was based on guarantees made when the original deal was struck. Some cuts were necessitated to mollify the MPAA ratings board. Back when he made *Taxi Driver*, Scorsese had desaturated the color in the climactic massacre scene to avoid an X rating. He had gotten cagier, more savvy on dealing with such concerns in subsequent years. In the scene in which Tommy is shot rather than made, he actually filmed an effect of Tommy's forehead blowing off in an exit wound after Tuddy shoots him in the back of the neck. It's likely he knew all along that this would not fly with the ratings board, and by putting it in, knowing they would ask for him to cut it, they'd probably overlook other instances of violence Scorsese considered more important for the film as a whole. He would go on to play a not-dissimilar game of bait and switch in *Casino*, showing an eyeball popping as a head is squeezed in a vise, fully aware the scene would have to undergo a trimming.

Warner's panic subsided once the movie began screening for audiences who were actually eager to see a new Scorsese picture, a new Scorsese picture set in a familiar milieu—and of course a new Scorsese picture that teamed him up with De Niro again, the unenthusiastic reception in many corners for *The King of Comedy* notwithstanding.

The movie's world premiere was in early September 1990 at the Venice Film Festival and netted it both the audience award and a jury Silver Lion to Scorsese for directing. (The jury was chaired by the writer Gore Vidal, a man skeptical of the theory of the Imperial Director ever since the time in the 1950s when he met Norman Taurog, a longtime and then still active Hollywood helmer who was in fact almost stone blind by the time he was introduced to Vidal. Other jurors included Argentine filmmaker Mariá Luisa Bemberg, longtime Cannes festival head Gilles Jacob, Russian filmmaker Kira Muratove, *Lawrence of Arabia* star Omar Sharif, and Italian director Alberto Lattuada, whose 1962 *Mafioso* was an antic black comedy about an Italian everyman recruited as an unwitting assassin who's shipped in a crate to Hoboken to carry out his task.)

De Fina, recalling the disastrous previews and their aftermath, notes, "The strange thing is that while it didn't do well in previews, if you go back and look at all the reviews, it only got one bad review."

Todd McCarthy's September 10 review from Venice, in the trade paper *Variety*, was not entirely a rave. He called it "simultaneously fascinating and repellent," noting "sympathy is not the issue here, empathy is." He praised Schoonmaker's "masterful editing" but complained that while the film "is taut in the first half" it "rambles seriously after that, wearing out its interest at least half an hour before it's over." Warming up his point, the reviewer complained that "the second half [...] doesn't develop the dramatic conflict between the character and the milieu that are hinted at earlier." Yes, *that* second half, which features the aftermath of the Lufthansa heist and the macro-detail of Henry's arrest day. In fairness to McCarthy, when you're filing reviews from film festivals it's generally on the day of the screening, and under that tight deadline pressure you might not have an entirely reliable assessment of certain aspects of a given picture.

When *Goodfellas* opened in US theaters soon after Venice (September 19), reviews from Scorsese's home turf of New York were enthusiastic indeed. In his September 20, 1999, review in the *New York Times*, Vincent Canby called the movie "breathless and brilliant.

"*Goodfellas* looks and sounds as if it must be completely authentic," he noted.

In the September 20 *Wall Street Journal* Julie Salamon wrote, "There's very little that's really new in *GoodFellas*, Martin Scorsese's latest film, which is what makes this gangster picture so astonishing. Like some half-mad visionary who finds new magic every time he paces the same street, Mr. Scorsese has made familiar territory seem thrilling and dangerous all over again." She continued: "The film doesn't glorify the gangsters or make their outbursts of violence seem anything less than shocking and horrible." Her whole review is a kind of Manifesto for Scorsese, especially interesting thirty years on in a film culture where several factions loudly insist that the director makes movies not just about white men but *only for* them: "The fierce humor and originality of *Goodfellas* is especially impressive if you consider how tempting it is in these days of multimillion-dollar contracts for a successful director to play it safe. Though one could argue that all Scorsese films are the same, one could just as easily argue that no two are alike. Sometimes they're almost too powerful to watch (*Raging Bull*) but they're always amazing. Compare *Alice Doesn't Live Here Anymore* with *New York, New York* and

Taxi Driver or *The Last Temptation of Christ*. Then, if you think one person couldn't stretch himself any further, rent the rest."

In the *New York Post* on September 19 David Edelstein astutely noted, "Scorsese has become so fluid a filmmaker that he creates his own syntax. Momentum is all, and he gets his effects quickly, without apparent wheezing. At times he accelerates the action, herky-jerkies it up. When Henry becomes a cokehead, the camera speeds up but the action crawls. No one in years has used a zoom lens as brilliantly as the in-and-out move on the helicopter tailing Henry." He was also responsive to its themes: "The brilliance of *Goodfellas* is in how the dread seeps into Henry's life without him realizing it—how the price of immediate gratification is immediate death."

In the same day's *New York Daily News*, Kathleen Carroll wrote, "One remains detached from the characters, but Scorsese succeeds in smashing all the foolishly romantic myths about the mob with this shocking, vigorously honest portrait of a slick yuppie gangster who couldn't stand being 'an average nobody.'" Henry Hill was hardly a yuppie, but one can't totally blame Carroll for the reach here. In a tandem "review," Jerry Capeci, the paper's crime reporter responsible for the engaging, popular "Gang Land" column, vouched for the movie's authenticity: "It's about real-life gangsters from Brooklyn and Queens whom we hate because they do anything for money and often kill for the fun of it." He continues: "The central story [...] is a familiar New York story, but I don't know of any movie that has told it as well. *GoodFellas* got the details right."

A notable dissent came from Andrew Sarris, the groundbreaking critic whose book *The American Cinema: Directors and Directions* championed the Hollywood directors that Scorsese and other male "movie brats" of his generation would call touchstones as they began making their own pictures. Sarris and Scorsese may have shared reverence for John Ford and Howard Hawks and Alfred Hitchcock but Sarris was an early Scorsese skeptic. His October 8 column in the *New York Observer* called *Goodfellas* "wildly overrated." Sarris had an aesthetic/philosophical objection to the movie's very concept: "Movie gangsters should be larger than life, as they are in *Miller's Crossing* and *King of New York*, and not smaller than life, as they are in *GoodFellas*." He went on: "I have encountered a few gangsters in my salad days, and I know almost as much as Jimmy Breslin does about Queens Boulevard, but I never felt the slightest twinge of involvement with the relentlessly mediocre hoods of *GoodFellas*. For the first time in his career, Martin Scorsese has fashioned a film utterly devoid of guilt, shame, redemption, and even low-grade romance. What he has made instead is a slyly derisive antigangster movie hobbled structurally by the lumpy details of Nicholas Pileggi's bestselling *Wiseguy*. After all, where does the 'plot' of *GoodFellas* go after more than two hours? Nowhere except a hastily devised ratlike escape into the witness protection program without the slightest trace of regeneration or dawning self-knowledge."

Sarris' subsequent mea culpa with respect to Scorsese's earlier work is not particularly convincing: "I must confess that I have missed the boat on some of Mr. Scorsese's previous hits, most notably with my thoughtful pans of *Mean Streets*, *Taxi Driver*, and *Raging Bull*. I have never doubted the director's enormous talent, particularly with actors exploding in scenes as if they were intuitive splotches of paint in a Jackson Pollock painting. Yet the lack of the kind of moral trajectory that produces narrative fluidity still strikes me as a conspicuously Scorsesian shortcoming. Mr. Scorsese is essentially more a scene assembler than a storyteller. The parts are invariably better than the whole."

Pauline Kael was very high on the movie: "It's like *Raging Bull* made in a jolly, festive frame of mind," she wrote in the September 24, 1990, issue of the *New Yorker*. "[Scorsese] loves the

Brooklyn gang milieu, because it's where distortion, hyperbole, and exuberance all commingle." It's Queens, not Brooklyn, at least for the most part. But as someone said in another movie, "Forget it, she's rolling."

"Is it a great movie? I don't think so. But it's a triumphant piece of filmmaking—journalism presented with the brio of drama. Every frame is active and vivid, and you can feel the director's passionate delight in making these pictures move." Great movie or not, *Goodfellas* got Kael excited, and in her review, her discursive enthusiasm practically flails; she supports her assertions with delightedly recounted detail. The notice is worth seeking out and reading in its entirety.

In the *Chicago Sun-Times*, after saying that no finer film had ever been made about organized crime than this one, Roger Ebert wrote, "It isn't about any particular plot; it's about what it felt like to be in the Mafia—the good times and the bad times." His counterpart at the *Tribune*, Gene Siskel, also gave it a rave. Even the notoriously dyspeptic Rex Reed called it "great entertainment."

Gossip columnist Liz Smith, in the *New York Daily News* of September 21, effused over the picture's New York premiere screening: "Seldom have I been to a more impressive premiere than the one at the Museum of Modern Art this week for Nick Pileggi's *GoodFellas*, based on his true-to-life book *Wiseguy*. Madonna arrived and seemed thrilled to be in the VIP audience along with her fellow Italian actors and peers. [...] You can read the analytical raves for *GoodFellas* everywhere but just let me say this is one of the best movies I have ever seen! [...] The person who has really 'arrived' with *GoodFellas* is author Pileggi, a much-respected, well-loved, and really excellent writer who has paid his dues with years of reporting. Pileggi and his famous wife, writer Nora Ephron, are a celebrity phenomenon. But not just for 'celebrity.' These two deserve their success." And in the

September 29 *Times*, op-ed columnist Russell Baker mused on the amusement early audiences seemed to derive from *Goodfellas*: "More amazingly, the chuckles became big belly laughs as the movie proceeded to expose a society, New York society, in fact, so utterly corrupt that the cops are bribed by a few cartons of cigarettes, truckers connive blandly with hijackers, and judges give most-favored-perpetrator treatment to gangsters. In this society everybody is entitled to rob New York blind without risking retribution, except from an associate with an ice pick to slide in the back of the neck or a sweet old Italian mom's butcher knife to plunge into a solar plexus.

"What was going on in that audience? Are New Yorkers, who pay top dollar for absolutely everything, including their government—are New Yorkers so resigned to being blatantly robbed that when Mr. Scorsese rubs their noses in their humiliation, they can only laugh?"

Between the reviews and a not spectacular but largely solid box-office take—a $6.3 million opening weekend in 1,070 theaters, and an ultimate domestic take of almost $50 million, representing a modest profit off a $20 million budget—*Goodfellas* gave Warner executives fresh enthusiasm for another "edgy" film on its roster. In her book *The Devil's Candy*, Julie Salamon writes of the studio's 1990 year: "Warner Brothers hadn't been having a good year. None of its pictures had 'opened.' Martin Scorsese's *GoodFellas* was the one bright spot; the movie had gotten great reviews and might have Oscar possibilities. But it wasn't exactly a huge hit, though it was doing better than they'd expected, financially."

Salomon's book is an unsparing account of the making of *The Bonfire of the Vanities*, an adaptation of Tom Wolfe's novel directed by Scorsese's contemporary and friend Brian De Palma. The film, a Christmas holiday release for Warner, would prove a critical and financial boondoggle. But, prior to its release, Salomon says, "*GoodFellas* had now become the beacon of hope for *Bonfire*. *GoodFellas* had scored poorly in test screenings. As [Warner advertising president Robert] Friedman put it, 'On an A to F scale it got at best a C-minus in the preview process.' Reviews saved it. 'They weren't good, they weren't great,' said Friedman. 'They were brilliant. So critically, *GoodFellas* was an A movie, and that's what put it over.'" The same would not hold for *Bonfire*, though. The picture was both a critical and box-office fiasco and has proven more resistant to revisionism than several other poorly-received-in-their-time De Palma movies.

As for the aforementioned Oscars: Scorsese's relations to the Academy Awards had and has long been fraught. It need not be entirely relitigated here, but these relations of course in part stem from the filmmaker's status of being with Hollywood but never quite of it. But let's just take it back to the Academy Awards ceremony of 1981, honoring the films of 1980, which had to be postponed by a day after an assassination attempt on then US president Ronald Reagan. Said assassination attempt was perpetrated by a disturbed young man named John Hinckley, Jr. Among several other symptoms of his unbalanced mental state was a fixation on the actor Jodie Foster, with whom he had become obsessed after seeing her play a teenage prostitute in Scorsese's *Taxi Driver*.

This fact was not known when the Oscars actually took place the following evening. Scorsese's *Raging Bull* had eight nominations, and the movie took home just two awards. One for Robert De Niro, for Best Actor, and the other, for Editing, going to Thelma Schoonmaker. Besides that, the picture was largely overtaken by *Ordinary People*, a family drama directed by the actor and megastar Robert Redford, making his debut in that capacity. Thus touching off one of the great (in terms of scale, if not intelligence) debates in awards history, centering on the conviction that Scorsese and company were robbed.

Ordinary People is a better than decent picture; it's not *How Green Was My Valley* but it's not nothing, either. In any event, it's not quite the self-evidently protean achievement that *Raging Bull* was—it's hardly as difficult, for one thing—and this makes people mad. This really began the longtime "Scorsese Was Snubbed" meme.

In his spectacular autobiography (the second half of his autobiography actually—its predecessor, *A Life in Movies*, only takes things up to the mid-1940s) *Million Dollar Movie*, Michael Powell describes an evening in his courtship of Thelma Schoonmaker, to whom he was introduced by Scorsese: "I made an Irish stew. I congratulated her on her Oscar. She was outraged. 'I didn't deserve it, and you know I didn't deserve it. Marty should have gotten the Oscar, not me.'"

At the 1991 Oscars, honoring the films of 1990, *Goodfellas* garnered six nominations, including Editing (Schoonmaker once more, of course), Adapted Screenplay, Director, Best Picture, Supporting Actress (Lorraine Bracco), and Supporting Actor (Joe Pesci).

And as if history were (perhaps farcically) repeating itself, the movie was all but shut out by *Dances with Wolves*, another directorial debut from another male movie superstar, this one Kevin Costner. An earnest epic of the American West with a special emphasis on Native American issues (as refracted through the view of a white man, played by Costner), the movie does not have quite as many now-hold-on-there defenders today as *Ordinary People* does.

The contemporary critical fallout from this was pronounced. From Mason Wiley and Damien Bona's *Inside Oscar*, 10th Anniversary Edition: "Janet Maslin denigrated the Academy as 'an

organization capable of deeming Kevin Costner a better director than Martin Scorsese (the evening's single biggest outrage).'
Gene Seymour of *Newsday* demanded to know 'What is it going
to take? What wheels does Martin Scorsese have to grease? Who
does he have to buy off? Or knock off?' *Premiere* characterized
Scorsese as being 'angry and disappointed' over his loss and he
told the magazine, 'I wish I could be like some of the other guys
and say, "No, I don't care about it." But for me, a kid growing
up on the Lower East Side watching from the first telecast of the
Oscars, there's a certain magic out there.' Two Scorsese veterans
expressed their opinions. Harvey Keitel reasoned that 'Maybe
he got what he deserves—exclusion from the mediocre.' *Taxi
Driver*'s Jodie Foster said, 'When you look at the ten old ladies
who put down *Dances with Wolves* instead of *GoodFellas*—I don't
know. The Oscars are like bingo. Who cares?"'

Joe Pesci won the Best Supporting Actor Award, and graced
the ceremony with a terse acceptance speech: "It's my privilege.
Thank you." Not the shortest Oscar acceptance speech, but as
of this writing it is in the top ten. Appearing as a presenter later
in the show, he pronounced, "I still can't talk." In the back-
stage press scrum, Pesci said that nerves made him tongue-tied.
"There were so many people to thank, I was afraid that if I
started I couldn't stop and I would get booed."

Goodfellas would not see its first home video release, on VHS
tape, until December of 1992, over two years after its theatrical
release. So far four iterations of the movie have been released on
DVD/Blu-ray. It has performed well on home video: according
to the website The Numbers, as of November 2009, *Goodfellas*
had sold 68,873 units. *Dances with Wolves*, as of January 2011,
had sold 22,023 units. So Scorsese's picture has that going for
it. Throughout the 1990s, the movie was referenced so consis-

tently and constantly, it seemed, by standup comics and in some sketch comedy that it felt like something that *everyone* had seen.

Its influence on other films is difficult to quantify. Certainly Quentin Tarantino got a lot out of it. The opening scene of his feature debut, *Reservoir Dogs*, in which its criminals sit in a diner and talk shit about their tipping practices and their sexual fantasies of Madonna, is a resourceful spin on the banter in *Goodfellas*, for instance the trash talk about Sammy Davis, Jr., in one of the Copa scenes in Scorsese's picture. Tarantino has also benefitted from the way Scorsese juxtaposed horrific violence with laugh-out-loud black humor, and has received disapprobation from cinema moralists about it.

In 1997 *Premiere* magazine, in its tenth anniversary issue, pronounced *Goodfellas* as one of "Ten Movies That Rocked the World" during those ten years. Martin Amis contributed an essay commemorating the movie, writing, "In its dealings with the Cosa Nostra, Scorsese's camerawork displays all its inimitable edginess and urgency; but we shouldn't overlook the director's steely moral wit. His goons see mob culture as a vibrant alternative to the schmuckville of nine-to-five. Scorsese insists, however, that they are money's slaves, and money's fools. And he has them bang to rights." (I suppose I ought to disclose that I was an editor at *Premiere* at the time, and that I commissioned this essay.)

"It's no secret, [show creator] David Chase has said many times there would be no *Sopranos* without *Goodfellas*," Michael Imperioli told me when I interviewed him. "*The Godfather* had this towering mythical storybook aspect; *Goodfellas* is a very contemporary street movie. These are in a sense people you know, people who live next door to you, and I think that really makes it resonant in a specific way." The hook of *The Sopranos*, which premiered on HBO in 1999, was that of a mobster seeing a psychiatrist; this is also the plot of the Harold Ramis movie, *Analyze This*, made in the same year and starring Robert De Niro. De Niro would play the same cartoonishly neurotic mobster in 2002's sequel, *Analyze That*. In 2012 *The Family*, directed by Luc Besson, explicitly references *Goodfellas* in a meta-movie moment that almost defies description.

Bill Hader, the actor and director whose HBO series *Barry*, about a hit man pursuing a new life in acting, deftly balances horror and (often absurdist) humor, told me that the hierarchies within the ranks of wiseguys in *Goodfellas* have loose analogies in the world of comic performance. "The guys in that movie, the way they relate to each other, is the way comedians relate to each other. It's a weird hierarchy, and there's something about the trivial points in the arguments they get into. Then there's that feeling of status and respect among comedians, that's kind of like when Jimmy Conway comes into the room when Henry is a kid. When somebody comes in the room, there's that. I was never a standup, but if I was somewhere and Steve Martin was there, it's not so much feeling starstruck as it is massive respect, something to live up to. Which, in crime, is kind of messed up, but has a little more moral standing in comedy."

Hader still marvels at the audacity of some of the film's scenes: "After Tommy shoots Spider to death, he actually jokes about it, saying, 'What can I say, I'm a good shot.' No matter how terribly Tommy acts he can't help be himself, and sometimes watching the movie with an audience you hear that the line still gets a laugh. But the key to that is letting emotions and character lead the way, and not thinking in terms of genre. That's the ultimate lesson for a filmmaker."

Eight:

THE EVENTUAL TRAGEDY OF HENRY HILL

In his book *Conversations with Scorsese* Richard Schickel observes to the director, after Robert Warshow's essay "The Gangster as Tragic Hero" comes up, "I'm not sure I completely buy into that in a movie like *Goodfellas*; there's actually nothing very tragic about these guys." Scorsese agrees: "No."

"What happens to Henry Hill is not tragic; he's just not having fun anymore," Schickel says. Scorsese, clearly amused, responds, "Right. Too bad for him!"

In each of Scorsese's examinations of money and power in America—*Goodfellas*, *Casino*, *The Wolf of Wall Street*, and *The Irishman*—the protagonists, each an antihero to at least some degree, make it out of their predicaments alive, albeit worse for the wear. Henry loses his identity, and also, like Vinnie in *My Blue Heaven* and Dominic (at least in his worst imaginings) in *Cookie*, his ability to eat well. "Ace" Rothstein in *Casino* survives a car bombing and loses most of his friends, not to mention the wife who was probably not a great match to begin with. Jordan Belfort in *The Wolf of Wall Street* takes a slide in his infinite–con man variant of Chutes and Ladders, and goes back into sales (and in real life wrangles a cameo in a Martin Scorsese movie, something the director himself seemed displeased with when Belfort's appearance in *Wolf* came up in a press conference I moderated). Frank Sheeran in *The Irishman* ages into some vague realization that his career in murder has been for naught, but can't find real remorse, which the movie does consider tragic.

Henry Hill is, after *Mean Streets*' Charlie, the first male character in a Scorsese film meant as an audience surrogate all the way through. In most of his films Scorsese dispenses, and most of the time radically, with that kind of mediation. Charlie is the docent of his movie's world, and it's arguably true that the more he screws up the more alienated the viewer becomes. Griffin Dunne's horndog everyman in *After Hours* is a guy you're supposed to have an affinity with, but again, he grows more selfish and conniving even as he plays the flummoxed victim. When he cries, "All I wanted was to meet a nice girl and now I have to die for it," the answer is, well, yes. Michael Powell told Scorsese that *After Hours* was a New York Kafka story, and one is reminded of Welles' *The Trial* and Welles' ruminations on Josef K.'s guilt: "The point isn't whether or not he's guilty or innocent. It's an *attitude* toward guilt and innocence." With *Taxi Driver*, *Raging Bull*, and *The King of Comedy*, you're tossed in the maelstrom with these characters, the only life raft of sanity or any such thing to be the viewer's psychological relief or control group is the viewer's own processing of the material. It's only in *Alice Doesn't Live Here Anymore* that you have, in this case, a heroine who's a genuine rooting interest *and* through whose eyes you can see the world coherently.

With Henry Hill it's not quite so comfortable, nor is it meant to be. But he's the closest thing to an ingratiating protagonist as has come up in the Scorsese body of work up until this time. Yes, Willem Dafoe's Christ in *Last Temptation* is spectacularly appealing, but he's *Christ*. As much as that movie makes you feel the character's pain, you're still at a divine remove, so to speak. But with Henry, he's your guy, for better or worse, the whole ride.

And as such, he can't be portrayed entirely accurately and still serve that function. Henry Hill was an alcoholic for a good portion of his life. He was a cokehead. He physically abused his wife. In the book *On the Run: Escaping a Mafia Childhood*, Gregg Hill, Henry's son, recalls a horrific night during the period Henry was first looking out of his witness protection hole: "Experience told me what was happening, what was going to happen next. How many times had he come home hammered and screamed at my mother, slapped her, taken a swing at her? I couldn't count that high. Was it getting worse, happening more often? Or was I just getting bigger, older, sick of it all?"

"Henry was a schmuck," former prosecutor Ed McDonald says—with not inconsiderable affection, mind you.

After he stopped working for the government, McDonald went into private practice, and he now has an office at a corporate law firm—one of those places touting offers of "global solutions" and such—with an impressive view of one of Manhattan's landmark parks. Sitting in his office listening to him spin his tales felt ever so slightly like being Thompson listening to Bernstein in *Citizen Kane*.

"I always called him the Beetle Bailey of mobsters," McDonald continued. "You know, he just couldn't get anything right. But Paul Vario loved him. Jimmy Burke, all these wiseguys in New York, loved him. Henry was inept, he couldn't do anything right. But they wanted him around, because he was funny, he was cracking jokes, he was doing silly things, and when he'd do something stupid he'd make fun of himself, and he was a really charming, self-deprecating guy...and he could be relied upon. For some things. And he was the same way with the guys in the witness protection program, the marshals, you know, they'd go, 'C'mon, baaaad Henry, baaad Henry,' they'd call him that. And he'd be, 'Fuck you, fuck you.' And they loved him, they'd get such a kick out of him. And the FBI agents who worked with him liked him. And he would still be inept. He'd be inept when he was supposed to be doing witness prep, but you know, the next day he'd be, 'I'm so sorry, I'm a schmuck, I'm a schmuck.' So, it was easy to have a good rapport with him.

"On the other hand, you know, you had to say to yourself, 'The guy is a gangster and a con man. And you can't get too close to him, or too friendly with him.'"

Wiseguy was a chance for Hill to come clean, but it was also a hustle for him. In addition to what Simon and Schuster, the publisher of the book, paid author Nicholas Pileggi, it had agreed to award Hill almost $100,000 for story rights. But the publisher was stymied by New York's so-called "Son of Sam" laws, named after the infamous serial killer of the late '70s. These statutes were designed to prevent criminals from "profiting" from their crimes via books, film rights, and so on. When Simon and Schuster moved to pay Hill royalties he accrued from *Wiseguy* sales—about $30,000—they were hence enjoined. Simon and Schuster sued, not just for Hill's sake, but for the larger principle. The publisher's case got all the way to the Supreme Court. Which resolved in Simon and Schuster's favor, allowing Hill to collect the funds. This cleared the path for Hill to pursue more book money with new projects.

Pileggi remembered the time prior to Hill's coming out, prior to their collaboration. "He couldn't not spend money. And he couldn't not get into schemes that ended up being total busts.

He once bought a vintage trolley car in St. Louis, or in Kentucky, I can't remember. And he was going to conduct tours on it. A total bust. And then he would need money. He'd call and say, 'I need money, I need money.' It turns out he 'needed' money because he wanted $7,000 to buy his daughter a pony."

That pony was named Bananas, and Hill bought the animal during his family's stay in Kentucky, for Gina, a passionate rider. When the family was relocated from Kentucky to Washington state, Hill contrived to have the animal shipped to them. Gina had no idea how. (Prior to Kentucky, the Hills had been in Omaha, Nebraska.)

The lure of criminality remained strong, despite the fact that one feature of witness protection was near-constant surveillance, or at least monitoring, by law enforcement.

"He rationalized living this way because around the corner he was gonna make a $50,000 score on a coke deal," Pileggi recalls, still wryly incredulous to this day. "He was being watched by the FBI twenty-four hours a day, and it didn't occur to him that he might not get away with such a thing. There was no consequence. He didn't understand how vulnerable he was. And I had talked to him about that, and his position was, 'Look, if I had to worry about every single thing, I would never have done anything.'"

Gina Hill writes, "Whatever money my dad got from the book was spent as soon as he got it." Gregg writes, "My father had an angle for everything. If there was a way to make a buck off a situation, he'd figure it out. And it was easy for him to pull it off because he never thought about or cared about the consequences. Plus, he had no shame."

In 1987 Hill was arrested for conspiracy to sell narcotics. At this point in time his family life was convoluted. Another woman had entered his life—referred to as Dawn in the account by Gregg and Gina, called Kelly Norblatt (presumably her real name) in Hill's *Gangsters and Goodfellas*. The movie hadn't happened yet, but the book had, and Henry had a kind of local celebrity, which also trickled down to Gina, who couldn't stand it. "Henry Hill had become a famous character," Gina wrote, "not even a real gangster anymore who inspired fear and dread. Strangers felt free to harass [me] in coffee shops. I was right about his being protected, though. The government didn't rescue him, but things always seemed to work out for my father. When he went to trial in September 1987, his lawyer argued that my father was actually a victim. The stress of witness protection, of being far from familiar places and constantly fearing for his life, led to drug and alcohol problems, which in turn caused his marriage to fall apart. The only reason he got involved with the conspiracy to sell cocaine, his lawyer said, was because he owed those drug dealers so much money that they were threatening him and molesting Dawn [Kelly]. 'He was scared,' the lawyer said. It worked, sort of. My father was convicted, but the judge sentenced him to five years' probation. As long as he stayed out of trouble, he'd stay out of trouble."

The making of *Goodfellas* and its subsequent release only led to more of the limelight, but it also provided a kind of bubble. "The truth is, if it hadn't been for Ed McDonald and Nick Pileggi, I'd have been twenty years in the ground already," Hill writes in *Gangsters and Goodfellas*. These guardian angels got Hill into the public spotlight, and one of them got him paid, too. Hill could luxuriate at least a little in the idea that these two genuinely good fellows had his back, up to a point. And there was more. "When I signed on the deal for *Goodfellas*, in 1989, Scorsese sent me a check, two weeks before principal photography, for $480,000. The feds didn't even know it. They knew about it, but not the amount. Scorsese made sure I got the check privately—that was also part of the deal."

Hill's account of other wiseguy survivors trying to get a piece of the action is amusing: "Just as we started gearing up to film *GoodFellas*, Jimmy Burke's fearsome daughter Cathy reared her ugly head. She tried to shake down De Niro for one hundred large to give him the right to use the name 'Burke.' We said, 'Fuck her, we'll change the name.' That's why the name is Jimmy Conway in the movie. Thank God this happened before they filmed all the Burke scenes."

Hill does not turn up in the production credits of *Goodfellas*, even as a consultant, but he arguably earned that half mil. "During this whole process I really came to respect De Niro. I was never much for celebrity worship, which is like a disease out here"—Hill was writing from Topanga, where he spent his last years; the town is close enough to Hollywood to pass for "out here"—"but De Niro was special. He was so intense about getting Jimmy Burke down right that he had me coaching him all the time. I was getting ten phone calls a day from De Niro or Scorsese. My own phone bill was $4,000-plus a month, which Scorsese covered. And the calls came at all hours. When Kelly was in delivery, who should call me but Bobby De Niro. You should have seen it, my girl is giving birth, and while she's yelling I'm trying to coach De Niro, who's about to shoot a scene where somebody gets whacked. I'm telling Bobby how to pistol-whip a guy's head at the same time my new kid's head is popping out. You could say it ruined the moment." (Joseph Reidy remembers that he was often the go-between for Hill and the filmmakers, and has a similar complaint about Hill: "Henry had my number. And unfortunately, he'd call me—you know, it'd be the landline in those days—call me at home at night, check in on how things are. And I had his number because once in a while Marty would ask me to call Henry about something.")

Hill, Kelly Norblatt, and their son, Justin, lived in Hollywood for much of the 1990s after the release of *Goodfellas*. "To be honest, the '90s are a huge blur," Hill wrote in *Gangsters and Goodfellas*. It was in Hollywood and Santa Monica that he first tried to make a go of working with recovery groups. But Hill was a chronic relapser, and it seemed he could only get a good amount of time under his belt under extreme conditions. He recounts two years in a sober living residence. In the early 2000s he moved to North Platte, Nebraska, where he opened a restaurant, a sort of coeval to his 2002 *The Wiseguy Cookbook*. He sought to get into e-commerce selling his "Sunday Gravy" on the internet. But he couldn't keep away from substance abuse, and in a 2005 interview from a jail cell in his new hometown, he says his brief time in stir once again saved his life. "It gave me a chance to sober up and get my stuff together again and move forward."

Ed McDonald has an anecdote from that period. "So he calls me, he was living in North Platte, Nebraska, with a woman there, and she owned a restaurant. I think they called it the Goodfellas Restaurant, or Wiseguy Restaurant, something like that. And he says, 'I'm gonna come to New York, and Howard Stern's gonna have me on his show.' And I say, 'That's great.' He says, 'I'd love to have dinner with you, I wanna have a New York steak.' I say, 'Sure, go to Smith and Wollensky's.'" McDonald is still a habitué of the legendary Manhattan steak house. "I go to Smith and Wollensky's all the time, in fact I was there last night," he told me in our interview.

"I get there, like, at 8:30, and I'm walking in, and David Cone, the pitcher"—Cone played for both the Mets and the Yankees, and in 1999 had pitched the sixteenth perfect game in the professional history of the sport; at around this time he was close to his last hurrah with the Mets—"is standing at the front, by the entrance. I remember thinking that I couldn't believe how short he was. In the meantime the maître d' is saying, 'Yeah, that's Henry Hill over there.' He was attracting some sort of attention. And I know the bartender, and he comes up to me and says, 'There's a guy here claims he's Henry Hill.' I say, 'He is Henry Hill.' And so here's Henry, with his wife, an attractive woman, and the first thing he says is, 'I gotta get a buckin' bink, I gotta get a buckin' bink.'"

Hill had been in such a rush to catch his plane out of North Platte that he had neglected to bring his dentures with him. "He's on his third martini in, like, twenty minutes. And he's making a scene, still wants another 'buckin' bink.' I give my credit card to the waiter, and I said, 'Just get me a shrimp cocktail and get them, you know, what they want.' So, I had got my shrimp cocktail, the woman orders, like, a big T-bone steak. Which Henry can't partake in because of his toothless state. He ended up with creamed spinach."

It was around this time, too, that McDonald and Hill got together in Burbank, at a recording studio at Warner Brothers, to record their *Goodfellas* commentary, one of several included on an anniversary edition of the home video version. The recording date was June 10, 2002, one day before Henry's fifty-ninth birthday and the day that John Gotti died in prison.

Throughout that commentary, Hill profusely, you might even say obsequiously, thanks McDonald for saving his life. Watching things like the stabbing of Billy Batts in the trunk, Hill almost shudders, and speaks of how he can't believe that it was he who was involved in such brutality, and how bad he feels about it. It gets to be a bit much. McDonald allows that it indeed was. "I certainly don't think Henry was remorseful. I never encountered that with him in any way. I don't think that he was sincere. As much as I liked him, you know, I liked him with my eyes open. If he hadn't been caught, you know, he wouldn't have gone through witness protection program. This wasn't like he got a conscience and had a 'Saint Paul on the road to Damascus' conversion. I never felt that about Henry at all."

When the two men emerged into the sunlight, both found their mobile phones were inundated with messages. Various media representatives were calling McDonald and Hill for their reactions to John Gotti's death. The two men played a brief game. Henry would say, "Sure, I'll give you a comment, but you really ought to talk to this guy," and hand his phone to McDonald. The former prosecutor in turn would say, "You really ought to talk to Henry Hill. I have him right here." Hill, working with the writer Daniel Simone, would tie Gotti into the Lufthansa heist (this is in Simone's book, published a few years after Hill's death). But at this point, Hill had mainly one thing to say about Gotti. "We had to go back to my hotel room," McDonald recalls, "because we're too far from where Henry was living, to be jointly interviewed in person. We were interviewed by the BBC. I remember this reporter with a plummy British accent asking, 'Did you know John Gotti, and if so, what did you think of him?' And Henry said, 'Yes, I did know him,' and the reporter says, 'What was he like?' and Henry says, 'He was a fucking homicidal maniac. Excuse me, he was a homicidal maniac.'"

And it was during this time, his witness protection strictures long severed, that Hill got back in the book business. *The Wiseguy Cookbook* (2002) is a remarkably dense recipes-with-memoirs work. In its introduction, Hill hits on a familiar theme: "Try buying arugula in Omaha, Nebraska, or good Italian sausage in Butte, Montana." *A Goodfellas Guide to New York* (2003) is a tour of his old world written with Bryon Scheckengrost, with whom Hill produced a short film during this period. *Gangsters and Goodfellas* followed in 2004.

In his 2019 book *Coming Clean*, introducing a partial transcript of a May 2002 interview, Howard Stern writes: "We first had him on the show back in the mid-'90s, and he'd been on three or four times since then. In those appearances, because Henry was an alcoholic and would come in drunk, we would just screw around with him and never get into any deep conversation.

"This time he was drunk again. I'd been thinking more and more about Henry. How much of his substance abuse had been self-medicating, trying to drown the guilt of having done the unforgivable? How did he feel about killing people? Did he carry that around with him? Was there remorse? He might not be in a physical prison, but he was clearly in a mental one. He was in hell. I wanted to understand how he was feeling. I thought, 'Let's see if I can get him to be real with me. Let me see if I can get him to go there.'"

In the transcript, Stern lightly chastises Hill for showing up with a can of Heineken—"You were doing so good"—and advises him to keep the swearing to a minimum (Stern's show was still on the public airwaves at this time). A guy identifying as a mobster, calling himself "Paulie," yet, calls Hill a rat, and Hill replies, "A happy rat."

"Is life so boring without alcohol?" Stern asks. "Yeah, it sucks," Hill says. In a desultory fashion, Hill recounts several murders he claims to have committed (his tales got very tall as the years went on, and he needed to keep whatever interlocuter he had on the hook interested; hence, I believe, a story of Tommy DeSimone shooting a random guy in the face). Near the end of the conversation he says, "Howard, I am so miserable," and "I'm a scumbag."

Ed McDonald would hear from Hill on the phone every now and then in a specific circumstance. The former wiseguy would tell the man who did not put him in jail that he was sitting on the edge of the Santa Monica pier, about to throw himself off. Ray Liotta, who kept a certain distance from Hill during the shooting of *Goodfellas*, posed with Hill in a photo shoot in 2006. During that time Liotta advised Hill to check into a rehab, and Hill claimed he did so.

During the last ten years of his life Hill's marriage to Norblatt dissolved, and he took up with Lisa Caserta, who would become his common-law wife and self-described manager. Caserta told me during one of our first phone conversations that Hill had been sober ten years when he died on June 12, 2012 (the day after his sixty-ninth birthday). It was Caserta who got Hill together with Daniel Simone to write *The Lufthansa Heist*, a novelistic and rather outlandish re-re-recounting of the affair, which was published in 2015.

Ed McDonald enjoyed playing himself in *Goodfellas*, to the extent that he kind of caught an acting bug, although the acting profession did not bite back. Some filmmaker friends did, around 2010, ask him to play a cameo in a film they were working on called *Sinatra Club*. Having had some recent contact with Hill, he thought it might be fun to bring the erstwhile gangster along. The movie was about a young John Gotti, and McDonald's hunch was right: the moviemakers were so delighted to meet Hill that they gave him a bit part—as "MOB GUY" as it's listed on the IMDb—on the spot. On the drive back from the location, Hill told McDonald that he considered the man his best friend. McDonald did not know quite what to say to that.

Nine:

UNOFFICIAL NARRATIVES

I first interviewed Barbara De Fina in May of 2019. De Fina is small-boned and gives an impression of shyness and modesty as soon as you meet her. This held throughout the actual interview. She had good memories of the making of *Goodfellas*, and told me about her background, working with Sidney Lumet, the affinities between Lumet and Scorsese, and more. She told me about her current project, an adaptation of Tommy James' memoir *Me, the Mob, and the Music*, a rock 'n' roll biopic with a strong crime element and a strong Oedipal one; much of the book details James' twisted relationship with Morris Levy, the very mob-affiliated head of Roulette Records, the label that broke, and subsequently controlled, James.

I was interested in the dynamic between De Fina and Scorsese—the fact that they married, divorced, but continued working together. De Fina has an executive producer credit on as recent a Scorsese movie as *Silence*. Their marriage had broken up around the time *Goodfellas* was made. For all that, I said I wasn't going to delve too deeply into the personal lives of the filmmakers, at least beyond which factors of these had an effect on the making of this particular movie. Still, I probed. I tiptoed around the "why did the marriage break up" question and De Fina made a reference to demons, and how everyone had them. I mentioned that I was curious that when Jay Cocks gave Scorsese a copy of Edith Wharton's *The Age of Innocence*, he told his friend Marty that the almost fatally scrupulous Newland Archer *was* the filmmaker, at least in certain ways. De Fina raised an eyebrow. "You'd have to ask Jay about that," she said, practically incredulous.

A little while after this first interview, De Fina got in touch. She wanted to meet again. We set a date for June.

"When you called about *Goodfellas*, in a way you just kicked a hornets' nest for me. Because I didn't want to sit back and say everything that's already been said. This is the opportunity to do whatever I can do to set it straight, or to be truthful, I don't know; as I told you I was thinking of writing my story. If there's a time to do it, it's now. Because I went through the '80s and '90s in a position I should not have been in.

"I mean, I love the movie, we had a great time making it and, you know, if I had gotten proper credit, it would have changed my life a lot. I mean, there's a British Academy Award, there's the Academy Award nominations… I think things would have been different."

Scorsese and Pileggi had collaborated on the script; Scorsese made *The Last Temptation of Christ* first, nevertheless, because that deal came together in a "now or never" fashion. De Fina picks up the thread from there:

"So we came back, we had the script, and we started, you know, prepping, and even in Morocco doing *Temptation* we were talking music, we talked about what to put on the end credits, the crazy 'My Way' by Sid Vicious thing. When we got back, I started producing the movie, and Irwin Winkler wasn't around. Marty had at this time other lawyers, which I wasn't aware of, separate lawyers, which was a problem. And so these lawyers sent out deal letters and somehow Irwin had gotten himself into it with, also through Ovitz—who deny, deny, denies it—they got Irwin in the picture. Which would have been fine, but after I had started the movie, started producing it, we started, you know, doing all the work, Irwin got me, like, demoted."

It should be noted here that Winkler had, sometime prior, acquired the movie rights to Pileggi's *Wiseguy*. This happened during the interstice that De Fina described, during which Scorsese and his assistant were calling Pileggi without De Fina's knowledge. Had she known this was going on, De Fina said, she would have made the correct calls. But as it happens, those calls were made, successfully, by Irwin Winkler.

And as Winkler himself told me, this was during a period, after his partnership with Robert Chartoff had dissolved, in which Winkler did not share the credit of "Producer." Scorsese's manager Harry Ufland had pushed for a "Producer" credit on *Goodfellas* and Winkler flat out said no. He had the power to do that because he had control of the book's movie rights. De Fina's credit was changed to "Executive Producer." Additionally, once CAA got into it, her profit participation points on the movie were decreased.

Recounting the situation thirty years after the fact, De Fina fumes. "He just—I mean, I—and everyone else that had been working on it. And then he wasn't even there. He visited the set a few times, got his picture taken in the director's chair."

In an interview prior to my second session with De Fina, Winkler readily allowed that he did not visit the set frequently. Joseph Reidy told me that as a rule Scorsese doesn't like having producers on his set. De Fina was there relatively frequently—

on the audio commentary for the twenty-fifth anniversary Blu-ray of *Goodfellas*, she speaks of enjoying the atmosphere, camaraderie, and even some of the craziness, while in person she told me while she did enjoy it she did so "within limits"—but the biggest presence from the production department was the customary one, the unit production manager, Bruce Pustin. Who, Reidy recalls, often served the function of "bad cop," which is also the customary one for an individual in this position.

De Fina said that Winkler was, and has been, "nothing but nasty" to her. She told the story of a party that Winkler and his wife, Margo, attended; on seeing Barbara, Margo said, "The two producers are here," and Winkler responded with words to the effect that there was only one producer. (De Fina retains affection for Margo, whom she calls "lovely.") Winkler denies making the remark, and denies snubbing De Fina, or denying her invitations to *Goodfellas*-commemorating events.

As for Scorsese, De Fina recalls, "The only thing he ever said to me about the whole thing, when it happened, was that he didn't think the movie would come to anything."

Winkler's responses to De Fina's assertions are polite and brief. "Barbara did a great job, as I said the first time we spoke. This production was thirty years ago, and at that time 'Executive Producer' was a real credit—it wasn't like these days when they give out Executive Producer credits like candy. If she feels that way, I can only repeat, she did a great job, and I have great admiration for what she did. As you mentioned, at that time I did not share 'Producer' credit, and the reason I could take producer credit was because I did what a producer does—I tracked down the right agents, who referred me to CAA, and I bought the rights to the property."

★ ★ ★

In the entertainment industry, personal and professional re-lationships often bleed into each other, and are often sundered with near-extreme prejudice. Brad Pitt's film production com-pany, Plan B, a prominent and successful entity as of this writing, was originally a joint venture between Pitt and his then-wife, Jennifer Aniston. When they broke up, Aniston was unattached from the company, which went on to back Scorsese's *The De-parted, 12 Years a Slave*, and more.

In the case of De Fina and Scorsese, the decision to main-tain the professional relationship after the marriage had dis-solved was perhaps not the best one, despite the fact that it yielded some classic pictures, among them *The Age of Innocence* and *Casino*. It was during work on *Casino* that De Fina saved the production oodles of money by concocting a way to shoot in working casinos, cordoning off certain sections during the wee hours, instead of constructing sets to simulate them. On these films and others, De Fina *did* receive sole credit as pro-ducer. But De Fina holds that *Goodfellas* was one that mattered in a different way.

The Scorsese–De Fina marriage was troubled before *Good-fellas*—in our second formal interview De Fina upgraded "he had his demons" to "endless womanizing"—and the profes-sional relationship took further hits once Scorsese signed with Artists Management Group, the company Mike Ovitz formed after leaving CAA, in 1997. She likens her situation to that of Tommy James, who, after entreating boss/father figure Morris Levy to pay him, would be doled out money on which to tour and record, but no greater spoils. That is, "I got paid for each individual movie but I never got any deal money. And once Marty signed with AMG, the guys there were really tough on me, they wanted to get rid of me. I could write ten chapters on that. Ovitz is strange. He wouldn't stand up for me on *Goodfellas*, he wanted me gone at AMG, but he gave me an overhead deal at Disney."

De Fina made the decision to step away for good once the ogre/mogul Harvey Weinstein became a participant in *Gangs of New York*. "I knew that I would not live through having to be the go-between in this situation," she says. "Oddly enough, prior to my stepping away, Harvey was always kind of pleasant to me." Settlements made between De Fina and Scorsese during both personal and professional separations meant that she would get credit on projects on which she had been involved with development—hence, her credit on *Silence*, the physical production of which she had no involvement in—and, in her account, right off the bat these agreements were not honored to her satisfaction.

"*No Direction Home*, the Dylan documentary. That started as a joint project, so I was supposed to get a credit, and he wouldn't let me work on it. I started on it, but then he wouldn't let me work on it. And I was supposed to get a producer credit, and when it finally came out, we saw the credits, I had gotten some peripheral executive production credit. And this was the first thing under the agreement. I wound up having to sue the production company. And it went on for, like, five years, and cost hundreds of thousands of dollars. Which—because he also then wanted to renegotiate everything—we finally settled, but it took years and years. And I think that was sort of the kind of nail in the coffin."

While De Fina appears in some short documentaries about the making of *Goodfellas*, and the making of *Casino*, and contributes pertinently to the audio commentary of the former film, her sense that she's been written out of a part of film history is not unsupported, to say the least. In the November 1991 issue of *Premiere* magazine, Peter Biskind contributed a set-visit feature on *Cape Fear,* which not only doesn't mention producer De Fina once, but contains a long bit in which Biskind contemplates how Scorsese's work ethic has affected his personal life. Scorsese speaks of divesting himself of personal "complication," which I imagine must have looked odd to one of *Cape Fear*'s actors, Illeana Douglas, who was dating the director at the time: "Your personal life, you know, you deal with it as best you can. But you even divest that. All the way up until, I'd say, '84, '85, every Sunday my mother and father, my friends, would come over. We'd have a big Italian dinner. Whatever different marriages— whatever was going on. It was really good, like the Italian family that I remember growing up. But I don't expect much from people anymore, and I don't really want them to expect much from me. Except when it comes to the work."

In the book *Scorsese on Scorsese,* Scorsese related how Bertrand Tavernier's *Round Midnight* came into being out of a lunch that he arranged with Irwin Winkler and director Bertrand Tavernier. "Which [movie] Bertrand asked me to be in," Scorsese said, "because he said that when I open my mouth, it's New York. I would save him a lot of establishing shots! He told me, 'You have to play the owner of the club because he's just like you, he's a nice guy, but he's ruthless.' I said, 'Gee, thanks.'"

In the introduction to Michael Powell's *Million Dollar Movie,* Scorsese pays moving tribute to his mentor while also hinting at the way in which moviemaking can be a kind of sickness: "He reassured that in me most of all. You believe in an idea, a concept, a story, a statement you want to make, and that's the foundation of the film. You do not waver from it. Whether it takes you all the way down, whether it takes you to the edge, then pushes you off, even to the point of not making another film for thirty years, you do not waver. You'd better make that picture even if you know it's suicide."

NINE: UNOFFICIAL NARRATIVES

★ ★ ★

I do not think that Lisa Caserta will object to my calling her a character. I got her number from Edward McDonald, who told me that she had been Henry Hill's companion and manager for the last ten years of his life. He thought that Lisa might be able to put me in touch with Karen Hill.

When we first connected, we spoke on the phone for a good thirty minutes. I was only calling to give her my email address, so we could conduct communications that way. I explained who I was and what I was doing. She told me that she had kept Henry sober for the last ten years of his life. This didn't square with what I had gleaned, but as others said, and Lisa eventually allowed, keeping Henry sober was a frequently provisional process at best.

I got the impression that since Henry's death in 2012, Lisa had been doing what Colonel Tom Parker said he was going to do after Elvis died: that is, go right on managing him. That said, she has always been completely aboveboard with me; she's made queries with respect to certain opportunities, but never asked for compensation for cooperation.

Still, it's been kind of a trip working with her. We've had about a half dozen conversations in which she's been generous and kind and chatty, and I have always ended them by saying, "Remember to email me," and she never emails me.

When Karen comes up, Caserta's natural ebullience sometimes plummets. "She's scared" or "She's scared for the kids" were two things I heard. I proposed using McDonald as a go-between to establish my own bona fides and good faith, but because of the frazzled nature of our exchanges, we never moved forward with the process.

When we texted in mid-February of 2020, Caserta said she was changing residences, and that it would be difficult to talk for a while. Then, out of the blue, she offered me the phone number of Joe Hill, Henry's brother. Henry was one of six children, but only his youngest brother Michael (Henry was born in 1943, Joe 1944, and Michael in 1950) is depicted in the book *Wiseguy* and the film *Goodfellas*.

"That was all worked out beforehand," Joe Hill said, his friendly voice still New Yawk–accented despite decades spent on the West Coast, when I called him a few days later. "None of us wanted any part of that." Joe tells me that Michael died in 1987—"the day after my first grandchild was born"—after the book was published, but of course before the movie. "At that time, he was the oldest surviving spina bifida patient in America. And that was because of the good medical care we were provided through my dad's union affiliations."

Joe has vivid memories of the people Henry knew as a kid, and grew up emulating, because Joe knew them, too. "My impression of that time is closer to what Chazz Palminteri did in *A Bronx Tale*, the closer depiction of how every Italian American neighborhood was run by an underboss whose main function, as we saw it, was to protect the neighborhood. And put money into legitimate businesses. Every little 'hood, those guys had control and gave protection. You see a lot of envelopes passed into the hand, to the local precinct commander, say. *Wiseguy* was Henry's version of it. Nick [Pileggi] did a wonderful job of translating it. The movie Hollywoodized it up a bit."

Joe Hill did admire the picture's depiction of addiction. He contends that Henry's subsequent, seemingly intractable problems with alcohol and drugs arose from his trauma at being backed into a corner from which the only exit was the betrayal of his wiseguy family. "Henry's alcoholism and drug abuse was perpetuated by the fact that he just never reconciled the fact that he had to do that. It wasn't just the friendships that factored in, either. The five Vario brothers, they were men of respect not just among the Italian community, the Jewish community; Henry retained his childhood admiration for them."

The brother also takes issue with Henry's, and the movie's, portrayal of their father. Henry Hill, Sr., was an electrical engineer for Tishman, the New York construction giant. "He helped put up the Trade Center. In fact, he put off retiring so he could get them finished. Every twenty or thirty floors they'd have a party for the workers. Barrels of beer and cocktails. These were extraordinary workers and craftsmen.

"Henry lived more in fear of punishment than what he actually received. Yes, the belt had a place in parenting then. It was convention. I saw my share of it. Henry used to give *me* up more than anything. But my dad wasn't angry with Henry. Disappointed with him, yes."

Hill mentioned to me that when Henry died, one of the sisters, Lucille, gave her local paper an interview corroborating this.

Sure enough, in the June 14, 2012, *Tampa Bay Times* is an item, "A sister mourns 'goodfella' Henry Hill in Spring Hill," in which Lucille Hill, now Lucille Chrisafulle, says that their father wasn't abusive, merely very frustrated with Henry. The boy was his dad's namesake, after all.

Lucille also remarks that their neighborhood was "actually [...] very safe" on account of the wiseguys, and that *Goodfellas* "couldn't show [Jimmy Burke] as bad as he really was. If you ever met pure evil, it was that man." (This observation may come in handy if you're ever wanting to take the "yes" side in the "Would Jimmy Have Killed Tommy Had It Come Down to It?" debate popular with some of the movie's fans.)

Their absence from both the book and the movie has managed, Joe Hill says, to keep much of the family happily inoculated from unwanted attention. When he traveled to Ireland it was his name's match with that of the labor organizer that was most remarked upon, he told me. A family leitmotif has been to "keep the children from discussing Uncle Henry." But an occasional niece or nephew will discover the movie and have to be walked through the actual situation.

As for Henry, in his book *Gangsters and Goodfellas* he recounts that he had to rely on Joe quite a bit once he parked himself in Hollywood, after the movie was made. Joe recalls his brother once blurting, "All I wanna be is the best fucking drunk in the world." Hill credits Lisa for a great deal: not only for helping Henry get straight sometimes, but for engineering a genuine reconciliation with Henry and his children. Joe observes, with an affectionate chuckle, that "Henry gets credit for writing or cowriting five books, and he'd only ever read three books in his life!" Nevertheless, Joe says, "He was very intelligent. And as they used to say, he was a good earner."

Finally I asked Joe about Karen. He told me they have not been in direct touch for a bit, and that she has been dealing with health issues. "On the advice of Gregg, she doesn't really talk to people about that time of her life. Gregg's attitude about the whole thing is 'enough is enough.'"

Ten:

FROM *GOODFELLAS* TO *THE IRISHMAN*

"I thought of it as being a kind of attack," Scorsese told Richard Schickel about *Goodfellas*. "Attacking the audience. I remember talking about it at one point and saying, 'I want people to get infuriated about it.' I wanted to seduce everybody into the movie and into the style. And then just take them apart with it. I guess I wanted to make a kind of angry gesture."

"Why were you angry?" Schickel countered. Scorsese's response is long and varied, but "I get angry about the way things are and the way people are" kind of sums it up.

But *Goodfellas* did not infuriate its audience. Some made objections to its violence, some to the portions with which Scorsese wanted to "seduce" viewers, but there was not, in the main, a reaction similar to Russell Baker's.

Scorsese's follow-up to *Goodfellas*, another collaboration with De Niro, *Cape Fear*, materialized quickly. It was released in November of 1991, barely a year after *Goodfellas*. Funnily enough, the sprawling remake of a semiclassic thriller directed in 1962 by J. Lee Thompson (and featuring several members of its original cast, including Gregory Peck, Martin Balsam, and Robert Mitchum in supporting roles) *did* make people angry, at least some media people.

Terrence Rafferty, then the film critic of the *New Yorker*, called the picture "a disgrace," while the political commentator George F. Will appeared on an ABC News program to condemn the movie's violence, which he considered a symptom of Hollywood depravity. Will, seething with fresh-off-the-*Mayflower* WASP-patrician indignation, pronounced the director's name "Scor-seeze."

Speaking to Schickel, Scorsese said, "Sometimes I try to make a picture for purely entertainment reasons, like *Cape Fear*." One imagines the emphasis here was on "try." The movie had originated out of Steven Spielberg's production company, Amblin, and as credited screenwriter Wesley Strick said, "I wrote it as an Amblin thriller," that is, "big-budget and conventional." De Niro was eager to throw himself into the role of vengeful convict Max Cady, but Spielberg was obliged to defer the project—he was too busy—so De Niro wrangled Scorsese in. As with *Raging Bull* and *The King of Comedy*, it wasn't a project the director was too keen on. He found his way into it by introducing a lot of dysfunction into the family menaced by Cady (played by Nick Nolte, Jessica Lange, and Juliette Lewis; Nolte had worked with Scorsese on 1988's *Life Lessons*). The galvanic violence, including a scene in which Cady not only rapes Lori Davis, a professional colleague of Nolte's character and also his side love interest, but bites a chunk out of her cheek and spits it out (that's the bit that really bugged George Will), was more typical of Scorsese—and De Niro—than of Spielberg or Amblin. (In her memoir, Illeana Douglas writes, "A lot of folks thought the [rape] scene was gratuitously violent. I can only say, sadly, that it was based on actual events Bob had researched. To make it truthful, I also spent time with a criminal attorney in Florida's Broward County Courthouse doing my own research to prepare for the scene and its aftermath.")

For all that, the picture was a hit. Scorsese then presented a passion project, an adaptation of Edith Wharton's *The Age of Innocence*, to Touchstone, where he retained a production deal; they passed on the period piece. The picture was made at Columbia. (*Innocence* is one of the movies that many contemporary Scorsese detractors pretend doesn't exist when they try to point out that he only makes gangster pictures; but it exists, and it is a superb piece of work.)

In 1994 Scorsese had a role in the Robert Redford–directed *Quiz Show*. The movie, derived from a real-life 1950s scandal about a rigged television game show, was Redford's impassioned "media corrupts" statement. Scorsese's role was as the show's sponsor, who in one of the early scenes is seen balking at a contestant he doesn't believe is telegenic enough. "I don't think he works anymore," the sponsor tells a producer over the phone, in Scorsese's brisk, staccato delivery. When the producer says the contestant is a credible representative of New York, the character, deemed Martin Rittenhome in the picture's IMDb entry but only called "Sponsor" in the end credits, says, "Queens is not New York." (A sentiment that continues to resonate, sort of, when you think about it.) Like his nightclub owner character in *Round Midnight*, this man is ruthless; in a climactic confrontation with a lawyer trying to expose the corruption (played by Rob Morrow), Scorsese plays the character as the cat who swallowed the canary. He reels off how many bottles of twentieth-century snake oil Geritol he has been able to sell, then repeats, for emphasis, "Of *Geritol*." He continues: "That's the kind of businessman I am." He concludes his conversation with "You're a bright young kid with a bright future. Watch yourself out there."

Quiz Show was shot by Michael Ballhaus, and features Illeana Douglas in a bit part. That Scorsese appeared in it demonstrated, if anyone noticed, that he had no hard feelings about Redford winning those Oscars in the year after *Raging Bull*.

Casino (1995) reunited Scorsese with Nicholas Pileggi, Robert De Niro, Joe Pesci, a smattering of *Goodfellas* players, and more. (Barbara De Fina had been with him all along, no longer Scorsese's wife, but a producer, and she receives the sole producer credit here; Alain Goldman was the executive producer and Joseph Reidy, in addition to being first AD, is also an associate producer here.) Frank "Lefty" Rosenthal, the Chicago gambler who was able to oversee the business of several Las Vegas casinos in the late '60s despite his ties to organized crime, was not quite the next Henry Hill. But Hollywood saw so much potential in Rosenthal's story that Pileggi was compelled to work on the screenplay for *Casino* prior to finishing what would be the book of that name. Scorsese told Schickel: "That was kind of a commission. I had a deal at Universal. We did *Cape Fear* there and they wanted another film. Tom Pollock and Casey Silver were there. And Nick Pileggi brought this newspaper article to me about the car blowing up in Las Vegas with Lefty Rosenthal in it."

Rosenthal, whose name was changed to Sam "Ace" Rothstein for the movie—almost all the names of the real-life central characters were altered, and the Chicago mob became the Kansas City mob—was not a violent criminal himself, but he knew an awful lot of them. In the film the most troubling one is Pesci's Nicky Santoro, who impulsively stabs a guy near to death with an unusually sturdy fountain pen, pops out another guy's eye by increasing tension on a vise into which he's placed the guy's head, and so on. The ostensible story is how a golden opportunity for wiseguys is blown by their own greed and filthy habits. For the taciturn Rothstein (De Niro), another contributing factor is his blind love for the dazzling hustler Ginger (Sharon Stone), who proves an untrustworthy mate and an almost fatal distraction.

But the movie's other stresses, in their way, try to summon the kind of indignation that Scorsese told Schickel he was aiming for in *Goodfellas*. The affinities between legalized vice and the ordinary rapaciousness of American capitalism are laid out in galvanic detail in the film's first fifty minutes or so, in which almost-documentary-style scenes of casino action (including a lot of money counting) are accompanied by Ace's voice-over narration explaining How It All Works. People speak of Vegas as a gambling mecca, and Ace invokes both Lourdes and the "holiest of holies" in his descriptions, at one point concluding, "It's all been arranged just for us to get your money." *Casino* is not Scorsese's most Godard-ian film just because it uses large swatches of Georges Delarue's score for Godard's 1963 *Contempt* on its soundtrack. It's in the mode of analysis; while Scorsese's style is far more dynamic, his aim, like Godard's in many of his post-1968 pictures, is pedagogic. (See the "how the sausage is made" sequences in Godard's 1972 *Tout va bien* for a pertinent example.) Sometimes the lesson is terrifying, as when Ace outlines how his casino dealt with would-be cheaters (the one who gets away with his hands intact is played by Reidy, in a spectacular character turn).

Once the movie's personal story lines start getting more attention, there's a nagging sourness that's different from the notes of exhilaration *Goodfellas* sometimes hits. With respect to Ginger and her endless compulsive treacheries, Ace is the dog who returns to his own vomit, not to put too fine a point on it. These are not glamorous people doing glamorous things, their expensive clothes notwithstanding. The looks of contempt Stone conjures for her character are almost literally withering. "I'm not a john, you understand?" Ace says to Ginger at one point. But of course he is. You can't blame Stone's character for taking the opportunity, for taking the mark for all she can get. But the movie offers up no rooting interest, and doesn't want to.

The scene in which Ace and Ginger scream at each other on the front lawn of their house, while their daughter, Amy, looks out silently from a bay window in a neighbor's house, anticipates the stares of Peggy, the daughter of Frank Sheeran in the 2019 *The Irishman*. All the personal upheaval, and the increasingly brutal violence, culminating in the live burial of the übersadist Nicky, are so shudder-worthy and engrossing that the viewer is apt to be less up in arms about the depredations of capitalism than they had been earlier, but in the movie's coda Ace has an observation to set us all straight, as he laments the theme-park, family-friendly Vegas that was the city's identity as of the mid-'90s: "Where did the money come from to rebuild the pyramids?" Ace asks over a shot of the Egypt-themed MGM Luxor. "Junk bonds."

After the *Goodfellas* shoot, Ray Liotta sent De Niro a thank-you card, which was inscribed "With sincere thanks and appreciation." Liotta's handwritten note in the card reads, "Bob, Now I can tell you how much of a trip it was to work with you. You're the Best. And I hope we can do it again. But I really mean Do it! Thanks for your help and support in getting me a shot at this." Liotta and De Niro subsequently worked together in *Cop Land*, a 1997 police drama written and directed by James Mangold and featuring Scorsese alums including Harvey Keitel, Cathy Moriarty (Vicky in *Raging Bull*), and Frank Vincent, with wild card Sylvester Stallone in the lead.

Surveying Scorsese's career up to the turn of the century,

Schickel said to Scorsese, "So even though you made *Gangs of New York* and it's historical, I mean, this in a certain sense completes… You have the criminal element of, let's say, *Mean Streets* as it's perceived by quite a young guy. Then you move on to *Goodfellas* and then [*Casino*]." And Scorsese responds, "Definitely *Casino* is the final one."

Like *The Last Temptation of Christ*, *Gangs of New York* had been a longtime dream project for Scorsese. In its way, *Goodfellas* had accomplished one of Scorsese's ambitions: it made him "a player." But even with that status, the sprawling period piece, based on a 1927 nonfiction account by Herbert Asbury and scripted by Scorsese with his old friend Jay Cocks, along with Steven Zaillian and Kenneth Lonergan, was difficult to make.

The film industry is such that to get even the most modest picture made, someone involved has to strike a Faustian bargain. For *Gangs* Scorsese needed to make an alliance with monster mogul Harvey Weinstein. "That's where I got off the bus," we have seen Barbara De Fina recall.

For years Weinstein announced himself as a booster of great directors, a real man of cinema. In practice this meant coopting filmmakers and then telling them that he knew best. To make a long story short (the creation of this film would make a very juicy book, were one able to worm all of its secrets out of the participants, which is unlikely at this juncture), that's why *Gangs* is the often impressive but more than slightly compromised picture it is. (Scorsese's vision did not include a romance subplot, for instance.) The movie was also the first time Scorsese worked with Leonardo DiCaprio, who was in his late twenties at the time. While "stuff the author heard personally at the time" suggests that the personality of the actor and that of the director did not mesh perfectly on this shoot, DiCaprio was sufficiently impressed with Scorsese that he wanted to work with the director again, and again, and again. And DiCaprio had, and still has, such movie star clout that he can get some very expensive and ambitious projects funded.

It was in working with DiCaprio, arguably, that Scorsese catapulted from a player to a megaplayer. Scorsese did not become a mogul as his contemporary Steven Spielberg did, but he doesn't have to go around with hat in hand like Brian De Palma, or found a profitable wine concern like Francis Ford Coppola. He oversees a production office with a high overhead and has not looked at a movie with the equivalent of a *Mean Streets* or *After Hours* budget in decades.

Around the time Scorsese made the inventive and involving Howard Hughes chronicle *The Aviator* in 2004, one did not have to be an entirely cynical observer of his career to note that it was starting to resemble that of another maverick American filmmaker in his later years, that is, Nicholas Ray's. The director, a man who had not been able to curb his epic tendency to self-destruction the way Scorsese managed, made some staggering personal films in the late '40s and the 1950s, including *They Live by Night*, *In a Lonely Place*, *The Lusty Men*, and *Bigger Than Life*. Interspersed among these were genre pictures that he imbued with an idiosyncratic perspective, like the female-driven Western *Johnny Guitar* and the rawer-than-usual Youth Crisis melodrama *Rebel Without a Cause*. By the early '60s, after a series of setbacks both personal and professional, he found himself allied with producer Samuel Bronston, making the large-scale epics *King of Kings* and *55 Days at Peking*, pictures that, while not necessarily showing the director's *disconnect*, were not so immediately aligned with what one inferred Ray's interests were at the time. In interviews Scorsese often spoke of "finding" his way into the projects that DiCaprio brought to his table.

One reason that 2006's *The Departed* wasn't considered by

either Schickel or Scorsese to be part of the director's personal gangster "cycle" is because the movie, a remake of the 2002 Hong Kong picture *Infernal Affairs*, was, almost up until the point that it got into preproduction, one Scorsese did not feel he was "right for."

It became the movie for which he wound up winning his only Best Director Academy Award, ironic because he almost always speaks of it as a movie that he felt disconnected from even as he was making it. Which is not to say he slacked off. The movie is one of his most formally daring, its editing style the most break-neck of any of his pictures, slicing and dicing sound and image to the point of abstraction. All this while retaining a homage to Howard Hawks' *Scarface* by placing large X's in the architecture or shadows in certain scenes. It is also the picture in which he definitively overplayed his "Gimme Shelter" hand.

As big as the pictures got, Scorsese evolved in ways that one might not expect from someone involved in endeavors of this scale. Bob Griffon, the property master on *Goodfellas*, has gone on to work with Scorsese on several other projects. "Over the years I've noticed him more willing to get input from crew members. On *The Departed*, at the end, the DiCaprio character, Costigan, gets this huge police funeral, full gun salute, all that. Which I, and a couple of other crew members, noticed made no sense given what was said in the script about his file and his whole identity having been wiped before his death. And I pointed this out to Marty, and he thought about it, and he said, 'Yeah, that's right.' And he concocted with a couple of actors in suits, and co-lead Matt Damon, the scene in which Damon's treacherous character gives a statement in which he says, 'I just wanna go on record. I'm recommending William Costigan for the medal of merit.'" The scene was shot in a van on the same day as the funeral scene, Griffon says.

★ ★ ★

2013's *The Wolf of Wall Street*, another DiCaprio-driven project that located the lifestyle excess and criminal-mindedness of *Goodfellas* in the ostensibly legal world of high finance, managed to irritate members of a whole new generation of film writers. In a piece in *The Atlantic* headlined "*The Wolf of Wall Street* Is a Douchebag's Handbook," Esther Zuckerman wrote, "Call me a prude, but I had a hard time seeing any indictment of Belfort's lifestyle and boiler room culture in the movie."

She states later in the review, "I felt that the filmmakers weren't put off enough. Scorsese and DiCaprio want to have their cake and eat it, too." One can appreciate (without agreeing with) her perspective, especially with respect to DiCaprio, a movie star whose advocacy for environmental issues still has not erased from the media's mind the fact that his post-teen Gang of Boys referred to itself as "the Pussy Posse." His current penchant for dating women half his age, or maybe less, arouses much disapprobation in social media. The conclusion of Zuckerman's notice, "I guess, at the tender age of twenty-three, I'm just an old fogey," suggests a resistance to further investigation of the movie, which is Zuckerman's prerogative, and anyone's.

The particular giddiness of the characters in the picture, and the movie's whiplash style, make the occasional instances of horror and tedium Scorsese injects—the Weegee-like photo of the dead body in a bathtub full of blood, the FBI agent's dismal ride home on the F train—more difficult to register, maybe. But these shots/scenes are not *not* there.

Oh, well. Back in 1992, Scorsese said to the critic David Ehrenstein, "My attitude as a film director has always been... provocation. I want to provoke the audience. Like in *Goodfellas*. What these people do is morally wrong, but the film doesn't *say* that. These guys are really just working stiffs. They understand that if you cross a certain line it's death. But that's 'business.' And it *is* business. In that world it's normal behavior."

During this interim, the reputation of *Goodfellas* has both grown and been diminished along lines slightly suggested by Zuckerman's review. As cultural discourse splinters into (sometimes valuable) arguments about who ought to tell which stories, and who certain movies are and are not "for," reactionary pieces like Kyle Smith's *New York Post* article of June 10, 2015, headlined "Women Are Not Capable of Understanding *Goodfellas*" become more probable. Which is unfortunate in and of itself. (Variations on this theme hark back to the past critical arguments about '50s melodramas, "women's pictures," and "male weepies," many of which considerations were in their way tinged by some form of sexist condescension.)

After an anecdote in which a Smith paramour (now erstwhile, of course) dismisses *Goodfellas* as a "boy movie," Smith avers that, well, of course it is. "Way down deep in the reptile brain, Henry Hill (Ray Liotta), Jimmy the Gent (Robert De Niro) and Tommy (Joe Pesci) are exactly what guys want to be: lazy but powerful, deadly but funny, tough, unsentimental, and devoted above all to their brothers—a small group of guys who will always have your back" is Smith's thesis. "Women sense that they are irrelevant to this fantasy, and it bothers them."

One infers that Smith is being at least one-quarter facetious here. He's a conservative, so he can't really believe that the criminal path is an ultimately desirable way of life. I guess.

But his how-is-it-funny argument is rooted in a fallacy, the one where the guys "will always have your back." Always have your back as in Tuddy Cicero shooting you in the back of the head? Or, conversely, as in ratting out your former crew to save your skin?

Smith's insistence on seeing the film strictly as a male fantasy is in keeping with an overall attitude among a large percentage of contemporary reviewers: that film is not really an art, or "art" form with potentially universal or at least broad-scale pertinence. That it ought not be taken too seriously. Smith ends his piece with a speculation:

"What would *GoodFellas* be like if it were told by a woman?

"Meet an at-risk youth called Henry Hill. Victimized by horrific physical abuse from an early age, and traumatized by the responsibilities of caring for a handicapped brother, he fell prey to criminal elements in his rough East New York neighborhood in a time when social-services agencies were sadly lacking. At an impressionable age, he became desensitized to violence when a gunshot victim bled to death in front of a restaurant where he was working. His turn to the Mafia was a cry for help—a need to find a family structure to replace the one he had never really known.

"And who would want to watch that movie?"

The general misogyny on display notwithstanding, this ignores the fact that the Martin Scorsese picture *Goodfellas* is a story that is to a not-insignificant degree *told by women*. Thelma Schoonmaker. Barbara De Fina. Kristi Zea. Lorraine Bracco. And so on. Smith insults them all.

In 2019 the online publication *The Ringer* posted a video program called "Shea Serrano's 15 Best Gangster Movie Moments." Meant as a promotional tool for Serrano's book *Movies (And Other Things)*, it offers precisely what its title promises. Serrano is primarily a sportswriter who came to prominence via Grantland, a website founded by Bill Simmons, who had been a columnist for ESPN. Both men are what you might call polymaths, or multimedia enthusiasts; in any event, they both apply a dudes-talking-about-the-game informality to all their discourse, regardless of the topic. As the title of Serrano's book suggests (this volume is a follow-up to Serrano's bestseller

Basketball (And Other Things); you see a pattern emerging here) movies are a frequent topic.

"We're going to draft actual moments from the movies," as in an NBA draft, Serrano says at the video's opening, after which he lists a few of the arbitrary rules he's applying as a form of diktat. One of these is there can be no Robert De Niro moments among these moments, because then you'd have nothing but Robert De Niro moments. Another is that there will be no films prior to *The Godfather* because while "Gangster movies stretch all the way back to the 1930s…we're not going to include those movies in there because most of those movies aren't that much fun to watch."

His pals, internet personalities Van Lathan, Lilliam Rivera, Amanda Dobbins, and Chris Ryan, all chiming in via cutaways, raise mild objections—Ryan tries to stick up for older movies—but it's Serrano's show. When I say informality, I do not kid; discussing the film *New Jack City*, Serrano refers to its protagonist as "the main person." The video runs a clip from *American Gangster* and follows it with Serrano describing the action of the clip—inaccurately. The panel hits on some truths; Charles Stone III's *Paid in Full* is indeed an underrated gem.

But overall "15 Moments" provides arguable proof that cinema is a failed art form. Serrano and his crew reduce movies to anthologies of "cool" or shocking moments, as opposed to fictions whose circumscribed worlds aspire to create beauty or sorrow or horror or joy in some formally coherent whole.

As when Serrano drones, "The number eight pick is the 'hand or foot' scene from *City of God*," a scene in which poverty-ridden children are goaded into shooting one another. "How do you pick that, Shea?" Lilliam Rivera says, laughing nervously.

In any event: "The number three pick is when Joe Pesci was 'funny like a clown' in *Goodfellas*," Serrano says. "Joe Pesci again"—he was previously featured in a *Casino* clip—"doing all of the things that Joe Pesci does, but this is the best version of him that we saw...ever. He's leaning on Ray Liotta, he is, again, intimidating a guy, but finally we get to watch him do it, with one of his friends, as a joke."

"That could be the greatest scene in movie history," Van says.

"I don't really understand how the Mafia works," Amanda says.

"My cousin's like that," Lilliam says.

Chris Ryan says, "For as much as *Goodfellas* is always zipping around, the camera's always moving, the cutting, the voice-over, the music, it's very cinematic"—!!!—"Scorsese just kinda gets out of the way and lets life play out."

The "it's very cinematic" stuff and the "Scorsese gets out of the way" observations (as if the scene directed itself) notwithstanding, Ryan's point manages to reach the heart of the matter for Scorsese: getting *life* into the frame. For better or worse. Even if it's suicide.

After *The Wolf of Wall Street*, Scorsese, so much of a player by this point that he was neck-deep in HBO documentaries and series, ad work, and other endeavors that, among other things, paid his office overhead (which is not small), stopped entertaining offers for feature films and dug in his heels. He was going to make *Silence*, a movie whose gestation period had by this time been longer than *The Last Temptation of Christ*, before he made anything else.

Based on a 1966 novel by Shūsaku Endō, the story of seventeenth-century Portuguese Catholic missionaries suffering persecution in Japan had been adapted into a film twice already, once by a Japanese director, then by a Portuguese one. Scorsese had read the novel in 1989 and its themes, not just of faith but of doctrine, stuck. He scripted the movie with Jay Cocks. In 2012, as it had been for almost the past twenty years, it was a movie Hollywood had zero interest in. (Might that have been the case had there been a way to get De Niro or DiCaprio in its cast? One can't really say.) Irwin Winkler came back into the fold (as he had been on *Wolf*), and tightening a variety of belts, Scorsese was able to make the complex, multilocation movie on a $50 million budget. It was distributed in the US by Paramount, and flopped; while for the most part critically praised, it is referred to by some younger assessors as Scorsese's "boring priest movie," and, again, summarily dismissed by those invested in characterizing Scorsese as only a director of gangster movies.

The Irishman (2019) is, of course, a gangster movie, and one that fits very snugly in the lineage of *Goodfellas*. *Casino* wasn't definitely the last one, after all. This movie's impetus was multi-headed. First, Scorsese and De Niro had not made a film together since *Casino*, and there was a feeling, on the part of director and actor, not to mention corners of the industry—not to mention a movie fandom that had grown more conspicuously vocal since the internet's amplifications of such entities—that this might not be a bad idea. An adaptation of the 2006 Don Winslow hit-man novel *The Winter of Frankie Machine* was floated, to the extent that the project was greenlit by Paramount. As the title suggests, this was a look at a criminal lion in winter; both Scorsese and De Niro were interested in exploring old age in their work together. Scorsese was already looking at pictures such as Jean Becker's *Touchez-pas le grisbi*, in which Jean Gabin plays a gang leader contending with certain modes of obsolescence.

But then De Niro read Charles Brandt's book *I Heard You Paint Houses*. The ostensibly nonfiction volume chronicled the life of Frank Sheeran, a teamster in the 1950s, '60s, and '70s who, to Brandt, confided that he had killed Jimmy Hoffa, the labor leader whose 1975 disappearance has never been officially solved. Brandt's book is slightly in the mode of Pileggi's *Wiseguy*, but it's not as good. It feels unvetted, it has no index; this and other features of the account fed into complaints about it (which accelerated mightily after it was made into a big-budget, all-star Martin Scorsese movie, of course) from other true-crime writers, and some survivors of the events described therein. Scorsese and De Niro have both stated that the veracity of the book was not their primary concern. (They did make a fiction film, in any event.) They felt this material had an even stronger potential than Winslow's for what they were increasingly seeking to convey.

Sheeran's confessions to Brandt were made in old age; they unwittingly added up to a grim portrait of a "greatest generation" assassin (Sheeran bluntly states that his service in World War II taught him to kill without getting too worked up over it) who did as he was told. Not only by a mob boss like Russell Buffalino, but by society. He got married, raised children, and tried to "protect" them...without ever questioning what he was doing, or what he was doing it *for*. There was money, there was some comfort, there was power (meted out in small portions), and there was work, which he did without much reflection. Up to the point where he was ordered to kill the man whom he considered a close friend—and he did it. Sheeran tells Brandt about his estrangement from one of his children. Trying to reflect on his works before he dies, Sheeran can dredge up very little. He's a cipher.

This personality and its circumstances provided riches for Scorsese, De Niro, screenwriter Steven Zaillian, and subsequent cast members such as Al Pacino, who plays Hoffa, and Joe Pesci. (The "getting the gang back together" aspect of the film was also part of its draw. Most specifically the teaming of icons De Niro and Pacino, who both appeared in *The Godfather Part II*, but had only been on-screen together in two other films: Michael Mann's landmark 1995 *Heat*—an epic crime picture whose tone is the ice to *Goodfellas'* fire, you could say—and the entirely less distinguished *Righteous Kill* in 2008.)

During the making and editing of *The Irishman*, several friends and colleagues of Scorsese said to me, "It's not *Goodfellas*." This is true, but it has many more affinities with *Goodfellas* than it does with, say, *When Harry Met Sally*. After seeing it I began thinking of it as *Goodfellas* strained through *Silence*. Not just in terms of themes, but style. This is not a film with *Goodfellas'* "zippiness." And that's not just because it's a film about old men, made by old men (old men who are frequently de-aged via a complicated technology, the results of which were largely, but not unanimously, deemed successful by critics and viewers).

At any of his ages, De Niro's Frank Sheeran is not a good-time guy like Henry Hill, or the other wiseguys of Scorsese's 1990 movie. Sheeran doesn't much laugh, and doesn't much make others laugh. He doesn't fire a shotgun into the sky after hijacking a truck. He doesn't try to keep a mistress. Instead, after having two children with one wife—just because it's the done thing—he meets a woman he likes better, divorces his first wife, marries the other woman, and stays married to her. There is nothing raucous about him. Aside from killing and stealing, the most he misbehaves is in dipping prosciutto bread into red wine with his friend and sponsor Russell. (Scorsese and Zaillian relieved Sheeran in the film of the alcoholism he suffered from in real life, correctly intuiting it would cloud the issues they wanted to foreground.) The movie is at its most crushing when it adds everything up, once Sheeran is looking at the end of it all.

Mortality, death—it's the no-exit exit, the inescapable...um, *dead end*. This is known to all, you'd think. The aim of *The Irishman*, then, is to compel the viewer to *feel* that, to confront it. To question where you might be when you get to the terminal, and how you'll feel when you get there. So, yes, another "boy movie."

In a January 15, 2019, interview on NPR's *Fresh Air,* host Terry Gross brought up the opening Steadicam shot of *The Irishman,* which goes through the hallway of a nursing home before locating a wheelchair-bound Sheeran. She seems to take it as a refutation of the Copacabana shot in *Goodfellas.* Scorsese is slightly dumbfounded: "It's not like now I look back and I realize gangsters are bad. I know they're bad!"

Scorsese has spoken of *The Irishman* as a culmination. Not merely of the gangster theme in his movies. Where Sheeran is unreflective, the movie itself is profoundly reflective. Another thing Scorsese said to Terry Gross was that the theme of hospitals and/or nursing homes was one that resonated deeply with him because at this point in his life he spent a lot of time visiting them. Sitting in waiting rooms.

The work is an attempt to come to terms. But *The Irishman* is not his last film. As the writing of this book finished up, Scorsese hoped to be in Oklahoma, shooting *Killers of the Flower Moon,* adapted from a book by David Grann, and starring Leonardo DiCaprio and Robert De Niro—the first time these actors have worked together since 1993's *This Boy's Life,* made when DiCaprio was in his late teens.

Scorsese's persistence resembles that of the character he played in Akira Kurosawa's 1990 film *Dreams:* Vincent van Gogh. In the movie, a young Japanese man of the twentieth century, a Kurosawa surrogate, meets an uninterested, abrupt Van Gogh in a wheat field as the great artist chases not just inspiration, but means. "The sun! It compels me to paint!" Scorsese/Van Gogh exclaims. And he storms away. Following the light.

Epilogue:
MARTIN SCORSESE, MARCH 2020

On the evening of September 18, 2018, I got an email from Jenna Chasanoff, a publicist with the firm 42 West, with the heading "Book Proposal." The text of the email read, "Hi, Glenn—Marty has approved this. Please keep us posted on your next steps. Thanks!"

This was most welcome news. While this project had not been conceived or pitched as an "authorized" account, obviously securing Scorsese's cooperation was crucial. I had some big ideas. I would request three interviews, each focusing on a specific aspect of *Goodfellas*, that is, preproduction, shooting, and editing. I would ask to sit down with Scorsese and Thelma Schoonmaker and screen the film, in Scorsese's office screening room, and ask about specific shots. In the almost thirty years since I first met Scorsese while he was editing *Goodfellas*, I had interviewed him a number of times, and had commissioned and edited an essay he wrote about the careers of Robert Mitchum and Jimmy Stewart shortly after those two icons of classic Hollywood had died. (This was all for *Premiere* magazine, where I was an editor and writer for over ten years, until the publication folded in 2007.) During these encounters I found that we had an easy rapport.

My research for this book had begun in earnest just as Scorsese began postproduction work on *The Irishman*. In this phase of his career, Scorsese and Schoonmaker work on editing over the course of a year or so. In the case of *The Irishman*, the process was complicated by the digital technology that had to be applied to alter the appearance of the principal actors, who are depicted at various ages. In the case of Robert De Niro, who plays the lead character Frank Sheeran, he goes from a World War II soldier in his twenties to an increasingly feeble nursing-home patient in his seventies, at least. De Niro himself is in his hardy mid-seventies.

And once *The Irishman* was finished, Netflix, the streaming service which backed the picture, would be rolling it out and promoting it. For its premiere at the New York Film Festival, the company even compelled the reclusive Joe Pesci to appear. The press conference following the screening featured much bonhomie and hilarity between Scorsese, De Niro, and Al Pacino, but the funniest moment was when moderator Kent Jones asked Pesci if he wished to recount how he had gotten involved in the project, and Pesci smiled (tightly) and said, "No." And that was it.

Scorsese was then obliged to spend a lot of time on the West Coast, to campaign for his film during awards season. While highly praised by critics, and deemed a success by Netflix, the movie did not garner much in terms of statuettes. What was the reason? I'm not an Oscar expert—my attitude toward the awards show is pretty much in line with what David Foster Wallace wrote in his essay "Big Red Son," that is, "Underneath it all, though, we know the whole thing sucks" (there was a lot more prefacing this obviously, but you might just want to read the whole thing of your own volition)—but two potential contributions to what some called a "backlash" were the social media participants fuming over Anna Paquin's minimal dialogue in the film (a lot of really ridiculous "Scorsese silences women" takes out there), and film industry and "fanboy" resentment over Scorsese's entirely reasonable comments concerning big-budget superhero movies, his view that they did not constitute "cinema" as he himself understood it. This moronic controversy climaxed when Disney CEO Bob Iger, whose pestilent corporation owns and finances films in the Marvel franchise and the *Star Wars* franchise, tut-tutted Scorsese and announced that he intended to take Scorsese to task at a "meeting." Iger announced he would leave his position some months after this. When the time came for my meeting, I somehow neglected to ask Scorsese whether this summit had taken place.

That time came on March 9, 2020, after much hurried juggling of appointments. Scorsese was preparing to start shooting *Killers of the Flower Moon* on location in Oklahoma. He and his staff at his production company, Sikelia, were also preparing to move their office, from the building that also houses the Directors Guild headquarters on West 57th Street, to a building several blocks east.

The office was quiet when I arrived in the late afternoon. I was greeted by Luis DeJesus, an intern at Sikelia who, it also so happened, was in 2017 a student in my Language of Film class at New York University, where I am an adjunct professor. We had a pleasant chat in the screening room. The office in general feels, in the Monty Python term, "very woody" and is of course decorated by many vintage movie posters. Soon I met in person Lisa Frechette and Jana Heaton, the two Sikelia people with whom I'd been negotiating the interview for many months.

I had been asked to submit a list of written questions so Scorsese could be well-prepared. In this exchange I was told that Scorsese did not want to discuss issues of producing credits, and in fact would prefer if I not bring up the name of his former producer and former wife at all. I had misgivings in this respect, of course. I decided I would not force the issue, and the fact that Irwin Winkler had already given me a response to Barbara De Fina's account made my resignation a bit less concerning.

Scorsese emerged from his office and Lisa led me inside as he paced around a little. A six-foot-tall poster for the 1942 classic *Cat People* made an immediate impression. Scorsese's very occupied desk faced east; catty-cornered from it was an easy chair and a sofa separated by a small coffee table and I was pointed to the chair. Scorsese was dressed in a white shirt with a small blue check, jeans, and elegant brown leather loafers. All Armani, I presume; Scorsese has a longstanding professional and personal association with the design firm. He immediately struck me as a little tired and a little preoccupied. He began with the first of two apologies, telling me he would have loved to have done this sooner, but…and he shrugged, and indicated his desk and the boxes around the room. I congratulated him on *The Irishman* and mentioned that my wife and I were frequently chuffed when Scorsese, when thanking crew members at screenings of the film, would mention Kip Myers, who was the locations coordinator on the movie and is an old friend of ours. "No kidding? Oh, Kip's great. Although I did yell at him a lot—'Kip, my God, what have you done!!!'" He laughed. In Tom Shone's coffee table book about *The Irishman*, he mentions that Kip put 5,000 miles on his Subaru Forester while scouting the over one hundred locations the film used; I told Scorsese I'd recently had the occasion to drive that same vehicle, and told Kip, "I'm driving a piece of film history!" Scorsese laughed again. "That's right!"

Lisa told Scorsese that she would interrupt the interview in the event that she got hold of "the doctor."

"Doctor?" I said. "My wife," Scorsese said matter-of-factly.

Since 1999 Scorsese has been married to Helen Morris, a book editor and producer; they have a daughter, Francesca, born in November of 1999. Francesca is now a college student at the same institution from which Scorsese came up, and where I now teach. Morris has Parkinson's disease (she was diagnosed in 1990) and this is a cause of constant concern and monitoring these days. I think it is both out of his own general sense of discretion and a protective instinct and respect for his family that when Scorsese refers to the personal life of his past, he doesn't mention any names.

He sat on the couch and we got started.

"I'm going to try to be as succinct at possible," he said. "I appreciate you doing this. It's very interesting and I'm sorry, because I could talk about this for days...but I don't have the time. Sorry. Sor-ry! And you should know, Marianne [Bower, Scorsese's print archivist] has so much in the archives..."

"Yes, I'd love to speak with her," I said. "I'm particularly interested in the annotated script. Joe Reidy let me look at his copy when I spoke with him."

"Joe really pulled it together. He knows. He and Michael Ballhaus really laid out the Copacabana shot for me in such a way... we knew where we were gonna go, and I'd go in the trailer and come back, and they'd have pieces of action plotted out, a little here a little there, and then ultimately by the end of the day we had it, but they did the legwork of staging stuff. *And* of course to make sure the table was flying right and to make sure that Mr. Tony the maître d' was in the right place. When we used to go to the Copa, we were young kids, we were maybe late teenagers. We didn't really frequent the lounge because that was for the...more mature crowd. Although the bar was run by Nicky De Faro, who was one of my best friends' fathers. And we put him in *Raging Bull*, in the bar scene. In any event, we'd go, for example, celebrations, graduation, high school, I saw Bobby Darin there. Whenever we went to see Joe E. Lewis or Sammy Davis or whoever, we would get in the line and go down and we'd get tables. And the tables were always very good. Until the last minute. And all of a sudden, other tables come flying in and it's all wiseguys. Or juiced-in people. And all of a sudden you couldn't see anything. And we couldn't believe we had such a great view, until the moment the performers came on, and then, gone. And so that had to be there. We did not go in through the back. We were kids."

"Everybody has wonderful things to say about Ballhaus," I said, "and because of his work with Fassbinder..."

"He could work very fast. And he wasn't afraid of camera movement. If the camera's freed by the use of lightweight equipment, whether it's *Shadows* to Godard and Truffaut...in Italy they didn't shoot with sound. Camera movement is less complicated with European thinking. American, in the '70s as soon as the camera got freed up, through the inspiration of European or Asian cinema—mainly Japanese, because there was not much South Asian film available to us at that time—it got complicated very quickly. Somehow, there was more equipment involved, it was heavier to move...but in the European mindset it was just a different way of working. And in the European films there was a roughness that was part of the shot. I'm not talking about handheld, I'm not talking about obvious attempts at shaking the camera. It wasn't supposed to be shaking. But you accepted it, and also it added to the energy of the shot, by being just a little off a bit. But in America, with a lot of the DPs, it became more arduous. And so Ballhaus had this freedom of thinking."

"I think of Godard's *A Woman Is a Woman*, the opening scene, when the camera follows Anna Karina through the Paris streets. It's a not too distant homage to Tashlin's *The Girl Can't Help It*, but much less slick..."

"Yes. That was exactly it. The camera was moving and it seemed so effortless, it seemed like the camera was flying. And I liked that. I always wanted to get to that. And now you can do it with an iPhone. You finally got there."

Scorsese took a look at the sheet that had my written questions on it. The first one was this: "It just so happened that you had to take the opportunity to make *Last Temptation* when it preempted *Goodfellas*. Both films have a cinematic language that is your own, but each film is also distinctly different from the other. You spoke of the attempt to create timelessness in *Last Temptation*, but in *Goodfellas* time is always hurtling ahead. Did making *Temptation* when you did help you hone the approach you would take in *Goodfellas*?" (In case you are wondering, almost all my written questions were that wordy.) He took it up.

"It was really the subject matter. *Last Temptation* was supposed to have been made in 1982, 1983. It was canceled, and in effect I had to start all over again. And I came back to New York. Honed my craft again to move faster on *After Hours*. Then, Mike Ovitz came into the picture. And that changed everything. And then what I applied to *After Hours* I applied to a studio picture, *The Color of Money*. Which is the only film I ever came in a day under and a million dollars under. Which I think betrays the mild nature of the film, which I'm not very satisfied with. It's a good picture, I like it. But it was marking time in a way. A workout. The whole thing was that I wanted to get *Last Temptation* made. The script had to be changed. Reconfigured in a more economical way. Obviously. I had been trying to combine both Hollywood elements, meaning bigger films, with the Italian style. All of that had to be eliminated. I use the term *Italian style* to mean Olmi, Pasolini, the last films of Rossellini, Taviani, all that sort of thing. Now we were looking at a smaller crew, minimal crowds. Minimalism, really, minimalism. That had a lot to do with the ancient towns, the life. Obviously not of the Senate class, or the aristocratic class or Herod, but the people on the street. So. That opened the way for me. And the intensity within something that's minimal. Camera movements included. And I had designed all the shots, they were all drawn. I enjoyed doing that but I was doing it to have control of the shoot. Knowing that if I was ever going to have it made, I wouldn't have much money to make it with.

"I was in Chicago, shooting *Color of Money*, and I was reading the *New York Review of Books*. And I certainly wasn't going to do an organized crime film again. But I read this review of the book, *Wiseguy*, in which it was described as mob life from the point of view of the foot soldier. And I thought, This is interesting. So I got a copy of it. And I read it. I think I told Mike Ovitz. This is how it works, I think. Ovitz is above all of this stuff, and he's behind all of it. Including *Last Temptation*. Including *Kundun*. Including *Schindler's List*. Including *Cape Fear*. All of that. His guidance and influence is there. He was very proud to resuscitate my life. And also to get my taxes paid. By '91 or '92. In any event he was putting me back on track. And so... I believe Irwin Winkler, who stayed a very good friend, because we met in 1972 at the New York Film Festival, with *Mean Streets*, which has a major reference to *Point Blank*, which he produced, so we met and talked and worked together. On a number of films, including *Raging Bull* and *New York, New York*. *New York, New York* was a life experience. Put it that way. So was *Raging Bull* but *New York, New York* was more trouble. And we all went through that together. *Raging Bull* we all went through together but we had it. With *New York, New York* we were flailing about. I had some thoughts, I had a certain way of doing it, Irwin supported me; Bob Chartoff was his partner and we went through some very hard times and some very wonderful times making it. And I think he wanted to work with me again. Thelma and I were editing in Chicago. And it wasn't an easy shoot, but it was easy enough, so that we could actually do some of the cutting as we were shooting. And I got a call from Irwin, who said, 'You like this book, *Wiseguy*?' and I said, 'If I were to do another film about organized crime in New York, this would be the way to do it.' Because that's how I knew it, when I grew up, through the street corner. Combined with confidential information I heard from my father. Telling stories of people, sometimes I didn't know their names. And that was only said at the kitchen table. Where nobody could hear.

"Irwin said, 'I'll buy it for you.' And that was that. Having said that, he was good friends with Nick Pileggi and Nora Ephron. And I was not. I was not in any way connected with the New York intelligentsia of the journalists, writers, for *New York* magazine. I knew a few people but I had horrible, horrible experiences with them. Understandably, though, under the circumstances. Still. I didn't know Nick. I didn't know his cousin Gay. Didn't know Nora, any of these people. The Elaine's group. I think I only went there twice. Once it was a little dinner to meet Isabelle Adjani, for Truffaut's *Story of Adele H.* And then another time. And then one other time Nick took me. All these *writers.* Flexing their muscles. Elaine was very nice to me. But I don't belong there. So I left.

"Nick called me in Chicago and he was very nice, very complimentary. He later told me that when he told his agent that I was interested in doing it and Irwin was buying the book for me, he told Nick, 'Don't bother, 'cause he can't get pictures made.' His agent was negative on it. But that was the take on me at that time. That was the take. *King of Comedy* was an unmitigated disaster, except for a few good reviews. *Last Temptation*, the first time around, from '82 to '83, when it was canceled, was considered a folly. We were laughed at by everyone in Hollywood. Irwin and Bob tried but eventually they had to give up. So I was sent packing then. I had been living in Los Angeles since '71. I couldn't get anything done. That's not to say that Paramount, when they canceled, because I was friendly with Jeffrey Katzenberg and Dawn Steel, that's not to say that they didn't offer me *Witness.* There was talk of *Beverly Hills Cop.* They tried to get me something that they had. I think even *The Golden Child.* But *Witness* was the one. And I...just couldn't take my... I had to start all over again on my own things. I just couldn't shift gears like that, especially after having the rug pulled out from under my feet. Because I was so into *Last Temptation*, it was all cast. And it wasn't all them. There were circumstances, and [the Gulf and Western CEO—G&W was then the parent company of Paramount Pictures] Marvin Davis getting all those letters from evangelicals. It was just circumstances. A perfect storm, to use the cliché. But that's what it was. I was talking after this for a little while with Gene Kirkwood, a friend of Irwin Winkler, nice guy, and dealing with Mark Helprin, the writer of *Winter's Tale*. He at least said to my face, when we were talking about doing that book, this was around '84 or '85, 'I've been talking to people in LA and they say you're washed up.' At this time I was doing *After Hours*, relegated to independent film, and at least David Geffen still believed in me and told me to go out and make that, for him.

"I don't mean anything negative about Helprin. He was concerned about his work getting on-screen. If this was the case, how are you going to get anything, especially a period movie with effects. And so that's what I was regarded as, in a way. So understandably Nick's agent was dubious. Even Irwin... Irwin came to visit me shooting one night on *After Hours*—it was all nights, forty nights—and he looked at me and said, 'You wanna come do a real film again?' And I said, 'I thought I was making a real film.' So he was very excited to do this. He got the rights and somehow Nick and I started working on it. I don't know how.

"You know what it was? In Chicago when I was reading it, I was taken up into the whirlwind of the last day. The way he was describing everything, I thought, This is the movie. This is the film. Everything builds to this. Forget all...the Lufthansa this...so and so being killed. None of it matters. What matters is the sauce. Sending her on the plane with her lucky hat. How much more can he take."

"You don't even show the Lufthansa heist," I said.

"No no no! It's not important! The money is important. They never found the money by the way!" Now, in the thick of his memories and observations, Scorsese could let go a little, and he began cackling with glee about the absurdity of the still partially unsolved case.

"There was a prosecution just a few years ago," I said, "a whole book is predicated on it, and they didn't get..."

"I can't believe it! They can never get a conviction!" Scorsese says. We are both amused with this.

"And the fact that none of them were made men. So they can behave badly. Especially in terms of Joe Pesci's character. Which, I've gotta say, is something I've experienced. There was a kid I knew, he was killed at twenty-one for that. Now whether he was killing people, I don't know, but he was the son of a major wiseguy. Then, about a year later, his father was killed. But we were with them, and that's how it happens. So I'm aware of all of that, and I was around it. It was the last days of the wiseguy, is how I saw it. And it became a movie more about the lifestyle than any main character. Henry Hill was Virgil taking Dante around."

Getting back to the matter of cinematic language, he continued. "Around this time I did a commercial or two for Armani. And I discovered that, doing this commercial, which I'm not very good at, meaning selling stuff, but we made little films in a way. But it was fun to be in Milan, enjoyable, the clothes are just so wonderful...getting back to Italy, having burned certain bridges in Rome in the late '70s, with my personal life, I was no longer welcome there...but I came back into the Italian scene through the Armani group in Milan. I made a commercial, and in Italy it can be a little longer, and then they tell you, you've got to have a minute version, and then they say, Oh, by the way you've got to do a twenty-second version, and then a ten-second. And I said, 'Wait a minute.' *But* I found a way to do it. And I found that shots could stay on...which I knew in a way...it's about the information in the frame. Let's say it's a pocketbook and a hand places something in it. How long does it have to be for it to register in an audience's mind? Knowing that, going back to Eisenstein. I know it, but I never did it. Or at least I did it in my first shorts at NYU, when I was playing with the medium. But they're juvenilia. *Murray, Nice Girl*...not *The Big Shave*, *The Big Shave* is different. And I'm thinking, the world is going so fast...what if we make something that's very fast? And I always talk about this: the first three minutes of *Jules et Jim*. It's pure cinema, and it's beautiful. And the language. The actual words. The voice-over is also part of the image. And each frame, each camera move, each expression of the actors, has a poetic nature to it that is...*poetic* is an overused word. But what I mean is that so much information, and I don't mean narrative information, is conveyed."

"But it's true, it's almost literally poetic, because ideas of line and meter are conveyed in the rhythm of the shots."

"Right, when the camera's zooming in, and they're saying, 'We went to this island to see this statue...'"

"And you have to pay attention, because if you don't pay attention you lose the thread, and the point of it. You do that in *Wolf of Wall Street*, with the poor guy who marries the woman who fellated him in the elevator, and the gruesome cut to the tub full of blood."

"Oh, that's right, that's right, I forgot that. In *Jules et Jim*, the narrative is as you point out, on another level. It's not direct exposition, I mean, he's saying certain things, 'I met Jules,' and so on, that's okay. But there's something about the frames, and every time I see it I think of the different production elements in that frame. There's not much to it. They're taking stuff out of a trunk, but in my mind's eye it's the entire fin du siècle."

"And it's the speed of thought."

"Yes, exactly, the speed of thought. Thank you."

"Nick said that both you guys went off after resolving to work together on the script and each outlined what needed cutting and you both came back with…"

"THE SAME THING. That's it, he's right. Forgot about that. So what the hell, the whole movie should be that way. And get even faster. Until it stops."

We moved on to a couple of the other written questions and Scorsese proceeded to poke little holes in some of my pet theories and interpretations. Of the moment of tenderness when Henry, in voice-over, remembers Tuddy, Scorsese said, "That's just how it was said. Henry was wistful about a lot of things. These guys were like gods to him." Of the hollowness of the laughter at the poker game before Morrie's death, he said, "We just wanted to capture late night, drinking, playing cards, laughing too hard at things that aren't that funny. We"—I am not entirely clear on just who "we" are—"still do that 'don't say it' bit from Tommy's story." I brought up Michael Imperioli's correct instincts on dealing with De Niro in his scenes and Scorsese nodded vigorously. "Don't mess with us. Just relate to the world that you're in. Do not bring yourself." He then expressed sympathy for what Imperioli had to go through with his hand and all, and laughed when remembering the emergency room story.

Getting back to the poker game, he said, "I needed them to be laughing at that, and then Bob says, We're not gonna kill him. And then they kill him, anyway. That's how arbitrary it was. In part because he was a sociopath, and also because he wasn't a made guy. All that stuff in the Mafia about honor, it's a lot of nonsense, there's no such thing. But. There was a sense of order. And the order was before you do anything like that you have to get permission. And you see what happens. I don't remember how I heard it but I heard somewhere that John Gotti thought the movie was bullshit because Tommy was tall, not Joe Pesci's size, and because Tommy was actually killed for killing a guy named Foxy, not Batts.

"*Goodfellas* was a great experience but it was also terrible. Joe Reidy and I had laid out a schedule of seventy days. And because I had all these short scenes, it's very difficult, a quarter of a page is harder to do than five pages of dialogue. Because you've got to go to all these different places. And the traffic was terrible. We had to really rush around. And I had it all planned, everything was annotated, all the freeze-frames, they were on the page because I knew I had to do this fast. I wanted to make this film quickly, not hastily. Warners said do it in fifty-five days. And we tried. And we were exhausted. And we kept going over schedule. And one day Mike Ovitz had to come on the set, Bob Daly came down, I think Terry Semel came down, too. We went to the trailer, they observed some of the shooting. My father was there. It was nice. But it was like, Can you cut anything, can you move any faster. And from that meeting on, we tried, but what happened was before we finally finished…at the same time I was supposed to act in *Dreams*, by Akira Kurosawa. And he had finished his film. And now he was waiting for me. The studio wants me to finish, and Kurosawa is waiting. So I was worried. And I thought I had palpitations. I went to see the doctor and he told me not to have any coffee. So the last two weeks of the shoot I didn't drink coffee. Which was pretty bad for me in the morning. Also Michael Ballhaus had to go on to another film. And Barry [Sonnenfeld] came in. Also De Niro had to leave. He had to be addressed as to his schedule and the way he had to shoot during the day. And he came first, and that was it. That was it. The pressure was enormous. But then they left me alone. And it turns out it was seventy days. Not that we were right and they were wrong. It's just the nature of the picture and the circumstances. This also—I don't want to be petty about it, but I think this tails with my reputation at the time. One they didn't want to give a wrap party. It was just like, 'Please finish. Please. Just. End it!' I think we made some T-shirts for everybody at our own expense. Also I remember making the deal for it. I wanted to get an extra amount, for my salary, and at the last minute they just wouldn't do it. I forget what it was I asked for. I know it was money, and I know it was an amount, and it wasn't that much but I just wanted it, out of respect. And no. So basically I was just glad to be making the film.

"But I still, during these times, had misgivings about making another film about organized crime. I was talking with Marlon Brando during that period, and he said, 'You don't wanna do that again.' So I was going sour on it a little bit. And then Mike Ovitz pulls *Last Temptation* together. With Tom Pollock, Casey Silver, and other Universal people. I was on my way to Tahiti to talk to Brando, he wanted us to go to the island to talk about a project he had. We're on the West Coast and Ovitz said, 'Meet with them, explain how you want to make *Last Temptation*. No salary.' And I did, and we then went on to Tahiti, and coming back from Tahiti we stopped in LA again and there was a deal. So then I had to go to Terry Semel and ask him to wait. And they were very kind about that. And also [then Paramount CEO] Frank Mancuso was a big help. Because a lot of money was owed to Paramount. And he called me and said, 'I'm going to do this because I know how much it means to you. I'll work it out with Universal.' They use the word *journey*, but boy was *Temptation* a journey. It was the best and it was the worst. And by the time we were editing it… I don't know. It's okay."

Scorsese made an abrupt gesture with his left hand, as if waving the whole thing away. "I don't wanna go into it because it's too layered. And then I was approached about *Schindler's List*. So I thought, I don't know. Do I really wanna do *Goodfellas*? I know it's a good script and all that. I don't know. There was a deal with Universal, too, I owed them another movie, and now I was going to go to Warner Brothers to make *Goodfellas*. The thing is, I had already planned it out in my head so thoroughly that it was almost like I'd already made it, so the shooting or the prospect of shooting was almost an afterthought!

"But Thelma had read the script to Michael Powell. And Michael was not a great fan of the gangster genre. And Michael called and told me, 'You must do this.' And that clicked. It shifted me back into the original energy and original impulse to make the picture, from when I'd read the book. And in a sense I approached it as unfinished work, unfinished business, just got to get done. And we got it done. We got it shot, we got it edited. Michael Powell died. Thelma stopped working. I, too, took a break...did a short film with Nestor Almendros on Armani. Thelma was away dealing with the sadness of the whole thing.

"And there was a weekend when Jay Cocks and I went to Washington. I think it was for the premier of the restoration of *Lawrence of Arabia*. We were at the event, and Roger Ebert and Gene Siskel walked by. Roger said, 'Did you hear?' I said, 'What?' He said, '*Raging Bull*, best of the decade. Two major film magazines. *Film Comment* and *American Film*, the AFI magazine.' And I think *Goodfellas* was ready to come out. And the advance screenings, aside from a couple of very, very bad previews, were very good. So the combination of the two, the recognition of *Raging Bull* by those two magazines—and one of them also had *King of Comedy* in there—and the good reaction to the new film...all of a sudden there was a reassessment. Of everything. And that was it."

"Since that time," I said, "there have been a not-quite alternating series of films you've made from your own personal impetus and films that come your way that you say you have to find your own way to. When I moderated a Q&A on *Wolf of Wall Street* you spoke of that in the case of the subject, and of Jordan Belfort, the protagonist..."

"Well, I had to do that with *Raging Bull*, too. I didn't know it was about me. I guess De Niro knew. He just needed to get me to make it. I KNEW *Taxi Driver*. I understood that. I understood *New York, New York*. But the problem with the dissatisfaction with the results of *New York, New York*, although that's my... inside, my personal relationship to that picture and that experience. It might be better than anything I ever made, and I don't know. And it's not for me to know. Just relate to it in a way that says I wanted to do something and it didn't get there. It went another way. I think I know why. And other people don't know it, they don't know anything about it, about the stylization of the sets and the color...mixed with the New Wave, not New Wave but improvisatory cinema..."

"Well, the restoration screened in New York recently and I moderated a Q&A with Irwin Winkler and when I introduced the movie I described it as a hybrid of Cassavetes and Vincente Minnelli."

"That's right. A lot of people say, well, you can't do that, well, we did it. But you know the names. People see it today, they might not know the names. But does it work for them? For some people it does. Fine. But that's beyond my care at this point but it's also out of my hands. People seeing *Paisan*, do they have to know about the Second World War? I mean, I knew about it, my uncles were in it. People see it now, what's left? What's there?"

"I screen the final section, with the partisans and the US and British troops, on the Po Delta, to my students, and they're moved by it."

"It's powerful." He thought back again to *New York, New York* and its cataclysmic personal aftermath.

"What was happening, the thing that kind of saved me for a while was *Last Waltz*. That was something that happened where I had the instinct and inspiration. Creative inspiration. All the inspiration I had had for *New York, New York* seemed to dissipate after I finished. And I didn't know if maybe I'd achieved what I thought I was after. It was so intuitive…the thinking about it didn't matter. I didn't know that at the time. But I did take on a very big production at the time, and the people involved, I feel like I failed them. And so I felt very bad about it. And what saved me creatively was *The Last Waltz* and even that collapsed. And then there was this hospital situation and De Niro came and said, 'Let's do *Raging Bull.*' And at that point, we had that script, six weeks' work that Paul Schrader had done on it, and we took that script and we went to an island, and re-found…how should I put it…found again, a reason to make another film."

"Which is why it's dedicated to Haig Manoogian."

"Yes. 'With resolution.' That's it. And I thought that would be my last film. I was involved with friends in Rome, personal life, and I was going to go to Italy and make films on the lives of the saints. So. There you have it. And De Niro grabbed me again for *King of Comedy.* And I had to find my way through that through the shooting. And then there was another…brick wall, in '82. It was very bad. And suddenly… Siskel and Ebert booked me in Toronto and gave me an award and that was another turning point. Not about the award, but my whole life had changed, anyway. I had gone through a very difficult period. I saw a lot of doctors and things, psychotherapy, and suddenly there was a freedom, that everything could start again. And that's when *Last Temptation* first became a possibility. And then that was crashed. But then, instead of collapsing, the thing to do was to go back to New York and suit up." He laughed.

"Suit up and show up," I said.

"Yes. Just go. Start working again. Beat them at their own game. And that happened with *After Hours* and *Color of Money.* And *Temptation* when it was made was not received. The only place that recognized the picture was the Directors Branch of the Academy. And that was more for, not the film or its art, but the tenacity to get it made. And freedom of speech. It was wonderful. Just to be there that night. Very enjoyable. But that was it. That was it."

"Every time I interview you, you speak as if you've made your last film. *Bringing Out the Dead...*"

Scorsese threw himself into the back of the sofa and extended his hands as if to shield himself.

"Oh! *Bringing Out the Dead!*"

"Or *Kundun...*" He did it again.

"Oh! *Kundun!*" He sat back up again, hugging one of the sofa's throw pillows.

"At the end of *New York, New York* and *Last Waltz*, the feeling was could I ever do it again. Could I feel anything strong enough to go through that process again. Not just shooting, which is very strenuous, arduous I should say, but also with the financiers. You have an obligation with the money. You want to make it a certain way. And also the cinema I came out of— the movies that I came out of, because *cinema* is a word that has strange connotations now—so. The movies I came out of in my period of living in LA were more oriented to a personal style. *Raging Bull* was one of two or three pictures that finished everything as far as the studios were concerned. But there were distractions. *Heaven's Gate* was one of the movies that distracted them from us. As did *Apocalypse Now*. That was a major effort as you know, and a great film. All UA, by the way. And when all that collapsed. Today, especially with the new fantasy films... The question becomes, where do you belong? It's not even where do you belong. It's where they'll let you work."

"So it never gets any easier. Not even with Netflix?"

"Netflix was the one. That was the one. That was the most support I've gotten since *Raging Bull*. I mean the production of *Raging Bull*. That doesn't mean other people didn't give you support. Like Tom Pollock on *Temptation* or Mark Canton on

The Age of Innocence. But invariably it was knock-down, drag-out fights, from *Taxi Driver,* to *Goodfellas,* to, well, I don't know. *Gangs,* of course. But that's part of the deal. That's part of the challenge. That's built in. The glove is on the ground. And I'm gonna pick it up. If you pick it up, you're in. Don't complain. That's *it.*"

"And now he's in jail," I said, referring to *Gangs of New York* producer Harvey Weinstein, whose glove was the one Scorsese picked up. The convicted rapist was incarcerated on Rikers Island as we spoke, awaiting sentencing a couple of days later. He got twenty-three years.

"Yeah..." Scorsese said, not sounding displeased.

"And there was a little bit on *Aviator.* In the last weeks of postproduction they did something to me and my crew that I didn't like. And he had something to do with it. And he wasn't the only one. It was all of them. And I said, 'That's it, I can't work with these people anymore.' Meaning, if this is the only way I can make a film, under these conditions... Let me put it this way: *Aviator* we finished on schedule, there was pressure, the editing, there was pressure, but it was good. And because I wouldn't do what certain people wanted me to, they did something in the last two weeks of post, when we went into mixing, that was...disgusting. And you've taken it all the way up to *there.* Then they become...at least on *Gangs of New York* it was *every day.*" He laughed. "Here, they were smiley one minute and at the last minute they came down like...what was that famous police force that Nicholas the Second had..."

We both got stuck on that. It was called the Okhrana.

"They just come in and they knock on the door in the middle of the night and say, 'Oh, you're coming with us.' And they do that *now*? It's a long story but I didn't even call their bluff. I just said, 'So just take it. Take it the way it is now.' And they said, 'It's not finished.' And I said, 'It's finished for me, if that's what you want to do with it.' They had some thoughts. Because I wouldn't cut anymore. And I said, 'It's good enough. A lot of people are looking at it now and they like it.' And then it stopped. It stopped not because they're afraid of me. It stopped because their major star, Leonardo DiCaprio, his reputation, his performance, which was wonderful, was then going to be compromised. When they understood that, that's when they stopped."

"Does DiCaprio bring more clout to these fights?"

"In that case he was not involved. It was the people around him who realized it. When I said, 'If you do *this*… I'm fine. I've had a pretty good career. It's good as it is but it needs to be finished.' But just think…you want it to be the *best*. The best it can be. My approach to *Aviator* was, after *Gangs*, I wanted to make a *movie*. *Gangs* was something that had been after me for so long, like *Last Temptation*, and I finally got it out of my system and I wanted to make a *movie*. And I decided that I would do this one, and it's really a vehicle for him. And he has to be treated right. So if you want to take a chance…and don't let me finish, the last few weeks…it's good enough for me, I don't know if it's good enough for *him*. Meaning, he's fine in the film. But to have the final voice right, to have the mixing right, to have the ADR right. You know, you want to…you know the phrase 'penny wise, dollar foolish'? Go ahead. I'm gonna go make a gangster film. I'm gonna shoot it in the streets. And it's called *The Departed*. And that turned out, it was the same studio." He laughed again. "And it was even worse! It was even worse. A worse experience with the studio. But it was a different kind of worse. In that the people involved were not unpleasant or mean-spirited. Just very different philosophies, and never the twain shall meet. We tried! We really tried! And so, anyway. That turned out the way it turned out. And it was another comeback, in a way. I don't know. Something happened. It's all about, I guess, bridges that are burned. *Gangs of New York* and *The Aviator*, that was it. When I did *The Departed*, I got the script, and I wanted to do it and Leo wanted to do it, and at the same time I was having health issues with my wife and all this going on…and I decided, That's it. No more. No more. And I was trying to mix the film. Thelma was in Los Angeles trying to get the answer print"—the first physical version of a finished film, back when they were made on celluloid—"with Michael Ballhaus. And I wouldn't even go there. I looked at some things they'd send me, but that's it. I did the mix. They finished the answer print. And I did one or two interviews, that was it. I went away. To shoot the Rolling Stones. That was it. I said, 'Leave me be now.' And people were reacting very well to it, and I was just like, 'That's great, I'm happy you're happy, but leave me alone. Maybe this does well, maybe people make some money, good. If not, I'm fine. Leave me alone!'

"And then things changed after that. And I decided to make different kinds of movies. *Shutter Island. Hugo.* The next big one I had in mind was *Silence*. I wanted to make *Silence* right after *Gangs* but I couldn't get Jay [Cocks] to lock in to write the script with me. There were so many legal problems." These were labyrinthine indeed, too much so to describe concisely here; among them was a dispute with the Italian company Cecchi Gori Pictures, which had the rights to the property and sued Scorsese several times after the project was delayed on multiple occasions. "And having had so many issues with the Italians, and having so many legal problems on *Gangs*, naturally people began to become shy about working with me. They didn't want to be included in the summons, if there was gonna be one. Understandable. Understandable. But we're old friends. You gotta help me out here. And once he was protected, by 2005, we finished the script about Christmastime. And in 2006 it was ready, and then *The Departed* hit. And *Silence* was caught up in extraordinary legal issues with the Italians. Extraordinary. The only person who ultimately was able—we all tried, Mike Ovitz, everybody, Rick Yorn, meeting after meeting, threats, talks, people doing things you couldn't even imagine—the only person who wasn't aware of the complexity of the Gordian knot was Irwin. So he sat there where you're sitting and he said, 'Why don't we make *Silence*, you always wanted to make that?' I said, 'Well, it's complicated,' and I realized he didn't know how complicated it was. So we open the door and said, 'Go in. Go into the room!' And a few months later he came back and said, 'Boy, is this complicated.' And [producer] Emma Tillinger, too, helped him out. But the thing about Irwin is he has that quality of an old-time producer. If you tell him 'no,' he'll go somewhere else. And he'll find something to get it done. His story about the first film he had to make. It's MGM and it's O'Brien or somebody. You know the story?"

"It's in Irwin's book. About *Double Trouble*. With Elvis. Which was originally to have been a vehicle for his client…"

"Yeah, it was with Julie Christie! Yes! And then all of a sudden, it's Elvis. And why not? His point is getting the film made. And he pursued it because he knew it was kind of a passion for me. And he said, 'Let's do it!' and I said, 'Great!' A year later we almost had it. But Graham King was holding it up, because he had put a lot of money in it and he wanted it back. And the times when someone like Frank Mancuso would make that go away for you—not these days. But Irwin tells a story in this room. 'This is it,' he says. Emma had come back from meeting with Graham, he won't go down on his price, there are other issues, they didn't tell me all of them because they were complicated, I really felt terrible. I said, 'What are we gonna do?' And Emma was depressed. And Irwin says, 'Well, look. There's a story.' And Irwin tells this story. Somewhere in the caliphate in the fifteenth century, let's say, there's a powerful Jewish person in with the court, of the sultan, or the caliph. And something had happened with the Jewish population in Baghdad, say. And the caliph sent out a decree: kill all the Jews. So his Jewish philosopher or astronomer or mathematician said, 'Hold off on that for a second.' The caliph says, 'Why?' The mathematician says, 'Think about it for a second.' The caliph says, 'I wanna do it.' The mathematician says, 'I tell you what. If I can get that dog that you like to speak, a year from now—' 'You're gonna get that dog to speak—' 'Yeah, I'm gonna get that dog to speak, gimme one year, and I'll get that dog to speak. You hold off on killing all the Jews.' The caliph says, 'Okay.' So. He takes the dog and goes home to his wife. He tells his wife what happened. She says, 'Are you crazy? That dog can't speak!' and he says, 'Yeah, but we got a year!' And that's film producing. We got ourselves a year. And he was right. Don't panic, don't go crazy, that's the way he is. And we had a year and we got it." Scorsese stood up.

It was almost time to wrap up. "And Brad Grey, too, he got *Silence* made by agreeing to distribute it." (Grey died in 2017, shortly after being ousted from Paramount.) "It's amazing how some people can be, it's very moving, because they know how much it means to you. And they came through. They came through.

"It all comes back to can you pull yourself together. For the next one, *Killers of the Flower Moon*, I think I can. I mean, I love the story. And the people involved. At seventy-seven there is an issue of physical stamina. Pictures take long to shoot. Although *Irishman*, that was a good, steady rhythm in shooting. We weren't too tired and we didn't waste any time. 'Cause I think we all reached a certain age. And Rodrigo Prieto was prepared, as was Emma, as was David Webb. And it was tough. But it was not tough for superfluous reasons. It was get there, Al, and Joe and Bob and Anna Paquin, all amazing."

I looked at my watch and saw our ninety minutes were almost done, so I decided to exercise the better part of valor and I turned off my recorder. Lisa was outside the office and I told her I figured I'd call it because...

"Oh, yes, I was just about to come in for you, anyway."

I mentioned to Scorsese that I was glad he had recently met my friend Farran Smith Nehme, the critic who the week before had interviewed him for a supplement on a Criterion Collection edition of his early short films. "Yes. She seemed very nice. I'm sorry I wasn't able to speak with her more personally but," and he shrugged again and gestured around, "you know."

I then told him that for the past couple of years Farran and I had been enjoying monthly lunches with Scorsese's old friend and collaborator Jay Cocks. "Really? I didn't know that." Then, with mock indignation: "Jay doesn't tell me anything anymore." After instructing me to touch base with Marianne Bower sooner than later, and pledging almost blanket permissions on using documentation and production stills, he continued in that vein when I said I'd be seeing Jay in a couple of days: "Don't tell Jay I said hi!"

As it happened, the lunch was postponed. By the end of the week, New York City would be in the process of shutting down to try to contain the coronavirus. The film industry would soon follow suit, and as I write this, the production of *Killers of the Flower Moon* is on hold.

Postscript:
A *GOODFELLAS* LIBRARY

Because Nicholas Pileggi's *Wiseguy* was a bestseller (and, better still for those with a stake in it, is still in print), it made sense for Henry Hill, who wasn't a complete dummy, to look once more to publishing after the well of get-rich-quick schemes he enacted in and out of witness protection ran dry. While it would be an overstatement to say that *Goodfellas* spawned a cottage industry in books, Hill himself has his name on four volumes, and several other figures associated with Scorsese's picture have capitalized on it in print. Here is a survey of such volumes, presented in chronological order of publication.

WISEGUY, NICHOLAS PILEGGI,
1985, Simon and Schuster

As Dobie Gray sang on "The In Crowd," "the original's still the greatest." Pileggi knows his turf backward and forward, blindfolded. His own prose style is terse, precise, direct. He doesn't just transcribe his subjects: he creates credible, recognizable, memorable voices for them. And he tells a compelling and frequently mind-boggling story.

Its considerable true-crime literary value aside, the *Goodfellas* fan will be struck by the often small deviations Scorsese and Pileggi took, in the screenplay, from the truth according to Pileggi/Hill. Omitting Hill's army stint, of course; the duo made this decision very early in the process, and agreed on it before even discussing it. It was for reasons relating to witness protection that the book did not go into much detail concerning the Hills' children. (Even though, according to the account of Gregg and Gina Hill, Henry had given up witness protection in 1984, before *Wiseguy* was published.) In the movie the kids were changed from a son and a daughter to two daughters, and their birth dates were fudged. This, too, was for their protection. Other changes were for reasons of dramatic coherence. Henry actually met Karen Hill on a double date with Paul Vario, Jr., the son of the actual underboss Paul Vario. In the film, Paulie Cicero's kids do not figure at all, except as background. So the double date partner became Tommy, and the offer of the double date that Henry refuses occurs during the torching of the Bamboo Lounge. While Scorsese has often expressed an indifference to, if not outright disdain for, plot, he is acutely conscious of story and story flow (if not "narrative arc"). Shifting Paul Jr. to Tommy moves things along organically; there's no sense of a component being shoehorned in as such.

TIN FOR SALE, JOHN MANCA AND VINCENT COSGROVE,
1991, William Morrow and Company

Nickey Eyes of the Bamboo Lounge gang, Manca, a gambler who'd had a long stint as an unusually crooked cop, was wrangled into the *Goodfellas* role by Nicholas Pileggi. This book, which is dedicated to Pileggi, followed shortly. It's in a similar format to *Wiseguy*: prose narrative surrounding long accounts in quotes from Manca.

Manca has a lot of crazy stories, going way back. A homicide cop in NYC in the late '50s, he was called to the scene of the murder-suicide of conservative muckraker Howard Rushmore and his wife, Frances—said scene being the back of a taxicab. On noting Rushmore's address, he took the man's house keys off his corpse and toddled up to the place, hoping to lift some valuables, but he found none there. (Had he been a little more knowledgeable about Rushmore he'd have known that a series of legal trials had largely cleaned him out already.) Because that's the kind of guy Manca was. Other characters include guys with names like Sal Cannoli and Dave Cadillac. Manca's misadventures with these sorts will bring to mind the Massachusetts sleazebags of George V. Higgins, although this book's coauthor, Vincent Cosgrove, is, it probably should go without saying, not quite the prose stylist Higgins was. For all that, this is very nearly in the same league as *Wiseguy*.

MAFIA COP, LOU EPPOLITO AND BOB DRURY, 1992, Simon and Schuster

Like most criminals, Henry Hill had what your mother might call "a lot of nerve." But he did not have nearly as much nerve as Louis Eppolito. Shortly after making his screen debut in *Goodfellas* as the placid wiseguy Fat Tony, he worked on this book, a fulsome self-justification of his career in law enforcement, a career he chose in spite of having been born into gangsterdom. The book, despite bearing Eppolito's name as a coauthor, toggles between close third person and first person, or more accurately stumbles between the two modes. To hear Louis, or Louie (the book also toggles between the two spellings of his name) tell it, he was one tough cop: "Patrolman Louis Eppolito adored the battle but despised the bureaucracy of his new profession. He had been taught by his father to care about people, to respect their feelings, to go out of their way to help others in need. He had also been primed to be combat-ready at all times. When murderers and rapists were banging on your door, Officer Louie Eppolito was the cop you wanted answering your 911 call."

Murderers and rapists banging on your door. It's a vivid image.

Anyway, there are some dustups on the force relative to Louie/Louis' mob ties, and these don't sit well with the fellow.

"As frightening as it may sound, I found more loyalty, more honor, in the wiseguy neighborhoods and hangouts than I did in police headquarters. The bad guys respected Louie Eppolito. Unfortunately, I cannot say the same for the good guys." What incredible irony.

The book concludes: "On December 14, 1989, Detective Second Grade Louis John Eppolito retired with full honors.

"The New York City Police Department had finally managed to rid itself of one of its worthiest cops."

Such indignation! Anyway, Louis, or Louie, found more than just loyalty and honor in wiseguy neighborhoods; he found employment as a hit man.

He was convicted in 2006 of executing eight murders for Anthony "Gaspipe" Casso of the Lucchese crime family. He died in November of 2019, in prison.

Mafia Cop remains in print as a mass-market paperback. There is no new foreword or afterword to update the reader or correct Eppolito's disgraceful (but also mordantly funny, if you think about it in a certain way) self-mythologizing. Instead, there's a block of text at the top of the front cover reading: "The book by the ex-NYPD detective whose recent arrest for multiple counts of murder made national headlines." Yeah, they did.

THE WISEGUY COOKBOOK: MY FAVORITE RECIPES FROM MY LIFE AS A GOODFELLA TO COOKING ON THE RUN, HENRY HILL AND PRISCILLA DAVIS (FOREWORD BY NICHOLAS PILEGGI),
2002, New American Library

Possibly the most practically valuable book that Hill ever put his name on. It contains nearly 200 discrete recipes, all detailed and coherent, and several that are genuinely daunting. And yes, "Michael's Favorite Ziti with Meat Sauce" is among them. Hill and Davis dot the book with anecdotes recounting an epicure's education from the US Army to prison to Hollywood. I don't know if Outsider Cookbooks is a genre, but if it is, this ought to be considered one of the best.

The difficulty of obtaining arugula in Middle America is once again addressed. If only Hill had lived to see Whole Foods. (Well, since the company was founded in 1980, he actually did, but not so much as he'd be able to appreciate its eventual transformative effect on grocery shopping nationwide.)

A GOODFELLAS GUIDE TO NEW YORK, HENRY HILL WITH BYRON SCHRECKENGOST,
2003, Three Rivers Press

An underwhelming follow-up to the cookbook. It's also pretty clear that poor Mr. Schreckengost did most of the heavy lifting. A lot of the book is formatted as a genuine guide, in the mode of Zagat's restaurant books, with addresses, and in the case of hotels and restaurants, indications in dollar signs of how expensive they are/were (a better than good number of the spots celebrated here have disappeared in the past decade and a half). There are some reaches, too, as in the late chapter (or "floor," as the never-not-cutesy volume would have it) "For the Little Goodfellas and Fellettes," which recommends the late unlamented sci-fi bistro Mars 2112 and the Queens Wildlife Center Sheep-Shearing Weekend. Abutting this chapter is the grisly "Unwritten Rules for the Street, Written" (the "14th Floor"—they even skip the 13th floor, how about that?), which includes the subsection "Best Ways to Hide a Corpse." ("7. Cement Boots. A classic.") Don't worry, though, a disclaimer at the beginning of these lists says, "DO not take the following lists literally. Although they come from years of experience, trial and error, this guide is meant to be a humorous take on the subject, not an actual guide for killing, robbing, intimidating, maiming, or causing discomfort to yourself or others." Okay.

Mr. Schreckengost has since migrated to the spirits industry.

GANGSTERS AND GOODFELLAS: THE MOB, WITNESS PROTECTION AND LIFE ON THE RUN, HENRY HILL AS TOLD TO GUS RUSSO,
2004, M. Evans

As freewheelingly entertaining as it is self-aggrandizing, Hill's unofficial sequel to *Wiseguy* backtracks to the early '60s and elaborates on some of the first book's Greatest Hits before moving on to tales tall and sometimes true. Among these are accounts of how helpful he was to Ed McDonald, and how he was sent to Italy to testify in a trial involving legendary Italian financier/crime boss Michele Sindona. This really happened.

The book is replete with mooky groaners. "When I met Jimmy Burke in 1964 [sic], he practically owned New York's Kennedy Airport. If you ask me, they named the place after the wrong Irishman." OH! as Andrew Dice Clay said. In the final chapters, he goes into his fight against the Son of Sam laws, his never-resolving problems with drugs and drink, and so on. Of his relationship with Howard Stern, he writes, "The trouble is, I usually call when I've fallen off the wagon and feel like I want to talk to somebody." After reeling off a list of celebrity friends ("People like Bobby De Niro, Ray Liotta, Melanie Griffith...") he says, "I'm still amazed that all these people want to meet me. Some are close friends, but others just want to schmooze. I just want to make money."

On his relationship with his children, Hill avers, "The kids are fine with me."

ON THE RUN: ESCAPING A MAFIA CHILDHOOD, GREGG AND GINA HILL,
2004, Penguin/Random House

Not so fast there, Henry. This harrowing book, told in a plain, blunt style that mostly conveys the emotional and physical exhaustion of its authors after having lived through the events recounted, is like a punch to the gut. Especially if you've spent a lot of time rolling with Henry Hill's bullshit. Gregg and Gina, both born in the late '60s, alternate in the telling, which begins in the 1970s and ends after the publication of the Pileggi book. The film isn't discussed. I've drawn upon this book for corroboration of/elaboration on some of the events depicted in the movie. Here's Gregg talking about an encounter that inspired the final scene between Karen and Jimmy in the movie: "When my father was in the Nassau County jail after the raid in Rockville Center, Uncle Jimmy tried to sell her some blank T-shirts for the silk-screening business. The shirts were supposedly in an empty storefront in a warehouse district in Queens, and Jimmy was standing on the sidewalk telling her where to

go, telling her he had great stuff for her. She got spooked—
something in Jimmy's tone, the way he was smiling at her—and
ran to her car. She knew too much. She could say too much. To
Uncle Jimmy, a friend for twenty years, she'd become almost as
much of a liability as my father. He would have killed her that
day. She believes that, and I do, too. It was business, like getting fired, only more permanent."

Henry Hill is almost entirely stripped of charm in this account, a heedless drunk and drug addict and a wife beater. His
presence alone is enough of a pall over the kids' lives. But even
with a better father, going through high school while in the
witness protection program would be a challenge. The procession of pushy friends and humiliating admissions goaded out of
Gregg and Gina is almost unbearable.

In the February 2, 2000, edition of the *New York Post*, four
years before *On the Run*'s publication, an item on page six announced, "Scorsese Tied to *Goodfellas*' Sequel."

The legendary moviemaker has inked a deal with Disney to
film the story of mob turncoat Henry Hill's kids, who grew up
in the witness protection program, Scorsese spokeswoman
Marion Billings told the *Post*.

The flick will be based on an untitled memoir to be penned
by Hill's thirty-one-year-old daughter and thirty-three-year-old
son, who've just signed a publishing deal with Warner Books
for $900,000.

The children, who've lived under assumed names since
their family entered the witness protection program, will tell
about growing up with their dad—whose experiences in the
mob were chronicled in Scorsese's 1990 box-office smash
Goodfellas.

Casting is now under way for the yet-to-be-named movie.
Lorraine Bracco, who played Hill's wife in the original—and

now plays Dr. Melfi on HBO's mob hit *The Sopranos*—has already been signed.

It is not known whether Ray Liotta will reprise his role as Hill or if Robert De Niro and Joe Pesci, who played bloodthirsty mob men, will be involved.

But a source at Disney told the *Post*, "I wouldn't be surprised if Bobby [De Niro] and Joe [Pesci] were involved, because Marty [Scorsese] is doing it and they have great respect for him."

The source added that "There's a fifty-fifty chance Scorsese will direct. Disney would love him to do it. They would be thrilled."

The movie never materialized, perhaps because its contents were too intractable to make a film palatable enough to bring to market.

A GUY'S GUIDE TO BEING A MAN'S MAN, FRANK VINCENT AND STEVEN PRIGGÉ (FOREWORD BY JAMES GANDOLFINI), 2006, Berkeley/Penguin

Because Frank Vincent was such an ingratiating character in real life, one feels inclined to root for this book. It is humorously intended, for the most part, a loose parody of self-help and how-to books.

But the material wobbles. From the dating advice section: "Now, when you're approaching a woman, it's important to be persistent, but not overly persistent. Overly persistent equals STALKER! Next thing you know, you're being locked up." Wow, that escalated quickly. (And, many women might note, if only the locking-up part were so simple.) Vincent offers some surprises—didn't see the recommendation of Terrence Malick's *The Thin Red Line* as a "man's man" war movie coming—but hits many clams throughout, as in this bit from his list of "man's man" songs: "'Red, Red Wine' (UB40): great song, especially if you're at Sparks Steak House (red is also better than white when having a steak)." No comment, except a jaw agape at the fact that Vincent didn't see fit to mention the song was written and originally recorded by Neil Diamond, a figure with a lot more wiseguy/mook clout than the British band UB40.

Also, the book leans on the phrase "man's man" a little heavily. For instance: "A treasured man's man 'collectible' of that era is the 1966 Reprise Records album *Sinatra at the Sands*, produced live on location by Sonny Burke and arranged and conducted by man's man Quincy Jones." One wonders just where Sonny Burke fell short.

THE LUFTHANSA HEIST: BEHIND THE SIX-MILLION-DOLLAR CASH HAUL THAT SHOOK THE WORLD, HENRY HILL AND DANIEL SIMONE,
2015, Lyons Press

This is a very odd book. It has an index, a note on sources, even a glossary of wiseguy argot. But it's written as a novel by Hill, or at least in first person as Hill, except when it's not. And then it's in omniscient third person, as in the opening of Chapter 57: "Ed McDonald was a devoted husband and father, and sadly his weekends dashed fleetingly into Monday morning." It also toggles a bit between tenses. And it reproduces reams of dialogue that cannot be considered verbatim under any circumstance. It introduces John Gotti into the world of Hill, with a chapter depicting Jimmy Burke requesting a favor from Gotti, then politely demurring when Gotti suggests a more substantial collaboration. In an epilogue, Lisa Caserta says, "Daniel Simone has buoyed Henry Hill's legacy in this book. Henry amassed fans all over the world, though some people view him as a pariah because, in the end, he became a 'rat.' Those dissenters, however, may not know that unlike most Mafia turncoats, he didn't inform on his associates merely to save himself; rather, he was slated to be killed whether he held his silence or not." This thread is hard to follow, logic-wise, but never mind. The book, with its outlandish elaborations, is a sort of "Here comes Mr. More" from Hill, a final storytelling session from a guy for whom stories were about the only things left.

THE BIG HEIST: THE REAL STORY OF THE LUFTHANSA HEIST, THE MAFIA, AND MURDER, ANTHONY M. STEFANO,
2017, Citadel Press

The most recent recounting of the famous crime was spurred by the 2014 indictment of Vincent Asaro for his supposed part in the heist, almost forty years after the fact. Asaro was acquitted in 2017. Stefano also loops in the murder of one Paul Katz, a truck driver whose remains were found in the ground below the basement in a house whose deed was once in the name of Jimmy Burke's daughter. This is not uninteresting stuff and Stefano is a solid veteran crime reporter with commendable insights, including this one: "[With Henry] Hill having gone through bouts of drug and alcohol abuse, a researcher has to be careful about his recollection of events. There is also a nagging suspicion that Hill in later years may have embellished events or had been confused."

Unfortunately, the book is overwritten throughout. From the beginning, in which Stefano goes into arguably tedious detail into the background of the forensic anthropologist who examined Katz's remains, to the end, in which he offers an explanation of jury nullification complete with a citing of the John Peter Zenger case (that was in 1733, people).

GOOD ADVICE FROM GOODFELLAS, D. X. FERRIS,
2017, 6632 Press

This self-published item opens with a series of confident assertions, not one of them deigning to address what many would consider the absurdity of its premise. Ferris begins by recalling an episode of *The Sopranos* in which Tony Soprano considers an Italian American alternative to the advice book *Chicken Soup for the Soul*, which Tony proposes to call *Tomato Sauce for Your Ass*. Ferris considers *Goodfellas* to be that very thing. He also insists that the movie is "a workplace drama," one "about businessmen." He waxes further in this vein: "Boss Paulie, executive Henry, and wife Karen all suggest ways to live a better life." Hoo boy.

How much good advice has Ferris gleaned or extrapolated from the film? Well, the book is over 300 pages but, n.b., once you get into the advice part, each advice module is announced in white type over black on the verso page, with nothing else there; on the recto page is Ferris' short text explicating the life lesson. For instance. After a verso page reading, "Tommy: 'I'm the Oklahoma Kid!'" Ferris writes:

Spider aggravates Tommy.
  Tommy—no surprise—is quick to let loose on Spider.
  Tommy berates the kid.

Spider's lackluster tableside manner escalates the situation.

Tommy goes full cowboy. He recalls a Humphrey Bogart movie, 1939's *The Oklahoma Kid*. In the flick, a wild-eyed cowboy shoots at a civilian, making him dance as bullets fly at his feet.

Tommy, as is his habit, starts acting like he's in a Western. He pulls out his revolver, waves it around, and fires at Spider's feet, telling him to dance.

As previously disclosed, the scene ends badly for Spider.

Don't play with guns.

They're not toys.

All right, then.

HOLLYWOOD GODFATHER: MY LIFE IN THE MOVIES AND THE MOB, GIANNI RUSSO WITH PATRICK PICCIARELLI,
2019, St. Martin's Press

The relationship of this memoir to *Goodfellas* is peripheral, but noteworthy. Russo is in *The Godfather*, not *Goodfellas*. In *The Godfather* he plays Carlo, the abusive husband of Corleone sister Connie, who clearly has a type. (In *The Godfather Part II* she'll take up with an oily creep played by Troy Donahue.) However. The book boasts a front cover blurb from Robert De Niro. And on the back cover, Nicholas Pileggi chimes in, as does Pileggi's cousin, the writer Gay Talese.

Russo has a lot of stories, many of which he tells with a special emphasis on the improbable detail, as when he has Elvis Presley bring up peanut-butter-and-banana sandwiches at the very beginning of their first substantial conversation. His account of an affair with Marilyn Monroe, begun when he was a teenage hairdresser, checks out, one supposes. And there's a lot of Vegas stuff, misadventures in the Moe Greene mode. Russo relishes sharing his lifelong Hungry Boy status; recounting his childhood stint in a polio ward, he toggles between fear of Harold, a reputed child molester on its staff, and lust for Delores, a candy striper nurse he befriends. These roiling interior states eventually yield this immortal sentence: "About a year passed and I hadn't had any problems with Harold, and with hormones beginning to rage like the Colorado River, all thoughts turned to Delores and her Magic Tits."

★ ★ ★ ★ ★

Appendix:
A *GOODFELLAS* TIMELINE

Marianne Bower, Scorsese's print archivist, very kindly compiled a timeline of pertinent dates in *Goodfellas*' history, which Scorsese signed off on before it was delivered to me via Barbara De Fina. I reproduce it below. Scorsese, De Fina, and Irwin Winkler all agree that there were two California previews (this may be the only thing that all three now agree on) but no verified locations or dates are in the papers.

GOODFELLAS SCHEDULE
INFO FROM SCORSESE ARCHIVE

STEP	DATE	NOTES
First Draft Outline	May 23, 1986	
Script, earliest (?) draft	November 4, 1986	
Warner Bros.–first production board Based on script dated 3-24-1987	May 4, 1987	
Warner Bros.–script timing	June 3, 1987	
Script Feedback from Studio	February 6, 1989	
Preproduction	February 14, 1989 (first correspondence)	
Location Scout	February 17-18, 1989	

STEP	DATE	NOTES
Preproduction continues	February 20-28, 1989	
Location Scouting Casting Props/Vehicles Meeting Wardrobe fittings ongoing	March 14-23 and April 3-13, 1989	
Marty Krugman TV Commercial "Morris Kessler"	April 12, 1989	
Dailies for Commercial Art Dept meetings	April 13, 1989	
Rehearsals City Center & "TBD"	April 17, 1989- April 29, 1989	(including weekend)
Tech Scouts	April 18, 19, 20, 21, 1989	
Hair Makeup Tests	April 24-25, 1989	
Production Meeting	April 26, 1989	
Principal Photography 68 days	May 1, 1989- August 4, 1989	(call sheets)
2nd Unit	August 5, 1989, or August 7, 1989	(call sheets)
Postproduction/ editing continue	September- December 1989	
Screening, Warner Bros. LA Film & trailer (MS, producers, editor)– + others on the 15th	January 14, 15, 1990	
Looping Session Warner Bros., LA	January 17, 1990	
Screenings, NY	January 31, 1990	PREVIEWS also during this time period
(Friends & Family)	February 5, 1990 March 5, 1990 April 11, 1990	
Press Screening & others, NY (work print)	June 29 and July 2, 1990	

APPENDIX: A *GOODFELLAS* TIMELINE

STEP	DATE	NOTES
Screenings, NY	July 12, 23, 24, 27, 31, 1990	
Screening, LA	July 31, 1990	
Screenings	August 13, 15, 16, 17, 20, 22, 23, 27, 29, 30, 1990	
Publicity Interviews	July–August 1990	
London Screening	August 30, 1990	
Screenings	September 5, 1990	
PREMIERE, Venice Film Festival	September 9, 1990	(Silver Lion Award for Best Director & Audience Award)
Trade Reviews Published	September 10, 1990	
Cast & Crew Screening	September 12, 1990	
Industry Screening, LA	September 17, 1990	
NY PREMIERE, MOMA	September 18, 1990	
WIDE RELEASE	September 21, 1990	
Press Junket	September 1990	
Screening, NY	September 24, 25, 1990 October 16, 1990	
BAFTA nominations (7 nominations, 5 wins)	February 12, 1991	
Oscar Nominations (6 nominations)	February 13, 1991	
Academy Awards announced (1 win for Joe Pesci)	March 25, 1991	

Notes/Sources

PROLOGUE

"The shorter attention span": "The Second Screen," Scorsese, Martin, *Video Review*, April 1990.

CHAPTER ONE

"I read in the *Village Voice* that Jim Jarmusch": Christie, Ian, and David Thompson, *Scorsese on Scorsese*, London: Faber and Faber, 2003, p. 88.

"There's a wonderful scene": Christie and Thompson, p. 32.

"I grew up on the East Side": Christie and Thompson, p. 88.

"Henry Hill frequently recounted how he 'kidnapped' the reclusive mob underboss": Wilson, Michael Henry, *Scorsese on Scorsese*, Paris: *Cahiers du Cinéma*, 2005. On page 164, Scorsese says: "This man, who lived like a feudal overlord, didn't even have a phone, never went to the movies, was carted off one day by Henry and his friends who wanted him to see... *Mean Streets*! He saw himself in it and loved it!"

"The only reason I was able to write *Wiseguy*": Author interview with Nicholas Pileggi, October 8, 2018. All other Pileggi quotations in this chapter are from this interview.

CHAPTER TWO

"I was getting my mail": Author interview with Barbara De Fina, June 19, 2019.

"My ritual was to visit the English-language bookstore": Winkler, Irwin, *A Life in Movies: Stories from 50 Years in Hollywood*, New York: Abrams Press, 2019, p. 153.

"We'd get all the magazines and newspapers": Author interview with Irwin Winkler, June 3, 2019.

"I read a review of *Wiseguy*": "Martin Scorsese: The *Rolling Stone* Interview," Anthony DeCurtis, *Rolling Stone*, November 1, 1990.

"When I was doing *The Color of Money* in Chicago": Schickel, Richard, *Conversations with Scorsese*, 2011, New York: Alfred A. Knopf, p. 186.

"Michael Ovitz at that time": Schickel, p. 160.

"And he smiled": Schickel, p. 163.

"It did not, however, result in another term in [...] 'movie jail' for Scorsese": This was emphasized for me in conversations with Barbara De Fina. As we shall see in the book's Epilogue, however, Scorsese's self-assessment of his career prospects at the time was markedly different from what De Fina laid out for me.

"He said, 'You know, I gotta be a producer'": Author interview with Winkler.

"I didn't think he had the charm": Winkler, p. 155.

"Like the date who says he'll call you, right?": "Lorraine Bracco on *Goodfellas*, therapy, and almost turning down *The Sopranos*," Leigh, Danny, *The Guardian*, February 20, 2017.

"I asked if Cruise had even read the script": Winkler, p. 155.

"The real difficulty there was the inner life": "One of the stars of *Goodfellas* almost quit right before it started filming," Ian Phillips, *Business Insider*, April 27, 2015.

"With our casting of Ray Liotta": Winkler, p. 156.

"In a note on the front page of one of the scripts": I examined many scripts annotated by De Niro, and related notes and correspondence, at the Ransom Center at the University of Texas in November of 2019.

"I was coughing on the floor": Christie and Thompson, p. 87.

"I had a good time making it": Author interview with Robert De Niro, September 21, 2019.

"On the first day of shooting": Christie and Thompson, p. 99.

"I want to be a player": "Goodfellas: Blood and Pasta," Taubin, Amy, *The Village Voice*, September 19, 1990.

"I was in Canada": Author interview with De Niro.

"Marty was very excited": Author interview with Pileggi.

CHAPTER THREE

"2014 biography": Levy, Shawn, *De Niro: A Life*, 2014, New York: Crown Archetype.

"De Niro dove": Levy, p. 351.

"Notes on the character": Levy, p. 352.

"Early approach to headshots": Levy, p. 66.

"So when we first started with De Niro": Author interview with Joseph Reidy, January 17, 2020. All Reidy quotes in this chapter derive from this interview.

"I worked with Sidney a lot": Author interview with Barbara De Fina, May 14, 2019.

"We did it the way he suggested": Christie and Thompson, p. 108.

"He expresses [...] defeat": "The Restrained Genius of a Joe Pesci Performance," Lucca, Violet, *The New York Times*, November 6, 2019.

"The producers introduced me": Christie and Thompson, p. 99.

"In the case of the crucifixion": Ebert, Roger, *Scorsese by Ebert*, 2008, Chicago: The University of Chicago Press, p. 192–93.

"He was always friendly and happy": Author interview with De Fina, May 14, 2019.

"[A] 1999 interview with the *Guardian*": "I guess I'm a whore, a masochist and a whore," Pulver, Andrew, *The Guardian*, August 12, 1999.

"Griffon withdrew $2,000": Author interview with Bob Griffon, January 18, 2020.

"The sequence took six hours": Author interview with Griffon.

"Well, we were comfortable": Author interview with De Fina, May 14, 2019.

CHAPTER FOUR

"Their insulation was a form of self-governance and self-protection": For more on this topic, see "How Italians Became 'White,'" Staples, Brent, *The New York Times*, October 12, 2019.

"Persico himself privately bragged of them": "Carmine Persico, Columbo Crime Family Boss, Is Dead at 85," Raab, Selwyn, *The New York Times*, March 8, 2019.

"Apparently they'd been looking to cast young Henry": Author interview with Christopher Serrone, September 27, 2019.

"*Goodfellas* 'cheats' a lot": The website Movie-Locations.com has reliable detail on such matters: https://www.movie-locations.com/movies/g/Goodfellas.php

"Geoffrey Macnab": "I Was in a Bad Place," Macnab, Geoffrey, *The Guardian*, July 6, 2006.

"Going and finding locations is one of the things I love to do most": Author interview with Kristi Zea, October 16, 2019.

"It was ancient": Douglas, Illeana, *I Blame Dennis Hopper*, 2015, New York: Flatiron Books, p. 136.

"Dingy and dirty": Author interview with De Fina, June 19, 2019.

"I don't remember fleas": Author interview with Reidy.

"2010 oral history": "Martin Scorsese's *Goodfellas*: A Complete Oral History," GQ Staff, *GQ*, September 21, 2010.

NOTES/SOURCES

"Word got around that I was working on the picture": Manca, John, and Vincent Cosgrove, *Tin for Sale: My Career in Organized Crime and the NYPD*, 1991, New York: William Morrow and Co., p. 280.

"Joe Pesci comes from that world": Christie and Thompson, p. 158.

"Entertainers were like booze": Tosches, Nick, *Dino: Living High in the Dirty Business of Dreams*, 1992, New York: Doubleday, p. 151.

"Terry Semel came to visit": Author interview with Winkler.

"We ended up shooting it in Queens": Author interview with De Fina, May 14, 2019.

"The real Tommy was six-foot-something": Kelly, Mary Pat, *Martin Scorsese: A Journey*, 1991, New York: Thunder's Mouth Press, p. 263.

"Before I thought about taking over The Suite": Pileggi, Nicholas, *Wiseguy*, 1985, New York: Simon and Schuster, p. 151.

"She had violet eyes": Pileggi, p. 85.

"Michael was one of those cinematographers": Author interview with De Fina, June 19, 2019.

"When you're doing a take that's this long in duration": Author interview with Larry McConkey, November 8, 2019.

"It was quite a feat": Author interview with Zea.

"Cheesy TV commercials": The creation of this hilariously cheesy fake spot was chronicled in admirable detail on the Tumblr website Mr. Godfrey: https://mrgodfrey.tumblr.com/post/157186647808/morries-wigs-behind-the-curtain

"The situation was exacerbated by the fact that Jimmy was a part-time insomniac": Pileggi, p. 255–56.

"*Exhilaration* is an apt term": Author interview with Kevin Corrigan, October 6, 2019.

"[She] was a very strong, demanding person": Pileggi, p. 181.

"They're very ornate on the outside": Author interview with Griffon.

"My show business knowledge": Author interview with Illeana Douglas, July 3, 2019. Illeana is paraphrasing material that's also in her book.

"[A] bloodcurdling scream": Douglas, p. 119.

"Word was spreading": Douglas, p. 139.

"Marty would talk to me about what was going on": Author interview with Douglas.

"They had missing teeth": Pileggi, p. 98.

"We'll come up with something" and **"We just all bonded"**: Author interview with Douglas.

"I was never afraid of my father's friends": Hill, Gregg, and Gina Hill, *On the Run: Escaping a Mafia Childhood*, 2004, London: Arrow Books, p. 56.

"They work more hours a day than if they had a nine-to-five job": Kelly, p. 274.

"On Shannon's classic": "A Chat with Frank Vincent," Harris, Will, Bullz-Eye.com, July 11, 2007.

"1996 profile of Vincent": "Frank Vincent's Two-Limo Night," Lewine, Edward, *The New York Times*, February 18, 1996.

"You're doing a film": Author interview with De Niro.

"Now don't forget": Kelly, p. 44.

"Tiger Mom": Author interview with De Fina, June 19, 2019.

"Scrambled eggs": Kelly, p. 271.

"For most wiseguys": Pileggi, p. 176.

"He did not like getting into costume": Author interview with De Fina, June 19, 2019.

"Everybody was at a different rhythm": Author interview with Reidy.

"Every take was different": Author interview with Michael Imperioli, August 8, 2019.

NOTES/SOURCES

"Sometimes on the set": Author interview with De Niro.

"Jimmy just made Tommy dig the hole": Pileggi, p. 168.

"I have pretty much every firearms license imaginable": Author interview with Griffon.

"I was supposed to turn myself in at nine a.m.": Hill, Henry, and Gus Russo, *Gangsters and Goodfellas: The Mob, Witness Protection, and Life on the Run*, 2004, Lanham: M. Evans, p. 83.

"My old girlfriend Linda": Hill and Russo, p. 255.

"The real trick": Christie and Thompson, p. 151.

"Semel was not around the set": Author interview with De Fina, June 19, 2019.

"Hustled like he had never hustled before": Pileggi, p. 204.

"Now take me to jail": The influence of *Goodfellas* extends far and wide, even into the world of pornography; "Now take me to jail" is spoken, in the back of a limo, by Tori Black at the end of *After Hours*, an extravagant 2018 adult video directed by Kayden Kross.

"They wanted me to become an ophthalmologist": Pileggi, p. 214.

"Crew names": Author interview with Griffon.

"The reality behind one very carefully thrown-away line": Marcus, Greil, *Mystery Train*, 1976, New York: E. P. Dutton, p. 95.

"Bobby Germaine": Pileggi, p. 241.

"Nothing is more exhilarating than philistine vulgarity": Nabokov, Vladimir, and Alfred Appel, Jr., editor, *The Annotated Lolita*, 1991, New York: Vintage, p. 315.

"One of the most satisfying things I did on the movie": Author interview with Zea.

"[A] really nice guy whom I liked a lot": Hill and Hill, p. 57.

"Christmas Day at the funeral parlor": Hill and Hill, p. 66.

"[A] longish story": Explained a bit more in "Eh, What's Up, Doc?" Kenny, Glenn, *The New York Times*, February 9, 2018.

"Williams recalls on his website": Its URL is: http://www.johnny-roastbeef.com/bio/

"I had a front-row seat watching Robert De Niro": Douglas, p. 135.

"Leo McCarey understood people": Sarris, Andrew, *The American Cinema, Directors and Directions 1926–1968*, 1968, New York: E. P. Dutton, p. 100.

"Well, yes": Author interview with De Fina.

"The scene was even shot to fit the song": Wilson, p. 168.

"Marty just had a shot": Author interview with De Niro.

"He sat down at my piano": Coolidge, Rita, *Delta Lady*, 2016, New York: Harper Collins, p. 121.

"What crane do you have?": Author interview with McConkey.

"The fact that Tommy gets killed that way": Christie and Thompson, p. 158.

"They were good friends": Author interview with De Niro.

"On the day I finally got arrested": Pileggi, p. 295.

"I just loved *Something Wild*, I wanted to be that kind of actor": Author interview with Corrigan, August 8, 2019.

"I was doing work at the Actors Studio": Author interview with Isiah Whitlock, Jr., December 9, 2019.

"Did I KNOW?": Author interview with Corrigan.

"There were some compensations for the agents": Volkman, Ernest, and John Cummings, *The Heist*, 1986, New York: Franklin Watts, p. 228.

"Well, it simply adds depth": Missy Robbins, in an email to the author, December 9, 2019.

"The state of anxiety and the way the mind races when on drugs": Christie and Thompson, p. 158.

"—and I still wasn't happy": "De Niro and Me," Scorsese, Martin, *Projections 7*, in association with *Cahiers du Cinéma*, 1997, London: Faber and Faber, p. 46.

"I went in to read for Ellen Lewis": Author interview with Welker White, May 21, 2019.

"The interior of that house": Author interview with Reidy.

"First real break": Pileggi, p. 328.

"Henry didn't have too much school spirit": Pileggi, p. 356.

"There was a researcher who came to my office": Author interview with Edward McDonald, April 25, 2019.

"Most amazingly, it concludes with a point-of-view shot": Adair, Gilbert, *Flickers*, 1985, London: Faber and Faber, p. 22.

CHAPTER FIVE

"For me, it's very, very serious": "Jerry Vale Sounds Like Family to Martin Scorsese," LeDonne, Rob, *The New York Times*, December 17, 2019.

"The man who cannot stop hurting himself": I wrote on this theme relative to 2010's *Shutter Island* in an essay on my weblog, Some Came Running: https://somecamerunning.typepad.com/some_came_running/2010/02/shutter-island.html

"These days every damn movie in America": Christie and Thompson, p. 110.

"Mitch and I came to an understanding": Bennett, Tony, *The Good Life*, 2010, New York: Simon and Schuster, p. 124.

"The most brilliant, and the classiest": Tosches, Nick, *The Unsung Heroes of Rock 'n' Roll*, 1984, New York: Charles Scribner's Sons, p. 101.

"Aside from Sinatra, Tony Bennett was the authority": *The New York Times*, December 17, 2019.

"In France the song is known as 'La mer'": Ocean Crossing," Friedwald, Will, *Vanity Fair*, November 2002.

"Sometimes we put the lyrics of songs between lines": Christie and Thompson, p. 161.

"A lot of music is used in movies today just to establish a time": Christie and Thompson, p. 161.

"After one particularly difficult night when nothing was happening": Shapiro, Harry, *Jack Bruce: Composing Himself*, 2010, London: Jawbone, p. 97.

"Tom Dowd" and **"psychedelic hogwash":** "Sunshine of Your Love," Churruca, Jason, Churruca Guitar website, September 19, 2019.

"I had to admit it sounded stunning": Coolidge, p. 132.

"That's not something that should happen even once": Coolidge, p. 97.

"There was no light, it was pure darkness": Coolidge, p. 94.

"What nobody knew at the time about Jim": Coolidge, p. 94.

"If I sound bitter, I'm not": Coolidge, p. 134.

"Paul Anka deemed it 'sincere'": "Paul Anka: One Song the Sex Pistols Won't Be Singing," McCormack, Neil, *The Telegraph*, November 9, 2007.

CHAPTER SIX

"Mary Patrick Kelly": Kelly, p. 50.

"He had much more": Kelly, p. 51.

"Anecdote recounted by Roger Ebert": "An Interview with Martin Scorsese and Paul Schrader," *The Chicago Sun-Times*, March 3, 1976, reprinted in *Scorsese by Ebert*, p. 42.

"The Only Dull Part of Moviemaking": Lumet, Sidney, *Making Movies*, 1995, New York: Alfred A. Knopf.

"*Raging Bull* was my first feature!": Kelly, p. 146.

"David Leonard": Author interview, March 5, 2020.

"I don't understand why people get so hung up on these issues": "Interview: Thelma Schoonmaker," Pinkerton, Nick, *Film Comment*, March 31, 2014.

"Thelma knows who I am": Schickel, p. 335.

"Thelma is the woman I trust": Schickel, p. 337.

CHAPTER SEVEN

"In his groundbreaking 1948 essay": Warshow, Robert, *The Immediate Experience: Movies, Comics, Theatre and Other Aspects of Popular Culture*, 2001, Cambridge: Harvard University Press, p. 97.

"Vehemently articulated by Manny Farber and Patricia Patterson": Farber, Manny, and Robert Polito, editor, *Farber on Film*, 2009, New York: Library of America, p. 752.

"Great independent filmmaker who's never made a film independently": On the audio commentary for the twenty-fifth anniversary Blu-ray of *Goodfellas*, Warner Home Video.

"The studio knew what the movie was": Author interview with De Fina, June 19, 2019.

"We were next door": Author interview with Winkler.

"The strange thing": Author interview with De Fina, June 19, 2019.

"Warner Brothers hadn't been having a good year": Salamon, Julia, *The Devil's Candy:* The Bonfire of the Vanities *Goes to Hollywood*, 1991, New York: Houghton Mifflin, p. 377.

"Janet Maslin denigrated the Academy": Wiley, Mason, and Damien Bona, *Inside Oscar: The Unofficial History of the Academy Awards, 10th Anniversary Edition*, 1993, New York: Ballantine Books, p. 812.

"There were so many people to thank": Wiley and Bona, p. 809.

"The guys in that movie, the way they relate to each other, is the way comedians relate to each other": Author interview with Bill Hader, September 30, 2019.

CHAPTER EIGHT

"I'm not sure I completely buy into that": Schickel, p. 189.

"The point isn't whether or not he's guilty or innocent": Welles, Orson, and Peter Bogdanovich, *This Is Orson Welles*, 1998, New York: Da Capo, p. 286.

"Experience told me what was happening": Hill and Hill, p. 267.

"Henry was a schmuck": Author interview with McDonald.

"'Son of Sam' laws": A good overview is provided in "Highlights of the Ruling That Struck Down New York's 'Son of Sam' Law," *The New York Times*, December 11, 1991.

"He couldn't not spend money": Author interview with Pileggi.

"He rationalized living this way": Author interview with Pileggi.

"Whatever money my dad got from the book": Hill and Hill, p. 281.

"My father had an angle for everything": Hill and Hill, p. 199.

"Henry Hill had become a famous character": Hill and Hill, p. 363.

"When I signed on the deal for *Goodfellas*": Hill and Russo, p. 223.

"Jimmy Burke's fearsome daughter": Hill and Russo, p. 224.

"De Niro was special": Hill and Russo, p. 224.

"Henry had my number": Author interview with Reidy.

"So he calls me": Author interview with McDonald.

"I certainly don't think Henry was remorseful": Author interview with McDonald.

"We first had him on the show back in the mid-'90s:" Stern, Howard, *Coming Clean*, 2019, New York: Simon and Schuster, p. 394.

"I'm a scumbag": Stern, p. 399.

"Quite what to say to that": Author interview with McDonald.

CHAPTER NINE

"When you called about *Goodfellas*, in a way you just kicked a hornets' nest for me": Author interview with De Fina, June 19, 2019.

"Bad cop": Author interview with Reidy.

"Winkler's responses to De Fina's assertions are polite and brief": Author interview with Irwin Winkler, January 31, 2020.

"Peter Biskind contributed a set-visit feature": "Slouching Toward Hollywood," Biskind, Peter, *Premiere*, November 1991.

"Which Bertrand asked me to be in": Christie and Thompson, p. 104

"He reassured that in me most of all": Powell, p. xiii.

"That was all worked out beforehand": Author conversation with Joe Hill, February 10, 2020. While Mr. Hill asked that I not record the conversation, he gave me permission to use quotes from my notes. Because of this provision I consulted with him about the accuracy of what I set down before finalizing my draft.

CHAPTER TEN

"I thought of it as being a kind of attack": Schickel, p. 188.

"[A] disgrace": "The Current Cinema," Rafferty, Terrence, *The New Yorker*, December 2, 1991.

"Pronounced the director's name 'Scor-seeze'": You're going to have to trust my word and my memory on this one, kids.

"I wrote it as an Amblin thriller": Levy, p. 377.

"It was based on actual events Bob had researched": Douglas, p. 140.

"Kind of a commission": Schickel, p. 203.

"Definitely *Casino* is the final one": Schickel, p. 210.

"That's where I got off the bus": Author interview with De Fina, June 19, 2019.

"More willing to get input from crew members": Author interview with Griffon.

"Call me a prude": *"The Wolf of Wall Street* Is a Douchebag's Handbook," Zuckerman, Esther, *The Atlantic*, December 18, 2013.

"My attitude as a film director has always been…provocation": Ehrenstein, David, *The Scorsese Picture*, 1992, New York: Birch Lane Press, p. 70.

"Shea Serrano's 15 Best Gangster Movie Moments": Help yourself: https://www.youtube.com/watch?v=j-k3aESXPQA

EPILOGUE

"The careers of Robert Mitchum and Jimmy Stewart": Scorsese's *Premiere* essay titled "The Men Who Knew Too Much."

"'Big Red Son'": The essay originally appeared in *Premiere*, and was reprinted in *Consider the Lobster and Other Essays*, 2006, New York: Little Brown and Company. I appear in the essay, in not-all-that thinly disguised form, as the character "Dick Filth."

"Take Scorsese to task at a 'meeting'": "Bob Iger Planning to Meet with Martin Scorsese Over Marvel Comments," Kilkenny, Katie, *The Hollywood Reporter*, December 12, 2019.

"He would leave his position": "Bob Iger steps down as Disney CEO. Bob Chapek replaces him," Pallotta, Frank, and Brian Stelter, CNN Business, February 26, 2020.

"Monty Python term": You may read the script for "The Woody Sketch" here: http://www.montypython.net/scripts/wood.php

"Coffee table book": Shone, Tom, *The Irishman: The Making of the Movie*, 2019, New York: Assouline.

"Parkinson's disease": "When Marty Met Helen," Susan Cheever, *Talk* magazine, February 2, 2000.

"There were so many legal problems": "Inside the Quiet Legal Battles Over Martin Scorsese's *Silence*," Gardner, Eriq, *The Hollywood Reporter*, September 28, 2016.

Acknowledgments

Joseph Veltre was a friend before he became my agent, and for as long as we've worked together he's shown me great kindness and dispensed a lot of wisdom. He and his assistant, Tori Eskue, were instrumental in making this book a reality. While I'm thanking him I should thank another wonderful friend, and a great and inspiring writer, Adrienne Miller, who is married to Joe.

Peter Joseph at Hanover Square Press, and his wonderful staff, brought the book to where it is now. Peter is a pleasure to know and a spectacular collaborator, as is his assistant, Grace Towery.

Scott Feinstein and Jenna Chasanoff at 42 West helped me a great deal with access to interview subjects and more.

Steven Wilson, Michael Gilmore, and the entire staff of the Ransom Center at the University of Texas were superb guides in my exploration of Robert De Niro's papers. Thanks to Gibby Haynes for recommending the magnificent Austin Tex-Mex restaurant El Caribe, a highlight of my trip.

R. Colin Tait, Tom Shone, Jason Bailey and Shawn Levy, gentlemen and film scholars all, were generous in sharing their own discoveries about the films under examination here.

Tony Scott, Manohla Dargis, Nicole Herrington, Mekado Murphy, Stephanie Goodman, Edward Marks, and all the individuals I work with reviewing films at the *New York Times* are treasures. Brian Tallerico, Matt Zoller Seitz, Nick Allen, Nell

Minow, and Chaz Ebert at Ebert.com have had my back for a long time and it's a good feeling.

I saw *New York, New York* at Manhattan's Ziegfeld Theatre on opening day with my friend Joseph Failla, a film-going buddy since third grade. I saw *Raging Bull* on opening night at The National in Times Square with Ron Goldberg. I don't get to see many movies with these fellows nowadays, but they will always be my favorite film-going companions.

I thank my family: my father, Allan, and his wife, Marjorie Kenny, my brother, Michael, my sister, Kathleen. My uncle Bob Relovsky, who we lost this year, and Cathy Relovsky, younger sister of my mother, Amelia, who's not around for this occasion. Jack Kenny. Richie and Chris Petrosino. There are a lot of you around and about—which I'm grateful for. Thanks, too, of course, to my loving and generous second family, Mary Alice Evans, Joe Evans, Jonathan Evans, Sarah Legg.

For friendship and moral support I thank Davitt Sigerson, Brian Koppelman, David Levien, Zach Barocas, Farran Smith Nehme, Jay Cocks, Kip Myers, Patrick Kyle, Brian Balderston, Rubina Hussain, Colleen McMillen, Nancy Chuang, Audra Gorman, Joe Mulligan, Colin Ungaro, Stewart Wolpin, John Fahey, Keith Uhlich, Dan Callahan, Christopher Risco, Ethan Iverson, Sarah Weinman, Tom Bissell, Owen King, Michelle Dean, Doug Brod, Ed Hulse, Jim Meigs, Kathy Heintzelman, Tim Apello, Tom Carson, Adam Hocker, Kate Kelly. David Koll kindly offered to proof a draft, and provided me with crucial corrections and perceptive and useful notes. I owe him a lot. I thank Doug Harvey, Tom Santamassino, and Daniel Burwasser for years of musical fellowship. Doug and Dan facilitated a particularly therapeutic jam session near the end of the writing of this book.

I especially thank all of my interview subjects. Particularly generous with her time and encouragement was Barbara De

ACKNOWLEDGMENTS

Fina. Another subject who was extraordinarily accessible and tolerant was Irwin Winkler. Go figure. Gillian Spear in Robert De Niro's office was especially helpful. And the great Joe Reidy's contribution was invaluable. At Sikelia, thanks to Lisa Frechette, Jana Heaton, my former student Luis DeJesus, and my old friend Gina Telaroli. Lisa Caserta and Joe Hill also have my undying appreciation. And a special thanks to Marianne Bower for assistance beyond the call of obligation or even reason with respect to illustrations.

In the process of writing this book, my admiration for Martin Scorsese—his artistry and his commitment, and during our interview, his consideration and his candor—only increased. I feel similarly toward Nicholas Pileggi.

This book's dedicatee, my wife, Claire, has blessed my life in every way possible, and is a paragon of brilliance, kindness, good humor, patience, and affection.

To paraphrase Nick Tosches at the end of his splendid book *Dino*: without Henry Hill we would be holding about a pound of blank pages right now. Rest in peace, wiseguy.

Index

INDEX

INDEX

INDEX

INDEX

INDEX

INDEX